Cervantine Futures

Cervantine Futures

Reading Cervantes after the Critical Turn

Edited by

NICHOLAS R. JONES AND
PAUL MICHAEL JOHNSON

VANDERBILT UNIVERSITY PRESS
Nashville, Tennessee

Library of Congress Cataloging-in-Publication Data

Names: Jones, Nicholas R., 1982- editor | Johnson, Paul Michael, 1982- editor
Title: Cervantine futures : reading Cervantes after the critical turn / edited by Nicholas R. Jones and Paul Michael Johnson.
Description: Nashville, Tennessee : Vanderbilt University Press, 2026. | Includes bibliographical references and index.
Identifiers: LCCN 2026008462 (print) | LCCN 2026008463 (ebook) | ISBN 9780826500441 paperback | ISBN 9780826500458 hardcover | ISBN 9780826500465 epub | ISBN 9780826500472 pdf
Subjects: LCSH: Cervantes Saavedra, Miguel de, 1547–1616--Criticism and interpretation | LCGFT: Literary criticism | Essays
Classification: LCC PQ6351 .C49 2026 (print) | LCC PQ6351 (ebook)
LC record available at https://lccn.loc.gov/2026008462
LC ebook record available at https://lccn.loc.gov/2026008463

FRONT COVER: Carl Chiarenza, *Peace Warrior (Don Quixote) 275* (2003). Gelatin silver print. Courtesy of Yale University Art Gallery; Gift of the artist in honor of Richard Albright, BA, 1961

This book will be made open access within three years of publication thanks to Path to Open, a program developed in partnership between JSTOR, the American Council of Learned Societies (ACLS), University of Michigan Press, and the University of North Carolina Press to bring about equitable access and impact for the entire scholarly community, including authors, researchers, libraries, and university presses around the world. Learn more at https://about.jstor.org/path-to-open.

For Reina, Eli, and Ethan—auspices of just futures.

P. M. J.

Contents

PART III. NEW MATERIALISMS

PART IV. BURIED HISTORIES

PART V: MEDIA FUTURES

Introduction

PAUL MICHAEL JOHNSON
AND NICHOLAS R. JONES

Challenging the popular conception of the archive as the static repository of a bygone era, Jacques Derrida once claimed that "the question of the archive is not . . . a question of the past. . . . It is a question of the future, the question of the future itself, the question of a response, of a promise and of a responsibility for tomorrow."[1] Beyond their flourish of deconstructive provocation, these words ask us to consider how the future inflects the past, and what is to be done with that past in the future. The ethical stance implicit in the "responsibility for tomorrow," in particular, prompts a deeper, more critical reflection on the stakes of premodern scholarship in the twenty-first century, as well as a set of related questions: How can a body of early modern writing like Cervantes's serve as a locus for thinking through, alongside, or against twenty-first-century critical theories and methodologies? How do the author's texts and their critical history engage, anticipate, challenge, or resist such methodologies? How might recent transdisciplinary movements serve to enrich our understanding of the Cervantine canon, and, conversely, how might Cervantes offer new yet uniquely premodern points of intervention and critique for thinking about contemporary issues and those of tomorrow? What possibilities might a temporal unshackling of Cervantes as a site for thinking through and with the future open for us? In more pragmatic terms, what is the future of Cervantes studies, and, with the flurry of the author's fourth centenary celebrations now behind us, where does *cervantismo* go from here? It might seem quaint, naïve, or misdirected to pose these questions now, when the world is besieged by no shortage of intractable crises, societal upheaval, ecological decay, paradigmatic ruptures, and existential threats, when the very future of the democratic global order appears to be on the line. But there is arguably no better time than now, in the midst of these pressing challenges, to ask where Cervantes fits, what "promise" the Cervantine archive might hold. Reworking Derrida's formulation, more pointedly, what "responsibility for tomorrow" should we as scholars of that archive carry forward?

"To write about the future is," as two historians of ideas have recently contended, "a critical act—though the degree to which any given writer, or genre, steps up to the critical challenge will vary widely."[2] We are inclined to agree with Frederick A. de Armas that Cervantes's writing is especially fertile terrain for the future.[3] The very anachronism of Don Quijote's existence is enabled by an implicit tension between a nascent modernity with which knight errantry is wholly incompatible, and which asserts itself in often ruthless fashion on his body and spirit. Technological, legal, bureaucratic, social, and linguistic novelties from an apparently distant future leave him bewildered, defiantly and often violently resisting his attempts to ascribe them to an earlier, albeit fictive, epistemological paradigm. Don Quijote remains intent on arresting the ceaselessly forward march of time, while Sancho is keener to hitch himself and his donkey to its locomotion as a vehicle for securing the wealth that in that emergent future will serve as the prime guarantor of comfort and power. Though the protagonists' deluded faith in the knightly enterprise ensures the futility of these efforts, each character, like the etymology of "adventure," remains guided by the tantalizing yet necessarily uncertain prospects of the future: Sancho pursues the governorship of an *ínsula* in part out of a patrilineal concern for his heirs, while Don Quijote, despite forging his identity in an antiquated fantasy of knighthood, is always preoccupied by his posterior reputation in the annals of his imagined historian. And Cervantes's novel itself has long been considered a landmark of literary modernity, one that foretold similar revolutions in science, philosophy, and aesthetics and thus has constituted a "literary longue durée."[4] If it is true that "the Renaissance was a period defined . . . by visions of the future," then Cervantes was surely an epochal visionary for his time and thereafter.[5]

Yet, beyond the routine definition of "future" to which these examples belong, we are much more interested in the political potential of "futures," and in the radical multiplicity suggested by its plural form. In their unspoken evocation of utopias or dystopias, futures are always already political. Even if it remains more abstract and unquestioned than the concreteness of territorial space, time has forever been a conduit of authority, domination, coloniality, and epistemic violence. Dipesh Chakrabarty, a leading voice in postcolonial and subaltern studies, has approached the Anthropocene as a planetary crisis demanding new models of time that challenge the humanist, linear underpinnings of cultural history, while scholars of queer studies, critical race studies, and Latinx studies have productively deployed dissident theorizations of futurity as a means of contesting Western-centric and heteronormative modes of temporality.[6] The technocultural aesthetic of Afrofuturism, while originating in African American science fiction, has grown into a multimedia ecosystem premised on envisioning, celebrating, and reclaiming Black futures as speculative hubs of liberation and resistance. These critical futures thus signal a more inclusive horizon, one which opens onto hitherto unseen and understudied vistas, subjects, and identities. "Futurity," as conceived by the critic Amir Eshel, "marks literature's ability to raise, via engagement with the past, political and ethical dilemmas crucial for the human future" and thus "to widen the language and to expand the pool of idioms we employ in making sense of what has occurred while imagining whom we may become."[7] Black feminist scholars like Kara Keeling and Tina Campt have similarly grounded their work in a proleptic register of liberation, one which can be realized, the latter explains, "in the form of acts and actions," or "in political movements and acts of resistance like those that have produced fundamental shifts in the status of subordinated, subaltern, and marginalized groups. But," according to Campt, "we must not only look but also listen for it in other, less likely places."[8] This book locates Cervantes as one of these "less likely places." Inspired by these varied, expansive, and imaginative futurities, we propose his writing as a site for activating critical alternatives, one populated by diverse identities and positionalities, and where the heuristic of futures drives a push to reimagine the political stakes and emancipatory possibilities of our collective scholarship.

The "futures" of the present volume's title finds its temporal complement in the subtitular "after the critical turn." This is intended not to delineate some datable watershed in the history of criticism but, rather, to place the study of Cervantes into conversation with a broad yet concerted movement in a number of humanities and social science fields to reexamine their disciplinary and ideological foundations in light of contemporary sociopolitical hierarchies. The intellectual seeds for such movements were in some cases sown by poststructuralist figures already familiar to, if not always embraced by, Cervantes scholars, though it was not until the first decade or two of the twenty-first century that they really began to flourish. Fourth-wave feminism, transgender studies, disability studies and crip theory, posthumanism, new materialism, migration and border studies, ecocriticism, and critical indigenous and critical race studies are just a few of the nomenclatural constellations that have been assembled or transformed by these developments. Such critical turns also encompass more radical efforts to rethink the very methodological foundations of our disciplines. What scholars like Rita

Felski have called postcritique, for example, seeks alternatives to the "hermeneutics of suspicion" that Paul Ricoeur ascribed to modern literary theory in favor of more affirmative, affective, and reparative methods of understanding literature. According to Felski and Elizabeth S. Anker, "the 'post-' of post- critique denotes a complex temporality: an attempt to explore fresh ways of interpreting literary and cultural texts that acknowledges, nonetheless, its inevitable dependency on the very practices it is questioning."[9] The drive to "undiscipline," as laid out by the Black studies scholar Christina Sharpe, similarly demands that we forge new, ground-up solutions for contesting the epistemic violence of traditional institutional practices.[10] These movements have not only transcended traditional disciplinary and methodological boundaries but, through profoundly intersectional approaches, also challenged ossified conceptions of race, gender, class, ability, citizenship, and other issues of political urgency.[11] Much socially engaged scholarship has likewise been inspired by concurrent local and global organizing in the public sphere, such as Black Lives Matter, LGBTQIA2S+ advocacy, land rights and climate change activism, #MeToo, and other justice-oriented action against systems of oppression. In sum, despite breathless predictions of the death of theory in the twilight of post-structuralism, the first quarter of the twenty-first century has witnessed a remarkable genesis and expansion of socially conscious theoretical movements.

Nowhere is this critical turn more discernible, perhaps, than in medieval and early modern studies, where such issues have intervened to enrich our understanding of the period through the diverse, theoretically driven work of multidisciplinary scholars.[12] This work has further eroded the timeworn opposition between historicist and theoretical schools, proving that cutting-edge analysis need not take place at the expense of rigorously historical, textual, comparatist, and philological methods. Yet, because the avatars of this critical turn coincided broadly with the several Cervantine anniversaries that occurred between 2005 and 2017, perhaps their impact on the field was overshadowed—and the critical reckoning they may have prompted, foreclosed—by the justifiably festive spirit of quatercentenary memorialization. Now that the confetti has settled, and with another two decades until the next commemorative milestone—2047 will mark half a millennium since Cervantes's birth—it seems to us an opportune moment to hold a mirror up to *cervantismo*; to ask how the field can engage with the growing body of critical work in premodern studies at large; and how Cervantes can supply new perspectives and points of inquiry to that work.

It has been more than twenty years since Steven Hutchinson—responding to the question of "what kind of Cervantes do we want?" first posed by George

Mariscal—diagnosed Cervantes's susceptibility to "ismosis," or the author's peculiar tendency "to absorb successively every -ism that comes along."[13] Writing in 2012, Francisco Layna Ranz and Antonio Cortijo Ocaña suggested that *cervantismo* was perhaps no longer ailing from such conditions, or at least that the field was on the mend, increasingly inoculated against the seasonal whims of an academy that had apparently lost its taste for theory, writ large. "Critical novelty," they opined, "is too ephemeral to allow for intense and constant observation of its products, but in the last few years one perceives a certain fatigue over the maintenance of critical factions, a kind of truce interwoven by eclecticism and dejection, perhaps disorientation."[14] While this assessment is not inaccurate, we would add that the guise of consensus can sometimes harbor an exclusionary conservatism at odds with that very impulse of scholarly rapprochement, as well as with more avowedly progressive tenets of diversity and inclusion. And though intellectual gatekeeping polices the borders of many an academic domain, it is perhaps more acute when those borders are drawn around the canonical darling of a relatively small but passionate cadre of devotees. At the very least, we should not allow aspirations of ideological unity to obscure or efface identities and perspectives whose apparent novelty might otherwise consign them to the margins of a field that, at times, has been resistant to change; been in the thrall of an uncritical, almost pious reverence to Cervantes; been beset by a transatlantic divide; or, more recently, been eager to transcend it through tacitly or overtly conciliatory methodologies.

Conscious of these varied perils, we seek here not to apply to Cervantes the latest theoretical fashion or passing trend, much less an exercise in intellectual sloganeering, but, as critics engaged in the current historical moment, to propose a more enduring—because purposefully more global and inclusive—framework. The chapters that follow do not always engage explicitly with the theoretical and methodological currents we have named in this introduction, even as they are enabled in many cases by the alternative modes of literary criticism that such currents have opened. *Cervantine Futures* purports to be neither prescriptive nor predictive, neither exhaustive nor exclusive. Eschewing more traditional models of the genre, rather, we envision this volume—composed of relatively short, incisive, and highly concentrated essays—as a heterogeneous collection of potential waypoints. If, as Layna and Cortijo contend, *cervantismo* has been beset of late by a sense of theoretical "disorientation," then another way to think about this book is as an operational field guide, an orientational vade mecum for researchers within and beyond Cervantes studies. This manifold quality of *variatio* should not be construed as auguring an anything-goes criterion of postmodern relativism.

By situating Cervantes in self-critical modes that acknowledge social and political forces operating on, beneath, and beyond his texts, the chapters that follow are anchored in close readings yet often perform antiracist, antiableist, and feminist praxis. Instead of hailing some shiny, radically innovative sea change for *cervantismo*, to be clear, much of this work has been ongoing, building on the firm foundations laid by *cervantistas* of generations past, even as many of the contributions propose to reinforce, reorient, repurpose, or, in some cases, raze and rebuild those foundations with new tools and materials.[15] Though we hope that this collection is representative of some of the most stimulating research in Cervantes studies today, it necessarily offers but a sampling of the exciting work scholars of, and adjacent to, the field are undertaking.

Each of the chapters that follow, authored by a diverse range of senior, midcareer, and emerging scholars, proposes theoretically, textually, and historically informed interpretations of Cervantes's texts, fashioning that literary past as a fulcrum for assembling a critical landscape of future possibilities. Although the volume is organized thematically into five sections, readers may discover among its chapters other fruitful parallels that cohere around such problems as race (Tweede and Lagresa-González; Johnson; Rigaux; Leahy), gender (Avilés; Burshatin; Johnson; Spragins), ability (Hicks-Bartlett; Boyle; Johnson), the senses (Alcalá Galán; Sierra Matute; García Piñar; Infante), the natural or nonhuman (Wagschal; Byrne; Rodríguez-Rincón), or modern adaptations and applications (Boyle; Laguna; Castillo and Egginton; Fernández-Blázquez; and Leahy). Users of this volume will also encounter intertextual references to several of Cervantes's prose narratives, drama, and poetry, despite the prominence of *Don Quijote* and several of the *Novelas ejemplares*. By design, a few of the essays even attend to the same character (Marcela, Luis, or Tomás Rodaja/Vidriera), thereby performing the perspectivism and exegetic plurality that are already manifest in Cervantes's writing and that, we suggest, light a worthy pathway for future scholarship.

The first section of the volume centers minor characters in Cervantes's writing that, by dint of their race, gender, sexuality, age, and ability, have also been minoritized. Luis F. Avilés opens the collection by providing an overview of recent theoretical developments advocating for a more expansive, human-centered approach to literary characters that breaks free from formalist orthodoxies. While this approach is implicitly applicable to the other characters treated in this first part of the volume, Avilés reads *Don Quijote*'s Marcela as a case study and gendered avatar of this characterological expansiveness, one which must necessarily confront, though certainly not endorse, the potential for both feminist and virulently anti-feminist readings. In his piece on "El celoso extremeño," Israel

Burshatin explores how the libidinal economies of empire continually underwrite the titular character's construction of a gendered and racialized regime of subjectivation. Yet by investigating how the *indiano* Carrizales wields his masculinist biopower over the bodies of his bride and the enslaved members of his household, the domestic fortress built on jealousy is revealed as a house of cards. Cornesha Tweede and Elizabeth Lagresa-González similarly foreground the otherwise marginal, racialized position of Black women in Cervantes's oeuvre. By studying the narrative and symbolic protagonism of Guiomar in "El celoso extremeño" and the unnamed Black servant in "El coloquio de los perros," however, they also recover a greater agential role for these intersectional characters while drawing connections to historical Afro-Iberian subjects and Black feminist thought. Intersectionality itself structures the final contribution of the first part of the volume. Through a fine-grained, historical analysis of the narrator's portrayal of "El celoso extremeño's" Luis as an old, Black eunuch, Paul Michael Johnson charts how race, gender, sexuality, age, and ability are all nested in such a deceptively simple portrayal, thereby validating an intersectional approach to Cervantes's oeuvre that likewise takes into account multiple categories of identity together.

Medical discourse, disability, and the bodymind inform the second set of essays. Alani Hicks-Bartlett begins with a rousing survey of corporeality across Cervantes's writing, from *La Galatea* to *Persiles y Sigismunda*, which in turn discloses a profound, integral, and sustained investment in bodily difference. Against the grain of largely conventional comic, ludic, and carnivalesque interpretations, she takes seriously the diverse bodies of differently abled others, including Cervantes's own. In doing so, Hicks-Bartlett makes a powerful case for the pairing of *cervantismo* with disability studies, one that the rest of the contributions explore from myriad angles. Margaret Boyle positions "El licenciado Vidriera" and its glass protagonist as an exceptionally fertile, albeit fragile, site for understanding the embodied links between physical ailment and psychiatric disorder. Drawing on Black feminists' notion of "slow loss" and a first-person model of disability, her reading advances both a more intimate account of the protagonist's illness and its relevance for today. A scopophiliac public is at stake in Pablo García Piñar's chapter, insofar as Cervantes's fondness for ekphrastic depictions of nonnormative bodies emerges across his writing. Fixating on *Don Quijote*'s Maritornes and Cervantes's rhetorical self-portrait of a permanently disabled veteran, this essay lingers on the inquisitive, impertinent, and often intrusive act of staring as a suggestive analogue for the critical gaze. For her part, Ana Laguna audits Cervantes's portrayal of medical science while probing its potentially salutary effects on an interdisciplinary readership. Her take on the author's empathetic representation of the lived experience of disease and illness in a number of his works reveals a Cervantes as aware of the clinical discourses of his time as poised to anticipate modern therapeutic practice and the future of carework.

Part Three of the volume draws on the theoretical assemblage known as new materialism, which, along with related movements in posthumanism, ecocriticism, and animal studies, rejects anthropocentric binaries of human/nonhuman, subject/object, and nature/culture to propose an integrated ontology of biological and material things. As the chapters gathered here demonstrate, the political upshots of such a project redound to our benefit as readers of Cervantes as well, beginning with a meditation by Luis Rodríguez-Rincón. For him, the material turn inspires a reexamination of Cervantes's engagement with the concept of *tercia naturaleza*, third natures that resist the excision of humans from the natural realm that is emblematic of modernity. Patent already in the author's early forays into pastoralism, what theorists have termed these "naturecultures," as well as adjacent investments in ecocriticism, also emerge in Don Quixote's encounters with an environment at once natural and aesthetic. Tarrying in a bucolic mode, Elizabeth Spragins interprets the material remains of Grisóstomo as an epistemological strategy of the "necropastoral," with the corpse becoming, as it were, vital to the juridical verdict of who is responsible for his demise. As with other contributions, Spragins's argument relies on the deft pairing of early modern historical context—in this case, legal traditions of witness testimony—with fresh, generative heuristics that always keep modern issues like gender and the Anthropocene in view. Cervantes's representation of nonhuman animals brings similar concepts into play, as Steven Wagschal demonstrates in an essay that surveys the many domestic and wild creatures populating *Don Quijote*. Placing the novel in dialogue with animal studies, Wagschal shows how its author pioneers an "animal embodiment" that invites readers into the cognitive workings of other species and, therefore, also into larger discussions in philosophy, biological science, and the environmental humanities. Catherine Infante looks to the Mediterranean world in her analysis of how material culture alternately endorses and complicates the social performances of its frontier characters. By reading various sartorial objects as actants that are pivotal for the narrative of "El amante liberal," Infante rescues not only the nuances of interfaith encounter in Cervantes's Mare Nostrum but those of the material things that have been similarly overlooked.

"Does Philology, backward looking to her core, have a future tense?"[16] The next grouping of essays could be seen to tender an affirmative response to that question, posed at the incipiency of what in the past few years has come to be known as post-philology. Though the contributors here do not align themselves explicitly with that movement, their interventions demonstrate the ongoing relevance of rigorously textual methods of excavating the literary past, not as a reactionary means of consolidating tradition but, crucially, of liberating new and previously subjugated forms of knowledge. While underscoring Cervantes's innovative and at times subversive use of rhetorical and allusive language, Susan Byrne defends the ongoing utility of a hybrid hermeneutics grounded in historically responsive, philological interdisciplinarity. In our current era, when flashy screens command our attention and the pursuit of evidence-based knowledge is imperiled, such practices of textual scrutiny may seem increasingly radical and gesture, however tacitly, toward study as a future-looking praxis of empowerment and critical consciousness. The materiality of corpses returns in the essay by Maxim Rigaux, who studies the entombed figure of *Don Quijote*, part I, chapter 19 as an intertextual linkage with the historic Juan Latino, the enslaved Black African scholar from Granada. By attending to authorial irony and considering seriously Cervantes's facility with Latin, Rigaux's chapter enhances both our comprehension of the episode and the visibility of the Afro-European diaspora. Mercedes Alcalá Galán similarly lifts the veil of Cervantine parody to study the painted *sargas* in *Don Quijote*, part II, chapter 71, aligning these painted canvases of often classical scenes with a broader visual aesthetic of the novel. But she also adopts a more critical stance toward visual studies to situate the *sargas* in their early modern socioeconomic context, in which these artistic objects were not restricted to the elite but instead were fixtures of everyday life for the masses. Hierarchies are toppled in Víctor Sierra Matute's essay, too, which offers a global overview of Cervantes's novel engagement with a multifaceted early modern sensorium. Marshaling various textual examples from *Don Quijote*, Sierra Matute establishes that, by elevating touch, smell, taste, and hearing, the author decenters sight and vision's conventionally privileged status among the senses as well as in critical treatments of the novel.

The final section of the volume assembles a theoretical toolbox for how we are to read Cervantes in an increasingly media-saturated world that readily takes assorted liberties with his oeuvre, not to mention with objective reality itself. David Castillo and William Egginton position Cervantes's writing as a potent means of deliverance from today's siloed media ecosystem, in which rampant mis- and disinformation undermine our collective ability to confront large-scale social, political, humanitarian, and ecological crises. Understanding Cervantes's wry metafictional response to theatrical spectacle, his revelation of artifice through artifice, the critics suggest, can similarly expose the charlatans peddling falsehoods and profiting behind the curtain of twenty-first-century synthetic media. This "reality literacy" would be indispensable for countering the literary hoaxes perpetrated in Cervantes's name by right-wing fabulists and dissected in the chapter by Ana Fernández-Blázquez. Though the apocryphal quotes promoting nationalist and populist ideologies are only the most recent example of how Cervantes and his most famous characters have been mythologized for fundamentalisms of all sorts, they raise pressing questions about the author's legacy in a technologically mediated future. Taking on the overlooked and dubiously authored *La conquista de Jerusalén*, Chad Leahy's chapter interrogates how Cervantes's name authorizes both modern stagings of the play and revisionist attempts to square its crusading ideology with twenty-first-century sensibilities of liberal multiculturalism. Noble though the motives may be for expurgating *La conquista*'s more zealous examples of ethnocentrism, the problem with such edits, according to Leahy, is that they "short-circuit the difficult and necessary labor of thinking through and sitting with the internal contradictions that characterize Cervantes' work."

That labor is an essential pillar of this volume as a whole and, we feel, a mandate of future *cervantismo*. The nineteen essays gathered here collectively make a compelling case for the ongoing vibrancy of Cervantes-centered scholarship and, because of how readily the author's writing appears positioned to intervene in twenty-first-century concerns, distinguish Cervantes as either a timeless figure or a man before his time. But these *Cervantine Futures* also suggest it is time to reckon critically with the author's legacy in order to make room for other, more inclusive vantages on his writing. For that, Cervantes should neither be exalted hagiographically nor dismissed reflexively for the canonical status that he, and we as enthusiastic readers, continues to enjoy. There is a scholarly tendency akin to the one Leahy describes by which we too sometimes avoid, willfully or otherwise, the thornier, more discomfiting aspects of Cervantes's corpus, bracketing off those texts or textual moments that clash with the modern progressivism that we are just as quick to exalt (of which the disregarded *La conquista de Jerusalén* is but one example). Such redemptive gestures can easily devolve into a casuistic exercise of relativity, from which Cervantes emerges triumphantly over his many contemporaries whose stance on such issues as gender or racial equality is much less equivocal. This is not to forfeit nuance, much less to righteously cancel Cervantes, but to remain clear-eyed about his complicity in a society that, not unlike our own, systematically sustained misogyny, racism, tribalism, and otherings of all sorts. If we are to elevate Cervantes for breaking with ideological dogma, then it seems only reasonable that he remain answerable for the ways in which he also perpetuates it. We need make of Cervantes neither a sacred cow nor sacrificial lamb.

"The consideration of the future," claimed the late cultural theorist Svetlana Boym, "makes us take responsibility for our nostalgic tales." What follows is premised on the conviction that whatever aesthetic or political insurgency we ascribe to Cervantes be utilized not for reinforcing his own canonicity, or for indulging our nostalgia for a bygone past, but for actualizing and performing that pathbreaking spirit in a more critical *cervantismo*, one whose engagement with difference opens onto radical, counterhegemonic possibility. Critique, after all, can be a potent act of devotion and admiration. In the words of Felski, "there is no reason why our readings cannot blend analysis and attachment, criticism and love."[17] In an era buffeted by war, climate change, global pandemics, unbridled capitalism, ethnonationalist violence, refugee crises, anti-immigrant sentiment, rampant disinformation, resurgent nationalisms, unchecked authoritarianism, and other existential threats around the globe, it would be as quixotic to seek salvation from these challenges in Cervantes as it would be reckless to cloister ourselves in the escapist comforts of his fictional worlds. But, as the following chapters underscore, these worlds of the literary past point actionably to the present and a vast array of possible futures.

NOTES

1. Derrida, *Archive Fever*, 36.
2. Andersson and Kemp, eds., *Futures*, 1.
3. De Armas, "Futurities, Empire, and Censorship." Along similarly futuristic lines, Brad Nelson has explored Cervantes's science fictional potential. Nelson, "Baroque Science Fiction" and *SciFi Cervantes*.
4. Egginton, *Man Who Invented Fiction*; Johnson, *Affective Geographies*, 51; 6–7. As Foucault famously pronounced: "With all their twists and turns, Don Quixote's adventures form the boundary: they mark the end of the old interplay between resemblance and signs and contain the beginnings of new relations." Foucault, *The Order of Things*, 46.
5. Villaseñor Black and Álvarez, *Renaissance Futurities*, 1.
6. One prominent example is Muñoz, *Cruising Utopia*.
7. Eshel, *Futurity*, 5.
8. Campt, *Listening to Images*, 17. See also Keeling, *Queer Times*, esp. 1–40.
9. Anker and Felski, *Critique and Postcritique*, 1. Felski's postcritical work also draws inspiration from Eve Kosofsky Sedgwick's distinction between "paranoid" and "reparative" reading. Sedgwick, "Paranoid Reading." See also Felski, *Limits of Critique*; Felski, *Uses of Literature*.
10. Sharpe, *In the Wake*, 13.
11. For another interdisciplinary example of this critical turn, see Gottesman, *The Critical Turn in Education*.

12. For merely a representative example, see Cefalu and Reynolds, *Return of Theory*; and Cefalu, Kuchar, and Reynolds, *Return of Theory*, vol. 2. Scholarship of this nature has already reoriented the early English literary canon, for which Shakespeare serves as a paradigmatic example: in the last few years, a panoply of conferences, colloquia, performances, special issues of journals, and edited volumes have placed the bard into extensive dialogue with many of the aforementioned movements.
13. Hutchinson, "What Kind," 89.
14. Layna Ranz and Cortijo Ocaña, "'¿Qué hay de nuevo, viejo?,' " i.
15. Previous edited volumes on Cervantes have provided valuable insights and state-of-the-field readings, including Cruz and Johnson, eds., *Cervantes and His Postmodern Constituencies*; Dopico Black and Layna Ranz, eds., *USA Cervantes*; and Burningham, ed., *Millennial Cervantes*. Yet, with notable exceptions (especially in Cruz and Johnson), such collections on the whole have not positioned themselves in the larger sociopolitical landscape. Monographs germane to that enterprise, among others, include Cascardi, *Cervantes, Literature, and the Discourse of Politics*; Childers, *Transnational Cervantes*; and Fuchs, *Passing for Spain*.
16. Frank, "The Unbearable Lightness," 513.
17. Felski, *Uses of Literature*, 22. See also Jones, *Cervantine Blackness*, 138.

BIBLIOGRAPHY

Andersson, Jenny, and Sandra Kemp. Introduction to *Futures*, ed. Andersson and Kemp. Oxford University Press, 2021.

Anker, Elizabeth S., and Rita Felski, eds. *Critique and Postcritique*. Duke University Press, 2017.

Boym, Svetlana. "Nostalgia and Its Discontents." The Uses of the Past. Special issue of *The Hedgehog Review: Critical Reflections on Contemporary Culture* 9, no. 2 (2007).

Burningham, Bruce R., ed. *Millennial Cervantes: New Currents in Cervantes Studies*. University of Nebraska Press, 2020.

Campt, Tina M. *Listening to Images*. Duke University Press, 2017.

Cascardi, Anthony. *Cervantes, Literature, and the Discourse of Politics*. University of Toronto Press, 2012.

Cefalu, Paul, and Bryan Reynolds, eds. *The Return of Theory in Early Modern English Studies: Tarrying with the Subjunctive*. Palgrave Macmillan, 2011.

Cefalu, Paul, Gary Kuchar, and Bryan Reynolds, eds. *The Return of Theory in Early Modern English Studies*, vol. 2. Palgrave Macmillan, 2014.

Chakrabarty, Dipesh. *The Climate of History in a Planetary Age*. University of Chicago Press, 2021.

Childers, William. *Transnational Cervantes*. University of Toronto Press, 2006.

Cruz, Anne J., and Carroll B. Johnson, eds. *Cervantes and His Postmodern Constituencies*. Routledge, 1998.

De Armas, Frederick. "Futurities, Empire, and Censorship: Cervantes in Conversation with Ovid and Orwell." In *Renaissance Futurities: Science, Art, Invention*, ed. Charlene Villaseñor Black and Mari-Tere Álvarez, 65–82. University of California Press, 2020.

Derrida, Jacques. *Archive Fever: A Freudian Impression*. Translated by Eric Prenowitz. University of Chicago Press, 1996.

Dopico Black, Georgina, and Francisco Layna Ranz, eds. *USA Cervantes: 39 Cervantistas en Estados Unidos*. CSIC/Polifemo, 2009.

Egginton, William. *The Man Who Invented Fiction: How Cervantes Ushered in the Modern World*. Bloomsbury, 2016.

Eshel, Amir. *Futurity: Contemporary Literature and the Quest for the Past*. University of Chicago Press, 2013.

Felski, Rita. *The Limits of Critique*. University of Chicago Press, 2015.

Felski, Rita. *Uses of Literature*. Blackwell, 2008.

Foucault, Michel. *The Order of Things: An Archaeology of the Human Sciences*. Vintage, 1973.

Frank, Roberta. "The Unbearable Lightness of Being a Philologist." *Journal of English and Germanic Philology* 96, no. 4 (1997): 486–513.

Fuchs, Barbara. *Passing for Spain: Cervantes and the Fictions of Identity*. University of Illinois Press, 2003.

Gottesman, Isaac. *The Critical Turn in Education: From Marxist Critique to Poststructuralist Feminism to Critical Theories of Race*. Routledge, 2016.

Hutchinson, Steven. "What Kind of Cervantes Do We Want?" Review of *Cervantes and His Postmodern Constituencies* (ed. Anne J. Cruz and Carroll B. Johnson, 1998), *Cervantes, the Novel, and the New World* (Diana de Armas Wilson, 2000), and *Cervantes and the Material World* (Carroll B. Johnson, 2000). *Journal of Romance Studies* 1, no. 2 (2001): 89–96.

Johnson, Paul Michael. *Affective Geographies: Cervantes, Emotion, and the Literary Mediterranean*. University of Toronto Press, 2020.

Jones, Nicholas R. *Cervantine Blackness*. Pennsylvania State University Press, 2024.

Keeling, Kara. *Queer Times, Black Futures*. New York University Press, 2019.

Layna Ranz, Francisco, and Antonio Cortijo Ocaña, "'¿Qué hay de nuevo, viejo?' o Cervantes after Theory." *eHumanista/Cervantes*, no. 1 (2012): i–xiii.

Muñoz, José Esteban. *Cruising Utopia: The Then and There of Queer Futurity*. New York University Press, 2009.

Nelson, Bradley J. "Baroque Science Fiction in Cervantes: A Proposal." *Revista Canadiense de Estudios Hispánicos* 41, no. 1 (2016): 193–213.

Nelson, Bradley J., ed. "SciFi Cervantes." Special issue, *Cervantes: Bulletin of the Cervantes Society of America* 40, no. 2 (2020).

Sedgwick, Eve Kosofsky. "Paranoid Reading and Reparative Reading, or, You're So Paranoid, You Probably Think This Essay Is About You." In *Touching Feeling: Affect, Pedagogy, Performativity*. Duke University Press, 2003.

Sharpe, Christina. *In the Wake: On Blackness and Being*. Duke University Press, 2017.

Villaseñor Black, Charlene, and Mari-Tere Álvarez, eds. *Renaissance Futurities: Science, Art, Invention*. University of California Press, 2020.

PART I

MINOR(ITIZED) CHARACTERS

CHAPTER I

Character Trouble

Theoretical Reflections on Don Quijote's Marcela

LUIS F. AVILÉS

The incentive to write about character stems from a sustained reflection on what for me has remained a mystery. How is it that a restrictive representation of a person in literary form can elicit so many diverse interpretations and perspectives? How is it that a limited number of personal traits can generate such an abundance of opinions? Why are so many readers invested in the destiny of literary characters? My intention is to review some of the most recent theoretical reflections on literary character in order to understand this dual and paradoxical nature of the relationship between a limited representation in language, and the wide range of interpretations that appear in the form of scholarly commentary. My aim is to show how thinking about character can help us understand some of the major complexities of fiction and its relationship to human beings and their lives. I would like to emphasize that I work with a notion of character that is intricately related to gender, power, social forces, language production, and literary productivity. The years of proposing purely formalist models of reading, or what Toril Moi has defined as a modernist formalist ethos, are frankly over.[1] Although we cannot exclude formal components from our readings, especially in the context of academic discussions, my interest in reflecting theoretically about media-based persons is to enhance our perspective of what otherwise could be seen as a traditional analytical category, one that has tended to circumscribe the interpretative possibilities of Cervantes's exceptionally rich, varied, and complex characters. As I demonstrate in what follows, and in line with the privileging of minor characters in other chapters of this volume, bringing these cutting-edge theories of character to bear on Cervantes's writing surfaces various psychological, moral, and identitary dimensions that have often been neutralized by more purely formalist readings.

As an illustrative example, I will focus on the minor character of Marcela in Cervantes's *Don Quijote de la Mancha*. Why Marcela? Because even though she is a highly restricted fictional representation, critics have nonetheless suggested a wide variety of interpretations of her, many of which revolve around her status as a proto-feminist icon.[2] Marcela is also a more manageable figure whose story begins and ends in three chapters of the novel, allowing me to explore an example of these theoretical trends within the limited scope of this essay. In this approach I will follow loosely the three fields of inquiry proposed by Jens Eder, Fotis Jannidis, and Ralf Scheider for the analysis of characters: the formal crafting of characters (or characterization), how they can be understood and interpreted, and a cultural approach that takes into consideration the sociohistorical context not only of production, but also of reception.[3]

We may begin our exploration of character by quoting the short definition suggested by Jannidis: "Character is a text- or media-based figure in a storyworld, usually human or human-like."[4] In three of the words that comprise this definition (media, storyworld, and human), we begin to see some of the complexities of what a character is: a media-based creation inhabiting a storyworld and "usually" constructed with reference to human life. The storyworld (or fictional world) is defined as "a system of non-real but possible states, or as a constellation, created by the text, of objects, individuals, space, time, events."[5] It is the world in which a character is embedded, affected by the diverse forces that come into play in the story, such as context, norms, moral imperatives, transgressions, points of view, and the existence of a plethora of other beings (including objects, animals, and the like). For Shlomith Rimmon-Kenan, a character "is a construct, put together by the reader from various indications dispersed throughout the text."[6] This definition adds another layer of complexity, since it is now the reader who has to reconstruct a figure by identifying a number of indications or "traits" that are revealed (directly or indirectly) in the story.[7] It is as if a character can only become one when the reader recovers the predicates "dispersed" in the text by an author. Such predicates may point to a prior social or literary construction reproduced (un)evenly in the fabric of discourse, one that will provide the reader with opportunities for extra-textual reflection. The accumulated predicates may point to what Alex Woloch has called a "referential personality," or "the unique sense and abiding impression that a character leaves us with."[8]

The referential force or representational nature of a character cannot be underestimated. In his reading of Marcel Proust's *In Search of Lost Time*, Peter Brooks explains that a character is "a simulation of what it would mean to inhabit another being."[9] For Brooks, what is truly important is representation itself, since represented persons "give us an understanding of life, and of ourselves, that real persons cannot."[10] In other words, fiction allows us to understand the complexity of life indirectly, through creative imagination and fiction. What sort of understandings does the creation of Marcela as a "represented person" (or media-based figure) provide us as readers? What are the bases of her allure as an imaginary being?[11]

The Formal Crafting of Marcela

For the purposes of clarity, I will follow a preliminary distinction between attributes related to formal aspects of character production (the design or textualization of the figure) and all those characteristics that may invoke a person or human being. According to Frow, this is a pervading distinction in theoretical reflections on character, understood as "verbal or visual constructs" or "treated as though they had lives independent of their textual existence."[12] Similarly, Woloch coins the phrase "character space" to define "the intersection of an implied human personality . . . with the definitively circumscribed form of a narrative."[13] From a formal perspective, Marcela is characterized following four preexisting literary forms that Cervantes is incorporating into the episode, and each one of them contributes specific character traits. They are: the topic of the Golden Age; elements from the idealized pastoral; the rustic world inhabited by goatherders and shepherds; and the *canzone disperata* borrowed from the Italian tradition.[14]

The Golden Age topic introduces a communal world where nature provides without having to till the land. It is a world dominated by peace, friendship, and "concordia" (harmony), where the simple shepherdesses were able to walk freely: "Las doncellas y la honestidad andaban . . . por dondequiera, sola y señera, sin temor que la ajena desenvoltura y lascivo intento la menoscabasen" (Maidens in their modesty wandered wherever they wished, alone and mistresses of themselves, without fear that another's boldness or lascivious intent will dishonor them).[15] From the beginning, Cervantes establishes the grounds for the construction of Marcela, for the Golden Age will contribute a crucial character trait and the opportunity for two worlds to coincide. This is achieved by Marcela's unique decision to live under conditions similar to the ones enjoyed by the young shepherdesses in the Golden Age and, in many ways, it reflects the literary genre of the pastoral. As an inhabitant of a small village in La Mancha, Marcela will actualize a life of freedom defined as the possibility of living without marrying, and at the same time refusing to exclude herself from the life outside her house by moving freely in public ("por dondequiera"). In other words, a conception of freedom inherent to Don Quijote's Golden Age discourse is replicated by Marcela. Consequently, she will begin to experience the constant following (and at times stalking) by her male suitors who live their lives in a different world.[16] The temporality of the Golden Age coalesces in a conflictive way with a contemporary world of the town and shepherds, a context that prescribes marriage as part of a culturally dictated life-sequence. This contemporary management of women's bodies and fortunes is shared by all social levels in the episode, by rich farmers, hidalgos, rustic goatherders, and university students. Marcela thus has created a social disruption in the novel that would have replicated a similar disturbance in the author and reader's contemporary world.[17]

In the context just described, the conditions created by Marcela's decision need further clarification. For her, freedom does not mean a complete rejection of or liberation from the presence of men or the world. On the contrary, her idea of living freely includes the possibility of treating men amicably, as long as they follow a linguistic contract: "Que puesto que no huye ni se esquiva de la compañía y conversación de los pastores, y los trata cortés y amigablemente, en llegando a descubrirle su intención cualquiera dellos, aunque sea tan justa y santa como la del matrimonio, los arroja de sí como con un trabuco" (For though she doesn't run from or avoid the company and conversation of the shepherds, and treats them with courtesy and friendship, if any of them reveals his desire for her, even one as honest and holy as matrimony, she hurls it away from her like a stone in a catapult).[18] Following models such as the one found in the topic of the Golden Age and in pastoral genres, Marcela does not flee the encounter with men and never rejects the possibility of having a relationship with them.[19]

With the juxtaposition of two different worlds, and the election of freedom as a way of life, Cervantes generates the conditions that will affect the character of Marcela for the remainder of the episode. Male characters will experience her actions as more than a transgression of a norm. It is as if Marcela has done something unlawful, close to committing a crime, and thus introducing the issue of responsibility. That is why she will be blamed for Grisóstomo's death, among several other complaints. All we know about Marcela from chapter 12 to her final appearance in chapter 14 is what other characters say about her, and most of what they say is negative. These emphatic and insistent opinions are so strong that characters who do not know Marcela, such as Vivaldo, are willing to accept them.[20] The hostility toward Marcela is further amplified by the appearance of another literary genre that serves as a supplement to the topic of the Golden Age and pastoral literature. I am referring to the genre of the *canzone disperata*.[21] As a topical genre, it depicts a cruel lady who ignores the advances of a suffering and desperate lover and, consequently, is deemed ungrateful. In the episode the topic appears in Grisóstomo's "Canción desesperada" (Song of Despair), his last written poem, one that anticipates his desperation and ultimate suicide.[22] As expected from the genre, the poem reproduces some of the negative adjectives associated with Marcela, echoing the dominant negativity assigned to her by other characters. Even though the formal aspects of the construction of Marcela seem to reinforce the indeterminate and schematic depiction of many characters, it is also true that there is a "one-to-many relation" between the construction of a character and its capacity to produce "a major source of readerly imaginative re-creation and of endless interpretative controversy."[23] In other words, the limiting aspects of form do not restrict the capacity of readers to produce contrasting and diverse interpretations. Furthermore, it is obvious that Cervantes did not want Grisóstomo's "Canción desesperada" to tilt the balance toward an overwhelming male perspective. Instead, he wanted to incorporate the poem as part of the narrative sequence to allow Marcela to respond to all the negative opinions against her that are circulating freely. This decision opened up the opportunity of expanding the generic and formal constraints of Marcela, giving her the possibility of being understood from the perspective of a singular woman who is able to voice her own perspective.[24] I want to argue that at specific moments, what Woloch understands as character space (the intersection of human complexity with the constraints of narrative form) seems at times to favor how a human being would or could act in a restrictive social situation. In other words, Cervantes allows Marcela to go beyond the formal aspects of her construction by not forgetting the complexity of the referential personality, the acknowledgment that human beings may respond in different ways to specific constraints.

Marcela's Offering to Men

The sudden appearance of Marcela affects not only all those attending Grisóstomo's burial, but also the readers of the novel. I believe that her speech is responsible for some of the strongest back-and-forth among critics who have worked on this episode, and in many ways, this reflects the referential understanding of the character as a representative human being. At times the referential potentiality is so strong that critics end up choosing a side between the two protagonists of the story based mostly on moral considerations. There is of course no absence of formal elements in Marcela's speech since the semblance of humanity is organized within a rhetorical argumentation. My contention is that those formal elements are no impediment for readers and critics to invest heavily in what Marcela represents.

Marcela's response to the opinions of others represents a shift from traits imposed by outsiders to self-revelations. She is understandably outraged by the circulation of a highly negative version of herself in the mouths of men. She has no other choice but to "volver por mí misma" (restore my own name) so that she may explain "cuán fuera de razón van todos aquellos que de sus penas y de la muerte de Grisóstomo me culpan" (how unreasonable are those who in their grief blame me for the death of Grisóstomo). In her own words, she directly accuses men of lacking reason. She asks for the attention of all those present and promises not to take much of their time "para persuadir una verdad a los discretos" (to persuade discerning men of the truth).[25] Notice how her response will not only be based on reason, but also has the intention to declare a truth that has been lost in the negative discourse of others.

The lack of a reasonable judgment on the part of all men is further amplified by another crucial quote from the beginning of her speech: "Hízome el cielo, según vosotros decís, hermosa, y de tal manera, que, *sin ser poderosos a otra cosa*, a que me améis os mueve mi hermosura, y por el amor que me mostráis decís y aun queréis que esté yo obligada a amaros" (Heaven made me, as all of you say, so beautiful that you cannot resist my beauty and are compelled to love me, and because of the love you show me, you claim that I am obliged to love you in return).[26] Marcela identifies an impossibility common to all men who complain about her way of life and her mode of living. Before explaining the implications of the phrase "sin ser poderosos a otra cosa," I would like to remind the reader that Marcela's decision to live freely and in the open is not a rejection of the possibility of having conversations with men. As I previously explained, Pedro's narrative had established this fact. In addition, Pedro explains that Marcela's "afabilidad y hermosura atrae los corazones de los que la tratan a servirla y a amarla" (her affability and beauty attracts the hearts of those who try to woo her and love her).[27] A key word here is "afable," which Sebastián de Covarrubias defines as "gracioso y agradable en sus pláticas y conversaciones, amoroso y blando en sus respuestas" (gracious and pleasant in dialogue and conversation, lovely and soft in their responses).[28] Men are attracted not only to Marcela's beauty, but also to the way she welcomes and talks to them. This is the contract that men are unable to accept, a revelation of Marcela's unique character zone, which I would like to define as an inviting space that offers conversation and affability on any topic other than love or marriage. Marcela defines all suffering men as powerless to accept such an offer, lacking the disposition to conceive alternate ways of interacting with her. This limitation has several detrimental effects. First, men are powerless before beauty, unable to avoid becoming suffering, pleading, persistent, and obstinate suitors.[29] This is why Marcela mentions alternate modes of beauty that preserve the will from its effects, because for her "no todas las hermosuras enamoran: que algunas alegran la vista y no rinden la voluntad" (not all beauties induce people to fall in love; some are a pleasure to the eye but do not surrender their will).[30] Second, men cannot accept a linguistic contract that promises affability and dialogue, incapable of conversing on other topics. And third, their intellect is severely affected, damaging their own capacity to reason.

If I am pressed to put a name to what Marcela is offering here, I would have to agree with Hernández-Pecoraro and define it as a form of friendship.[31] Not the humanistic conceptualization of the friend as a male counterpart, highly similar in character, able to exchange their deep secrets. It is what I would call a more casual exchange consisting of the possibility to have a dialogue guided by a verbal contract. Marcela's response has identified an impossibility of this type of friendship between men and women, but it is an impossibility that stems from what is defined as an unfortunate (and consistent) response to beauty by male characters, one that disables their capacity to reason. Cervantes echoes here both the mention of friendship in Pedro's narrative, and in Don Quijote's discourse of the Golden Age, where he says that at that time "Todo era paz entonces, todo amistad, todo concordia" (In that time all was peace, friendship, and harmony).[32] Peace and harmony are precisely what is being destroyed by this incapacity of men to explore Marcela's offering of friendship.

Conclusion

In an essay on the relationship between literature and life, Gilles Deleuze proposes that literature "discovers beneath apparent persons the power of an impersonal," which he defines as "a singularity at the highest point." For him, the characters' individual traits "elevates them to a vision that carries them off in an indefinite, like a becoming that is too powerful to them."[33] Marcela is a historical creation that through literature transcends history itself, in the sense that it proposes something bigger, a possible world under construction. Her openness to male characters conceives a new space of interaction that remains precarious and contentious even to this day. Remarkably, this possibility stems from a playful combination of traditional narrative and poetic topoi that resulted in a not-so-unusual creation in Cervantes's writing, since, as other chapters in this volume attest, several minor characters have captured the imagination of readers and critics, such as Zoraida, Ruy Pérez de Viedma, Dorotea, Ricote, and many others. In the case of Marcela, the literary genres combined by Cervantes reproduce conflicting gender traits and sexual expectations. What is described as free movement of women in the topic of the Golden Age is not remotely compatible with the highly emotional male expectations of the Italian *disperata*. Restrictive structures such as literary genres become vehicles for producing innovative particulars in Cervantes's continuous experimentation.[34] Marcela is given the capacity to adopt and at the same time resist literary prescriptions, resulting in the disruption of traditional expectations that would limit her choice of a way of life. In addition, her resistance to a traditional representation replicates sexual impositions and spatial distributions of bodies in the lived reality of readers. Marcela behaves in a fashion similar to what Sara Ahmed has described as a "problem character," one that exerts her willfulness and disposition "to deviate [and] to will the wrong way" within the constellation of all other characters who participate in the episode.[35] And I believe this is why Marcela is such an enduring character.

Unfortunately, this forward-looking possibility opened up by fiction, or what Derek Attridge calls "accommodating the other," continues to be misunderstood and even rejected by many critics, especially male scholars who were or still are unable to understand the cultural exploration that is offered in the episode.[36] Yvonne Jehenson and Ruth El Saffar have documented a strong gender divide between male and female critics of the episode.[37] For example, Cesáreo Bandera accused Marcela of "supreme indifference" toward Grisóstomo; Harry Sieber states that she has a "closed mind and world, a world of madness"; and Thomas Hart and Steven Rendall suggest that Marcela is "rejecting society itself."[38] More recently, Roberto González Echevarría has proposed that Ambrosio is right when he describes Marcela as "the mortal enemy of the human race" because she avoids having children, thus not reproducing and multiplying humanity.[39] It seems to me that, for this critic, marriage and reproduction are unavoidable moral choices imposed by biblical imperatives on women. In other words, he echoes the distribution of cultural imperatives operative in the episode and during Cervantes's time. One critic that has displayed an especially radical, fundamentalist position toward Marcela is Jesús G. Maestro. In the year 2017, he posted two diatribes against the character of Marcela (and feminist critics as well) in video format.[40] First, he states that Marcela is incapable of accepting a life in the world, and that this choice is impossible to defend or to follow in real or fictional life, as if Marcela's intention is to prescribe for everyone the way of life that she has chosen for herself. He argues that in such a world there is no possibility of action, a consequence of Marcela's androphobia and misanthropy. He even goes so far as stating that feminist critics have not only deluded themselves, but also "prostituted" the character in order to defend an absurd notion of freedom. In fact, he claims that if Marcela had lived in our contemporary world, she would have been a member of a cult, or work for a nongovernmental organization (NGO). I think we are dealing here with a purely moralistic, quasi-religious, and highly compromised way of reading. Such an approach does not even consider significant clues provided by the text itself, available to any careful reader of literature. However, this is precisely the expansive nature of literary characters at the interpretative level, allowing readers to propose multiple interpretations of limited fictional personalities. Unfortunately, there is a price to pay for this interpretative freedom, and Maestro's reading is doomed to replicate the critic's own prejudices and hatreds.

I am sure that the character of Marcela will continue to provide readers with alternate interpretative possibilities in the future, even ones that I am unable to grasp at this moment. As argued by Moi, we need "analyses that realize that literary forms always come embedded in world-building language that conveys specific meanings, themes, and subject matter, analyses that realize that texts are never just forms but also expressions, actions, and interventions."[41] Character analysis proves useful when reflecting on both the familiarity and alterity of the construction of singularities within a fictional constellation. The future of Cervantes criticism would do well to embrace this more expansive conception of character, as I have outlined here. If we are going to contribute as critics to the continued work of evaluating the cultures of the past as well as our own, we need to be attentive to the theoretical reflections on this magical capacity of characters to illustrate the complexities of life.

NOTES

1. Moi, "Rethinking Character," 30.
2. For an excellent review of these interpretations of Marcela, see the first chapter of Martí Caloca's *'Yo nací libre.'*
3. Enders, Jannidis, and Schneider, "Characters in Fictional Worlds," 4.

4. Jannidis, "Character." For Heidbrink, a character is a "*figuration of signs* that is able to elicit an idea within the spectator that under certain conditions tends to 'tip over' and appear *human or personlike*." Heidbrink, "Fictional Characters," 79. See also Margolin, "Character," 66–79.
5. Eder, Jannidis, and Scheider, eds., "Characters in Fictional Worlds," 7–8.
6. Rimmon-Kenan, *Narrative Fiction*, 36.
7. Philippe Hamon stated that a character is "as much a reconstruction by the reader as it is a textual construct," quoted in Frow, "Character," 109.
8. Woloch, *The One vs. the Many*, 12.
9. Brooks, *Seduced by Story*, 81.
10. Brooks, *Seduced by Story*, 86.
11. I borrow "allure of an imaginary being" from the title to the fourth chapter of Brooks's *Seduced by Story*, 79.
12. Frow, "Character," 107. Marvin Mudrick has categorized this distinction as the "purist" and the "realistic" arguments in the approach to character; quoted in Rimmon-Kenan, *Narrative Fiction*, 31–32. Woloch's intention is to go beyond this distinction, in *The One vs. the Many*, 17. Expanding the arguments of Woloch, Moi states that characters are either treated as people (what she calls the ethical answer) and as textual constructs (the structuralist answer), and that in both cases what we are confronted with is what she considers a prescription, in Moi, "Rethinking Character," 53. For Brooks, the crucial importance of the representational (fictional) nature of characters would make this distinction difficult, because there is a strong differentiation between a fictional person and a real person. He states that fiction provides a clarification and understanding of the complexities of knowing real human beings, in Brooks, *Seduced by Story*, 89.
13. Woloch, *The One vs. the Many*, 13. For Woloch, the human personality can be "infinitely complex" in comparison to the formal restrictions of narrative form.
14. For other sources of the character, see Martí Caloca's second chapter in *'Yo nací libre.'*
15. Cervantes, *Don Quijote*, I, 11: 123. All quotes in Spanish are from Cervantes, *Don Quijote*, edited by Francisco Rico. Quotes from Spanish will be followed by English translations from Edith Grossman's edition of *Don Quixote*. Each quote will be followed by volume, chapter: page number for the Spanish edition.
16. Marcela's uncle experiences this once she is of marrying age: "era rogado, solicitado e importunado" (asked, begged, and implored). Cervantes, *Don Quijote*, I, 12: 132.
17. In the episode there is a clear parallel between representing aspects of living human beings and a literary construct that replicates those same recognizable social and cultural imperatives. As stated by Frow, a character is "a composition of person based in norms of social personhood and elaborated according to the conventions of particular genres; they are technically quasi-persons." Frow, "Character," 113.
18. Cervantes, *Don Quijote*, I, 12: 133. Similar verbal contracts appear in *Don Quijote*, Book I. For example, Sancho's joke in chapter 20, and the conversation with Cardenio in chapter 24. In all instances the contract is not fulfilled.
19. A point made by Hernández-Pecoraro in "The Absence of the Absence of Women," 37.
20. For example, Vivaldo does not want to destroy Grisóstomo's papers so that they may serve as examples of Marcela's cruelty in the future. Cervantes, *Don Quijote*, I, 13: 145.
21. The genre and its relationship to Grisóstomo's song has been studied by Alonso, "La *Canción desesperada* de Cervantes." See also Avilés, *"No al concertado son, sino al ruido."*

22. Cervantes, *Don Quijote*, I, 14: 146–51.
23. Margolin, "Character," 69.
24. This has been convincingly argued by Jehenson, "The Pastoral Episode in Cervantes' *Don Quijote*," 16.
25. Cervantes, *Don Quijote*, I, 14: 153.
26. Cervantes, *Don Quijote*, I, 14: 153; my emphasis. I must make a correction to the English translation. The phrase "sin ser poderosos a otra cosa" more literally means "without being powerful to do anything else." This is crucial for the interpretation that will follow.
27. Cervantes, *Don Quijote*, I, 12: 133.
28. Covarrubias, *Tesoro*, 49 (my translation).
29. On this persistence, see Cortijo Ocaña, "Acerca del episodio de Grisóstomo y Marcela."
30. Cervantes, *Don Quijote*, I, 14: 153. I have emended the translation.
31. Hernández-Pecoraro, "The Law of Genre/Gender," 294. She coins the word "esquivamiga" (similar to *baciyelmo*) to define this friendship and its capacity to deconstruct the expectations of the pastoral genre.
32. Cervantes, *Don Quijote*, I, 11: 122.
33. Deleuze, "Literature and Life," 227.
34. On the relationship between structures and the production of particulars, see Hogan, "Characters and Their Plots," 137.
35. Ahmed, "Willful Parts," 240. For Ahmed, the willful character "is the one who poses a problem for a community of characters, such that willfulness becomes that which must be resolved and even eliminated." Ahmed, "Willful Parts," 233.
36. See Attridge, *The Singularity of Literature*, 27–28. For Attridge, cultural creation depends on the combination of both the familiar and alterity.
37. See Jehenson, "The Pastoral Episode," 16–17; El Saffar, "In Marcela's Case," 158–59, notes 2, 4, and 5.
38. All quotes in El Saffar, "In Marcela's Case," 159nn4–5.
39. González Echevarría, *Love and the Law in Cervantes*, 87. He also states that Marcela's fortune will be lost due to a lack of a successor.
40. Maestro, "Personajes anómicos," and "El falso feminismo."
41. Moi, "Rethinking Character," 67.

BIBLIOGRAPHY

Ahmed, Sara, "Willful Parts: Problem Characters or the Problem of Character." *New Literary History* 42, no. 2 (Spring 2011): 231–53.

Alonso, Álvaro. "La *Canción desesperada* de Cervantes: Cancioneros, modelos italianos y sensibilidad romántica." In *Cervantes y su tiempo*, vol. 1, edited by Juan Matas Caballero, José María Balcells Doménech and Desirée Pérez Fernández. Universidad de León, 2008.

Attridge, Derek. *The Singularity of Literature*. Routledge, 2004.

Avilés, Luis F. "*No al concertado son, sino al ruido*: La acústica ruidosa en la 'Canción desesperada' de Grisóstomo." *Bulletin of Spanish Studies* 100, no. 2-3 (2023): 431–56. https://doi.org/10.1080/14753820.2023.2177005.

Brooks, Peter. *Seduced by Story: The Use and Abuse of Narrative*. New York Review of Books, 2023.

Cervantes, Miguel de. *Don Quijote de la Mancha*, edited by Francisco Rico. 2 vols. Instituto Cervantes/Crítica, 1998.

Cervantes, Miguel de. *Don Quixote*. Translated by Edith Grossman. Harper Collins, 2003.

Cortijo Ocaña, Antonio. "Acerca del episodio de Grisóstomo y Marcela (I, 12–14): La *porfía airada*." *eHumanista/Cervantes* 1 (2012): 514–36.

Covarrubias, Sebastián de. *Tesoro de la lengua castellana o española*, edited by Ignacio Arellano and Rafael Zafra. Iberoamericana Vervuert, 2006.

Deleuze, Gilles. "Literature and Life." *Critical Inquiry* 23, no. 2 (1997): 225–30.

El Saffar, Ruth Anthony. "In Marcela's Case." In *Quixotic Desire: Psychoanalytic Perspectives on Cervantes*, edited by Ruth Anthony El Saffar and Diana de Armas Wilson. Cornell University Press, 1993.

Enders, Jens, Fotis Jannidis, and Ralph Schneider. "Characters in Fictional Worlds: An Introduction." In *Characters and Fictional Worlds: Understanding Imaginary Beings in Literature, Film, and Other Media*, edited by Jens Eder, Fotis Jannidis, and Ralf Schneider, 3–64. De Gruyter, 2010.

Frow, John. "Character." In *The Cambridge Companion to Narrative Theory*, edited by Mathew Garrett. Cambridge University Press, 2018.

González Echevarría, Roberto. *Love and the Law in Cervantes*. Yale University Press, 2005.

Heidbrink, Henriette. "Fictional Characters and Media Studies: A Survey of the Research." In *Characters and Fictional Worlds: Understanding Imaginary Beings in Literature, Film, and Other Media*, edited by Jens Eder, Fotis Jannidis, and Ralf Schneider. De Gruyter, 2010.

Hernández-Pecoraro, Rosilie. "The Absence of the Absence of Women: Cervantes's *Don Quixote* and the Explosion of the Pastoral Tradition." *Cervantes: Bulletin of the Cervantes Society of America* 18, no. 1 (1997): 24–45.

Hernández-Pecoraro, Rosilie. "The Law of Genre/Gender in *Don Quixote*: Cervantes' Feminism Reconsidered." In *Sexo y género en Cervantes / Sex and Gender in Cervantes*, edited by Esther Fernández Rodríguez and Mercedes Alcalá Galán. Edition Reichenberger, 2019.

Hogan, Patrick. "Characters and Their Plots." In *Characters and Fictional Worlds: Understanding Imaginary Beings in Literature, Film, and Other Media*, edited by Jens Eder, Fotis Jannidis, and Ralf Schneider. De Gruyter, 2010.

Jannidis, Fotis. "Character." In *The Living Handbook of Narratology*, edited by Peter Hühn et al. Hamburg University, 2013. https://www-archiv.fdm.uni-hamburg.de/lhn/node/41.html.

Jehenson, Yvonne. "The Pastoral Episode in Cervantes' *Don Quijote*: Marcela Once Again." *Cervantes: Bulletin of the Cervantes Society of America* 10, no. 2 (1990): 15–35.

Maestro, Jesús G. "El falso feminismo de la pastora Marcela en el *Quijote* de Cervantes." Posted by Jesús G. Maestro to YouTube, February 21, 2017. https://www.youtube.com/watch?v=ehqtk53A7KQ.

Maestro, Jesús G. "Personajes anómicos del Quijote: Ni Grisóstomo es racional ni Marcela es feminista," Posted by Jesús G. Maestro to YouTube, February 14, 2017. https://www.youtube.com/watch?v=U_5LqJzrR2M.

Margolin, Uri. "Character." In *The Cambridge Companion to Narrative*, edited by David Herman. Cambridge University Press, 2007.

Martí Caloca, Ivette. *'Yo nací libre': Tras los pasos de Marcela en el Quijote*. Iberoamericana Vervuert, 2023.

Moi, Toril. "Rethinking Character." In *Character: Three Inquiries in Literary Studies*. University of Chicago Press, 2019.

Rimmon-Kenan, Shlomith. *Narrative Fiction: Contemporary Poetics*. Methuen, 1983.
Woloch, Alex. *The One vs. the Many: Minor Characters and the Space of the Protagonist in the Novel*. Princeton University Press, 2003.

CHAPTER 2

Imperial Discontents and Biopower in "El celoso extremeño"

ISRAEL BURSHATIN

The spectacular failure of the curative project undertaken by Felipo Carrizales, the protagonist of Cervantes's "El celoso extremeño," allows us to interrogate the trappings of a deficient masculinity that neither property, New World gold, nor nubile bride can possibly remedy. Carrizales's prodigal youthful wanderings—from his native Extremadura to other parts of Spain, Italy, Flanders and, most profitably, the Indies—are imbued with the hollow promise of an early modern biopower that upon the wanderer's return is sustained by a largely enslaved and racialized labor force, a motley collective that overturns the master's disciplinary regime by ingenious expressions of subaltern desire. While the Indies may be synonymous with imperial salvationism, the Cervantine narrator swiftly challenges the notion in the opening pages, even if its allure resists the sweeping authorial indictment. A vague, but all the more tempting *remedio* is a fiction of empire: "engaño común de muchos y remedio particular de pocos" (the common cheat of many and the particular remedy of few).[1] And it remains a stubborn, if mendacious elixir, one whose promised relief endures even beyond the narrative frame, as the reader learns at the story's rondo-like conclusion, when the interloper Loaysa follows in the extremeño's footsteps and sets out to secure his own remedio abroad. The promise of a cure-all is a topos in Indies-centered discourses—recall that Bartolomé de las Casas "wrote about six memorials titled *remedios* and many more with other titles that also pertain to this subgenre."[2] And along with the protagonist, the false promise of a boon loops back to the metropole, enabling Cervantes to stage the mechanics of biopower in this exemplary novella. The newly rich and very old bachelor Carrizales not only seeks remedio, but fashions it according to the scale of his ambition—literally, his *mañas* (manipulations, hands-on governance)—and these instantiate the worldview of Spanish privilege.[3] Having chosen Seville as the proper place to find his groove and sire a dynasty, his own brand of biopower now straddles both a marriage plot and suitable mise-en-scène; the latter is a hermetic and imposing abode. His ostentatious fortress/ seraglio is fitted out with bespoke architectural elements, such as clerestory windows and an entryway secured with a *torno* (revolving dumbwaiter). Often used in convents to facilitate commercial transactions while honoring the residents' seclusion, the *torno* here serves to obstruct the gaze of other males upon Leonora, the objectified and confined bride, as well as to constrain the sequestered household staff. The edifice is thus a paradox: eyecatching and concealing—"a gloomy false paradise."[4] Thus securely housed, Carrizales seeks to consolidate wealth and exert mastery over time by siring progeny—hence the discipline imposed on his household, in which humans are reduced to efficient labor and reluctant vigilantes. These are exclusively female, with the exception of Luis, the Black eunuch, who is confined to a correspondingly liminal space between inner and outer doors. Enslaved or not, all are shut in, subjected to the remedio seeking discipline imposed by the *indiano* master. While the built environment is silo-like, Cervantes's language, especially as articulated by two of the enslaved actors—Luis and Guiomar, a Portuguese speaker who enacts the *habla de negros* trope and is described as *negra bozal*—enables a parodic release from the old extremeño's version of remedial coloniality.[5] The master's program is smoothly aligned with the biopolitical imperative "to make live" rather than "to let die."[6]

The female staff are first introduced, simply, as racialized and diverse chattel; and four of these he branded: "Compró asimismo cuatro esclavas blancas y herrólas en el rostro, y otras dos negras bozales" (he also bought four white female slaves, whom he branded on the face, and two Black women, who did not speak Castilian).[7] While in the culture at large the unmarked term was *negros/as*—whereby the word for skin color also denoted the chattelized condition—here the term *esclavas blancas* points to a biological referent and asserts a "naturalizing" designation by skin color. According to historian Aurelia Martín Casares the focus on the somatics of the enslaved was common in early modern Iberia and re-defined bonded subjects "exclusively through a biological referent (skin color) under the pretense of naturalizing the inferior status; on the other hand the biological erased cultural differences among Black Africans."[8] Carrizales as slave-master expands upon this strategy by inscribing the chattelized condition in the architecture of the household. But this takes an unexpected turn as the master's domain is appropriated by choreographed acts of *cimarrón* (maroon) resistance on the part of the multi-ethnic staff. Their collective assertion of what assumes the features of a carnivalesque, topsy-turvy reckoning is one enhanced by an eroticized theatricality that results in the collapse of Carrizales's dynastic ambitions. In his demise, the diminished master is entrapped by both his architectural folly and his unquestioning adherence to the biopolitical strategies of Spanish imperial endeavors—the colonizer ensnared in coloniality's deathly grip.

If, as Foucault has shown, the sovereign's prerogative is "to take life or let live," Carrizales assumes a similar role by virtue of his control over the lives of his bride and household attendants.[9] His version of "letting live" requires that precise measure and control be exerted over bodies regimented for work, vigilance, or procreation; their movements and field of vision are circumscribed to such an extreme that any intruder would surely be greeted as a savior of sorts. A telling example of Carrizales's modus operandi—one that focuses strategically on embodiment and visual signs of class, gender, and race—occurs early in the novella. As soon as he gains his future in-laws' assent Felipo notices with disgust his bride's shabby costume. In this emblematic moment of clothing as a trope for the master's own signature, the sore spot that needs immediate attention is young Leonora's skirt, which most likely is the only one in her wardrobe. This most elementary of markers of the feminine is found to be utterly abject and it just won't do for the *señora* of a wealthy *indiano*. With the same sort of snappy, decisive turn witnessed earlier during his perambulations around Seville, when Felipo resolved to marry the teenage Leonora—"Alto, pues: echada está la suerte, y ésta es la que el Cielo quiere que yo tenga" (Enough now: the die is cast and this is the path that Heaven wants me to follow)—he quickly revises his plan to have a tailor come and style the new garments directly on the young woman's person, suddenly anxious over the imagined intimacy between tailor and client.[10] The alternate scheme, which we'll examine in greater detail, introduces the guiding principle that also informs the house make-over: the totality of objects in the master's ken is to be scaled to his grasp, his *mañas*.[11] His mission is now clear: "Casarme he con ella; encerraréla, y haréla a mis mañas, y con esto, no tendrá otra condición que aquella que yo le enseñare" (I shall take her as my wife, shut her away and mould her to my ways).[12]

Carrizales's belated accession to the seigneurial ranks entails frantic if highly rational forms of husbandry. His exertions are closely reasoned acts even if his ability to make rational choices is often impaired. Prone to making rash judgments, he is equally given to deferrals; he returns again and again to a decision yet to be implemented. His choice of Leonora as his bride is a key example of this unstable amalgam of impetuosity and stasis; and it is in this context of push and pull that he repeatedly utters what the narrator dubs his *soliloquio*, cited above. The opening imperative—*alto pues* (enough now)—the narrator slyly points out, Felipo utters not once, but one hundred times before asking Leonora's parents for the hand of their just barely nubile daughter. His initiatives beyond requesting the teenager's hand in marriage stay within the pattern of anxious strivings to secure a home base in which he alone would possess the phallus and thereby exercise absolute authority over the lives of his subjects. Along with the noun *remedio*, *medida* keeps popping up right from the start. A perceived remedy or cure that would bring desired equilibrium, humoral or merely moral, along with the accurate rendition of an object or person in an act of representation or performance, both concepts, *remedio* and *medida*, point to a hegemonic ideal. But for the melancholy Carrizales, confidence is an elusive trait, albeit one that he tenaciously pursues. Hence his single-minded "prepping"—the intricate precautions taken to avert shame, theft, penetration, loss, or, in the case of intimacy, deferrals that we are led to regard as symptomatic of the master's irreversible sexual impotence:

> Y la primera muestra que dio de su condición celosa fue no querer que sastre alguno tomase la *medida* a su esposa de los muchos vestidos que pensaba hacerle, y así, anduvo mirando cuál otra mujer tendría, poco más o menos, el talle y cuerpo de Leonora, y halló una pobre a cuya *medida* hizo hacer una ropa, y probándosela a su esposa, halló que le venía bien, y por aquella *medida* hizo los demás vestidos, que fueron tantos y tan ricos, que los padres de la desposada se tuvieron por más que dichosos en haber acertado con tan buen yerno, para *remedio* suyo y de su hija.
>
> The first sympton he betrayed of his jealous temper was that he would not have any tailor to take his wife's *measure* for the many dresses he proposed to bestow on her; and so he went looking about for some woman who was pretty much about the height and figure of Leonora. He discovered a poor girl to whose *measure* he had a gown made, and his bride having tried it on he found that it fitted her well, and by the same means he had the rest of her dresses

> made, which were so many and so sumptuous that the bride's parents considered themselves more than fortunate in having met with so good a son-in-law for their own *advantage* and that of their daughter.[13]

As noted earlier with regard to the soliloquio, Carrizales here again performs an act of quick visual reconnaissance that yields a properly scaled female shape, *poco más o menos* (pretty much), like Leonora's, so that the tailor could cut the dress patterns to scale and perform proper fittings on the bride's body-double, while also evoking the foundational moment of surveillance in the story, when the elderly gentleman's explorations around Seville take him by chance in front of Leonora's family house, the visibly dilapidated abode of an impoverished noble family. Carrizales may be old and his vigor irremediably compromised by both his age and dissolute youth, but he is still eagle-eyed as he initially observes his bride-to-be at an open window:

> Quiso su suerte que pasando un día por una calle, alzase los ojos y viese a una ventana puesta una doncella, al parecer, de edad de trece o catorce años, de tan agradable rostro y tan hermosa, que sin ser poderoso para defenderse el buen viejo Carrizales, rindió la flaqueza de sus muchos años a los pocos de Leonora.
>
> Destiny willed that one day passing along a street he lifted up his eyes and beheld a damsel standing at a window who was apparently between thirteen and fourteen years of age, and so agreeable and lovely a countenance that, quite unable to defend himself, good old Carrizales surrendered the feebleness of his many years to the few years of Leonora.[14]

In the blink of an eye he takes in Leonora's charms—as well as her family's scant resources, circumstances he considers propitious for his own prospects. His quasi-scientific gaze—seemingly infallible when it comes to any sort of calibration or *medida*—initially casts the old man's governance in a confident light, until, of course, it ceases to be so in the story's traumatic denouement when Carrizales is shocked to discover that his fortress/ seraglio—a supposedly "immune and impenetrable space"—has been breached and finds his wife in bed and in the arms of Loaysa, the *virote* (studly *sevillano*).[15]

Among Carrizales's works of husbandry, it is the couple's home that stands as the most elaborate of his feats of surveillance and defense. But as we enter his realm, we encounter a site that impresses less as a secure environment than a chronotope of conflicting temporalities and valences—elegant interiors, pleasure house, fortress, slave quarters. In one important respect his abode hews to the technologies of the self already on display in Carrizales's make-over strategy for Leonora's wardrobe. As we saw in the bride's posh outfits, made to the body-double's measure, her costumes do not principally provide comfort or protection from the elements; rather, they enact the husband's ambitions. In the world of the Jealous Extremaduran, both the wardrobe make-over and the house's remodeling materialize hierarchy; from his elevated vantage point, mastery of the self is el celoso's overriding concern and one that is subject to insistent iterations. He is, after all, conditioned by nearly a lifetime spent as a settler-conqueror in the Indies, experiences which he systematically applies to a domestic space that recalls a conquered island, colony, or *ínsula.*[16] He is, in short, "a technician of sequestration, an architect of imprisonment."[17]

It should not surprise us, then, that Carrizales's insistent gendering of the couple's home is not a unique event in the history of architecture, as it reproduces some key principles of domestic architectural theory that are gender specific; these were articulated in the fifteenth century by Leon Battista Alberti in two of his treatises, *On the Art of Building in Ten Books* and *Della Famiglia.* As Mark Wigley observes, Alberti's treatise "contains an overt reference to architecture's complicity in the exercise of patriarchal authority by defining a particular intersection between a spatial order and a system of surveillance which turns on the question of gender."[18] For Alberti, surveillance is part and parcel of masculine authority, while woman, imagined as immobile and situated in the home, serves as both object and adjuvant—a compliant monitor in the service of masculinist vigilance. She may be visually alert, but she is presumably—and there's the rub in Cervantes—lacking in agency: "The woman, as she remains locked up at home, should watch over things by staying at her post, by diligent care and watchfulness. The man should guard the woman, the house, and his family and country, but not by sitting still."[19]

The genius of Cervantes's recasting of Alberti's architectural master narrative is the extent to which he infuses the worlds of both servants and masters with the cultural politics of early modern empire. The subordinate actors—especially Marialonso, an astute *dueña*, Guiomar, a witty Portuguese-speaking *negra bozal*, the ballad-loving eunuch Luis, and even the cloistered bride, Leonora—get to display their own forms of agency in a context so imbued with combined aesthetic and sensual pleasures that one begins to wonder about the time and place in which they occur. It is this upbeat dimension of the narrative, linked as it is to subaltern desire, that brings criticality into the picture. Pertinent to our undertanding of these acts of subaltern performativity is Joan Scott's characterization of the politics of experience: "emancipation is a teleological story in which desire ultimately overcomes social control and becomes visible."[20] As we discuss further, the attendants' emphasis on the jouissance of the visible not only interferes with the master's monitoring schemes, but also opens the floodgates to peripheral actors and desires; in the end these overturn the Extremaduran's regime. Equally compromised is the assiduously constructed house, erected *a medida de sus celos* (befitting his obsessions) as it turns into a peculiar and paradoxical ruin, its collapse as real as can be, but, one retrofitted peephole aside, showing no visible traces of such—the obverse of Leonora's family home, a crumbling shell that still asserts claims of blood purity and class privilege.[21]

Let us take a closer look at the *cimarronaje* (marronage) enacted by subaltern actors as they explore the opportunities now open before them, the master's gaze and his physical restraints temporarily suspended. As we shall see, those confined to Carrizales's "prepper palace" find ways to act out their desires. Marialonso, the older *dueña*, and Luis, who inhabits and manages the *casapuerta* (passageway), seize the opportunity to pursue their own pleasures as well as to arouse their fellow attendants and the confined mistress. How fitting, then, that these two pseudo-lieutenants should also be actors whose genders are interstitial; both fall under Loaysa's spell and disarm the master's carceral design. Luis's enthusiasm for *romances moriscos* (Morisco ballads)—especially those featuring the celebrated enamored Moor of Granada, "del moro Abindarráez"—place him in the sweet spot of homosocial affect, which the wily Loaysa, in his guise as a street performer and guitar and singing instructor, cannily exploits in order to penetrate the house and enjoy its treasures.[22] Marialonso, for her part, appropriates the masculine gaze, to the delight of her mistress and the assembled *doncellas*. We begin with Luis's musical seduction. With Loaysa disguised as a mendicant and physically disabled singer of ballads, his choice of a Moorish ballad does the trick and captures Luis's heart, thereby turning him into an accomplice:

> Con este talle se ponía cada noche a la oración a la puerta de la casa de Carrizales, que ya estaba cerrada, quedando el negro, que Luis se llamaba, cerrado entre las dos puertas. Puesto allí Loaysa, sacaba una guitarrilla algo grasienta y falta de algunas cuerdas, y como él era algo músico, comenzaba a tañer algunos sones alegres y regocijados, mudando la voz por no ser conocido. Con esto se daba priesa a cantar romances de moros y moras, a la loquesca, con tanta gracia, que cuantos pasaban por la calle se ponían a escucharle, y siempre, en tanto que cantaba, estaba rodeado de muchachos; y Luis el negro, poniendo los oídos por entre las puertas, estaba colgado de la música del *virote*, y diera un

> brazo para poder abrir la puerta y escucharle más a su placer: *tal es la inclinación que los negros tienen a ser músicos.*
>
> In this guise he began to plant himself nightly at the hour of *Ave Maria* at the door of the house of Carrizales, which was already shut, the Black attendant, whose name was Luis, remaining penned between the two doors. Thus posted, Loaysa was in the habit of taking out a small guitar, rather greasy and lacking some strings, and as he was a bit of a musician he began to play merry, lively tunes, disguising his voice so as not to be recognized. He also took care to sing some ballads of Moors and Moorish women in burlesque style, but with so much grace that those who passed along the street stopped to listen to him, and always while he sang he was surrounded by boys. Luis, the Black, putting his ears between the doors, was arrested by the music of the bachelor, and would have given his arm to have been able to open the door, and listen more at his ease; *such is the liking of Blacks for being musicians.*[23]

We might wonder what the narrator is up to here in characterizing Luis's affinity to music as a matter of "race." Is the conjunction of aesthetics and affect the exclusive privilege of blackness, as we've just been told? Well, not at all if we recall that in a foundational text of the poetic discourse of "romances de moros y moras," (ballads about Moorish men and women) *La historia del Abencerraje y la hermosa Jarifa* (1561; 1565), we witness a similar phenomenon that captivates not subaltern actors, but those valiant Christian knights who guard the Granadan frontier. Readers of the so-called Moorish novel will recall that the elite fighters under the command of Rodrigo de Narváez spy upon a richly attired Moorish knight and are mesmerized by his equestrian grace, posh outfit, and, especially, the sentimental ditty he sings as he rides along:

> Nascido en Granada,
> criado en Cártama,
> enamorado en Coín,
> frontero de Álora
>
> First in Granada I was borne,
> In Cartama brought up and bred,
> To Allora fronter,
> And in Coyn enamoured.[24]

What Cervantes's narrator and that of the anonymous author of *El Abencerraje* share as hegemonic privilege is the notion that the ethnic other's aesthetic competence falls short of some unspecified standard. In the latter "the music lacked artistry," while in the former the string instrument (*guitarrilla*) was "rather greasy and lacking some strings," which would call into question the enslaved gatekeeper *Luis el negro*'s aesthetic delight in the *guitarrilla*'s tones. Interestingly, as both narrators stake out their own critical distance from their respective singers, their auditors are swept away. And yet, this notion of excess of affection is precisely what captures the *Abencerraje*'s enthralled audience of "Old Christian" antagonists: "Aunque a la música faltaba el arte, no faltaba al moro contentamiento; y como traía el corazón enamorado, a todo lo que decía daba buena gracia. Los escuderos, transportados en verle, erraron poco de dejarle pasar, hasta que dieron sobre él" (Although the music lacked artistry, the Moor did not lack for happiness, and his heart, which was full of love, gave charm to his every word. The squires, transported by the sight of him, almost let him through before they set upon him).[25]

Surely, we as readers—not to mention the crew confined to quarters in the Extremaduran's prison-house—also share in the Black eunuch's enthusiasm for Moorish ballads. As we have just seen in the passage from *El Abencerraje*, Luis's devotion to *romances de moros y moras* reproduces the thrill experienced by Rodrigo de Narváez's *fronteros* (borderland knights)—and one that is overdetermined in the literary history of Iberian Orientalism. Viewed in this context, the ethnic othering in the passage quoted from "El celoso" doesn't quite stick since Narváez's band of *fronteros* are as prone as the Black eunuch to swoon over the lyrics recounting the lovesickness of a dashing Moorish suitor. In an interesting twist of biopower, we find in both Cervantes and the *Abencerraje* the authority to administer death or to grant or guard a life suddenly upended in the presence of affect released by aesthetic rapture.

Turning now to Marialonso, her desire is also awakened by Loaysa's transgressive presence inside the residence and, like Luis's own admiration for the inventive bounder, will result in a witty and theatrical performance; she leads the band of assembled *doncellas* in a burlesque version of the familiar poetic device of *blason anatomique*. In Carrizales's vigilance-intensive setting theatricality assumes elements of a drag performance, thereby opening up the gender binary to multiple points along a spectrum of such expressions. Marialonso is the mistress/ master of ceremonies whose "shtick" consists in the appropriation of the masculine gaze. Taking on lyric poetry's familiar enumeration of a female beloved's body parts (*blason anatomique*), the older *dueña*, enacts the trope, literally, by illuminating handsome Loaysa's physical charms, one by one, with the aid of a lit candle. She thereby usurps the traditionally male role of poetic fashioner of desirable bodies. These are now her *mañas*, not the master's. She manipulates the light, but refrains from speaking. The translation of the visuals into verbal language is a task for the sisterly attendees. Several get to express their pleasure in words; these are fan-generated *blasones*. Leonora, the confined mistress, watches in silence as she now realizes what she has been deprived of in her marriage to the doddering Carrizales:

> Fuéronse a la sala, donde había un rico estrado, y cogiendo al señor [Loaysa] en medio, se sentaron todas. Y tomando la buena Marialonso una vela, comenzó a mirar de arriba abajo al bueno del músico, y una decía: "¡Ay, qué copete que tiene, tan lindo y tan rizado!" Otra: "¡Ay, qué blancura de dientes! ¡Mal año para piñones mondados que más blancos ni más lindos sean!" Otra: "¡Ay, qué ojos tan grandes y tan rasgados! ¡Y por el siglo de mi madre que son verdes, que no parecen sino que son de esmeraldas!" Ésta alababa la boca, aquélla los pies, y todas juntas hicieron dél *menuda anotomía y pepitoria*. Sola Leonora callaba, y le miraba, y le iba pareciendo de mejor talle que su velado.
>
> [They] went off to the drawing room where there was a splendid dais, and putting the gentleman in the middle, they all sat down. Whereupon the good Marialonso took a candle and began to inspect the worthy musician from top to bottom. "Oh what a quiff he has, it's so handsome and curly," said one. "How white his teeth are! You won't find peeled pine nuts whiter or prettier than those!," said another. "Oh what big, wide eyes he has! And upon my mother's soul, they are so green that they look like emeralds!" said another. This one praised his mouth, that one his feet, and all together they made a detailed *anatomical study and fricasee* of him. Leonora alone was silent; she looked at him and gradually perceived him to be better proportioned than her husband.[26]

We've already remarked on the parallels between Marialonso and Luis. Their gemination as actors who disrupt the hierarchy of genders is very much a function of their respective peep shows of *anotomía y pepitoria* (anatomical study and fricasee).

A preceding episode of show-and-tell features Luis as precursor in Marialonso's role as presenter and light technician in displaying Loaysa as both singer of ballads and boy-toy. This earlier instance takes place prior to opening the doors from the liminal *casapuerta* to the house proper, which granted Loaysa access to the inner sanctum. Here we witness an echt peep show, enabled by a small opening through which the confined women, regardless of rank or ethnicity, can leer at the masculine intruder. Having drilled a hole into the *torno* ("revolving dumbwaiter") adjacent to Luis's cramped quarters, the *doncellas* line up and approach the aperture one by one to gaze at Loaysa's illuminated body parts. This suggestive guided tour of Loaysa's physique, mediated by the peephole-enhanced *torno*, is, in the words of Eduardo Olid Guerrero "an irresistible synecdoche for the feminine gaze."[27] For this special occasion the rogue intruder has shed his beggar's rags and ditched his crutches, replacing them with a courtier's flashy costume, "con cuello almidonado con grandes puntas y encaje" (with a starched lace ruff, elongated tips and lace).[28] In the eyes of those assembled, the young intruder is a veritable angel:

> Poníanse una al agujero para verle, y luego otra; y porque le pudiesen ver mejor, andaba el negro paseándole el cuerpo de arriba abajo con el torzal de cera encendido. Y después que todas le hubiesen visto, hasta las negras bozales, tomó Loaysa la guitarra, y cantó aquella noche tan extremadamente, que las acabó de dejar suspensas y atónitas a todas, así a la vieja como a las mozas . . .
>
> They took turns at looking through the hole, and so they might see him better, Luis the Black moved the lighted wax taper up and down the length of his body. And once everybody had seen him, including the *negras bozales*, Loaysa took up his guitar and sang so charmingly that night, that he left them all, from the old woman to the young girls, enchanted and amazed . . .[29]

The visual and auditory pleasures generated by Loaysa's illicit performance, enhanced by Luis's canny lighting effects, displace the joyless architectural order of husbandry. Recall that Carrizales had built his house *a medida de sus celos* (befitting his obsessions) as labors of "retentive anxiety."[30]

Carrizales may indeed be a clinical case and his control over his domiciled subaltern staff fatally compromised, but his strategies recall the established practices of early modern Iberian enslavement. Indeed, the variety of ethnic backgrounds found among his household workers corresponds to what historians have taught us about the practices of subjugation and their corporeal imprint. Like other petty sovereigns of his time and place, Carrizales employs the branding iron to inscribe his authority over the flesh of those who, owing to a light complexion (most likely Moriscas), might slip away and undermine the state's biopolitical regime of surveillance that we have seen is so strategic a component even on a smaller, more local scale in the Extremeño's assertions of biopower. If we heed Hortense Spillers's now classic study of the cultural meanings produced by forms of violence visited upon enslaved bodies—specifically, her reference to the "hieroglyphics of the flesh" of those branded—we can begin to entertain relevant questions regarding the cursory account of Carrizales's most dastardly of his soliloquios, his snap decision to brand the faces of his white female slaves.[31] Why does he do it? Are the context and other specifics omitted since branding was so familiar a practice in the sixteenth and seventeenth centuries? I would hazard a guess that Cervantes did not bother to add any context or psychological specifics to this fundamental enactment of the colonizer's privilege over commodified bodies since it was, indeed, widely practiced in the Iberian Peninsula; branding was as unremarkable to them as vanity plates are to today's automobile drivers. Indeed, so terse a description might be just enough to signal that we are in the presence of lives reduced to the barest of the bare; think again of Leonora's prickly skirt and place that alongside the scarification that would over time take the place of the burned flesh, presumably still healing over, of those chosen to be branded. From Carrizales's perspective, his spouse's shabby garment was beyond the pale, while his enslaved attendants' freshly inscribed facial tissue was just par for the course.

Turning once again to the staff's joyful *blasones* during Marialonso's drag act and Luis's peep show, we observe that both exemplify an eventful sort of mimicry, one that produces a provisional but truly festive display of what female sovereignty would feel like. The *doncellas*' masculine-like gazing through the peephole, along with their assumption of linguistic and poetic authority as they call out Loaysa's body parts, condition their display of subaltern *jouissance*—and they act without any hesitation, with no need for soliloquios. It is in these now smoothly installed episodes of female workers at play—aided and abetted by the strategically placed eunuch Luis—that the master's abode achieves its full polyvalent potential, with *remedio* and *medida* most emphatically displaced, even if the woeful humiliation cast by the branded hieroglyphs on the faces of some of the women re-connect to the wider world of grotesque forms of surveillance and subjugation.

NOTES

1. Cervantes, "El celoso extremeño," 89; "The Jealous Estremaduran," 3.
2. Jáuregui and Solodkow, "Biopolitics," 137. For Américo Castro, "The Indies thus appear . . . as nursery and dumping place of human flaws," Castro, "Cervantes," 214; this and all other uncredited translations are mine.

3. Castro situates both Carrizales and his rival Loaysa among the ruling elite: "The two male protagonists symbolize the dominant class," Castro, "Cervantes," 214.
4. Forcione, "El celoso," 36.
5. For other approaches to Luis and Guiomar, see the chapters in this volume by Johnson and Tweede and Lagresa-González, respectively. Guiomar's blend of pungent critique and linguistic mastery instantiates Nicholas R. Jones's insight regarding the speech of Ibero-African subjects, which "animates black Africans' agency, empowers their resistance, and highlights their African cultural retentions in early modern Spain." Jones, *Staging 'Habla de Negros,'* xiii.
6. Jáuregui and Solodkow, "Biopolitics," 142, 146.
7. Cervantes, "El celoso," 98. I cite from the English translation by Thacker and Thacker, "The Jealous Old Man," 347, with my own emendations.
8. Martín Casares, *La esclavitud,* 150.
9. Foucault, "Society," 62.
10. Cervantes, "El celoso," 94; "The Jealous Old Man," 345.
11. For José Manuel Hidalgo, Carrizales evokes the figure of Pygmalion. He cites a sculptor's "defining flourish" (rasgo moldeador), which he locates in the use of mañas, "with its semantic implication of manual activity." Hidalgo, "El engaño," 507.
12. Cervantes, "El celoso," 94; "The Jealous Old Man," 345.
13. Cervantes, "El celoso," 95–96; "The Jealous Estremaduran," 6; emphasis added.
14. Cervantes, "El celoso," 93–94; "The Jealous Estremaduran," 5.
15. Medina, "Cervantes, América," 71.
16. Fernández, "The Bonds," 974.
17. Molho, "Aproximación," 752.
18. Wigley, "Untitled," 332.
19. Alberti, quoted by Wigley, "Untitled," 334.
20. Scott, "The Evidence," 778.
21. The phrase, "a medida de sus celos," is uttered by the servant-gracioso Mosquito in the comedia by Pedro Calderón de la Barca, *El escondido y la tapada*: "Esta es la casa, sin duda / Que aquel famoso extremeño / Carrizales fabricó / A medida de sus celos, / Pues no hay puerta ni ventana, / Guarda, patio ni agujero / Por donde salga un mosquito." Jornada II, quoted in Cervantes, ed. Rodríguez Marín, n11, 97.
22. Cervantes, "El celoso," 114. On the crafting of the homosocial in the *Abencerraje,* see Bass, "Homosocial Bonds and Desire."
23. Cervantes, "El celoso," 108–9; "The Jealous Estremaduran," 10, emphasis added. The text cited from Maccoll's translation includes my emendations.
24. I cite, with emendation, from Yong's English translation of Montemayor's *Diana* (1598), which includes the *Abencerraje* as an intercalated tale; Kennedy, ed., *A Critical Edition,* 162.
25. López Estrada, ed., *El Abencerraje,* 134–36; Fuchs et al., ed. and trans., *'The Abencerraje,'* 29.
26. Cervantes, "El celoso," 148–49; "The Jealous Old Man," 375, emphasis added.
27. Olid Guerrero, *Del teatro,* 70.
28. Cervantes, "El celoso," 132; "The Jealous Old Man," 365, with my emendations.
29. Cervantes, "El celoso," 133; "The Jealous Old Man," 365.
30. Weber, "Tragic," 40.
31. Spillers, "Mama's Baby, Papa's Maybe," 67.

BIBLIOGRAPHY

Bass, Laura R. "Homosocial Bonds and Desire in the *Abencerraje*," *Revista Canadiense de Estudios Hispánicos*, 24, no. 3 (2000), 453–71.

Castro, Américo. "Cervantes se nos desliza en 'El celoso extremeño,'" *Papeles de Son Armadans*, Febrero–Marzo 1968, 204–22.

Cervantes Saavedra, Miguel de. "El celoso extremeño," *Novelas ejemplares*, vol. 2, edited by Francisco Rodríguez Marín, 85–171. Espasa-Calpe, 1969.

Cervantes Saavedra, Miguel de. "The Jealous Estremaduran," *Exemplary Novels*, vol. 2, edited by James Fitz-Maurice-Kelly, translated by N. Maccoll, 3–33. Gowans & Gray, 1902.

Cervantes Saavedra, Miguel de. "The Jealous Old Man from Extremadura," *The Complete Exemplary Novels*, edited by Barry Ife and Jonathan Thacker, translated by Michael Thacker and Jonathan Thacker, 337–89. Liverpool University Press, 2013.

Fernández, James D. "The Bonds of Patrimony: Cervantes and the New World," *PMLA*, no. 109 (October 1994): 969–81.

Forcione, Alban K. "El celoso extremeño and the Classical Novella: The Mystery of Freedom," 31–92. *Cervantes and the Humanist Vision*. Princeton University Press, 1982.

Foucault, Michel. "'Society Must Be Defended': Lecture at the Collège de France," 61–81. *Biopolitics: A Reader*, edited by Timothy Campbell and Adam Sitze. Duke University Press, 2013.

Fuchs, Barbara, Larissa Brewer-García and Aaron J. Ilika, eds. and trans. *'The Abencerraje' and 'Ozmin and Daraja': Two Sixteenth-Century Novellas from Spain*. University of Pennsylvania Press, 2014.

Hidalgo, José Manuel. "El engaño del sentido ocular en la 'Novela del celoso extremeño': Pigmalión y Narciso," *Revista de Estudios Hispánicos* 46, no. 3 (2012): 505–25.

Jáuregui, Carlos A., and David Solodkow. "Biopolitics and the Farming (of) Life in Bartolomé de las Casas." In *Bartolomé de las Casas, O.P.: History, Philosophy, and Theology in the Age of European Expansion*, edited by David Thomas Orique OP and Rady Roldán Figueroa, translated by Juliet Lynd. Brill, 2019.

Jones, Nicholas R. *Staging 'Habla de Negros': Radical Performances of the African Diaspora in Early Modern Spain*. Pennsylvania State University Press, 2019.

Kennedy, Judith M., ed. *A Critical Edition of Yong's Translation of George of Montemayor's 'Diana' and Gil Polo's 'Enamoured Diana.'* Clarendon Press, 1968.

López Estrada, Francisco, ed. *El Abencerraje: Novela y romancero*. Cátedra, 2000.

Martín Casares, Aurelia. *La esclavitud en la Granada del siglo XVI: Género, raza y religión*. Universidad de Granada, 2000.

Medina, Alberto. "Cervantes, América y el contagio del vacío." *Arizona Journal of Hispanic Cultural Studies*, no. 7 (2003): 67–73.

Molho, Maurice. "Aproximación al 'Celoso extremeño,'" *Nueva Revista de Filología Hispánica*, no. 38, Número Monográfico Dedicado a Cervantes (1990), 743–92.

Olid Guerrero, Eduardo. *Del teatro a la novela: El ritual del disfraz en las 'Novelas ejemplares' de Cervantes*. Instituto Universitario de Investigación Miguel de Cervantes and Universidad de Alcalá, 2015.

Scott, Joan W. "The Evidence of Experience." *Critical Inquiry* 17, no. 4 (1991), 773–97.

Spillers, Hortense. "Mama's Baby, Papa's Maybe: An American Grammar Book." *Diacritics* 17, no. 2 (1987): 64–81.

Weber, Alison. "Tragic Reparation in Cervantes' 'El celoso extremeño.'" *Cervantes* 4 (1984): 35–51.

Wigley, Mark. "Untitled: The Housing of Gender," In *Sexuality and Space*, edited by Beatriz Colomina. Princeton Papers on Architecture 1. Princeton Architectural Press, 1992.

CHAPTER 3

From the Margins to the Center

Black Women in the Novelas ejemplares

CORNESHA TWEEDE
AND ELIZABETH S. LAGRESA-GONZÁLEZ

This chapter employs an intersectional critical approach to problematize the representation of marginalized Black, Afro-descendant women in Cervantes's *Novelas ejemplares* (1613). While recent early modern scholarship has begun to address the gap in studies dedicated to Black women, there is still much work to be done to understand their presence in the early modern Spanish context.[1] The present study aims to contribute to this endeavor by relocating Black women from the periphery to the center, examining the intersection of race, gender, and class through case studies of two novellas. We first bring to light how the Black enslaved character Guiomar disrupts imperial and colonial structures within "El celoso extremeño," and then we turn to "El coloquio de los perros" in order to reclaim the relevance of *la negra*, the story's unnamed Black woman. Both readings engage with Nicholas R. Jones's call to action in *Cervantine Blackness*, in which he underscores that "contemplation of the cycle of life and death that absorbed, claimed, and consumed both enslaved and free black communities remains central to any understanding of Cervantes's literary corpus and should not be permitted to hover at the margins of scholarly literary criticism."[2] To this end, the future of Cervantes studies must reckon with the representation of Black women through an intersectional lens in dialogue with critical Black studies and Africana studies, an objective to which the following analysis seeks to contribute.

Seeing Guiomar: Intersections of Race, Class, and Gender in Cervantes's "El celoso extremeño"

Set in seventeenth-century Seville, an Iberian hub of transatlantic commerce and enslavement, "El celoso extremeño" ostensibly revolves around the figure of Carrizales, an old *indiano* who is driven by jealousy to construct with wealth extracted from the Americas what has been compared to a prison-convent and, more recently, an island-colony.[3] Created with the explicit purpose of isolating his noble child-bride, as well as his fortune, the house is also inhabited by an array of domestic staff: a *dueña*, six female enslaved servants—two of African descent and four identified as white—and Luis, a Black eunuch that stands guard at the periphery of the property and, as Paul Michael Johnson contends in this volume, is yet another eminently intersectional figure. While new studies have focused on the important role played by such marginal figures as the latter, little attention has been given to Guiomar, a sub-Saharan African *bozal*-speaking enslaved woman.[4] We argue that this 'minor' character, by acting on her own desires, sets off a chain of events that precipitate from within the collapse of Carrizales's imperial fantasy.

Referencing Cervantine fiction, Nicholas R. Jones and Chad Leahy ask, "what if we insisted on putting in its place—in the center of the narrative—Black African and Afro-descendant voices?"[5] In *Staging Habla de Negros*, Jones clarifies his intention "to highlight the agentive subject positions of *habla de negros* speakers and to examine their voices as viable discourses," arguing that, despite differing authorial ideologies, texts in which these characters appear "do, in fact, render legible the voices and experiences of black Africans."[6] Similarly, Cornesha Tweede, turning to María de Zayas, asserts that "black African women literary characters play a major role as they function as subjects who wield agency within the shaping of the plot and direction of the prose narrative's storyline."[7] Still, in his most recent publication on the topic, *Cervantine Blackness*, Jones forges a transtemporal connection between Cervantes and Black diaspora studies from the early modern period to the present and future. He presents "an incisive refusal of the dominant frames within which blackness and its adjacent proxies become studied" by embracing collaborative and collective methodologies driven by a sense of critical and political urgency.[8] We present our analysis of Cervantes's novella in dialogue with these recent studies on the representation of marginalized figures, with the aim of finding new ways of seeing Guiomar. Through the examination of early modern Iberian Black female characters and the significant spaces they inhabit, a forward-looking path can be forged to enrich both Cervantine and early modern Spanish scholarship.

Unlike the homonymous character featured in Lope de Rueda's *Los engañados* (1556), who only appears in one of the ten brief scenes that make up the play, Cervantes's Guiomar reappears intermittently throughout the novella.[9] The main point of contrast between these two iterations of enslaved sub-Saharan African women, however, revolves around the role these characters perform within the narrative.[10] According to Antonio M. Rueda's sociolinguistic analysis, "Lope de Rueda goes one step further with the character of Guiomar in his most famous play, *Los engañados* (*The deceived*, 1556), in which an African domestic slave is placed, for the first time in Spanish theater, in a position of mediation between white upper-class members."[11] Though this Guiomar makes for an ineffectual negotiator, Rueda goes on to note that Lope de Vega would later include the character of the "mulata indiana" as an intermediary that successfully brought together young nobles in love, in plays such as *Servir a señor discreto*, *La vitoria de la honra, El Arenal de Sevilla*, or *Amar, servir y esperar*, among others.[12] However, the role played by Cervantes's Guiomar is considerably more difficult to define.[13] She is not the embodiment of a facilitator. In effect, she might even be the very opposite, a kind of anti-go-between, whose function in the novella's plot is to obstruct rather than enable the attainment of others' desires by prioritizing her own.

Her voice first appears in the narrative as an affirmation of her longing to enjoy entertainment in the form of music, something in direct opposition to the laws Carrizales established to preserve his dominium.[14] As the group of women that makes up the domestic staff are debating whether to let Loaysa, the picaresque performer, into the house, Guiomar declares: "Por mí, más que nunca jura, entre con todo diablo; que aunque más jura, si acá estás, todo olvida" (For me, sure he swear, and in come devil, no matter he swear, if he here, he forget all).[15] Her statement underscores the fickleness of oaths and speech acts in general, as well as the primacy of her own personal needs, well in spite of the consequences. This brief introduction to her character is followed by the addition of two labels, one pertaining to her gender and the other to her race.[16] First the narrator describes her as a "doncella," alluding to her virginity, albeit sarcastically: "a perder tanta virginidad como aquí se encierra; porque hasta esta negra, que se llama Guiomar, es doncella" (to risk all the virginity confined here; even this black girl, whose name is Guiomar, is a maiden).[17] She then receives a second classification, that of a "negra bozal," where the term *bozal*, "defined by markers of linguistic marginality," means "a person of sub-Saharan origin who had been brought to the Peninsula as a slave and could hardly speak Spanish."[18] This specific designation gives readers indications about her recent trafficking from Africa, through Portugal, and into Spain.

During the late fifteenth and sixteenth centuries, the booming trafficking of the enslaved by the Portuguese and Spanish became a pillar on which the imperial economy was built. While a majority of enslaved Black people arrived to Seville and other Spanish cities from Africa with stopovers in Lisbon and Evora, some were born in Portugal, as might have been the case of Guiomar, even if her speech does not seem to reflect familiarity with the Portuguese language.[19] As both material goods and people were forcibly brought from Africa and the Americas to Iberian cities, they began forming part of everyday life. Representations of Black Africans in Spanish literature became commonplace, reflective of the growth of the Afro-Hispanic population in sixteenth- and seventeenth-century Spain.[20] Guiomar is a testament to the place Black women occupied in this transatlantic market dominated by Portuguese and Spanish enslavers. However, specifics about her unique journey through this system of human trafficking are omitted. As Jones notes, "Seville's black African population was ethnically diverse, originating from Angola and the Congo Basin, the Cape Verde Islands, the Kingdom of Dahomey, the Senegambia and its Rivers of Guinea, as well as Mozambique and neighboring Portuguese outposts in East Africa and Goa."[21] According to Alfonso Franco Silva's studies on Iberian enslavement, most African groups in Seville originated from Guinea as well as other regions with a high population of Wolof and Mandinka peoples.[22] Yet no details are given about where Guiomar calls home or how she came to form part of Carrizales's domestic staff. Beyond her speech, Cervantes provides no further clues to Guiomar's origins. However, as much as these silences obscure her figure, they also connote a sense of interiority and even privacy that renders her figure more tangible. As readers, we must get to know Guiomar through her actions instead of the narrator's often dismissive perspective that inscribes her as one more of Carrizales's possessions.

According to Shifra Armon, "'El celoso extremeño' may be read as an 'allegory of containment' in which Leonora represents wealth unprofitably hoarded rather than invested in international trade. From this perspective, the newlyweds' house . . . becomes a bank or vault into which Carrizales 'deposits' Leonora."[23] Yet, in this economic reading of the novella, Guiomar's presence is eclipsed, even as her actions throughout the narrative clash with her supposed roles as material object reflective of her owner's wealth, and as property in service of sustaining a declining empire. Subverting readers' expectations, it is none other than Guiomar who joins Luis in leading the group of female revelers within Carrizales's home, "alumbrándolos el negro y Guiomar la negra" (Luis the black man and Guiomar the black girl lighting their way), in direct defiance of established rules.[24] If what the *indiano* has attempted to build is a microcosm of Spain's colonial empire, it is one determined by women and their desires.[25] Yet, when the moment comes for all female subjects to enjoy Loaysa's much awaited musical performance, it is only Guiomar that is singled out by Leonora and given the duty to stand guard, while the rest enjoy themselves: "pero quédese aquí Guiomar por guarda" (but have Guiomar stay here to keep watch and let us know whether Carrizales wakens), to which she replies, "¡Yo, negra, quedo; blancas van: Dios perdone a todas!" (Black girl stay, white girls go; God forgive all!).[26] While the group of women dissect Loaysa's body with their gaze, making "pepitoria" of him, Guiomar remains out of view (125).[27] Once the first song and dance are concluded, the plot takes a puzzling turn.[28] Guiomar's absence from the merry-making does not last long at all. She abruptly, and without any notice, returns of her own accord: "llegó Guiomar, la centinela, toda turbada, hiriendo de pie y de mano como si tuviera alferecía y con vos entre ronca y baja, dijo: ¡Despierto señor, señora; y, señora, despierto señor, y levantas y viene!" (when Guiomar, the sentry, came in, completely agitated, her hands and feet and mouth convulsing as if she suffered from epilepsy, and in a voice between a rasp and a whisper, she said: 'Señora, Señor woke; Señora, Señor woke, and got up, and comes!').[29] Her "no esperada nueva" (unexpected news) warning that Carrizales has awoken from his opiate-induced sleep results in chaos.[30] What turns out to be a false alarm cuts short the entertainment and sets in motion the events that will lead Carrizales to believe his young wife has slept with the interloper, leading to his eventual death and final will, which will grant freedom to all enslaved members of his household. If, according to Ballestero, "Cervantes demonstrates that the architectural artifice created by Carrizales to enclose women, representative of patriarchal/imperial discourses, collapses in the face of female desire and sexuality," then Guiomar's actions place her front and center as a pivotal agent in this demise.[31]

It is Marialonso, the duenna, who soon discovers that Carrizales is still asleep in his room, peacefully snoring.[32] No justification is provided to explain why Guiomar cries wolf, and yet, at the next gathering that ensues, "no faltó de la junta Guiomar la negra" (Guiomar the black girl was not missing from the group).[33] She rejoins the group of women that had excluded her; however, the entertainment does not resume. The plot moves forward to the schemes of the picaresque characters of Loaysa and Marialonso. Still, the narrator includes one last mention of Guiomar before her freedom is granted at the end of the exemplary tale: "pero lo que mas risa causara a quien entonces las oyera, eran las razones de Guiomar la negra, que, por ser portuguesa y no muy ladina, era extraña la gracia con que la vituperaba" (but what would have most amused anyone who heard them then were the words of Guiomar the black girl who, because she was Portuguese and not very Castilian, reviled her in a very strange fashion).[34] Cervantes withholds from the reader Guiomar's stock comedic speech, just as he withholds the rationale behind her behavior, and yet her individual will to resign from her assigned job as lookout and rejoin the others on her own terms is patent through her actions. Guiomar subverts all roles she is prescribed to play by others, and she becomes an integral catalyst in the final downfall of her impotent master and the repressive edifice he built through the work and sacrifice of others. Reading from the margins allows Guiomar to occupy a central role in the development of the narrative, bringing into focus tensions between the domestic and global, the human and material, which resonate as a possible critique of exploitative racial and gendered imperial policies. Employing the female-centric space of the home as a microcosm, Cervantes places a spotlight on the fraught relationship between Iberia, Africa, the Americas, and their far-reaching human impacts, as embodied by the only enslaved woman who receives a name and a speaking role.

Conceptualizing Cervantes's Black Woman in "El coloquio de los perros"

Recent studies of "El coloquio de los perros" have noted the sinful portrayal of its Black characters, but *la negra*, the unnamed Black woman of the story, has received scant attention. We argue that, through her use of *dádivas* (bribes), *la negra* fights to uphold her reputation and her womanhood in the novella. Audre Lorde's concepts of eroticism and pleasure guide this analysis of the actions of the Black woman. In her essay "Uses of the Erotic," Lorde contends that a "Black female power has been suppressed."[35] For his part, Jones asserts in *The Routledge Companion to Black Women's Cultural Histories* that "Black women characters—or the 'negra,' as they are commonly called in early modern Spanish theater studies—also fight to protect their womanhood and social standing in early modern Spanish society."[36] Building upon Lorde's uses of eroticism and Jones's assertion of Black women characters' resilience, we argue that Black female power shows up in various ways in Cervantes's story, and that this power is more influential than the lack of scholarly assessments of the anonymous character would suggest.

The novella recounts a conversation between two dogs, Berganza and Cipión, that touches on various themes including greed, dishonesty, servitude, and racialization. In the related episode of "El casamiento engañoso," the protagonist Campuzano tells his friend Peralta, a soldier, that while he was in the Hospital of the Resurrection in Valladolid he witnessed a dialogue between two dogs.

After he attentively listens to the canine conversation, believing himself to be in full command of his faculties, Campuzano attempts to convince his friend of this occurrence by opening up his notebook, which contains the title of the following episode, the "Novela del coloquio de los perros." While the dogs' dialogue is the central focus of the episode, the unnamed Black woman is a minor yet substantive character, introduced as follows: "Dígolo porque *la negra* de casa estaba enamorada de un negro, asimismo esclavo de casa, el cual negro dormía en el zaguán, que es entre la puerta de la calle y la de en medio, detrás de la cual yo estaba"[37] (I say this because the black woman was in love with a black man who was also a slave in the house; and this black man slept in the portico between the street door and the one in the middle, behind the one where I was[38]). The narrator reports that the domestic Black woman was in love with a Black male servant who, not described in any detail, is solely the receiver of her actions. The movements, behavior, and protagonism of the woman are thus comparatively magnified.

Further evidence of the character's stature and resilience in the narrative can be found in the following passage, which is worth quoting at length. Berganza states:

> Digo, pues, que habiendo visto la insolencia, ladronicio y deshonestidad de los negros, determiné, como buen criado, estorbarlo, por mejores medios que pudiese; y pude tan bien, que salí con mi intento. Bajaba la negra, como has oído, a refocilarse con el negro, fiada en que me enmudecían los pedazos de carne, pan o queso que me arrojaba . . . a la cual, bajando una noche muy escura a su acostumbrado pasatiempo, arremetí sin ladrar, por que no se alborotasen los de casa, y en un instante le hice pedazos toda la camisa y le arranqué un pedazo de muslo: burla que fue bastante a tenerla de veras más de ocho días en la cama, fingiendo para con sus amos no sé qué enfermedad. Sanó, volvió otra noche, y yo volví a la pelea con mi perra, y, sin morderla, la arañé todo el cuerpo como si la hubiera cardado como manta. Nuestras batallas eran a la sorda, de las cuales salía siempre vencedor, y la negra, malparada y peor contenta. Pero sus enojos se parecían bien en mi pelo y en mi salud: alzóseme con la ración y los huesos, y los míos poco a poco iban señalando los nudos del espinazo. Con todo esto, aunque me quitaron el comer, no me pudieron quitar el ladrar. Pero la negra, por acabarme de una vez, me trujo una esponja frita con manteca; conocí la maldad; vi que era peor que comer zarazas, porque a quien la come se le hincha el estómago y no sale dél sin llevarse tras sí la vida. Y, pareciéndome ser imposible guardarme de las asechanzas de tan indignados enemigos, acordé de poner tierra en medio, quitándomeles delante de los ojos.[39]

> I'll say, then, that having seen the insolence, thievery, and dishonesty of the blacks, I decided, as a good servant, to hinder them by the best means I could; and I could so well that I achieved my purpose. The black woman would come down as you have heard, to take her pleasure with the black man, certain that the pieces of meat, bread, or cheese that she threw to me would keep me silent . . . one very dark night, when she was coming down for her customary amusement, I attacked her without barking so the household would not be disturbed, and in an instant I ripped her blouse to shreds and tore off a piece of her thigh; a bit of fun that was enough to keep her in bed for more than a week, pretending some illness or other for her masters. She got better, returned on another night, and I renewed the fight with my bitch, and without biting her I scratched her entire body, carding her as if she were a blanket. Our battles were silent, and I always came out the victor, while she was always injured and not at all happy. But her anger was certainly noticeable in my fur and my health. She cut off my ration and the bones, and mine slowly began to appear along my spine. With it all, though they took away my food, they couldn't take away my bark. But to finish me off once and for all, she brought me a sponge fried in lard; I recognized the evil act; I saw it was worse than eating poison paste, because if you eat it your stomach swells and there's no way out except to die. And thinking it was impossible to defend myself against the snares of such unworthy enemies, I thought of putting land between us, removing them from my sight.[40]

Because the Black woman and the Black manservant reside in different places, the Black woman sneaks out to meet him outside of her home. Berganza states that the female Black servant gives bribes to appease him and keep him silent during these nocturnal liaisons. Believing the Black servants to be rude, dishonest, and thieving, Berganza eventually charges at the Black woman—without barking so as not to disturb other residents of the house—tears her shirt to pieces, and bites off a piece of her thigh. Yet, despite being ill for days after the attack, the Black female returns to the Black male servant. As she resumes the nightly visits, she neglects to provide Berganza with bribes, leading him to break his silence with persistent barking. One day, out of frustration, Berganza attempts to attack the Black woman again, but this time she brings him a sponge soaked in fried grease. Recognizing this as an attempt to harm him, Berganza becomes frightened at the prospect of being killed and decides to leave the household in search of a new master.

What is significant throughout this narrative is how the Black woman, against all odds, creatively navigates her circumstances to protect her lifestyle and continue enjoying her relationship with the Black manservant. She goes to great lengths to do so, offering Berganza bribes, suffering bodily injury from a physical assault, and risking further aggression from the dog. Presumably, she also risks untold punishment from her enslavers, who would not approve of her movements, as suggested by the need for secrecy and by Berganza's own critique of her behavior. While the text does not detail the specific activities shared by the two Black characters, it does reveal the strong, authentic desire of the Black woman, her determination to stop at nothing to safeguard her reputation, her lifestyle, her romantic relationship, and her womanhood. The influence of the Black woman in this episode is so acute that Berganza ultimately decides to flee, fearing a risk to his own life.

To recognize this subtle yet consequential protagonism is to affirm *la negra* as a human character, and thus to push back against more abstract or negative interpretations of her role in the narrative. Luis Rodríguez-Rincón, in a recent essay on human-animal relations and theriophily in the novella, mentions the Black enslaved woman in Seville and posits that "the dog is not speaking of just one slave but potentially all Black people, *los negros*."[41] It is true that the demographics of Seville included many Black people, freed and enslaved, and Jones makes a solid case that "Berganza's comments . . . cannot be disentangled from this broader social history that influenced Cervantes."[42] As a former resident of the city, Cervantes was keenly aware of these dynamics, and it is no accident that his fictional narrative takes place in a setting abundant with Black people. Nevertheless, an allegorical reading such as Rodríguez-Rincón's, by which two Black characters come to define a racialized group, tends to flatten the actions of *la negra* and to elide her womanhood. In similar fashion, John Beusterien asserts that "Berganza judges an Afro-Hispanic woman's dark skin to be a sign of sin and lust, and he also violently and brutally attacks her."[43] Later, Beusterien states that this episode animalizes the Black woman and thus affects our perception of the animal-human relationship. Berganza's attack positions both the Black woman and the dog on the same plane, and Berganza certainly betrays an antiblackness through his violent attack on the Black woman. Yet the interplay of gender and racialization in their encounter highlights how such symbolic generalizations can overlook the experience of the Black woman entirely. Although sin and lust may underpin the rationale by which Berganza justifies his actions against the Black woman, this character is ultimately constrained by not only the racial stereotypes prevalent in seventeenth-century Spain, but also by the interpretative paradigms of critics.

Though Berganza's framing of her actions casts them as sinful and driven by lust, an alternative perspective, informed by the work of Lorde and other Black feminists, redeems them as expressions of pleasure. Lorde redefines the erotic as a powerful force beyond mere sexual sensation, arguing that the erotic is a vital source of knowledge, power, and transformation, particularly for women. In the face of daunting adversity, Cervantes's Black woman enjoys by night the freedom to live as she chooses. She surreptitiously, cleverly, and confidently continues her encounters with the Black male servant, fully embracing the *jouissance* of life and her desire for human, interpersonal connection. Indeed, for Lorde the sharing of joy acts as a bridge between individuals, enabling a deeper understanding and lessening the potential threat of difference. This shared vulnerability can form the basis for strong coalitions and concerted political action, such that the erotic can be a powerful motivator for pursuing genuine change and a crucial step in resisting oppression.[44] The resilience of *eros* in Cervantes's unnamed *negra* offers a different, more affirmative way of understanding the character, of reclaiming her human agency from its tendentious displacement by talking dogs.

Conclusion

Instead of permitting Black women in these episodes of the *Novelas ejemplares* to hover at the margins, our reading has centered Guiomar and the unnamed Black woman. Positioning them in such a way reveals how their actions set off a chain of events that are vital to the narrative and, therefore, to the literary history of Cervantes. These narratives prompt a discussion that integrates intersectional studies, animal studies, Black studies, Africana studies, and Black feminism. Such approaches can help transform the field and make scholars more attentive to what Cervantes does with Black women and other marginalized characters that inhabit his corpus while reflecting on the historical complexities of the broader Atlantic world. Bringing to the fore the critical analysis of Black women not only enriches the interpretation of Cervantes's works, but also aligns them with broader, more inclusive methodologies for understanding early modern literature, history, and culture. We urge scholars to look beyond traditional European and Spanish-centered frameworks and to engage with African and critical Black studies as conceptual horizons essential to the future of Cervantine scholarship.

NOTES

1. See Hobson, *The Routledge Companion*; Earle and Lowe, *Black Africans*; Morgan, *Reckoning with Slavery*. Some notable contributions on the topic in the Spanish context include Berruezo Sánchez et al., *Iberia negra*; Martín Casares and Periáñez Gómez, *Mujeres esclavas*; Jones and Tweede, "Black Women in Early Modern Iberia"; Jones, *Staging Habla de Negros*; and Owens and Mangan, *Women of the Iberian Atlantic*.
2. Jones, *Cervantine Blackness*, 34.
3. See Ruiz, "Cervantes's *Celoso*"; Ballesteros, "El imperio desde el centro"; and Fernández, "The Bonds of Patrimony."
4. For the most recent scholarship on Luis, see Jones, "Meditation 3"; Johnson, "Cervantes's Black Castrato" and, in this volume, Johnson, "Cervantine Intersectionality." For a study that combines an analysis of Luis and Guiomar, focusing on "the linguistic and erotic energies of the female Guiomar, and the erotic and musical ones of Luis," see Ruiz, "Counter-Discursive and Erotic Agency," 194.
5. Jones and Leahy, "Cervantes y la materia." This translation, as well as all others below, are our own, unless otherwise noted.
6. Jones, *Staging*, 4–5.
7. Tweede, "Women and Blackness."
8. Jones, *Cervantine Blackness*, 138.
9. Lope de Rueda's Guiomar is present only in the third scene of the play, never to reappear, making her singular performance noteworthy. For an in-depth discussion on Guiomar and other Black female figures in Lope de Rueda's plays, see Jones, *Staging*, 119–58.
10. Other points of contrast between the two figures include that while Rueda's Guiomar goes on to itemize her daily work routine, from sweeping, to cooking, to setting up the table, to washing the dishes, to assisting the young lady Clavela with the distillation of flowers or her latest hobby (179–80), Cervantes's Guiomar appears to have a more ambiguous service role in her household and seems to suffer from the same boredom that afflicts all other women living with her in confinement. More notably, the dialogue of Rueda's Guiomar also revolves around her personal goals, where Gerardo, the head of household, asks, "¿Qué's aquesso de casar? Qué, ¿ya no quieres ser monja?" to which she replies, "No, siñor, que ya tenemo un prima mía contrita na religiona monja priora nabadessa ayá en mi terra de Manicongo muy honradas. Yo, señor, queremos muntipricar a mundos" (180), ("What's this about getting married? What, you don't want to be a nun anymore?"; "No, sir, we already have a cousin of mine who is contrite in the religion, a nun prioress and abbess there in my land of Manicongo, very honorable. I, sir, want to multiply the worlds"; our translation). The exchange serves as an affirmation of her motivations and desires, looking toward a life outside the constraints of servitude, something wholly absent from Cervantes's characterization, whose desire for greater freedom manifests rather through her actions instead of her words.
11. Rueda, "From Bozal to Mulata," 100.
12. Rueda, "From Bozal to Mulata," 102–3.
13. Cervantes's Guiomar shares similarities with earlier literary representations of enslaved Black women, akin to those of Lope de Rueda, written in the mid-1500s, instead of those created by his contemporaries in the first decades of the 1600s. Cervantes's character employs earlier patters of *habla de negros* stressing her lack of knowledge of Castilian Spanish, which

stands in contrast to the representation of similar figures by Lope de Vega, which feature "mulattas" that are fluent.

14. All quotations for the novella are from the edition by Sieber. All English translations, unless otherwise noted, are by Grossman.
15. Cervantes, *Novelas ejemplares,* 123. Grossman, *Exemplary Novels,* 231. For consistency, we reproduce Grossman's translation here and below while acknowledging that the decision to translate *habla de negros* speech into stilted English is problematic.
16. According to James D. Fernández, "in early modern Spain it is impossible to disentangle the discourses of race and gender, the concerns of colonialism and humanism–the architecture of harem, convent, and island." "Bonds of Patrimony," 978.
17. Cervantes, *Novelas ejemplares,* 123; Grossman, *Exemplary Novels,* 231.
18. Cervantes, *Novelas ejemplares,* 117; Grossman's translation, however, equates "bozal" to "dim-witted," 227. According to Rueda, "Linguistic communication, then, was understood by authors and audience as a sign that defined the individual and distinguished the Spanish self from the Afro-Hispanic self." "From Bozal to Mulata," 99.
19. See Silva, *La esclavitud en Sevilla.*
20. According to Jones, "The city of Seville and the kingdom at large had a voluminous black population that reached a height of 11 percent. In a one-year period, between 1569 and 1570, 1,100 slaves were sold annually, of whom more than 85 percent were purchased by neighboring cities across Andalusia. Primarily dominated by Portuguese merchants and traffickers of black bodies." Jones, *Staging,* 2–3. Rueda notes, "There are no official statistics for the population in Spain in the early 1600s, however the 1565 census taken by church officials indicated that there were 6,327 slaves, one slave for every fourteen inhabitants." "From Bozal to Mulata," 109n25.
21. Jones, *Staging,* 3.
22. Silva, *La esclavitud en Sevilla,* 204. Silva states, "the majority of the sub-Saharan residents of Granada derived from the geographic space then called Guinea (50%). Among them, groups of the Wolof and Mandinga were the most numerous." *La esclavitud en Sevilla,* 204.
23. Armon, "The Paper Key," 101. Reinforcing this reading from a different perspective, Fernández writes, "'El celoso extremeño' is, after all, a tale of the dangers and failures of containment." Fernández, "The Bonds of Patrimony," 978.
24. Cervantes, *Novelas ejemplares,* 124; Grossman, *Exemplary Novels,* 232.
25. James Fernández concludes, "if Carrizales's house is a harem and a convent, it is also a colony, or, if you prefer, an *ínsula.*" Fernández, "Bonds of Patrimony," 974. Ballestero describes the household similarly, albeit stressing the central role of women: "la "colonia" de mujeres—esclavas blancas, negras, la dueña—que crea de Carrizales." Ballestero, "El imperio desde el centro," 122.
26. Cervantes, *Novelas ejemplares,* 125; Grossman, *Exemplary Novels,* 233.
27. Edith Grossman's translation of the term is "and all together they made a slow, detailed examination of his anatomy." Cervantes, *Exemplary Novels,* 233.
28. Serving as an echo to the themes of the novella, the *coplas* revolve around the subject of the dangers of confinement without the will of the subject being confined or guarded (125–26).
29. Cervantes, *Novelas ejemplares,* 126; Grossman, *Exemplary Novels,* 235. Sieber defines *alferecía* as "enfermedad peligrosa que suele dar a los niños . . . y caballos." Cervantes, *Novelas ejemplares,* 53n36.
30. Cervantes, *Novelas ejemplares,* 127; Grossman, *Exemplary Novels,* 235.

31. Ballestro, "El imperio desde el centro," 116.
32. Cervantes, *Novelas ejemplares*, 127.
33. Cervantes, *Novelas ejemplares*, 128; Grossman, *Exemplary Novels*, 236.
34. Cervantes, *Novelas ejemplares*, 128; Grossman, *Exemplary Novels*, 236. While Grossman opts to translate the term "extraña" as "strange," an alternative would be to translate it as "remarkable," which changes the tenor of the narrator's account of Guiomar, opening new lines of interpretation.
35. Lorde, *Selected Works*, 29.
36. Jones, "Black Women," 62.
37. Cervantes, *Novelas ejemplares*, 252.
38. Grossman, *Exemplary Novels*, 382.
39. Cervantes, *Novelas ejemplares*, 256, 258–59.
40. Grossman, *Exemplary Novels*, 384–85.
41. Rodríguez-Rincón, "Berganza's 'Buen Natural,'" 122.
42. Jones, *Cervantine Blackness*, 118.
43. Beusterien, *Canines in Cervantes*, 52.
44. Lorde, "Uses of the Erotic," 32–33.

BIBLIOGRAPHY

Armon, Shifra. "The Paper Key: Money as Text in Cervantes's *El celoso extremeño* and José de Camerino's *El pícaro amante*." *Cervantes: Bulletin of the Cervantes Society of America* 18, no. 1 (1998): 96–114.

Ballesteros, José R. "El imperio desde el centro: Representaciones indianas sexualizadas en 'El celoso extremeño' de Miguel de Cervantes." In *Estas primicias del ingenio: Jóvenes cervantistas en Chicago*, ed. Kerry Wilks and Francisco Caudet Roca. Editorial Castalia, 2003.

Berruezo Sánchez, Diana, Manuel Olmedo Gobante, and Cornesha Tweede, eds. *Iberia negra: textos para otra historia de la diáspora africana (siglos XVI y XVII)*. Routledge, 2024.

Beusterien, John. *Canines in Cervantes and Velázquez: An Animal Studies Reading of Early Modern Spain*. Routledge, 2016.

Cervantes, Miguel de. *Exemplary Novels*. Translated by Edith Grossman. Edited by Roberto González Echevarría. Yale University Press, 2016.

Cervantes, Miguel de. *Novelas ejemplares II*. Edited by Harry Sieber. Cátedra, 2007.

Earle, T. F., and Kate Lowe, eds. *Black Africans in Renaissance Europe*. Cambridge University Press, 2005.

Fernández, James D. "The Bonds of Patrimony: Cervantes and the New World." *PMLA* 109, no. 5 (1994): 969–81.

Hobson, Janell. *The Routledge Companion to Black Women's Cultural Histories*. Routledge, 2021.

Johnson, Paul Michael. "Cervantes's Black Castrato and the Racial Politics of Timbre." In "Early Atlantic Soundings," edited by Sarah Finley and Elisabeth Le Guin. Special issue of *Atlantic Studies: Global Currents* (2025): 1–14. http://dx.doi.org/10.1080/14788810.2025.2583246.

Jones, Nicholas R. "Black Women in Early Modern Spanish Literature." *The Routledge Companion to Black Women's Cultural Histories*. Edited by Janell Hobson. Routledge, 2021.

Jones, Nicholas R. *Cervantine Blackness*. Pennsylvania State University Press, 2024.

Jones, Nicholas R. "Meditation 3: Rethinking Luis." In *Cervantine Blackness*. Pennsylvania State University Press, 2024.

Jones, Nicholas R. *Staging Habla de Negros: Radical Performances of the African Diaspora in Early Modern Spain*. Pennsylvania State University Press, 2019.

Jones, Nicholas R., and Cornesha Tweede. "Black Women in Early Modern Iberia." Routledge Resources Online, *The Renaissance World*, June 18, 2023. https://doi.org/10.4324/9780367347093-RERW92-1.

Jones, Nicholas R., and Chad Leahy. "Cervantes y la materia de las vidas negras." *Ctxt: Contexto y acción*, no. 262, July 2020.

Lorde, Audre. "Uses of the Erotic." In *The Selected Works of Audre Lorde*. Edited by Roxane Gay. W.W. Norton, 2020.

Martín Casares, Aurelia, and Rocío Periáñez Gómez, eds. *Mujeres esclavas y abolicionistas en la España de los siglos XVI al XIX*. Iberoamericana, 2014.

Morgan, Jennifer L. *Reckoning with Slavery: Gender, Kinship, and Capitalism in the Early Black Atlantic*. Duke University Press, 2021.

Owens, Sarah E., and Jane E. Mangan, eds. *Women of the Iberian Atlantic*. Louisiana State University Press, 2012.

Rodríguez-Rincón, Luis. "Berganza's 'Buen Natural' and the Theriophily of *El Casamiento Engañoso* and *Coloquio de Los Perros*." *Hispanic Review* 90, no. 1 (2022): 107–29.

Rueda, Antonio M. "From Bozal to Mulata: A Sociolinguistic Analysis of the Black African Female Slave in Early Modern Spanish Theater." *Critical Multilingualism Studies* 5, no. 2 (2017): 87–110.

Ruiz, Eduardo. "Cervantes's *Celoso*, a Tale of Colonial Lack." *Hispanic Review* 81, no. 2 (2013): 45–63.

Ruiz, Eduardo. "Counter-Discursive and Erotic Agency: The Case of the Black Slaves in Cervantes's 'El celoso extremeño.'" *Hispania* 97, no. 2 (2014): 194–206.

Silva, Alfonso Franco. *La esclavitud en Sevilla y su tierra a fines de la edad media*, vol. 14. Diputación Provincial de Sevilla, 1979.

Tweede, Cornesha. "Women and Blackness in Early Modern Iberia." Online talk, presented by The Center for the Study of Women and Society and the Society for the Study of Women in the Renaissance, CUNY, Nov. 18, 2021. https://www.gc.cuny.edu/events/women-and-blackness-early-modern-iberia.

CHAPTER 4

Cervantine Intersectionality

Race, Gender, Sexuality, Age, and Ability in "El celoso extremeño"

PAUL MICHAEL JOHNSON

Intersectionality, according to Kimberlé Crenshaw's foundational formulation of the concept, affirms that discrimination and exclusion do not always emerge along a singular axis of identity. Rather, such categories as race, ethnicity, religion, gender, sexual orientation, class, and ability interact in cumulative, more complex fashion to determine the positionality of a given individual. As Crenshaw asserted decades ago from the perspective of Black feminism and antiracist legal reform, dismantling the structures of oppression that continue to marginalize minoritized populations requires considering multiple aspects of identity together.[1] Yet, as Roland Betancourt explains in his acclaimed 2020 book *Byzantine Intersectionality: Sexuality, Gender, and Race in the Middle Ages*, "intersectionality . . . does more than flesh out the subjectivities" of these communities, as it "also alerts us to the subjects whose privilege keeps them away from the public eye." "Privilege, and the privacy it often enables," Betancourt argues, "create the greatest lacunae in the historical record."[2] These dynamics recall the titular character of Cervantes's novella "El celoso extremeño," Carrizales, whose vast economic privilege, coupled with paranoid jealousy, enables him to construct a veritable fortress around himself and his young bride, with such warily guarded privacy designed to underwrite marital fidelity. The ironies and inversions innate to fictional literature, and to Cervantes's writing in particular, entail that not only the narratorial voice but also a dashing interloper, Loaysa, will penetrate the home, spoiling Carrizales's private life, hastening his death, and vitiating the "early modern biopower that," as Israel Burshatin contends in his contribution to this volume, "is sustained by a largely enslaved and racialized labor force." Though Loaysa ultimately fails in his bid to seduce Carrizales's wife, his entrance and its ensuing mayhem depend on Luis, an enslaved, Black eunuch porter who resides in an antechamber and facilitates the lothario's furtive access to the domestic space. As I will contend in what follows, the multiple identities occupied by this minor character, along with his physical and symbolic positioning in the narrative, make Luis eminently intersectional, and a far more interesting and elaborate figure than the dearth of preexisting scholarship on him would suggest.[3] Rather than mine a fuller extent of his characterization, however, here I will limit myself in the main to considering but the narrator's introduction of Luis as an "old Black eunuch." Dwelling on these three words—as well as sketching their historical resonances and new affiliations with theoretical concepts in critical cultural studies—reveals differences of race, gender, sexuality, age, and ability.[4] For organizational purposes, I consider each of these categories in turn, yet, as will become clear, an intersectional approach by design precludes doing so in a strict fashion. Overall, I aim to develop a proof of concept that illustrates the payoffs and pitfalls of such an approach to other of Cervantes's characters who, like Luis, are traversed by multiple marginal identities. Cervantes's penchant for incorporating such characters, in all their deceptive simplicity, into his writing constitutes what, riffing on Betancourt, might aptly be called Cervantine intersectionality.

Cervantes's text declines to supply an origin or backstory for Luis, introducing him merely as a *negro viejo y eunuco*, or "old Black eunuch."[5] Yet each word of this designation would have been sufficient to trigger an array of associations in the minds of early modern readers. It should be noted that, in Spanish, each of these words could be either nouns or adjectives, depending on context and syntax. This allows for absolute interchangeability among the three, which could result in such alternative orderings as "un viejo negro y eunuco" or "un eunuco viejo y negro." That the nominal component in Cervantes's phrasing is "negro," placed before its adjectival modifiers, suggests this is the most consequential element of Luis's identity. Along with the dearth of narrative detail—marked only by the color Black—his enslaved status vexes attempts to determine even the continent of his birth. Black chattel slaves not born into bondage in Iberia were deracinated from multiple regions of Africa, while the complexities of trans-Mediterranean and trans-Atlantic human trafficking, of which the character is an implicit product, entailed a violent, tortuous life trajectory. Whether Luis's heritage derives from Northern, Western, or sub-Saharan Africa—and whether he might have resided on the American continent before accompanying Carrizales on his return voyage to Spain—are questions left unanswered by the narrative. Yet for it do otherwise would indeed be the purview of fiction, since such genealogical and geographical uncertainties are of a piece with the historical realities of the enslaved. His eunuchism, to which I will return momentarily, further obscures any effort to get a definitive fix on his hypothetical origins.[6] Eunuchs, both Black and white, routinely safeguarded Ottoman seraglios and harems, and, given Cervantes's own intimate experience in the Maghreb and Eastern Mediterranean as well as other details in the narrative, critics like Cory Reed have persuasively allegorized Carrizales's zealously shielded home as a sultan's palace, casting Luis as the Kızlar Ağası or Chief Eunuch.[7]

By turning to the presence of Iberia's own domestic population of both Black Africans and castrated boys and men, however, I want to advance another possible origin for Luis. Although traditional historiography largely ignored these populations, often as an implicit or explicit endeavor to whitewash Spain's historical complicity in the trafficking of the enslaved, there is evidence of a robust Afro-diasporic community in early modern Iberia. Already in his mid-sixteenth-century history of Seville, the setting of "El celoso extremeño," Luis de Peraza remarked on the presence of "enslaved Moors, Christian and infidel, from all parts of Africa" and "an infinite multitude of Black men and women from all parts of Ethiopia and Guinea."[8] My strategic reading elsewhere of the character of Luis as a castrato—based on Cervantes's pointed depictions of his high-pitched voice and penchant for music as well as on growing historical evidence of a legion of male sopranos in imperial Spain—aligns him with a vibrant network of Afro-diasporic musicians and vocalists active in early modern courtly, liturgical, and popular venues. Many of these vocalists were, like Luis, gonadectomized, since a high tessitura was especially prized and women were usually excluded from chapel choirs, and there is evidence to suggest that Spain was a principal source of castrati who later were exported to Italy, where many garnered lasting fame. In addition, legal documents attest to the practice of castrating the enslaved on Iberian soil. The body of laws known as the *Siete Partidas* levied for the royal treasury the seizure of enslaved servants known to have been castrated by their enslavers. Following reports in 1559 of the practice among Spanish *moriscos*, who were believed to be trafficking in enslaved Black people that they castrated for export to North Africa, where emasculation was also illicit, King Philip II legislated further monetary deterrents for the practice.[9] What I wish to underscore with these historical details is that, instead of imagining Luis necessarily as hailing from distant, foreign lands or symbolizing an abstract, generalizable other, the Black eunuch porter is plausibly as much the progeny of Iberia as is his enslaver Carrizales.[10] If Luis is a homegrown reflection of the racially diverse, albeit far from racially integrated, urban environment of Cervantes's day, then exoticizing the character risks orientalizing the cultural practice of prepubertal emasculation and disavowing Iberia's own domestic population of both Black Africans and castrated boys and men.[11] An historically informed intersectional approach alerts us to these dual perils.

"Viejo." As scholars in the growing interdisciplinary field of age studies have established, age comprises another differential category of identity and a potentially determining factor of privilege and oppression. Beyond natural biological processes of maturation and decline, old age is a culturally and historically constructed concept, such that the significance of the statement that Luis is "old" is more associative than numerical. Though it could also connote wisdom and prudence, more often than not, as José Cartagena Calderón has demonstrated, old age was portrayed unfavorably in prominent writings of the period, from the humoral theory of Juan Huarte de San Juan to the extended trope of the *senex amans*, of which Carrizales is a prime example.[12] Ageism and gerontophobia, in other words, were as much a reality of early modernity as they are today. On one hand, Luis's senescence aligns him with his enslaver, as well as the many other characters of advanced age across Cervantes's oeuvre, including Don Quijote, not to mention the author himself, whose own elderliness became an object of ridicule.[13] On the other hand, when we consider the ways in which age was intimately entangled with race and gender, and in particular with normative standards of masculinity among white, European, and intact men, the limitations of such comparisons become evident. For example, while neither Carrizales nor Luis adhere to the social expectation that men procreate to produce heirs to their estate, the latter is presumably incapable, due respectively to his castration and enslavement, of both siring children and amassing wealth.[14] To fixate on merely one category like age risks not only effacing other important differences of identity but also, as this example shows, perpetuating a potentially racist and ableist narrative that reifies whiteness and non-disability as neutral, unmarked norms.

"Eunuch" is perhaps the most deceptively simple of the descriptions applied to Luis, for within it nest four major axes of identity: sexuality, gender, race, and ability. In terms of the latter, a eunuch by definition would imply a genitally altered individual, usually through varying surgical means, and a correspondingly diminished sexual potency and functionality. Yet there were significant historical variations in terms of method and outcomes; for example, castration could signify the complete ablation of the penis and gonads or a more limited procedure of testicular removal. These and similar variations meant that, though sterile, many castrates were capable of erection, ejaculation, and sexual activity, such that eunuchs belong on a more inclusive and nuanced spectrum of disability. Prepubertal castration could lead to a number of physiological traits, some of which were readily visible—such as sallow skin, elongated limbs, and larger hips and breasts—or audible, such as a high tessitura. This is the most salient feature of Luis's voice—described by the narrator as high-pitched ("atiplada")—and, of course, was for castrati both the purpose of their castration and reason for their privileged status. But we must consider not just biomedical, physical impairment but also social disability. In his highly influential treatise on humoralism, Huarte remarks on the effects of castration and the cold, dry disposition of those who have undergone the procedure:

> Pues vemos por experiencia que luego se le cae el vello y la barba; y la voz gruesa y abultada se le vuelve delgada; y con esto pierde las fuerzas y el calor natural, y queda de peor condición y más mísera que si fuera mujer. Pero lo que más conviene notar es que, si antes que capasen al hombre, tenía mucho ingenio y habilidad, después de cortados los testículos lo viene a perder como si en el mismo celebro hubiera recebido alguna notable lesión.
>
> Indeed we see through experience that afterward their body hair and beard fall out; their thick and bulky voice becomes thin; and with this they lose their force and natural color, and end up in worse condition and more miserable than if they were women. But what is most important to note is that, if before they castrate a man he has much wit and ability, after the testicles are cut he comes to lose it as if in the very brain he had received some serious injury.[15]

Huarte's aspersions prove that, beyond the degree to which eunuchs were physically disabled, they were also subject to attitudinal hostility and disparaging treatment in the social realm.[16]

As was the case with preceding examples, the categories of ability and gender are deeply intertwined, even mutually reinforcing, in Huarte's censure. Francisco Narváez de Velilla's early seventeenth-century *Diálogo intitulado El Capón* (Dialogue entitled The Castrate) similarly vitiated castrati, in particular for defying normative gender expectations. While his gender grants him the highly dubious privilege of access to Carrizales's home, it would have further marginalized him in a society often suspicious of emasculated men, who "provided important foils against which masculinity could be defined."[17] That Luis is permitted inside a gendered space that, save for Carrizales himself, is strictly forbidden to other men suggests that Luis is regarded as existing outside the bounds of adult masculinity and, perhaps, of heteronormative sexuality. If for historian Kathryn Ringrose early Byzantine eunuchs occupied "an alternative gender category" to mediate between men and women, then recent scholarship has established that the gender variance and fluidity of eunuchs challenge the very concept of a gender binary.[18] For Abdulhamit Arvas, a specialist in early modern English and Ottoman culture, eunuchs may constitute "a distinct gender category," while Betancourt sees them "less as a third gender than as embodiments of genderqueer figures."[19] Yet both scholars coincide in framing premodern eunuchism as a transgender identity and in advocating for understanding it from the more inclusive vantage of modern trans* theory.[20]

Though I have been advocating for the need to consider multiple categories of identity together, care must be taken not to conflate ambiguity of gender with that of sexual object choice.[21] Contrary to many modern, phallocentric assumptions about the desirability or sexual functionality of castrated men, historical sources reveal that castrati sometimes sought to marry, were often eroticized, and attracted and desired both men and women (and quite possibly others across the gender spectrum).[22] Crawford signals that, like other disabled people, eunuchs were regarded "as at once sexually deficient and sexually excessive . . . enabling the development of a double bind in which castrates were simultaneously incapacitated and held responsible for sexual transgressions of all sorts."[23] According to the musicologist Emily Wilbourne, moreover, "The voluntary castrato is quintessentially queer, for he slips between the cracks of heteronormativity: he modifies his body to suit his desire and he abdicates the procreative responsibilities of the heterosexual."[24] Arvas similarly observes that some Ottoman eunuchs voluntarily opted to undergo castration and thus to embrace an available means of gender transition and nonconformity. Yet, even if castration historically was performed to remedy various medical illnesses, and despite Cervantes's narrator remarking that Carrizales had also purchased white slaves for his household, the fact of Luis's enslavement almost certainly means that he would have exercised no consent over the surgical alterations to his body, manifesting once again the intersections between gender and race. The racialized distinctions between white and Black eunuchs in the Ottoman court indeed reveal for Arvas "an emerging race-making process that constitutes blackness as intricately interlinked with non-normative gender."[25]

In Cervantes's story, Carrizales appears to presume that Luis will neither pique the sexual interest of his young bride nor desire her for himself. Given the jealous old man's paranoid suspicion of other men, the strictly feminine quality of his household, and its resemblance to an Ottoman harem, scholars have typically assumed that Luis's access hinges on his gender. But thinking about the character intersectionally, and therefore about how other categories of identity were routinely denigrated as ugly, monstrous, and undesirable, suggests that his suitability as a sexually nonthreatening member of Carrizales's tightly controlled enclave might just as well relate to assessments of his race, age, a presumed physical deformity, or a combination thereof. In raising this possibility of an anti-Black, ageist, and ableist hierarchy of beauty operating in the veiled motives of white, able-bodied characters, I want also to acknowledge the risk of reifying a teleological assumption that early moderns espoused necessarily more conservative or retrograde attitudes toward nonnormative gender, differently abled people, or racial others. Such fallacies have been amply rebutted by other critics (not to mention overturned by the vitriol and growing right-wing backlash against non-white and LGBTQIA2S+ communities in contemporary US political and social media discourse). Nor do I wish to flatten Luis's identities into a monolith of subjectivation, or to imply that the character is an exclusive product of these identities. "Intersectional identity," according to Betancourt, "is byzantine—it is infinitely complicated, and it is often characterized as devious, deceitful, and corrupt."[26] If not Byzantine, then Luis's identity certainly is byzantine in each of these senses, given the narrative's depiction of his devious assistance to Loaysa. If Luis is thus an ideal candidate in theory for Carrizales, then, given his placement in the domestic and symbolic geography of the story, he would likewise seem an ideal theoretical avatar for Cervantine intersectionality: like the liminal position of the vestibule he is forced to inhabit, he exists in between, as an interstitial linkage between interior and exterior. But there are certainly other characters in Cervantes's body of work that might benefit from a similarly intersectional analysis, or that might challenge us to rethink the politics of identity.[27] To understand these characters in all their complexity is to recognize how racial otherness, gender nonconformity, differently abled bodies, and other marginalized identities were mutually constitutive of the consolidation of social hierarchies, in Cervantes's day as well as ours.

NOTES

1. Crenshaw, "Demarginalizing the Intersection." I want to acknowledge, yet unfortunately do not have the space here to engage more fully, recent debates over Crenshaw's paradigm, which the scholar of Black feminism Jennifer C. Nash has christened the "intersectionality wars"; Nash, *Black Feminism Reimagined,* 33–58. While the nuances of such critiques are important to bear in mind, my aim in this chapter is to prompt an initial yet sustained conversation around intersectionality and Cervantes that has yet to take place.
2. Betancourt, *Byzantine Intersectionality,* 15.
3. Prominent exceptions include Johnson, "Cervantes's Black Castrato"; Jones, *Cervantine Blackness;* and Ruiz, "Counter-Discursive."
4. Unfortunately, I am unable to adequately account here for the growing bibliography of valuable work on queer of color critique and similar issues but, as a starting point for readers, I offer a limited sample of recent, groundbreaking monographs on some of the entangled identities analyzed in this essay: Bey, *Black Trans Feminism;* Kafer, *Feminist, Queer, Crip;* and Snorton, *Black on Both Sides.*
5. Cervantes, *Novelas,* 416.
6. Johnson, "Cervantes's Black Castrato."
7. Reed, "Harems and Eunuchs," 208.
8. Peraza, *Historia de Sevilla,* 131, 134.
9. Phillips, *Slavery,* 130–31; 38.
10. Molho, "Aproximación," 756–57; Prendergast, "Fear and Control," 11.
11. Johnson, "Cervantes's Black Castrato."
12. Cartagena Calderón, "Aging Masculinities," 346. For more on the representation of age in early modern drama and Cervantes, see Cartagena Calderón, *Masculinidades;* and Alonso, *Envejecimiento.*
13. In the prologue of *Don Quijote* of 1615, Cervantes defends his old age and disability against the aspersions cast by Alonso Fernández de Avellaneda, author of the unauthorized sequel to the 1605 novel.
14. Though Luis expresses a desire to hire Loaysa for musical instruction, his use of the imperfect subjunctive mood—"Harto mejor os lo pagara yo . . . a tener lugar de tomar lición"—would seem to make his ability to pay as futile as that of leaving Carrizales's premises. Cervantes, *Novelas,* 423.
15. Huarte, *Examen de ingenios,* 619–20.
16. For a more general approach to early modern Spanish representations of disability, see Juárez-Almendros, *Disabled Bodies.*
17. Behrend-Martínez, "Manhood," 1080.
18. Ringrose, *Perfect Servant,* 3.
19. Arvas, "Early Modern Eunuchs," 117; Betancourt, *Byzantine Intersectionality,* 109.
20. Other scholars of early modernity have recently established that trans identity is far from simply a modern phenomenon; see Chess, Gordon, and Fisher, *Early Modern Trans Studies;* and LaFleur, Raskolnikov, and Kłosowska, *Trans Historical.*
21. For the entanglements between gender and sexuality, see Loomba and Sanchez, "Feminism," especially 29–31.
22. See Freitas, "Eroticism of Emasculation"; and Wilbourne, "Queer History."
23. Crawford, *Eunuchs and Castrati,* 6.

24. Wilbourne, "Queer History," 448.
25. Arvas, "Early Modern Eunuchs," 117.
26. Betancourt, *Byzantine Intersectionality*, 15.
27. For the case of Maritornes, see Aronson, "Intersectional Identities."

BIBLIOGRAPHY

Alonso, Ismael, ed. *El envejecimiento en y desde "El Quijote."* Grupo Ars XXI de Comunicación, 2006.

Aronson, Stacey Parker. "Intersectional Identities of Maritornes in Don Quijote." *Cervantes: Journal of the Cervantes Society of America* 45, no. 1 (April 2025): 55–76.

Arvas, Abdulhamit. "Early Modern Eunuchs and the Transing of Gender and Race." *Journal for Early Modern Cultural Studies* 19, no. 4 (2019): 116–36.

Behrend-Martínez, Edward. "Manhood and the Neutered Body in Early Modern Spain." *Journal of Social History* 38, no. 4 (2005): 1073–93.

Betancourt, Roland. *Byzantine Intersectionality: Sexuality, Gender, and Race in the Middle Ages.* Princeton University Press, 2020.

Bey, Marquis. *Black Trans Feminism.* Duke University Press, 2022.

Cartagena Calderón, José R. "Don Quixote and the Performance of Aging Masculinities in Early Modern Spain." In *Drawing the Curtain: Cervantes's Theatrical Revelations*, edited by Esther Fernández and Adrienne L. Martín, 331–53. University of Toronto Press, 2022.

Cartagena Calderón, José R. *Masculinidades en obras: El drama de la hombría en la España imperial.* Juan de la Cuesta, 2008.

Cervantes, Miguel de. *Novelas ejemplares.* 2nd ed. Edited by Jorge García López. Crítica, 2010.

Chess, Simone, Colby Gordon, and Will Fisher, eds. "Early Modern Trans Studies." Special issue of *Journal for Early Modern Cultural Studies* 19, no. 4 (2019).

Crawford, Katherine. *Eunuchs and Castrati: Disability and Normativity in Early Modern Europe.* Routledge, 2019.

Crenshaw, Kimberlé. "Demarginalizing the Intersection of Race and Sex: A Black Feminist Critique of Antidiscrimination Doctrine, Feminist Theory, and Antiracist Politics." *University of Chicago Legal Forum* 1, no. 8 (1989): 139–67.

Freitas, Roger. "The Eroticism of Emasculation: Confronting the Baroque Body of the Castrato." *Journal of Musicology* 20, no. 2 (2003): 196–249.

Huarte de San Juan, Juan. *Examen de ingenios para las ciencias.* Edited by Guillermo Serés. Madrid: Cátedra, 1989.

Johnson, Paul Michael. "Cervantes's Black Castrato and the Racial Politics of Timbre." "Early Atlantic Soundings," ed. Sarah Finley and Elisabeth Le Guin. Special issue of *Atlantic Studies: Global Currents* 23, no. 3 (Sept. 2026): 1–14. http://dx.doi.org/10.1080/14788810.2025.2583246.

Jones, Nicholas R. *Cervantine Blackness.* Pennsylvania State University Press, 2024.

Juárez-Almendros, Encarnación. *Disabled Bodies in Early Modern Spanish Literature: Prostitutes, Aging Women and Saints.* Liverpool University Press, 2017.

Kafer, Alison. *Feminist, Queer, Crip.* Indiana University Press, 2013.

LaFleur, Greta, Masha Raskolnikov, and Anna Kłosowska, eds. *Trans Historical: Gender Plurality before the Modern.* Cornell University Press, 2021.

Loomba, Ania, and Melissa E. Sanchez. "Feminism and the Burdens of History." In *Rethinking Feminism in Early Modern Studies: Gender, Race, and Sexuality*, edited by Ania Loomba and Melissa E. Sanchez, 15–41. Routledge, 2016.

Molho, Maurice. "Aproximación al *Celoso extremeño*." *Nueva Revista de Filología Hispánica* 38, no. 2 (1990): 743–92.

Nash, Jennifer C. *Black Feminism Reimagined: After Intersectionality*. Duke University Press, 2019.

Peraza, Luis de. *La historia de Sevilla de Luis de Peraza*, edited by Francisco Morales Padrón. *Minervae Baeticae: Boletín de la Real Academia Sevillana de Buenas Letras*, no. 6 (1978): 75–173.

Phillips, William D., Jr. *Slavery in Medieval and Early Modern Iberia*. University of Pennsylvania Press, 2014.

Prendergast, Ryan. "Fear and Control in 'El celoso extremeño.'" *Hispanic Journal* 31, no. 2 (2010): 9–22.

Reed, Cory. "Harems and Eunuchs: Ottoman-Islamic Motifs of Captivity in *El celoso extremeño*." *Bulletin of Hispanic Studies* 76, no. 2 (1999): 199–214.

Ringrose, Kathryn M. *The Perfect Servant: Eunuchs and the Social Construction of Gender in Byzantium*. University of Chicago Press, 2004.

Ruiz, Eduardo. "Counter-Discursive and Erotic Agency: The Case of the Black Slaves in Cervantes's 'El celoso extremeño.'" *Hispania* 97, no. 2 (2014): 194–206.

Snorton, C. Riley. *Black on Both Sides: A Racial History of Trans Identity*. University of Minnesota Press, 2017.

Wilbourne, Emily. "The Queer History of the Castrato." In *The Oxford Handbook of Music and Queerness*, edited by Fred Everett Maus and Sheila Whiteley, 441–54. Oxford University Press, 2018.

PART II

OTHERED BODIES

CHAPTER 5

"El manco sano," Corporeal Variance, and the Problem of Transparency

For a Disability-Centered Approach to the Body and Health in Cervantes

ALANI HICKS-BARTLETT

While Miguel de Cervantes is widely recognized as an author preoccupied with the body, a point of inquiry that has been persistently overlooked in critical literature is how his authorial voice not only proclaims an interest in bodily matters, but also overtly privileges bodily difference. To wit, even in a text as indisputably bodily-centric as the *Ingenioso hidalgo don Quijote de la Mancha* (1605 and 1615), Cervantes's corporeal preoccupations and the full extent of the theoretical underpinnings that they reveal are often treated elliptically or summarily by critics.[1] His bodily investments are viewed more as a prop than as an integral component of the plot's denouement; they are frequently understood as a thematic vehicle that helps mobilize and support Cervantes's narratological humor; and they have often been cursorily taken as yet another instantiation of Cervantes's prevailingly ludic orientation.[2]

Countless scenes of bodily manipulation and physical suffering in the *Quijote* often appear to be firmly situated as comical, such as Sancho's famous "manteamiento," or "blanketing" (I:17); the ingestion of Fierabras's balsam and its surprising emetic properties (I:17–18); and Don Quijote's dramatic suspension by his hand due to Maritornes's trickeries (I:43 and I:44); as well as the wayward knight's fears that his brain is melting when curdled cheese drips from his helmet

(II:17), to name just a few.[3] Notwithstanding the humoristic vein seemingly uniting episodes such as these, the prioritization of humor in critical interpretations of the *Quijote* disdains Cervantes's study of the body and his thoughtful and continual exploration of bodily integrity and solvency. Surely, even Don Quijote's gaunt, wizened body, contraposed as it is against his round squire's corpulence, bears all the signs of humoral imbalance and melancholic excess.[4] The different challenges the pseudo-knight and squire have in navigating the terrain before them and mounting on horseback; their varying susceptibility to falling, injury, and disorientation; and Sancho's firm inscription within the gustatory, gastroenteric, and the scatological that his surname "Panza" further dramatizes, all stand as clear indications of Cervantes's far more sustained and attentive meditation on health and bodily variance than is usually acknowledged.[5]

Cervantes's commitment to exploring corporeal variance is also revealed in the *Quijote*'s representation of gendered bodies, which are often negotiated through binary extremes. Namely, Cervantes insists upon the stark contrast between Dulcinea's imagined hyperbolic pulchritude and the discomfiting, "real" unattractiveness of the shepherd girl Aldonza upon whom he bases his fantasy. Dulcinea's idealized, unreachable body circulates throughout the text in a manner that renders the contradictory blazon made of her even more fragmentary and fleeting than standard Petrarchan paeans to female beauty, for example, for though Don Quijote claims her as his aesthetic and affective ideal, believing her to be "la más hermosa mujer del mundo" (II, 64: 534; the prettiest woman in the world), who is "supernaturally" attractive, and "sobre las bellas bella" (I, 4: 99; [even] more beautiful than beautiful women), she is also described as "fea" (ugly), "pestífera" (pestiferous), and excessively hirsute and malodorous, which encourages various characters to repeatedly call into question any of Don Quijote's proclamations about her singular "beauty."[6]

Moreover, perhaps as a coy metaphorization of the transferable, penetrative objectives of *innamoramento* and a wry literalization of the symptomatology of the ocular moorings of *aegretudo amoris* so often taken as diagnosable evidence of one's commitment to love, Dulcinea's body is constantly portrayed as nonnormative, pathognomic, leaky, and infectious.[7] Rather than crying the silvery rivulets of tears that a devoted lover would shed, for instance, it seems that Dulcinea's eye oozes *something* that is noxious, which Don Quijote idealizes nonetheless. Countering hypotheses that her reddened eye is leaking a pus-like poison as she is imaged to weep "bermellón y piedra azufre" (red and yellow sulfur), Don Quijote defends the discharge from her infected eye: "No le mana, canalla infame . . ., no le mana, digo, eso que decís, sino ámbar y algalia entre algodones" (I, 4: 100–101; Nothing is leaking from her, you vile scoundrel, I mean she's not leaking what you say she is, but rather amber, and civet musk among cottons).[8] Like Ginés de Pasamonte/Maese Pedro whose strabismus causes him visual difficulties, Dulcinea too is cross-eyed, and potentially partially blind.[9] She is also textually linked to the servant maid Maritornes, who is described as being "del un ojo tuerta y del otro no muy sana" (I, 16: 198; crossed in one eye and not very healthy in the other).[10] Furthermore, similarly to Maritornes, whose back and shoulders point toward the ground ("las espaldas, que . . . la hacían mirar al suelo más de lo que ella quisiera" [I, 16: 198; her back, which made her look at the ground more than she would like]), Dulcinea is also likely "corcovada" (hunchbacked), despite Don Quijote's suspiciously unprompted insistence that she is not: "y no es tuerta ni corcovada, sino más derecha que un huso de Guadarrama" (I, 4: 101; she is neither cross-eyed nor hunchbacked; rather, she is as straight and upright as a Guadarraman peak).

As various myths about Dulcinea as hale and toothsome (or not) proliferate throughout the novel, readers are provided with an image of a body that does not correspond to the fanciful blazon that Don Quijote has situated as his fantastical ideal. For instance, the varying signifiers and ever-changing renderings categorizing Dulcinea's beauty and that of the text's other female characters emphasize the "inherent mutability of bodies," along with the binary extremes that idealized chastity exploits.[11] As such, they reinforce what Ruth El Saffar persuasively deems the "essential insubstantiality of the female object of desire."[12] These extremes and the ephemerally coded, imagistic portrayal of the desired female body are then juxtaposed to assertive corporeality and bawdy speech of many of the *Quijote*'s other eccentrically nonnormative women as well. From Don Quijote's shock upon discovering Dulcinea's "real" nature to his bashfulness before female nudity, and his commitment to and desire for the "monstrous" bodies that he idealizes, the various textual moments staging his simultaneous discomfort and curiosity regarding corporeal matters are commonly thought to be humorous, intended as they are to delight and elicit the laughter of the novel's homodiegetic and heterodiegetic readers. Yet, the critical inclination to read these moments only ludically often minimizes or disregards the explicit fleshly critique, the serious nosological explorations, and the pointed bodily arguments these episodes meaningfully lay bare.[13] Cervantes's extensive corporeal commentary in the *Quijote* as in all other Cervantine texts, I argue, can productively be read as offering a serious engagement with what we now call premodern disability studies.

Undoubtedly, disability provides a fundamental lens from which to reconsider the Cervantine corpus, starting even as early as the attempts at authorial "self-fashioning" that Cervantes's prologues and self-referential comments show.

"Self-fashioning," as it is typically understood, connotes an easy suppleness of a malleable, moldable self, over which the powerful *artifex*—the author or artist, usually—has deft mastery and control.[14] Assessing the "conditioning" of the self, and the febrile contours of the body (which is often pliant, but also frequently elusive, fragile, infirm, or out of one's control), through the framework of disability thus allows us to better see the inherent connection between what is often regarded as a stylized trend or rhetorical sensibility in early modern literature but has a much greater theoretical embrace. In particular, this approach uncovers the explicit disability framework that considering "self-fashioning" only rhetorically elides.

If we reorient ourselves around disability, taking it as an ideological and thematic priority in the Cervantine corpus, and if we consider the body as a key, suffuse component of the premodern "bodymind," it is helpful to again signal the simultaneous vastness and centrality of the unmistakable corporeal critique that Cervantes puts forth throughout his entire oeuvre.[15] To be sure, even just the contributions that bookend Cervantes's literary career manifest his deep and sustained investment in the body and disability. Cervantes's first published work, the *Galatea* (1585), opens with expressions of corporeal instability through lamentations about a body and a voice, which, charting a certain commensurability with pathetic fallacy, are both physically and affectively unsupported by the surrounding environment. In the *Galatea*'s opening verses alone, for example, the adjective "cansado" comes up three times in rapid succession, evoked as it is in references to the shepherd Elicio's "cansado aliento"(I, 3: 165; tired breath), "cansados ojos"(I, 9: 166; tired eyes), and a depleted plain, which, reflecting the tiredness of the human body, is similarly fatigued as well: the land supporting the wearied body "se ha cansado" (I, 14: 166; has gotten tired).[16] Tellingly, the first characters whom readers meet all bemoan the effects that lassitude and fatigue have upon body and spirit. Along with corporeal fatigue, literal and metaphorical "falls" are coupled with laments about the cumbersome weight and weariness of the body and voice ("la pesada carga deste miserable cuerpo, y la voz cansada," I:183; "the weighty burden of this wretched body, and tired voice"), as well as with the psychic or emotional "weight" that runs in parallel with the text's descriptions of corporal fragility. Frequently evoked along with a comedic play on words that is formative for the text's ensuing discussions of illness, lovesickness, and melancholy, the consideration of maladies that are physical, mental, and emotional all dovetail with discussions of suffering, doctors, and potential remedies—that is, with the hope for a cure in an evocation of "Dios que todo lo cura" (God who cures all), and the inevitable pull of "locura" (I:174; madness).

In Cervantes's final text, the *Trabajos de Persiles y Sigismunda*, published posthumously in 1617, the authorial voice of the prologue cites numerous symptoms of ill health in comments referencing corporeal febrility, dropsy, a flickering pulse, the aging process, and death. Reversing the more ingenuous hopes for a cure expressed by the enamored swains at the beginning of the *Galatea*, these complaints are invoked alongside a more practical and skeptical discussion of the healing potential, or lack thereof, of "remedies" and "cures." In this prologue, Cervantes receives compliments through the voice of a "comedido estudiante" (attentive student). The youth is full of praise for Cervantes's literary efforts, and upon discovering that Cervantes is near, rushes to him, shouting: "'¡Sí, sí; éste es el manco sano, el famoso todo, el escritor alegre, y, finalmente, el regocijo de las Musas!'"(48; "Yes, yes; this is the wise one-handed man, the famous in everything, the happy writer, and finally, the delight of the Muses!").[17]

Since one of many pleonasms used in this brief prologue is "sano," Cervantes performatively highlights the injured hand he cannot use to write. Surely, alongside notions of sanity and health, "sano," also recodifies the values of "soundness," "intactness," "wholeness," and "worthiness" that Cervantes is directly interrogating throughout the prologue in the pointed attention he gives to his body, wounds, and the fame that the quality of his writing represents.[18] Moreover, Cervantes underscores these many valences of "sano" and "sanar" by anticipating the student's enthusiastic identification of him as a famous, excellent, wounded writer, with his awkward attempt to "asir" ("to grasp") Cervantes's injured hand. Most darkly, the student's gesture could also signal an instinctive, suspicious attempt to verify that Cervantes's hand is indeed wounded.[19] Yet, given that the student leaps from his horse, drops his belongings, and interrupts the author,[20] his efforts to take Cervantes's hand also open the possibility that he is simply so excited about their encounter that he momentarily forgets about the injury, as he dramatically—albeit fleetingly—puts Cervantes's name and authorial achievement over his inoperational hand even prior to voicing the exuberant encomium of his literary hero.[21]

Notwithstanding the fact that Cervantes feints at modesty regarding his literary impact by calling the "alabanza" ("praise") that he receives "un error donde han caído muchos aficionados ignorantes"(48; an error into which many ignorant admirers have fallen), the student's praise allows Cervantes to draw even more attention to his situation as an esteemed author, and also to the vitally important hand with which he writes. Insisting that he is just Cervantes, the author claims that he lacks all of the other qualities the student hyperbolically granted him: "Yo, señor, soy Cervantes, pero no el regocijo de las musas, ni ninguno de las demás baratijas que ha dicho vuesa merced. Vuesa merced vuelva a cobrar su burra y suba, y caminemos en buena conversación lo poco que nos falta del camino"(48; I, sir, am Cervantes, but not the delight of the muses nor any one of the rest of the silly things you said. You should go and get back on your donkey, and we can travel along together in good conversation for this little bit of the road we have left). The figurative and corporeal instability suggested by the "error" into which the susceptible fall is an indication of the bodily fragility that metaphorizes the tenuousness of authorial identity—which, in this case is grandiosely subsumed by "demás baratijas" (silly things).

Additionally, while the invocation of error and the "camino" or path that must still be traversed plays on the familiar trope of the story-to-be narrated qua physical trajectory, the laudatory attribution that Cervantes does *not* correct, is that of being a "manco sano" (the "sound," "wise," or "healthy one-handed man"). Given the structure of the sentence, "éste es el manco sano" (48; this is the sound one-handed man) is most closely aligned with "Yo, señor, soy Cervantes" (48; I, sir, am Cervantes). In other words, Cervantes rejects the appellation of being the "regocijo de las musas" (delight of the muses), yet revindicates being interpellated as the "manco sano": a proud designation he highlights even further by using "éste" as a deictic reference spotlighting both himself and his body. This pairing of identity and disability is especially pertinent to our present ends since it explicitly brings together physical disability and mental health, relating both not only to Cervantes's authorial identity, but to his authorial success as well.

Moreover, in this prologue so important to Cervantes's representation of disability, the matter of his advanced age and his own illness also comes about directly as a natural part of his conversation with the student: "y con paso asentado seguimos nuestro camino, en el cual se trató de mi enfermedad"(48; and with a leisurely pace we continued on our way, during which we discussed my illness). The intimacy established between student and author gestures toward contemporary understandings of carework.[22] In particular, along with underscoring the interrelationality and emotional engagement between the student (as carer) and himself (as recipient of care), the author's description of their exchange insists upon a certain complicity that unites himself and the student through their mutual awareness of Cervantes's ailment.[23] It also highlights their shared knowledge of symptoms and medicinal practices, which becomes a dynamic point of connection as they exchange evaluative comments about how Cervantes might best cure himself or find relief: "Esta enfermedad es de hidropesía, que no la sanará toda el agua del mar Océano que dulcemente se bebiese. Vuesa merced, señor Cervantes, ponga tasa al beber, no olvidándose de comer, que con esto sanará sin otra medicina alguna"(48; "This malady is dropsy, which cannot be cured even by drinking the sweet waters in all the Oceans of the world. Your grace, Mr. Cervantes, you must limit what you drink, without forgetting to eat, because with this you will be healed without any other medicine").[24] Not only does the student's unusually intimate knowledge of Cervantes's personal health present an argument for carework in that it shows how affective engagement, attention, and care abet accurate diagnosis, the student's skeptical stance toward common medicinal practices also revindicates traditional medicine while validating the empirical experience of the individual. So doing, the student reprises the frequent excoriation of doctors and iatrophobic take on medical knowledge that Cervantes offers elsewhere in his oeuvre and which correspond to larger premodern tropes inveighing against doctors and the problematic hierarchies that medical "authority" presumes.

In the prologue to the *Trabajos* specifically, Cervantes mentions appropriate gaits, diagnostic evaluations of the body, effective cures and remedies, the inconstant thrum of his beating heart, and the relatively short time—correctly assessed, in this instance—that remains for him on the "path" of life: "Mi vida se va acabando, y, al paso de las efeméridas de mis pulsos, que, a más tardar, acabarán su carrera este domingo, acabaré yo la de mi vida"(48; My life is already ending, and ceases to the pace of my pulse, which, at the very latest, will stop running this Sunday, thereby stopping the course of my life as well).[25] Just like Cervantes's mounting corporeal lassitude, the disability-centered comments of the relatively short prologue keep accumulating.[26] Overtly authorial remarks continue to foreground disability in the rest of the prologue, exemplifying the range of representations of corporeal variance, vigor, and illness that Cervantes persuasively examines throughout the *Trabajos*, just as he has done in all of his earlier works, from the prologemena and authorial asides of the *Quijote* to the *Novelas ejemplares*.

In offering a final word on the *Trabajos de Persiles y Sigismunda*, I would like to emphasize that along with voicing his accord with the bleak prognosis the student grants him, as he passes away mere days after penning the prologue, Cervantes is quite accurate in properly diagnosing the fatal lassitude and terminal decrease of his body.[27] Fueled by his mounting corporeal fatigue, his presentiment of death is so great that rather than any genuine introductory orientation to the *Trabajos*, what his prologue offers instead is a touching *valediction*. Accentuating the precipitous, continuous threat of death with a striking use of the gerund, as if in a final epic gesture Cervantes triply voices his leave-taking and closing *adieux*: "¡Adiós, gracias; adiós, donaires; adiós, regocijados amigos; que yo me voy muriendo, y deseando veros presto contentos en la otra vida!"(49; "Farewell, charms; farewell, graces; farewell, my delightful friends, for I am dying, though I remain hopeful I will see you soon and happily in the next life!"). While this last salute coupled with the timely dedication of his book to the Count of Lemos immediately after receiving extreme unction certainly comprises the most dramatic and moving example of Cervantes's perspicacious understanding of his bodily limits ("Ayer me dieron la Estremaunción y hoy escribo ésta," 45; ["Yesterday I was administered final rites and today I am writing this"]), readers should note that just like the emphasis bodily fragility receives throughout the *Persiles*, the frequent and pointed mentions of bodily ills are found in all of Cervantes's earlier texts as well.[28]

By way of illustration, in the *Novelas ejemplares* (1613), the confrontation between newness and traditional models, between singularity and exemplarity, aberrance and normativity, provides a helpful point of departure for Cervantes's exploration of matters relevant to bodily health, corporeal vigor, and disability. Like "hysteria," melancholy, and the "disease" of maniacal jealousy that he investigates in the *Quijote*'s intercalated "Curioso impertinente," Cervantes offers an ample repertoire of disability experiences in the *Novelas*, many of which similarly link amorous and affective reactivity to corporeal responses.[29] For instance, he probes everything from humoral imbalance and potential cases of jaundice, excessive sweating, limping, pustules, witchcraft, birthing methods, and venereal disease in the *Novelas*'s "Casamiento engañoso," which he relates to the medical setting and "broken and contaminated corporality of female prostitutes" that he represents in the "Coloquio de los perros."[30] Readers of the *Novelas* also encounter Cervantes's dramatic staging of melancholy, the performative feigning of illness and the debilitating effects of pregnancy and birth in "La señora Cornelia," as well a near-fatal fall from horseback, attempts at rehabilitation, frequent episodes of syncope, and concerns regarding genetic resemblance and dissemblance in "La fuerza de la sangre," through which he again proves himself deeply concerned with illness and disability. He centers both in his representations of youth, health, healing, and vitality, and the bodily strength of others and of his own.

A key example of Cervantes's negotiation of disability and infirmity is found in the story of the glass graduate, "El licenciado Vidriera." At first blush, the tale of the *licenciado* might seem to propose a fictive account of absurd embodiment, since the protagonist, Tomás Rodaja, comes to believe that he is entirely made of glass after ingesting an ill-fated love potion. However, Cervantes situates the malady from which the *licenciado* "suffers" (the glass delusion), and the attendant commentary on poison, medicinal thought, cures, and remedies that the novella features, within a larger philosophical and alchemical discussion of "transparency."[31] As such, the novella's opening descriptions of health and bodily sensations symptomize the tenuous dance between the protagonist's wisdom, madness, and "imaginación," while Rodaja's belief that he is "transparent" dialogues with important understandings of the materiality and malleability of glass, which reached an apogee during the late medieval and early modern periods.[32] While "transparency" and metaphorical "darkness" in the "Licenciado Vidriera" characterize Rodaja's fluctuating delusions and harken back to the lack of clarity and nebulous characteristic of Don Quijote's own 'clouded' mind, the material, metaphorical, and even metaphysical implications of transparency also reprise classical and medieval debates situating rhetorical clarity as a sociopolitical objective.[33] Specifically, transparency serves as metaphor for the desired honesty and limpid motivations of political and religious leaders. Moreover, especially with the details that Rodaja is transported to court in a carriage carefully lined with hay to better protect the body he believes could easily shatter, and that he similarly requests loose clothing for the "vaso quebradizo de su cuerpo" (II:54; the fragile vessel of his body), the symptomatology Cervantes attributes to the "glass delusion" recalls the famous historical example of Charles VI of France, who also suffered from the same malady, thus intensifying the political implications of Cervantes's portrayal of the glass graduate's illness.[34]

Additionally, however, not only is the political critique and commentary on good governance that lies at the heart of the *licenciado*'s delusions too frequently overlooked in most scholarly approaches, the novella's interrogation of philtres, cures, and diagnostic evaluation, of mental and bodily health, and of enteric and alimentary concerns related to ingestion, are also frequently disregarded.[35] The preoccupation with consumption is revealed in the discourse surrounding purges, poison, contamination, and even the eating disorder "malacia" or pica (geophagia, in this case), which is gestured toward in the description of a woman who fell ill "porque la había probado la tierra" (71; because she had eaten dirt).[36] Furthermore, the "transparency" that characterizes the glass graduate's particular vein of madness is directly related to the representation of health, transparency, bodily ills, and melancholy central to the larger Cervantine oeuvre and to Cervantes's implementation of metaphors of clarity, brilliance, and transparency in his rendering of his own bodily health and the "health" of his writing.[37]

As regards his own body and fitness, in the prologue to the *Novelas ejemplares*, Cervantes details his tendency to stutter and his flagging strength, and he proffers a catalogue of other corporal "complaints" as well. Among these number many of the expected discomforts of aging, such as his cracking joints, his mounting lassitude, and the increasing trouble that he has walking, for example, along with what he perceives as a decline in his general appearance. However, he also claims that he neither regrets his aspect—citing the "deformity" caused by his scars and battle wounds—nor should visible "impediments" such as his wounded arm, "aunque parece fea"(I:51; although it looks ugly), ever be perceived as uncomely or burdensome.[38] Rather, and similarly to the perversely heroic joy that Cervantes feels by continuing to wage a naval battle despite suffering from "calentura" (fever) and being deemed too ill to fight by his friends ("no estaba sano para pelear," 221; I wasn't healthy enough to fight) as one of the "Interrogatorios" of the *Información de Argel* details, wounds are a mark of honor and pride.[39] Recovering the positive designation that they had in classical accounts of triumph and war, wounds become a testament of strength rendered tangible through the body. Thereby, they are only positive, Cervantes avers, as they offer visual and material proof of his heroism, virtue, and glory.

Yet instead of asserting his authority unequivocally in the *Novelas ejemplares*, Cervantes complains about needing to write prefatory material in the first place since the prologue he included in Part I of the *Quijote* did not happen to turn out so well for him: "Quisiera yo, si fuera posible, lector amantísimo, excusarme de escribir este prólogo" (I:50). Nevertheless, despite not wishing to supply a prologue, he recognizes that he must write one. Since the necessary portrait of himself that he was to include as a frontispiece for his collection of stories was never delivered to him, he finds himself left to rectify what seems like a gaping, "faceless" space. Thus, at the beginning of this witty prologue, Cervantes explains that it has become his task to machinate ways to present his own body, and he does so in the following way, which I report in full:

> Éste que veis aquí, de rostro aguileño, de cabello castaño, frente lisa y desembarazada, de alegres ojos y de nariz corva, aunque bien proporcionada; las barbas de plata, que no ha veinte años que fueron de oro, los bigotes grandes, la boca pequeña, los dientes ni menudos ni crecidos, porque no tiene sino seis, y ésos mal acondicionados y peor puestos, porque no tienen correspondencia los unos con los otros; el cuerpo entre dos estremos, ni grande, ni pequeño, la color viva, antes blanca que morena; algo cargado de espaldas, y no muy ligero de pies; éste digo que es el rostro del autor de *La Galatea* y de *Don Quijote de la Mancha*, y del que hizo el *Viaje del Parnaso*, a imitación del de César Caporal Perusino, y otras obras que andan por ahí descarriadas y, quizá, sin el nombre de su dueño. Llámase comúnmente Miguel de Cervantes Saavedra. Fue soldado muchos años, y cinco y medio cautivo, donde aprendió a tener

paciencia en las adversidades. Perdió en la batalla naval de Lepanto la mano izquierda de un arcabuzazo, herida que, aunque parece fea, él la tiene por hermosa, por haberla cobrado en la más memorable y alta ocasión que vieron los pasados siglos, ni esperan ver los venideros, militando debajo de las vencedoras banderas del hijo del rayo de la guerra, Carlo Quinto, de felice memoria. (I:51)

This man that you see here, with an aquiline face, dark hair, a smooth and clear forehead, cheerful eyes, and a hooked nose, although it is well proportioned, and a silver beard, which lost its gold color some twenty years ago, a large mustache, a small mouth, teeth neither too small nor too large, because he actually only has six, and those six are in bad condition and arranged even worse, since they have no alignment at all with one another; his body is between the two extremes, neither tall nor short, his color is bright, he is somewhat more fair than dark; he is somewhat hunchbacked, and not very light on his feet; this, I say, is the face of the author of *La Galatea* and *Don Quijote de la Mancha*, and the face of he who wrote the *Viaje del Parnaso*, in imitation of that César Caporal Perusino, along with other works that wander around, misguided and astray, and perhaps, even without the name of their owner. He is commonly called Miguel de Cervantes Saavedra. He was a soldier for many years, and for five and a half he was a captive, which is where he learned how to have patience in adversity. In the naval battle of Lepanto he lost his left hand from an arquebus, which is a wound that, although it looks ugly, he considers to be quite beautiful since he earned it during the most memorable and magnificent occasion that past centuries have ever seen, and which the coming centuries can ever hope to see, as he was fighting under the victorious flags of the son of that lightning bolt of war, Charles the Fifth, of happy memory.

Although Cervantes wryly toys with Renaissance artistic and representational ideals of proportion and *misura* as he laments the failed promise of his friend to provide him with the desired portrait, and instead foregrounds all that his friend did not give him, Cervantes draws attention to what he believes is the poor aspect of his body, his body's uncertain presence in the text vis-à-vis his writing, and his concerns about how he is seen by others. This destabilizes him literally, metaphorically, and artistically, leaving him "en blanco y sin figura" (I:51; blank and body-less).[40] That is, he is left unsupported and unrealized, without a friend in whom to trust, and without the portrait he was promised, which he insists he needs in order to satisfy standard protocol, "como es uso y costumbre" (I:50; as is practice and custom).

Since the promised portrait has prosthetic implications for Cervantes, he mitigates his complaint about its absence by insisting upon his authorial agency despite the odds, and extolling the novelty of his approach: "yo soy el primero que he novelado en lengua castellana, que las muchas novelas que en ella andan impresas todas son traducidas de lenguas estranjeras, y éstas son mías propias, no imitadas ni hurtadas: mi ingenio las engendró, y las parió mi pluma, y van creciendo en los brazos de la estampa" (I:52; I am the first to have written novels in the Spanish language, as the many novels that have previously been printed are all translated from foreign languages, and in difference, these are my very own, not imitated or stolen; my genius engendered them, my pen birthed them, and [now] they are growing up in the arms of the press).[41] Along with the literal exemplarity of his novellas, which proliferate and have a type of *sui generis* maturation since they "van creciendo en los brazos de la estampa" (are growing up in the arms of the printing press), the portrait's lack, which leaves the author "blank and faceless," thus also coincides with Cervantes's recurring evocation of bodily diversity through references to monstrosity, parthenogenesis, and monstrous births.[42]

Emphasizing his paternal relationship to the *Novelas*, while Cervantes privileges the tighter familial and genetic relationship that binds him to his literary "product," he also describes his texts as having some autonomy since they "andan impresas" and then "deambulate" more freely in the press. In contrast to the *Quijote* where he casts himself as the text's somewhat unwilling stepfather, Cervantes is their "genitor," in the truest sense of the word. Nevertheless, in addition to his discussion of the engendering capacity of his "ingenio" ("ingenuity") that not-so-subtly links the exemplarity of the *Novelas* to the *Quijote*'s "ingenioso" protagonist once again, Cervantes promises to cut off his hand if the reading or consumption of the stories he writes were to lead his readers astray: "Una cosa me atreveré a decirte: que si por algún modo alcanzara que la lección de estas novelas pudiera inducir a quien las leyera a algún mal deseo o pensamiento, antes me cortara la mano con que las escribí que sacarlas en público. Mi edad no está ya para burlarse con la otra vida, que al cincuenta y cinco de los años gano por nueve más y por la mano" (I:52; I will dare to tell you one thing: that if in any way it were possible that the reading of these novels could induce the person who was reading them to some bad desire or bad thought, I would sooner cut off the hand with which I wrote them than bring them before the public's eye. I am already too old to play around with my eternal life, since I am already sixty-four"). While the violence he claims he will do to himself should his didactic intentions flop is already extreme, it becomes even more so when we recall that at the moment in which he pens this declaration, Cervantes is only able to write with one hand, having lost the use of the other at the 1571 battle of Lepanto.

In the prologue to Part II of the *Quijote*, Cervantes vehemently rails against Avellaneda, the author of the 1614 apocryphal continuation of the *Quijote*, who attempted to insult him by calling him "viejo" and "manco" ("old" and "one-handed").[43] Cervantes insists that he finds no shame or vility in either his age or his injury; instead, with a play on words that draws attention to his missing hand, he casts aging as a privilege since he would never have been able to halt the passage of time ("como si hubiera sido en mi mano haber detenido el tiempo"; as if it had been in my power [literally, "hand"] to hold back time).[44] Repeating the exultant view of the bravery and excellence on which he congratulates himself in the prologue to the *Novelas ejemplares*, Cervantes again exalts the heroic reasons that earned him his wounds in the first place. Certainly, it is not that his "manquedad hubiera nacido en alguna taberna" (II:33; loss [disablement; defect] was born in some tavern); rather, it was gained "en la más alta ocasión que vieron los siglos pasados, los presentes, ni esperan ver los venideros" (II:33; in the most sublime occasion that past centuries and present centuries have ever seen, and which the future can ever hope to see).

Along with serving as a bellicose and ennobling reorientation of the longstanding "orden de búsqueda" (search and arrest warrant) pronounced against Cervantes in September of 1569, which, as a punishment for wounding Antonio de Sigura in what was likely a "reyerta a espada o cuchillo en la corte" (sword or knife-fight at court) called for the "amputación de la mano derecha" (amputation of his right hand)—and which Cervantes suggestively alludes to in the *Novelas*'s prologue, as we have just seen—he frequently endeavored to reinscribe charges of delinquency or ignoble activity as lofty feats and prodigious action.[45] To be sure, some of Cervantes's proudest authorial comments harken back to the well-known incidents of his wounding, captivity, and bellicosity that he references at numerous reprieves.[46] In addition to the psychic weight of captivity detailed in "La española inglesa" ("Bien se me podrá creer si digo que sentía en el alma mi cautiverio . . ." (I:281; "You should really believe me if I say that I felt my captivity in my soul"), for instance, Cervantes also provides fictionalized explorations of his own captivity, wounds, and suffering in *El trato de Argel*, *Los baños de Argel*, and the *Quijote*'s "Historia del cautivo."

Cervantes also references his injury in his "Epístola a Mateo Vázquez," where he cites the "cansada mano" (v.8; tired hand) that he links to his overall corporeal experience. He describes himself as "cansado y laso" (v.10; tired and weary) and links his fatigue and chest wound to his "siniestra mano / . . . por mil partes ya rompida" (vv.137–38; left hand . . . already broken into a million pieces). He is thus using the only hand of which he continues to have use as an authorial guarantee of his good intentions. Ostensibly, as he claims in his discussion of his injured hand in the "Prólogo al Lector" to Part II of the *Quijote*, if he does incite readers to evil, then he must pay the appropriate price: his *novelas* should neither be read, nor should he write again; he should lose both his hand and his authorial agency. Finally, it has even been suggested that Cervantes dramatizes the limitations ascribed to his hand by punishment or injury through the addition of "Saavedra" to his name.[47] Notably, this important act of renaming takes place after the "crisis del cautiverio" ("crisis of captivity") and of identity that he endures in Algiers.[48] Indeed, the proximity between "Saavedra" and an "antiguo apellido argelino que significa 'brazo defectuoso, herido'" (ancient Algerian surname meaning 'defective, wounded arm') was precisely the "epíteto" (epithet) ascribed to him during his captivity and a name he began using thereafter.[49]

Yet leaving aside the promise to self-harm and hinder his writing career in a way that risks his authorial commitments and identity for the time being, the complexity of Cervantes's violent vow to cut off his hand before he moves on to recount "exemplary" stories challenges the very meaning of deviance and exemplarity. The authorial pledge put forth in the *Novelas ejemplares* becomes even more peculiar if one remembers that while many of the stories contained within the volume are indubitably presented as examples, they largely stand as negative models of comportment, and present negative understandings of trust-based relationships between characters. Nonetheless, they primarily feature the *bad* behavior of the characters whose actions are propelled by a "mal deseo o pensamiento"(I:57; bad desire or thought) from which, ostensibly, readers are expected to learn through negative example.[50] Theatrically staging the peril into which one can fall by misunderstanding the narratives of others, and mistaking the body for what it is not, the pessimism that stems from the frustration Cervantes describes in the prologue bleeds over to all other relationships. His desire to avoid inducing both the "descuidado" (careless) and the "cuidadoso" (careful) who read the *Novelas* to a "mal pensamiento," or any bad desire or impulse, toys with readerly expectations while calling into question authorial integrity, since this, of course, is not a truthful aspiration. Not only is the relationship between the author and his text thus weakened, or that between the author and the audience, or between author and reader, friends are no longer friends, teachers no longer teachers, servants no longer bound to their masters, the most devoted student no longer an accurate reader of texts and of bodies, and so forth.

The link between physical disability and Cervantes's ability to write becomes particularly poignant since he makes repeated references to his hands, which are of course integral to the writing process. Yet Cervantes also stakes them as a gauge or punishment for any failed narratological promise. Indeed, he pronounces an intricate series of authorial promises in this prologue that underscores both the corporeal integrity and salubrity (or lack thereof) of his body and the unique nature of his "exemplary" tales. To this end, the representation of health and related medical thought become something of a fulcrum of the *Novelas*, as the unstable body both catalyzes and justifies the instability of Cervantes's arguments, and the incongruous nature of many of the stories contained within.

Not only does the reprioritization of the body and disability in all of Cervantes's work abet the reassessment of his ludic aims, as mentioned earlier, it allows readers to have an even better appreciation of the breadth of the Cervantine oeuvre, and of premodern representations of disability, as it insists upon Cervantes's serious and sustained corporeal critique, which not only attends to the disabled body or passively describes it, but gives explicit attention and subjectival priority to it. What contemporary criticism offers to premodern literary and historical representations of disability is substantial, and premodern representations of disability likewise help inform our contemporary critical priorities and concerns. Cervantine studies thus has much to gain from direct engagement with disability studies, just as the methodological approach that the field of disability studies proposes offers tools that are indispensable to all studies of Cervantes, be they grounded in literary criticism and reception, historical approaches to the Early Modern period, or pedagogical and theoretical objectives. To regard Cervantes as purely humoristic is not only superficial, but a harmful erasure of the varied and extensive examination of disabled bodies and disability, capaciously understood, that Cervantes centers in every one of his works.

NOTES

I would like to thank the University College London Institute of Advanced Studies and the Huntington Library for the hospitality, support, and intellectual energy offered to me as I completed this article as a Visiting Fellow and a Dibner Research Fellow in the History of Science and Technology, respectively. I am also deeply grateful to Alexander Samson, Laura Bass, Tom Conley, and Jean Canavaggio for generously sharing their expertise and for the invaluable feedback and conversation.

1. Notable exceptions are Davoine, *Don Quichotte*; Quinn, "Handless Maidens"; López-Muñoz et al., "'Than all the herbs'"; and Presberg, *Adventures in Paradox*, 193–229. The greatest exception, Elizabeth Bearden's excellent *Crip Authority: Disability and the Art of Consolation in the Renaissance*, which dedicates a chapter to Cervantes, disability gain, and consolatory practices related to war injuries, was published after the completion of this article.

2. See, for instance, the chapters on the *Quijote* and the *Novelas ejemplares* in Scham's *Lector Ludens*. Although the context studied is Alfonso X's court, Serrano's "Visual Frames and Breaking the Rules of the Reconquista" helpfully evinces the frequent recurrence to the stuff of games (billiard tables and chess, for example) in Cervantine literature, 261–75.
3. References to the text are to vol. I (2021) or vol. II (2010) of Luis Andrés Murillo's edition of the novel.
4. On bodily size in the *Quijote*, see Cárdenas-Rotunno, "Mirth of Girth."
5. One important area of exception is the work that has been done on Cervantes and medicine, for which there is a considerable bibliography. As a point of departure, consider: Correa Fernández, *Las ciencias médicas*; Omedilla y Puig, *Cervantes en ciencias médicas*; Restrepo, "Médico y medicinas"; C. Johnson, "Psychoanalysis and Don Quijote"; Reverte Coma, "Antropología médica"; Redondo, "La melancolía y el *Quijote*"; and Osterc, "Cervantes y la medicina." More recently, see the excellent contributions by Domínguez, "A Window onto the Heart"; García Santo-Tomás, *Science on Stage*; and García Barreno, "La medicina en *El Quijote*."
6. As we will see in the *Quijote*'s discussion of Dulcinea's eye infection, to give just one example, more than just a parodic recodification or humoristic inversion of traditional literary representations of idealized female beauty, Dulcinea's body, like that of many of the *Quijote*'s female characters, is simultaneously pathologized as aberrant and lauded both despite and for those ostensible signs of aberrance and difference. Katritzky's "'A Wonderfull Monster Borne in Germany'" pertinently charts the numerous connections between "pathological hirsuteness" and premodern representations of corporeal diversity, particularly as related to: the "Wild Man" tradition; hagiographic and anchoritic accounts; and travel narratives depicting monstrosity, deformity, and "marvellous races." Katritzky, "'A Wonderfull Monster,'" 467–71. See also Velasco, "Hairy Women," especially 62–63, and 69–73; and Garland-Thomson on spectacularity and "freakery" in *Staring*, 161–67, and *Freakery*, 2–5.

   On ugliness, specifically, see Baker's detailed survey of nonnormative early modern bodies that challenge "the borders of subjectivity": *Plain Ugly*, 106. In addition to Garland-Thomson, cited above, Schweik and Sontag offer the most extensive analyses of the problematic connection between ugliness, notions of licitness and illicitness, disability, and visibility in *The Ugly Laws* and *Regarding the Pain of Others*, 95–99, respectively.
7. On the perceived "instability" of the female body, and the infective potential of female emotions, see Paster, *Body Embarrassed*, 25. See also Shildrick, *Leaky Bodies*, 14, 40–45; Baker, *Plain Ugly*, 2–5; and Juárez-Almendros, *Disabled Bodies*, 17–55.
8. For "amber," think, etymologically, "ambergris" ("ambergrease")—a lumpy intestinal excretion from sperm whales frequently used in perfumery and pharmacopoeia, considered valuable for its fixative aromatic properties in perfumes, and for its aphrodisiacal, humoral, physiological, and medicinal properties. Ambergris developed a sweet scent over time, but when freshly excreted had a fetid, fecal odor, Kemp, *Floating Gold*, 5–19 and 50–66, especially. See also Cole, "Scent from the Sea," 23–244.

   "Civet musk" refers to the potent paste drawn from the perineal glands of civet cats, used in exotic luxury perfumes, as well as the *materia medica* utilized for fumigations and remedies for plague, noxious wounds, and uterine problems. Civet was also often an integral component of aphrodisiacal potions, and of vitality-, fertility- health-, and humoral balance-restoring remedies," for instance. Dannenfeldt, "Europe Discovers Civet Cats."
9. González Echevarría cites Cervantes's continual portrayal of "problems of vision and

perception" (218), and the positive affordances Cervantes ascribes to literal and metaphorical strabismus: "Cervantes' is a happy cross-eyedness. . . . To him, the origin of vision is always already a double vision, with irony being congenital to it and with representation depending on it." González Echevarría, "*Don Quixote*: Crossed Eyes," 253.

10. In his edition, Francisco Rico draws attention to the ambiguity of "tuerta," which connotes both strabismus and blindness, 15n74.
11. Mitchell and Snyder, *Narrative Prosthesis*, 24.
12. El Saffar, "In Praise of What Is Left Unsaid," 207.
13. Surely, even this fascination before the corporeal has both philosophical and medical implications, as *curiositas* was commonly situated as either proof of the individual's sophisticated intellectual aperture or an unquittable humoral imbalance that exacerbated epistemological and moral maladies. On the important stakes of curiosity during the Early Modern period—which corresponds not just to the more literal takes on inquisitiveness, but also to the curiosity related to expanding *worldviews* as a result of maritime exploration, inquisitorial greed and colonial expansion, technological advancement, and new negotiations of the limits and liberties of the individual—see Benedict; Blumenberg; and Harrison. Neuhauser also provides a useful overview and history of curiosity.

    Curiosity is also aligned with theoretical investigations of the power and control granted to those privileged enough to obtain knowledge—as well as the contentment and (often) ignorant satisfaction of those willing to live with uncertainty. Recalling Augustine's warning against the relationship between the *libido sciendi* and pride in the *Confessions* X (10.35 [54] 160), Michel de Montaigne famously argues against curiosity, which he casts as a vain, presumptuous, and prideful vice in many of the *Essais*, and notably in: "De la praesumption" ("La curiosité de connaître les choses a été donnée aux hommes pour fléau"; "The curiosity to know things has reached men like a plague"), and in "C'est folie de rapporter le vrai et le faux à notre suffisance" ("La gloire et la curiosité sont les deux fleaux de nostre ame"; "Glory and curiosity are the two poxes on our soul"). This is similar to the stance articulated in Cervantes's "Curioso impertinente," which draws from Herodotus, Ovid, and Ariosto, to showcase curiosity's degrading effects. Not only do other characters debate the story's utility, the title of the *novela* alone ironizes on the idea of curiosity as a vain, fruitless enterprise, given the double valence of "impertinence" as both relentless and irrelevant. See Wilson, "Passing the Love of Women," 10, and Wardropper, "The Pertinence of *El curioso impertinente*."
14. See Greenblatt, *Renaissance Self-Fashioning* and Greene, "The Flexibility of the Self." On Don Quijote's fictional process of self-fashioning, see also Martinez, "I Know Who I Am," and Harney "Ludology, Self-Fashioning."
15. On the "bodymind," see Price, "The Bodymind Problem," Schalk, *Bodyminds Reimagined*; and Clare, *Brilliant Imperfection*, xvi. On the premodern bodymind, in particular, see Hobgood, *Beholding Disability*, 1–6, 20–21.
16. The text cited here is Francisco López Estrada and María Teresa López García-Berdoy's 1995 Cátedra edition of the *Galatea*.
17. All citations are from the 1969 Juan Bautista Avalle-Arce edition of *Los trabajos de Persiles y Sigismunda*.
18. "Sano," is of course related to the verb "sanar" designating the acts of "curing," "healing," and "recovering."
19. Although the student's profound affection for Cervantes somewhat mitigates the negative potential of this scene, his dive for the author's hand and potential "test" of the author's

"manquedad" nonetheless gesture toward the deeply problematic stereotype of the "disability con," wherein "'real' and 'fake'" disabilities were "distinguished" from one another based on ableist principles of exclusion and control fueled by a heightened apprehension toward "disability fakers" and concerns about "disability imposture." Samuels, *Fantasies of Identification*, 18, 68; Row-Heyveld, *Dissembling Disability*, 1–3.

20. Brownlee, in "Interruption and the Fragment," is especially helpful on fragmentation and interruption.
21. The student's brief disregard for Cervantes's wounded hand that allows him to orient his praise toward Cervantes's other qualities, is, of course, in stark contrast to Avellaneda's insensitive critique of Cervantes's age, body, and injury, which Cervantes angrily rebukes in the "Prologue" to Part II of the *Quijote*.
22. See especially Piepzna-Samarasinha, *Care Work*; Kelly, "Intimate Assemblages"; Ahmed, "Affective Economies"; and Shildrick, *Dangerous Discourses of Disability*.
23. On interrelationality and intersectional care, see Piepzna-Samarasinha, *Care Work*; and Ahmed, "Intimate Assemblages"; on relationality and the affective imbrication that appropriate carework requires, see Kelly, "Building Bridges," 787–88; on disabled-abled carework and its sociopolitical implications, see Fritsch, "Intimate Assemblages."
24. Curiously, the student vacillates between declaring Cervantes terminally ill ("el buen estudiante me desahució al momento" [112]), offering ways Cervantes might find relief, and insisting that he will be cured. Canavaggio, in "De la dédicace au prologue du *Persiles*," emphasizes the finality of the verb "desahuciar" (6), which Covarrubias, in the *Tesoro de la lengua castellana, o española* gives as "desafiduciar, perder la esperãça de alguna cosa. Desahuciado, el despedido de todo punto de su pretensión, y particularmēte el enfermo de cuya salud desconfían los Medicos" (306; *desafiduciar*, to lose hope in something. *Desahuciado*, someone utterly dismissed as a lost cause, and particularly a sick person for whom physicians see little hope of recovery).
25. While Close takes the fact that Cervantes has already received final rites and is quite literally on his deathbed as reason enough to believe that this exchange with the student was not invented, Canavaggio far more convincingly accentuates both the implausibility that Cervantes would have been able to "se tenir en selle tout au long des quelque douze lieues qui séparent Esquivias de Madrid" ("remain saddled up the entire twelve or so long leagues separating Esquivias and Madrid"), at the advanced stage of infirmity that he describes, and the accuracy of his prediction of an imminent death, which given the dating of the prologue and the dedicatory letter, was some forty-eight hours away. Canavaggio, "De la dédicace," 5.
26. The space that Cervantes dedicates to his body and the various discussions of disability is noteworthy given that the prologue only consists of seventeen sentences.
27. On the days leading up to Cervantes's death, see Dopico Black, "La Historia del ingenioso hidalgo." On Cervantes's acceptance or resignation before death, see Canavaggio, "De la dédicace." Canavaggio brilliantly reads Cervantes's citation of the "ancient *coplas*" "Puesto ya el pie en el estribo" ("Puesto ya el pie en el estribo / con las ansias de la muerte, / gran señor, esta te escribo" ["With my foot already in the stirrup, and preoccupied with death, dear Sir, I begin this letter to you"]) in the dedicatory letter that precedes the *Trabajos de Persiles*, as an intentional valediction, voiced almost *in extremis*, 6–8.
28. Indeed, Cervantes writes his dedication to the Count of Lemos on April 19, 1616, just one day after receiving extreme unction, and shortly after concluding the *Persiles*'s prologue, where he makes a similarly poignant withdrawal from his readers and the world. He dies on April 22, 1616.

29. On the Curioso's "hysteria" and its Freudian resonances, see Wey-Gómez, "Anselmo's Eating Disorder."
30. On symptomology, somatic response, and venereal disease in these *novelas,* see Carrera, "Embodied Cognition"; Albers, "La razón de los desmayos"; and Juárez-Almendros, *Disabled Bodies,* 56.
31. Speak, "An Odd Kind of Melancholy."
32. Schnapp, "Crystalline Bodies."
33. We recall that just one of the "clear" signs of Quijano's burgeoning "madness" is that he finds Feliciano de Silva's "entricadas razones" ("intricate reasonings") like "La razón de la sinrazón que a mi razón se hace" (The reason of the unreason that is made to my reason—so clear that they seem like pearls to him. Meanwhile, it is precisely the twisted logic of this literature that concretizes his derangement: "Con estas razones perdía el pobre caballero el juicio, y desvelábase por entenderlas y desentrañarles el sentido," (I.1: 72; With these reasonings the poor knight lost his senses, for he was trying to understand them and unravel their meaning).
34. One of the symptoms of the indisposition that left Charles VI (1368–1422) unable to reign consistently, beginning around 1392, when he had a first infamous spell of "maladie," was precisely his glass delusion, which contributed substantially to the political instability of the French court. See Autrand, *Charles VI;* and Famiglietti, *Royal Intrigue.* On Charles's euphemistic "absences" that "became longer and more frequent over time, undermining almost completely his effectiveness as a ruler" see Delogu, *Theorizing the Ideal Sovereign,* 153. See also Singer, *Representing Mental Illness,* 87; and Hicks-Bartlett, "War, Tears, and Corporeal Response," 242–44.
35. The novella links the difficulty of understanding the *licenciado's* illness and how to treat it, with numerous scenes of hypothesis evaluation, assessment, and experimentation: "Quisieron algunos experimentar si era verdad lo que decía" (II:53; Some people wanted to investigate to determine if what he was saying was true).

    Through his staging of Tomás's illness and a fraught process of recuperation, Cervantes proposes a frictious and dualistic mind-body connection: "aunque le hicieron los remedios posibles, sólo le sanaron la enfermedad del cuerpo, pero no de lo del entendimiento, porque quedó sano, y loco" (II: 53; [although they administered every possible cure to him, they only cured him of bodily, not mental illness, for he was left sound, and unsound]). Consider, for example, Aristotle's discussion of the (in)separability of body and soul in *De Anima* III: 642; Descartes's famous sundering of mind and matter in the *Méditations métaphysiques;* and the aforementioned discussions of the "bodymind" (Price, "The Bodymind Problem"; Schalk, *Bodyminds Reimagined;* Hobgood, *Beholding Disability* especially).
36. In his popular 1578 *Examen de ingenios para las ciencias,* Juan Huarte de San Juan provides an overview of this "appetitive perversion," which was deemed gendered in nature and often caused women "particularly young virgins, to eat the clay of which certain drinking vessels were made," 480–81, also cited in Wey-Gómez, "Anselmo's Eating Disorder," 818. See also Sieber, "On Juan Huarte de San Juan," 1–3.

    Unconvincingly, the argument has been made that the reference to eating dirt is merely a metaphorical description of the lady's difficult adjustment to a new city ("así como había entrado en Valladolid, había caído . . . muy enferma" [71; just as she had entered Valladolid, she had fallen . . . very ill]). It has also been read as the woman's attempt to cure herself. Although pica can sometimes be related to remedies, Cervantes casts the ingestion of "tierra" (dirt) as a symptom of disorder and illness, particularly since Anselmo of the "Curioso impertinente" admits that he too suffers from this "malady" even despite the gendered predisposition that commonly makes women more susceptible to it. As Anselmo specifies: "yo padezco ahora la enfermedad que suelen tener algunas mujeres, que se les antoja comer tierra, yeso, carbón y otras cosas peores, aun asquerosas para mirarse, cuanto más para comerse; así que es menester usar de algún artificio para que yo sane"(I, 26: 412; I am suffering now from the illness that some women tend to have, which makes them crave eating dirt, plaster, coal, and other things that are worse, or even disgusting to look at, let alone eat; so it is necessary to find some artifice for me so that I can heal).

37. On the etiology that aligns Rodaja's "más extraña locura que entre las locuras hasta entonces se había visto" (53; strangest madness that had ever been seen among all of the madnesses up to that point in time) with melancholy, see Fabietti's excellent "A Body of Glass," 331–32.
38. Citations of the "Prólogo" to the *Novelas ejemplares* and the *Novelas* themselves are from Sieber's Cátedra edition.
39. Cervantes, *Información de Argel*, 221.
40. Definitionally, in addition to "body," "figura," also means "shape," "form," "role," "statue," "portrait," or "person of reknown."
41. An indispensable text on prosthesis and the prosthetic implications of narrative supplements is, of course, the aforecited *Narrative Prosthesis* by Mitchell and Snyder. See also Shildrick's excellent *Visceral Prostheses*, 23–43.
42. While I note the connection between disability and monstrosity, as well as monstrosity and its coalescence with the Early Modern investment in *copia*, imagination, and exemplarity, I find many critical equivalations of disability and monstrosity troubling at best, and meritorious of greater study and nuance regardless.

    Exempted from these qualms are contributions like Cohen's Monster Theory: Reading Culture; Bates's Emblematic Monster; Río Parra's *Una era de monstruos*; Bearden's meticulous *Monstrous Kinds*; Davies's "The Unlucky, the Bad and the Ugly"; and Godden and Mittman's *Monstrosity, Disability, and the Posthuman.*
43. On Avellaneda's "false Quijote" or "Counter-Quixote," see especially Canavaggio, "Cervantes's Life," 16; and Iffland, "Quixote and Counter-Quixote," 149.
44. Another key "correction" that Cervantes makes of Avellaneda is in his re-establishment of the etiology of Don Quijote's "madness." On which, see Sicroff: "Cervantes does not waste time in determining the direction that he needs to go in the continuation of his novel. To do so, he first addresses the fundamental problem that reading Avellaneda's book would have posed for him: the need to reestablish the authentic meaning of his hidalgo's madness. If Avellaneda had started with a Quijote who was swiftly cured of his madness and who had then fallen mad again—as can occur in a "real" illness—Cervantes now transforms this vacillation between madness and sanity into an extraordinary equivocation that sets the tone for the denouement of the work." "La Segunda muerte de don Quijote," 276.
45. See Rodríguez, "Un ejercicio de lectura"; McCrory, *No Ordinary Man*, 47; and Dopico Black, who helpfully reports the "sentencia instruida" against Cervantes: "Know that the mayors of our house and court have undertaken and proceeded against an absent Miguel de Cervantes, on the grounds that he has given some wounds in our court to Antonio de Sigura, . . . about which the aforementioned Miguel de Cervantes was condemned by our aforementioned mayors, with great public shame, to have his right hand cut off, and to be exiled from our kingdoms for a period of ten years, along with other penalties that are contained within the aforementioned sentence." Dopico Black, "La Historia del ingenioso hidalgo," 25.

46. Rodríguez, "Un ejercicio de lectura," 60n2; see also Sliwa, *Documentos de Miguel de Cervantes*; and McCrory, *No Ordinary Man*, 47.
47. Garcés, "Los avatares de un nombre," 364. Expanding upon Salinas, who accentuates Quijote's recurrence to naming and renaming as if it were a "mágico utensilio de metamorfosis" Garcés describes Cervantes's likely adoption of "Saavedra" during his captivity as "un clamor o grito de guerra" (a cry or shout of war) that simultaneously attests to his bravery at Lepanto and Argel, and validates the "experiencia traumática del cautiverio argelino" (364; traumatic experience of captivity in Algeria). For Salinas, see "El polvo y los nombres,"13. See also López-Baralt, "El tal de *Shaibedraa'*," 420.
48. In his biography of the author, Canavaggio persuasively elucidates Cervantes's identification with his injury, tracing it to the petition that his mother (Leonor de Cortinas) makes when she asks for the rescue of the "manco de la mano izquierda," 106. On the connection between Cervantes's captivity and his subsequent identitary "crisis," see López-Baralt, "El tal de *Shaibedraa'*," 411–14.
49. Sáez, Introduction, 61; see also López-Baralt, "El tal de *Shaibedraa*'": "But it is not only that there is in Algeria an Arabic surname that is phonetically consonant with the Spanish surname Saavedra, it is that Cervantes, maimed in one arm during the great victory at Lepanto, could have been given the surname *Shaibedraa'* during his captivity. It is that the word *shaibedraa'*, used as a phrase, specifically means 'defective arm.' The word *al-ḍirā'* means 'arm' (Cowan 356), while *'šaīb'* comes from the verb *šūb* or *šiāb* which means 'to alter, to falsify, or to make gray' [Cortés 601; Cowan 574; and Corriente 77]. The word *šāi'ba*, comes from this verb, which, according to Cowan (574), means 'defect, lack, stain,' and according to Cortés [601] means 'defect, imperfection, damage/harm'" (416; see also 359–61). For more on this act of naming, see Sáez, "Introducción," 61. See also Garcés, "Los avatares de un nombre," 360; and Zmantar, "Saavedra et les captifs."
50. On didacticism, skepticism, and belief in the *Novelas ejemplares*, see Fuchs, "Suspended Judgments," 447–50; Thompson, "*Eutrapelia* and Exemplarity"; and Johnson, *Affective Geographies*, 161–63.

BIBLIOGRAPHY

Ahmed, Sara. "Affective Economies," *Social Text* 22, no. 2 (Summer 2004): 117–39.

Albers, Irene. "La razón de los desmayos en 'El celoso extremeño' de Cervantes." In *Escenas de transgresión: María de Zayas en su contexto literario-cultural*. Edited by Irene Albers, Uta Felten, and Hans Ulrich Gumbrecht. Iberoamericana, 2009.

Augustinus, Aurelius. *Confessions*, vol. II, books 9–13. Loeb Classical Library. Edited by Carolyn J.-B. Hammond. Harvard University Press, 2016.

Autrand, Françoise. *Charles VI: La folie du roi*. Fayard, 1986.

Aristotle. *De Anima*, book III, translated by J. A. Smith. Clarendon Press, 1931.

Baker, Naomi. *Plain Ugly: The Unattractive Body in Early Modern Culture*. Manchester University Press, 2010.

Bates, A. W. *Emblematic Monsters: Unnatural Conceptions and Deformed Births in Early Modern Europe*. Rodopi, 2005.

Bearden, Elizabeth. *Monstrous Kinds: Body, Space, and Narrative in Renaissance Representations of Disability*. University of Michigan Press, 2019.

Bearden, Elizabeth. *Crip Authority: Disability and the Art of Consolation in the Renaissance.* University of Michigan Press, 2025.

Benedict, Barbara. *Curiosity: A Cultural History of Early Modern Inquiry.* University of Chicago Press, 2001.

Blumenberg, Hans. "Curiositas und Veritas." *Studia Patristica*, no. 81 (1962): 294–302.

Brownlee, Marina. "Interruption and the Fragment: Heliodorus and Persiles." In *Cervantes'* Persiles *and the Travails of Romance.* Edited by Marina Brownlee. University of Toronto Press, 2019.

Canavaggio, Jean. *Cervantes.* Espasa-Calpe, 1987.

Canavaggio, Jean. "Cervantes's Life." In *The Oxford Handbook of Cervantes*, edited by Aaron Kahn. Oxford University Press, 2021.

Canavaggio, Jean. "De la dédicace au prologue du *Persiles*: Le fin mot de Cervantès." *e-Spania* 18 (2014): 2–10.

Cárdenas-Rotunno, Anthony. "The Mirth of Girth: Don Quixote's Stout Squire." *Rocky Mountain Review* 68, no. 1 (Spring 2014): 9–31.

Carrera, Elena. "Embodied Cognition and Empathy in Miguel de Cervantes' 'El celoso extremeño," *Hispania* 91, no. 1 (2014): 113–24.

Cervantes, Miguel de. "Epístola a Mateo Vázquez," edited by Schevill and Bonilla. *Cervantes: Bulletin of the Cervantes Society of America* 23, no. 1 (2003): 215–22.

Cervantes, Miguel de. *La Galatea.* Edited by Francisco López Estrada and María Teresa López García-Berdoy. Cátedra, 1995.

Cervantes, Miguel de. *Información de Argel.* Edited by Adrián J. Sáez. Cátedra, 2019.

Cervantes, Miguel de. *El ingenioso hidalgo don Quijote de la Mancha*, vols. I and II. Edited by Luis Andrés Murillo. Cátedra, 2021.

Cervantes, Miguel de. *Don Quijote de la Mancha.* Edited by Francisco Rico. Biblioteca Clásica de la Real Academia Española, 2015.

Cervantes, Miguel de. *Novelas ejemplares.* Edited by Harry Sieber. I and II. Cátedra, 2004, 2002.

Cervantes, Miguel de. *Los trabajos de Persiles y Sigismunda.* Edited by Juan Bautista Avalle-Arce. Castalia, 1969.

Clare, Eli. *Brilliant Imperfection: Grappling with Cure.* Duke University Press, 2017.

Close, Anthony. "Cervantes: Pensamiento, personalidad, cultura." Centro Virtual Cervantes, accessed May 19, 2026, https://cvc.cervantes.es/literatura/clasicos/quijote/introduccion/prologo/close.htm.

Cohen, Jeffrey Jerome. *Monster Theory: Reading Culture.* University of Minnesota Press, 1996.

Cole, Georgina. "Scent from the Sea: Ambergris in Eighteenth- and Nineteenth-Century Medicine, Perfume, and Natural History." In *Sea Currents in Nineteenth-Century Art, Science and Culture: Commodifying The Ocean World*, edited by Kathleen Davidson and Molly Duggins. Bloomsbury Visual Arts, 2023.

Correa Fernández, Antonio. *Las ciencias médicas en tiempo de Miguel de Cervantes.* Sesión solemne, 1905.

Covarrubias, Sebastián de. *Tesoro de la lengua castellana, o española.* Luis Sánchez, 1611.

Dannenfeldt, Karl. "Europe Discovers Civet Cats and Civet." *Journal of the History of Biology* 18, no. 3 (1985): 403–31.

Davies, Surekha. "The Unlucky, the Bad and the Ugly: Categories of Monstrosity from the Renaissance to the Enlightenment." In *The Ashgate Research Companion to Monsters and the Monstrous*, edited by Asa Mittman and Peter Dendle. Routledge, 2012.

Davoine, Françoise. *Don Quichotte pour combattre la mélancolie.* Stock, 2008.
Delogu, Daisy. *Theorizing the Ideal Sovereign: The Rise of the French Vernacular Royal Biography.* University of Toronto Press, 2008.
Descartes, René. *Méditations métaphysiques.* Edited by Marie Frédérique Pellegrin. Flammarion, 2021.
Domínguez, Julia. "A Window onto the Heart: Cervantes and the Cardiocentric Self." *Hispanic Review* 91, no. 4 (2023): 517–39.
Domínguez, Julia. *Quixotic Memories: Cervantes and Memory in Early Modern Spain.* University of Toronto Press, 2022.
Dopico Black, Georgina. "La Historia del ingenioso hidalgo Miguel de Cervantes." In *España en tiempos del Quijote,* edited by Antonio Feros and Juan Gelabert. Taurus, 2004.
El Saffar, Ruth. "In Praise of What Is Left Unsaid: Thoughts on Women and Lack in Don Quijote," *MLN* 103, no. 2 (1988): 205–22.
Fabietti, Elena. "A Body of Glass: The Case of El Licenciado Vidriera." *symplokē* 23, no. 1–2 (2015): 327–40.
Famiglietti, Richard. *Royal Intrigue: Crisis at the Court of Charles VI 1392–1420.* AMS Press, 1986.
Fritsch, Kelly. "Intimate Assemblages: Disability, Intercorporeality, and the Labour of Attendant Care." *Critical Disability Discourses* 2 (2010): 1–14.
Fuchs, Barbara. "Suspended Judgments: Skepticism and the Pact of Fictionality in Cervantes's Picaresque Novellas." *Modern Language Quarterly* 76, no. 4 (2015): 447–63.
Garcés, María Antonia. "Los avatares de un nombre: Saavedra y Cervantes." *Revista de Literatura* 65, no. 130 (2003): 351–74.
García Barreno, Pedro. "La medicina en *El Quijote* y su entorno." In *La ciencia y El Quijote,* edited by José Manuel Sánchez Ron. Crítica, 2005.
García Santo-Tomás, Enrique, Ed. *Science on Stage in Early Modern Spain.* University of Toronto Press, 2019.
Garland-Thomson, Rosemarie. *Freakery: Cultural Spectacles of the Extraordinary Body.* New York University Press, 1996.
Garland-Thomson, Rosemarie. *Staring: How We Look.* Oxford University Press, 2009.
González Echevarría, Roberto. "*Don Quixote*: Crossed Eyes and Vision." In *Cervantes' Don Quixote: A Casebook,* edited by Roberto González Echevarría. Oxford University Press, 2005.
Greenblatt, Stephen. *Renaissance Self-Fashioning: From More to Shakespeare.* University of Chicago Press, 1980.
Greene, Thomas. "The Flexibility of the Self in Renaissance Literature." In *The Disciplines of Criticism,* edited by Peter Demetz, Thomas Greene, and Lowry Nelson Jr. Yale University Press, 1968.
Harney, Michael. "Ludology, Self-fashioning, and Entrepreneurial Masculinity in Iberian Novels of Chivalry." In *Self-Fashioning and Assumptions of Identity in Medieval and Early Modern Iberia,* edited by Laura Delbrugge. Brill, 2015.
Harrison, Peter. "Curiosity, Forbidden Knowledge, and the Reformation of Natural Philosophy in Early Modern England." *Isis* 92 (2001): 265–90.
Hicks-Bartlett, Alani. "War, Tears, and Corporeal Response in Christine de Pizan." In *Literatures of the Hundred Years War,* edited by Daniel Davies and R.D. Perry. Manchester University Press, 2024.
Hobgood, Allison. *Beholding Disability in Renaissance England.* University of Michigan Press, 2021.

Huarte de San Juan, Juan. *Examen de ingenios para las ciencias*. Cátedra, 1989.
Iffland, James. "Quixote and Counter-Quixote: The Cervantes-Avellaneda Duel and Its Impact on the History of the Novel." In *The Oxford Handbook of Cervantes*, edited by Aaron Kahn. Oxford University Press, 2021.
Johnson, Carroll. "Psychoanalysis and Don Quijote." In *Approaches to Teaching Cervantes'* Don Quixote, edited by R. Bjornson. Modern Language Association of America, 1984.
Johnson, Paul Michael. *Affective Geographies: Cervantes, Emotion, and the Literary Mediterranean*. University of Toronto Press, 2020.
Juárez-Almendros, Encarnación. *Disabled Bodies in Early Modern Spanish Literature: Prostitutes, Aging Women, Saints*. Liverpool University Press, 2017.
Katritzky, M. A. "'A Wonderfull Monster Borne in Germany': Hairy Girls in Medieval and Early Modern German Book, Court and Performance Culture." In "The Feminine in German Culture," special issue of *German Life and Letters* 67, no. 4 (2014): 467–71.
Kelly, Christine. "Building Bridges with Accessible Care: Disability Studies, Feminist Care Scholarship, and Beyond." *Hypatia* 28, no. 4 (2013): 787–78.
Kemp, Christopher. *Floating Gold: A Natural [and Unnatural] History of Ambergris*. University of Chicago Press, 2012.
López-Baralt, Luce. "El tal de *Shaibedraa'* (*Don Quijote* I, 40)." *eHumanista/Cervantes* 2 (2013): 407–26.
López-Muñoz, Francisco, Cecilio Álamo, and Pilar García-García. "'Than all the herbs described by Dioscorides . . .': The Traces of Andrés Laguna in the Works of Cervantes." *Pharmacy in History* 49, no. 3 (2007): 87–108.
Martinez, Felicia. "I Know Who I Am: Don Quixote, Self-Fashioning, and the Humanness of Ordinary Identity." *Philosophy and Literature* 41, no. 2 (2016): 511–25.
McCrory, Donald. *No Ordinary Man: The Life and Times of Miguel de Cervantes*. Dover, 2005.
Mitchell, David, and Sharon Snyder, *Narrative Prosthesis: Disability and the Dependencies of Discourse*. University of Michigan Press, 2000.
Montaigne, Michel de. *Les Essais*, edited by Pierre Villey and V. L. Saulnier. Presses Universitaires de France, 2004.
Omedilla y Puig, Joaquín. *Cervantes en ciencias médicas, brevísimas consideraciones acerca de sus conocimientos en este asunto*. Administración de la Revista de Medicina y Cirugía Prácticas, 1905.
Osterc, Lúdovik. "Cervantes y la medicina." *Verba Hispanica* 6, no. 1 (1996): 17–22.
Paster, Gail Kern. *The Body Embarrassed: Drama and the Disciplines of Same in Early Modern England*. Cornell University Press, 1993.
Piepzna-Samarasinha, Leah Lakshmi. *Care Work: Dreaming Disability Justice*. Arsenal Pulp Press, 2018.
Presberg, Charles. *Adventures in Paradox: Don Quixote and the Western Tradition*. Pennsylvania State University, 2001.
Price, Margaret. "The Bodymind Problem and the Possibilities of Pain." *Hypatia* 30, no. 1 (2015): 269–84.
Quinn, Mary. "Handless Maidens, Modern Texts: A New Reading of Cervantes's the Captive's Tale." *MLN* 123, no. 2 (2008): 213–29.
Redondo, Augustin. "La melancolía y el *Quijote* de 1605." In *Varia lingüística y literaria*, edited by Martha Elena Venier. El Colegio de Mexico, 1997.

Restrepo, Miguel. "Médico y medicinas al través de la obra de Cervantes." *Revista Universidad de Antioquia*, no. 145 (1961): 255–79.
Reverte Coma, José Manuel. "Antropología médica del *Quijote*: Farmacopea en el *Quijote*." Previsión Sanitaria Nacional 76 (1992): 38–44.
Río Parra, Elena del. *Una era de monstruos: Representaciones de lo deforme en el Siglo de Oro español.* Iberoamericana-Vervuert, 2003.
Rodríguez, Juan Carlos. "Un ejercicio de lectura: El Quijote en el siglo XXI." In *Territorios de la Mancha: Versiones y subversiones cervantinas en la literatura hispanoamericana*, edited by Matías Barchino. Ediciones de la Universidad de Castilla-La Mancha, 2004.
Row-Heyveld, Lindsey. *Dissembling Disability in Early Modern English Drama.* Palgrave, 2018.
Sáez, Adrián. Introduction to *Información de Argel*, edited by Adrián Sáez. Cátedra, 2019.
Salinas, Pedro. "El polvo y los nombres." In *Ensayos de literatura hispánica: Del* Cantar de Mio Cid *a García Lorca*, edited by Juan Marichal. Aguilar, 1961.
Samuels, Ellen. *Fantasies of Identification: Disability, Gender, Race.* New York University Press, 2014.
Schalk, Sami. *Bodyminds Reimagined: (Dis)ability, Race, and Gender in Black Women's Speculative Fiction.* Duke University Press, 2018.
Scham, Michael. *Lector Ludens: the Representation of Games and Play in Cervantes.* University of Toronto Press, 2014.
Schnapp, Jeffrey. "Crystalline Bodies: Fragments of a Cultural History of Glass." *West 86th: A Journal of Decorative Arts, Design History, and Material Culture* 20, no. 2 (2013): 173–94.
Schweik, Susan. *The Ugly Laws: Disability in Public.* New York University Press, 2009.
Shildrick, Margrit. *Dangerous Discourses of Disability, Subjectivity and Sexuality.* Palgrave, 2009.
Shildrick, Margrit. *Leaky Bodies and Boundaries: Feminism, Postmodernism and (Bio)ethics.* Rutledge, 1997.
Shildrick, Margrit. *Visceral Prostheses: Somatechnics and Posthuman Embodiment.* Bloomsbury Academic, 2023.
Serrano, Nhora Lucia. "Visual Frames and Breaking the Rules of the Reconquista: Chess and Alfonso X, el Sabio's *Libro de ajedrez, dados y tablas*." In *Playthings in Early Modernity: Party Fames, Word Games, Mind Games*, edited by Allison Levy. Western Michigan University, 2017.
Sicroff, A. A. "La segunda muerte de don Quijote como respuesta de Cervantes a Avellaneda." *Nueva Revista de Filología Hispánica* 24, no. 2 (1975): 267–91.
Sieber, Harry. "On Juan Huarte de San Juan and Anselmo's Locura in 'El Curioso Impertinente.'" *Revista Hispánica Moderna* 36, no. 1–2 (1970–1971): 1–8.
Singer, Julie. *Representing Mental Illness in Late Medieval France: Madness, Machines, Metaphor.* D. S. Brewer, 2018.
Sliwa, Krzysztof. *Documentos de Miguel de Cervantes.* Universidad de Navarra, 1999.
Sontag, Susan. *Regarding the Pain of Others.* Picador, 2003.
Speak, Gill. "An Odd Kind of Melancholy: Reflections on the Glass Delusion in Europe (1440–1680)." *History of Psychiatry* 1, no. 2 (1990): 191–206.
Thompson, Colin. "*Eutrapelia* and Exemplarity in the *Novelas ejemplares*." In *A Companion to Cervantes's* Novelas Ejemplares, edited by Stephen Boyd. Boydell & Brewer.
Velasco, Sherry. "Hairy Women on Display in Textual and Visual Culture in Early Modern Spain." *South Atlantic Review* 72, no. 1 (2007): 62–75.
Wardropper, Bruce. "The Pertinence of *El curioso impertinente.*" *PMLA* 72, no. 4 (1957): 587–600.

Wey-Gómez, Nicolás. "Anselmo's Eating Disorder." In *The Norton Critical Edition of Don Quixote,* edited by Diana de Armas Wilson. Norton, 1999.

Wilson, Diana. "'Passing the Love of Women': The Intertextuality of *El curioso impertinente*." *Cervantes: Bulletin of the Cervantes Society of America* 7, no. 2 (1987): 9–18.

Zmantar, Françoise. "Saavedra et les captifs du Trato de Argel de Miguel de Cervantes." In *L'Autobiographie dans le monde hispanique*. Honoré Champion, 1980.

CHAPTER 6

Shattering Glass

Cervantes Between Diagnosis and Disability

MARGARET E. BOYLE

> Structuring experiences and emotions through language makes life tolerable, meaningful; it allows you to escape your condition through fantasy, only to find yourself confronting the condition you're trying to escape.
>
> GLORIA ANZALDÚA, *Light in the Dark*

Miguel de Cervantes engages extensively with the topic of health status and identity, as Alani Hicks-Bartlett also demonstrates in her contribution to this volume. He does so most famously, perhaps, in the interplay between the real and fictional selves of Alonso Quijano / Don Quijote. Readers that begin to form relationships with this lead character grapple with a range of diagnoses for bodily and mental ailments. The novel likewise contemplates potential causes of illness—most famously the overconsumption of chivalric literature—and of course a range of treatment methods and proposed cures from balms and tinctures to book-burning and self-avowal.[1] Certainly throughout *Don Quijote*, Cervantes firmly establishes his narrative engagement with the construction of self in relationship to the realities of an aging body and the specter of mortality. Within this specific context of health and illness, identity is fragmented and precarious, and placed into the complex network of imagination, desire, and sociopolitical norms.

This engagement with identity in terms of fragmentation, vulnerability, and transparency is most provocative in "El Licenciado Vidriera" (The Glass Lawyer), a short story from Cervantes's collection *Novelas ejemplares* (The Exemplary Novels), published between parts I and II of *Don Quijote* in 1613. Here readers witness the protagonist Tomás's bodymind transform after an unexpected encounter with severe illness, prolonged episodes of convulsions, and physical paralysis, conditions that, when finally resolved, are replaced with the psychological terror of being made of glass. Early modern European literature—both medical and fictional texts—offered its readers numerous examples of individuals enduring similar ailments, particularly what is known as the tradition of the glass delusion.[2] My reading follows Black feminists' conceptualization of Jennifer Nash's "slow loss" to describe "multiple and overlapping forms of time—waiting, anticipation, the chronic, durational—all of which decenter the primacy of the event and instead focus on the quotidian and the endured."[3] In this case, the glass delusion manifests for Tomás as an after-effect of extreme illness. He grapples with how to make his life meaningful, addressing the topics of perception (how we are seen, understood, and valued) and memory (how we are remembered, legacy). Throughout these meditations, there is a palpable and ongoing encounter with mortality, the limitation of bodies and health status in relationship to narrative. That is to say that the narrative is concerned both with the circumstances of a disabling event, but also the inevitability of disability through the process of aging.

My reading of Cervantes's short story engages with the first-person model of disability—that is the intimacy of how Tomás narrates his story—versus medical models of disability through diagnoses from Cervantes's day. Several critics have highlighted Spanish physician Alfonso de Santa Cruz's *Dignotio et cura affectuum melancholicorum* (Diagnosis and treatment of melancholic diseases, 1569) as a medical text that closely correlates with symptoms experienced by the protagonist of the short story, and this comparative reading between literary and medical texts allows us to think broadly about the interactions between scientific and popular knowledge. Moreover, it is compelling that all the accounts in this medical text are presented in the first person. Treatments for manifestations of melancholy are described via personal testimonies of the doctor, including the patient whose symptoms align with those of Tomás.[4] While there is much to be gained from this wider understanding of how physicians conceptualized and treated parallel elements, it is also worth reflecting on how to trace more directly patient testimonies concerning their own experiences and the extent to which literary accounts broadly allow for this kind of comparative work, as in Tomás's first-person narration of his own experience.

Certainly, Cervantes's personal contact with medical practice and treatment experiences also offer needed context for his writing about disability. As

Francisco López-Muñoz and others remind us, and as Ana Laguna's chapter in this volume also explores, Cervantes's family contacts with the scientific and medical world profoundly shaped his knowledge about modes of treatment and patient experiences. He was the son of a surgeon-bloodletter (Rodrigo de Cervantes, 1509–1585) and brother of a nurse (Andrea de Cervantes, 1545?–1609). Cervantes's private library would have contained several medical texts, including Dionisio Daza Chacón's *Práctica y teórica de cirugía* (Practice and theory of surgery, 1584), Juan Huarte de San Juan's *Examen de ingenios* (The examination of men's wits, 1575), as well as a copy of the famous edition of the *Dioscorides* (1555) annotated by Andrés Laguna (1494–1560) in the mid-sixteenth century.[5] Moreover, there is evidence that Cervantes frequently visited Seville's Hospital de Inocentes, a custodial institution that served a wide population including those classified as sick, poor, and criminals.[6] Outside of these experiences as a student or observer, Cervantes's own health experiences could inflect his narratives; for instance, how his health related to shifting socioeconomic status and access to care and nutrition, more formal diagnoses including diabetes and liver cirrhosis, and, as Pablo García Piñar argues in his chapter in this collection, his physical disability occasioned by war-time injury.[7]

Cervantes and Naming Practices: "Así decía él que se llamaba"

For reasons obscured in the narrative, Tomás leaves home (or is possibly abandoned) at eleven years old. The narrator tells us that our protagonist earns a living as a servant in Salamanca in exchange for access to education. As the years pass, as an adolescent and young adult Tomás's motivation for scholarship grows to earn himself a reputation: once he is famous for his intellect, he says he can disclose the truth about his origins and self, about his parents and his home. Access to this level of recognition will allow his parents to fully see him as the person he wishes and knows himself to be, and it is this ambition that drives the first half of the narrative. In eight short years, Tomás transforms from "criado de sus amos" (servant) to "compañero" (companion) and unlocks his stated goal: "se hizo tan famoso en la universidad, por su buen ingenio" (he became so famous in the university for his good mind.)[8] Having achieved some excellence in letters, he accepts an invitation by the soldier-lieutenant Don Diego to join his crew of soldiers (now with just two books in his pocket), travels across Italy and France, and returns to Salamanca to complete his education as a lawyer.

We next meet an unnamed, nefarious woman who manages to woo everyone in town but Tomás. Spurned, she seeks the love potion of a Morisca. After Tomás consumes it, the unexpected happens, and he falls severely ill: "comenzó a herir de pie y de mano como si tuviera alferecía" (immediately his feet and hands and mouth began to convulse as if he had epilepsy). The unnamed woman flees the story, and Tomás is bedridden for six months. Cervantes writes in gruesome detail about the physical transformation, the injuries of his skin, the brittleness of bones. At this point in the story, his bodymind moving in and out of disability, Tomás renames himself: "Vidriera" or "glass window" ("así decía él que se llamaba").[9] Though after time his body seems to finally recover from the experience, his mind lingers with early modern diagnoses of the glass delusion: "aunque le hicieron los remedios posibles, sólo le sanaron la enfermedad del cuerpo, pero no de lo del entendimiento" (only the disease of his body was cured, not the disease of his mind.)[10]

In as much as Cervantes is concerned with perceptual tricks throughout his body of work, the particularity of the glass metaphor forces us to think about the instability of belief.[11] I call out the metaphor of glass as a critical term for reading both diagnosis and disability in early modern literature in the context of Joanna's Bourke's *The Story of Pain*, where she lifts up the usefulness of metaphors as a way to understand pain: "By using metaphors to bring interior sensation into a knowable, external world, sufferers attempt to impose (and communicate) some kind of order onto their experiences."[12] Tomás describes various experiences of pain throughout the short story: the immediacy of the physical pain in the first weeks of illness, as well as the anguish of isolation and social confusion he experiences later in the story as he tries to make sense of his new ways of occupying space in the world. The glass metaphor also extends outside of Cervantes's narrative and can be found in various early modern Spanish mystical texts where glass is symbolic of the soul's purity. In Tomás's words: "por ser hombre de vidrio y no de carne: que el vidrio, por ser de materia sutil y delicada, obraba por ella el alma con más promptitud y eficacia" (he said he was a man of glass and not flesh, and because glass was a subtle and delicate material, the soul acts with greater speed and efficiency).[13] Transparency here is upheld as a key tenet of spiritual practice, both for confession and the material of glass itself, yet the precarity of his material and spiritual condition is also emphasized to explain the discipline and order required to protect him.

In the latter half of the story, an increasing number of friends, practitioners, and onlookers offer a wide range of practices and treatment measures. As a glass man, he begins to engage widely with his audience, offering aphorism after aphorism to an increasingly growing audience that seeks out his advice. Cervantes points to the disjuncture between illness and impact: "viendo que en un sujeto donde se contenía tan extraordinaria locura como era el pensar que fuese de vidrio, se encerrase tan grande entendimiento" (seeing that an individual suffering from so extraordinary a madness that he thought he was made of glass would have such great intelligence).[14] And almost as quickly in the latter paragraphs of the story, Vidriera moves from a public position to relative anonymity when he imagines himself to be cured.

Cervantes, Glass and Present

Upon the 400th anniversary of the deaths of Cervantes and William Shakespeare in 2016, Deborah Levy authored a reimagining of *El licenciado Vidriera* titled *The Glass Woman*. It is one of the stories that forms part of *Lunatics, Lovers and Twelve Stories after Çervantes and Shakespeare*, a collection that speaks to continuities between the early modern and the present as well as linguistic and canonical boundaries between Spanish and English. In her adaptation, Levy fused Cervantes's story with the documented experiences of nineteenth-century Princess Alexandra Amalie of Bavaria (1826–1875), noted for a variety of eccentricities including an obsession with cleanliness, the color white, and belief that she had swallowed a piano made of glass. At the end of the story, Princess Alexandra is at least temporarily cured through the expression of love for her doctor. Though that love is not reciprocated, the cure and the conclusion offer a provisional explanation: "We make our phantoms in every century and if encouraged it is possible they can speak for us but it is better if we can speak for ourselves. I am a traitor to love, but an honourable physician."[15] In other words, the physician describes a model of illness caused by the absence of expression, and frames self-knowledge and expression as therapeutic. Princess Alexandra, like Tomás, needs to name (what is most true about) themselves.

By attending to first-person descriptions of disability experiences within both narratives, early modern and contemporary, my readings are informed by a variety of theorists in disability justice, including, for example, Eli Clare's *Brilliant Imperfection: Grappling with Cure*, Rosemarie Garland-Thomson's *About Us*, and Alice Wong's *Disability Visibility*. A dialogue between past and present in literary and disability studies provides a fruitful path forward to center the experience and ethics of care practices and disparities throughout Cervantes's writing and in subsequent adaptations. Reading personal accounts of disability through

Cervantes builds on the framework of disability justice as a way to interrogate and document experiences of diagnosis, corporality and translation. Engaging with Cervantes both via early modern texts and contemporary adaptation allows for tracing modes of resistance and transformation.

The heroine of *The Glass Woman* is concerned not only with breaking, as is Cervantes's Vidriera, but also with the sounds that the piano might emit through her mouth. In Levy's adaptation, we read stories of encounters between a physician and the Princess as well as the tensions between diagnoses and the patient's lived experience.[16] The reimagining also parallels Cervantes's original story in dialogues that relate to origins and class, when for example the doctor remarks: "She is an aristocrat. I am a physician."[17] After multiple visits with the Princess, the physician describes in detail the physical sensations he has heard and observed and offers context for others with parallel delusions—other glass people—even one made of butter, with little interest from the patient, even as she is described as the first woman with the diagnosis ("no records of women who suffer from glass delusions").[18] Over time the Princess begins to recover by recognizing the disconnect between her own physical and social experiences. One diagnosis offered by the physician is fantastical and complicated: her interior glass piano has a different sort of morality than her physical body.[19] The elaborate metaphor of a music that cannot be contained again calls the reader to reflect on the protagonist's willingness to express truths about the lived experiences of their bodies, and the ability of others to observe and listen.

Both Tomás and Princess Alexandra request special clothing to protect the fragility of their bodies, refuse shoes, radicalize their diets, and observe how their experience of sensory perception is increasingly altered over time (sensitivity to light, crowds, noise, materials). In both cases, physicians are for the most part unable to resolve the concerns of the patients. In these interactions, readers reflect on limits of control, power of belief, and perhaps most acutely the trauma of sickness. Cervantes confronts the reader with a fusion of the lived experience of fear with memoir, poetic writing, and lyrical prose. The acuteness of the fragility extends to unexpected moments, when for example Cervantes writes about Tomás's responses to weather: "Cuando tronaba, temblaba como un azogado, y se salía al campo y no entraba en poblado hasta haber pasado la tempestad" (When it thundered, he shook like a leaf, and went out into the countryside, and would not come back among buildings until the storm had passed.)[20] Cervantes sensitively attends to the echoes and ramifications of severe illness, that is the relationships between trauma, disability, and identity. In this moment of the outsider looking in, we are allowed to see and even empathize with the slow losses that Tomás experiences. Through the metaphor of glass as both fragile and transparent, the reader stands in as cautious witness. And through the process of narrating, via Cervantes and his adaptations, we give visibility and history to these lived experiences of disability.

NOTES

1. I write at greater length about health and disability in *Don Quijote* in Boyle and Owens, eds., *Health and Healing in the Early Modern Iberian World*; see especially the introduction and chapter 7.
2. Both Augustin Redondo and Gill Speak provide a thorough introduction to the medical and literary tradition of the glass delusion in early modern Europe, describing a host of patients believing they were breakable as glass or embodied as other kinds of fragile receptacles, including clay pitchers. Speak describes how the condition had taken on "epidemic proportions" during this time period. Speak, "El licenciado Vidriera," 852. Among notable examples, consider the first medical treatise on melancholy to describe this delusion, written in 1561 by the Dutch physician Levinus Lemnius; King Charles VI of France's noted experience of a parallel delusion; and, in the Spanish context, Agustín Moreto's *El licenciado Vidriera* (1654), which takes up Cervantes's original tale.
3. See Jennifer Nash, *Slow Loss*, 2–5: "I use the term slow loss to describe the durational and even seemingly endless nature of loss, and how it is marked by the unknown."
4. Through his reading of Alfonso de Santa Cruz in relationship to Cervantes, Or Hasson has persuasively made the argument for "the value of close, contextualized, and narratologically sensitive readings of medical texts," demonstrating that it is not likely that Cervantes had access to this medical text as an inspiration for his story, but rather that there were cultural markers that might have informed both works. Hasson, "Between Clinical Writing," 160. A Spanish translation of the *Dignotio* by Raúl Lavalle was published under the title *Sobre la melancolíca: Diagnóstico y curación de los afectos melancólicos*. An unpublished critical edition of the Latin text, together with an annotated Spanish translation and a biographical study on Santa Cruz, can be found in Ana Saéz Hidalgo's *Dignotio*.
5. López-Muñoz et al., "Psychotropic Drugs," 226–34.
6. See Alonso Fernández, "Dos especies psicopatológicas," for a description of Cervantes's encounters with this institution.
7. See Montes Santiago, "Saberes medicos" for additional context concerning the process of reconstructing Cervantes's medical experiences.
8. Cervantes, *Novelas ejemplares*, 173.
9. Cervantes, *Novelas ejemplares*, 179.
10. Cervantes, *Novelas ejemplares*, 179.
11. Elsewhere I describe how within the context of Inquisitional Spain, preoccupation with belief and its implications saturated almost every aspect of everyday life and challenges readers to consider relationships between belief, diagnoses, and identity in relationship to sixteenth-century Spanish mystic Teresa of Ávila. Boyle, "Chronic Denial."
12. Bourke, *The Story of Pain*, 279.
13. Cervantes, *Novelas ejemplares*, 179.

14. Cervantes, *Novelas ejemplares*, 180.
15. Levy, *Lunatics*, 192.
16. The story was adapted to the stage by Alix Sobler in 2019, with the play premiering at the Coronet Theatre in London, again speaking to the ongoing interest in the metaphor of glass as a means of engaging with experiences of illness. In an interview about the 2020 US premiere, Sobler describes parallels between herself and the protagonist: "I am a person who struggles with anxiety. I'm a playwright and a New Yorker, so that almost goes without saying. It's something I've grappled with throughout my life and I thought, wow, what does it mean to have a big thing inside of you, something that's so fragile? To feel like it could always break, to feel like you're always in danger, to feel like just one false move and you'll wreak everything. And I thought, 'Wow, I relate to that feeling.'" Erstein, "Playwright's."
17. Levy, *Lunatics, Lovers and Twelve Stories*, 177.
18. Levy, *Lunatics, Lovers and Twelve Stories*, 185.
19. Levy, *Lunatics, Lovers and Twelve Stories*, 192.
20. Cervantes, *Novelas ejemplares*, 179.

BIBLIOGRAPHY

Alonso Fernández, Francisco. "Dos especies psicopatológicas: Don Quijote y el Licenciado Vidriera." *Torre de los Lujanes, Boletín de la Real Sociedad Económica Matritense de Amigos del País*, no. 56 (2005): 45–64.

Anzaldúa, Gloria. *Light in the Dark / Luz en lo Oscuro: Rewriting Identity, Spirituality, Reality*. Edited by AnaLouise Keating. Duke University Press, 2015.

Bourke, Joanna. *The Story of Pain: From Prayer to Painkillers*. Oxford University Press, 2014.

Boyle, Margaret. "Chronic Denial: When Making Change Means Saying the Whole Truth." *postmedieval* 11, no. 2 (2020): 189–94. https://doi.org/10.1057/s41280-020-00167-8.

Boyle, Margaret, and Sarah Owens, eds. *Health and Healing in the Early Modern Iberian World: A Gendered Perspective*. University of Toronto Press, 2021.

Cervantes Saavedra, Miguel de. *Novelas ejemplares*. Edited by Jorge García López. Real Academia Española, 2013.

Cervantes Saavedra, Miguel de. *Novelas ejemplares*. Edited by Roberto González Echevarría. Translated by Edith Grossman. Yale University Press, 2016.

Clare, Eli. *Brilliant Imperfection: Grappling with Cure*. Duke University Press, 2017.

El Saffar, Ruth. *Novel to Romance: A Study of Cervantes's Novelas ejemplares*. Johns Hopkins University Press, 1974.

Erstein, Hap. "Playwright's 'Glass Piano,' at FAU Theatre Lab, Offers a Fairy Tale of Anxiety." *Palm Beach Arts Paper*, February 5, 2020. http://palmbeachartspaper.com/playwrights-glass-piano-at-fau-theatre-lab-offers-a-fairy-tale-of-anxiety.

Garland-Thomson, Rosemarie, and Peter Catapano, eds. *About Us: Essays from the Disability Series of The New York Times*. Liveright Publishing, 2019.

Hasson, Or. "Between Clinical Writing and Storytelling: Alfonso de Santa Cruz and the Peculiar Case of the Man Who Thought He Was Made of Glass." *Hispanic Review* 85, no. 2 (2017): 155–72.

Lavalle, Raúl, trans. *Sobre la melancolía: Diagnóstico y curación de los afectos melancólicos (ca. 1569)*, by Alonso de Santa Cruz, edited by Juan Antonio Paniagua. Ediciones U de Navarra, 2005.

Levy, Deborah. *Lunatics, Lovers and Twelve Stories after Cervantes and Shakespeare.* And Other Stories, 2016.

López-Muñoz, Francisco, Cecilio Álamo, and Pilar García-García. "Psychotropic Drugs in the Cervantine Texts." *Journal of the Royal Society of Medicine* 101, no. 5 (2008): 226–34. https://doi.org/10.1258/jrsm.2008.070269.

Miñana, Rogelio. *Monstruos que hablan: El discurso de la monstruosidad en Cervantes.* University of North Carolina Press, 2007.

Montes Santiago, Julio. "Miguel de Cervantes: Saberes médicos, enfermedades y muerte." *Anales de Medicina Interna* 22, no. 6 (2005): 293–97. https://scielo.isciii.es/scielo.php?script=sci_arttext&pid=S0212-71992005000600010.

Nash, Jennifer C. "Slow Loss: Black Feminism and Endurance." *Social Text* 40, no. 2 (2022): 1–20. https://doi.org/10.1215/01642472-9631103.

Redondo, Augustin. "La locura del cervantino licenciado Vidriera: Tradiciones, contexto histórico y subversión." In *Revisitando las culturas del Siglo de Oro: Mentalidades, tradiciones culturales, creaciones paraliterarias y literarias.* Ediciones U de Salamanca, 2007.

Saéz Hidalgo, Ana, ed. and trans. "Dignotio et cura affectuum melancholicorum," by Alfonso de Santa Cruz. Licenciatura thesis, Universidad de Valladolid, 1993.

Saéz Hidalgo, Ana. "Una visión renacentista de la melancolía: Alfonso de Santa Cruz." *Revista de la Asociación Española de Neuropsiquiatría* 15 (1995): 87–93. https://uvadoc.uva.es/handle/10324/51822.

Speak, Gill. "El licenciado Vidriera and the Glass Men of Early Modern Europe." *Modern Language Review* 85 (1990): 850–65. https://doi.org/10.2307/3732644.

Wong, Alice, ed. *Disability Visibility.* Vintage, 2020.

CHAPTER 7

Cervantine Staring

From Maritornes's Divergent Body to Cervantes's Self-Portrait

PABLO GARCÍA PIÑAR

Throughout his literary works, Miguel de Cervantes's representations of bodies invite readers to engage with them through a blend of wonder and curiosity. His attention to unusual physical traits—whether deviant or exquisite—is never arbitrary. In early modern thought, the body, whether conforming to or deviating from a corporeal canon, was laden with meaning. Excess or deficiency in bodily matter, extremes in height and corpulence, bodily disproportions, and congenital deformities were believed to reflect temperament, intellect, and moral character. A master of physical characterization, Cervantes meticulously maps the corporeal topography of deviant bodies, shaping the reader's perception and emotional response. Yet he does not treat bodily divergence uniformly: at times, it provokes laughter, repulsion, or even fear; at others, it invites compassion or admiration.

Although Cervantes frequently depicts bodily difference, scholarship has paid comparatively little attention to his representations of characters marked by physical difference. Considerable research has explored literary pictorialism and visual elements in his work—particularly the influence of Renaissance Italian and Flemish painting, as well as broader visual culture, as Mercedes Alcalá Galán's chapter in this volume also highlights. Less attention, however, has been given to how Cervantes constructs physical difference through rhetorical portraiture.[1] His depictions of bodily deviance—and their narrative and interpretative effects—remain largely unexplored. This chapter asks how Cervantes portrays divergent physicalities and, more importantly, how he shapes the reader's perception and emotional response. I argue that readers' mental images of Cervantine characters are shaped not only by his physical descriptions but also by narrative tone. The curiosity and wonder these portraits evoke, I suggest, mirror the reactions people experience when encountering unusual bodies. Furthermore, the process of constructing these mental images parallels the act of staring—a phenomenon I term "figurative staring."

Rosemarie Garland-Thomson defines staring as an instinctive response to the unexpected or novel, driven by curiosity.[2] When directed at individuals with unusual bodies, it creates a temporary connection between the starer and the staree, forming a circuit of communication and meaning-making. Such interactions, she argues, can cause discomfort for both parties but may also foster mutual understanding, depending on the context and those involved. Despite being a natural impulse, staring often clashes with social norms that discourage overt or prolonged eye contact, as it is often perceived as intrusive or rude.[3] Here I posit that Cervantes's steering of the reader's figurative gaze toward divergent bodily features mirrors the intrusive act of staring described by Garland-Thomson. It highlights the ambivalence in his treatment of bodily deviance: the emotional responses depend not only on the nature of the character's physical difference but also on the tone used. To illustrate this, I examine two case studies: the unabashed gaze directed at Maritornes's sexually repulsive body in *Don Quijote* I, 16, and the carefully controlled response Cervantes seeks from the reader in his self-portrait in the "Prologue to the Reader" of the *Exemplary Novels*. Ultimately, I argue that Cervantes's treatment of bodily deviance is shaped by the cultural distinction between congenital bodily differences and those resulting from external causes.

Unsettling: Maritornes Through the Narrative Voice

In *Don Quijote* I, 16, the narrator introduces Maritornes, a young Asturian servant at Juan Palomeque's inn who provides sexual services to the guests. She is described as having a broad face, flat head, and stubby nose, blind in one eye and with poor sight in the other.[4] Short in stature, she also has slightly hunched shoulders that cause her to lean forward. Maritornes's appearance plays a key role in the humor of the inn episode, as Don Quijote imagines her as a noblewoman who visits him in his bed to profess her love. As night falls, captivated by the beauty of the innkeeper's daughter, Don Quijote fantasizes that the girl is in love with him. Meanwhile, on her way to a rendezvous with a mule driver, Maritornes accidentally stumbles into Don Quijote's bed. Mistaking her for the innkeeper's daughter, Don Quijote pulls her onto the bed and attempts to politely decline her imagined advances. During the encounter, Maritornes is depicted with increasing repulsiveness, her odor so overpowering that it could make anyone but a mule driver feel like vomiting. The humor stems from the incongruity between Don Quijote's idealized perception of Maritornes and the reality of her perceived unattractiveness.

Scholarship has traditionally interpreted Cervantes's portrayal of Maritornes's body as integral to the farcical design of the inn episode, in which misunderstanding, slapstick, and exaggerated physical portrayals generate the scene's comedy.[5] Some critics, however, have challenged this interpretation as overly simplistic. Ernesto Veres d'Ocón argues that Maritornes's portrayal conveys more wit than humor, a position echoed in Paul Michael Johnson's recent work.[6] Johnson critiques the reductionist reading of the novel as merely a "funny book," instead presenting laughter as a complex, multidirectional emotional experience.[7] Building on this shift in perspective, scholarship has increasingly emphasized Maritornes's complexity rather than treating her merely as an object of ridicule. In doing so, it has sought to recover her from a male-driven critical gaze that mirrors the narrative voice and reduces her to an object of scrutiny.[8] In this reassessment, her role in exposing Don Quijote's anxieties about masculinity takes center stage, particularly in chapter 43, where she deftly ensnares him, leaving him bound atop Rocinante in a scene of symbolic emasculation. Other analyses highlight how her characterization deepens in chapter 17, where she shows compassion for Sancho, bringing him water after his blanket-tossing ordeal at the inn.[9]

These interpretations underscore the evolving complexity of Maritornes's character, but that depth emerges from an initial moment in which Cervantes carefully shapes the reader's first perception of her. While her characterization deepens throughout the novel, my focus remains on her introduction—specifically, how Cervantes constructs the reader's first mental image of her and shapes the emotional response that follows. Encarnación Juárez-Almendros has observed that some readers find Maritornes's portrayal unsettling.[10] My interest lies precisely in the discomfort evoked by this mental image of her body. Unlike the innkeeper's daughter, whose beauty is briefly mentioned at the start of chapter 16, Maritornes is subjected to explicit physical scrutiny. This disparity reflects Cervantes's gendered approach to characterization: while beautiful women are left comparatively undescribed, female characters with divergent corporealities receive heightened descriptive attention.[11] Clothing often signifies social status for male characters, whereas descriptions of beautiful women are typically confined to brief mentions of their hair, face, or head.[12] By contrast, Cervantes provides more detailed descriptions of women marked by bodily difference. André Michalski attributes this asymmetry to Cervantes's reliance on a Petrarchan ideal so familiar to his readers that elaborate depictions of female beauty were unnecessary. Such reticence, he argues, also preserved decorum by avoiding the arousal of lustful thoughts.

Cervantes's detailed descriptions of divergent female bodies engage with and ultimately subvert Petrarchan conventions, reflecting his growing weariness with Petrarchan ideals. While he initially embraced this tradition enthusiastically, as seen in *La Galatea*'s portrayals of Galatea and Nísida, he later distanced himself from its idealizing tendencies, ultimately satirizing the trope from *Don Quijote* onward.[13] Maritornes's depiction exemplifies this rejection, functioning as a subversion of the *descriptio puellae*, a medieval and Renaissance literary trope that presents a woman's attributes in a gradual, often descending sequence.[14] While Cervantes preserves the *descriptio puellae* structure, he repurposes it to shape the reader's emotional response to the servant's physical divergence. Following its conventional descending order, the narrator first describes Maritornes's facial features—broad face, flat head, stubby nose, and impaired eyes—before shifting to her stature and concluding with her posture. He systematically pairs these features with adjectives that emphasize asymmetry, irregularity, and impairment ("ancha de cara," "nariz roma"), creating an accumulation of traits that ultimately render Maritornes's body as sexually repulsive.

Cervantes further heightens this effect by blending unflattering characterizations with euphemistic expressions, creating an ironic contrast that makes Maritornes's divergent traits more conspicuous and underscores their misalignment with conventional expectations of female desirability. This irony is most evident in the transition from her facial features to her body, where he inserts incongruous praise—referring to her "gallardía" (elegance) before ultimately calling her "gentil" (charming). Rather than softening her perceived flaws, this juxtaposition amplifies them, reinforcing the passage's wry humor. By directing the reader's gaze so explicitly, Cervantes turns Maritornes's body into an object of scrutiny, initiating a figurative act of staring that reinforces her bodily divergence and mirrors the power dynamics inherent in looking. The narrator's use of understated language and euphemisms, combined with ironic distance and an observational tone, creates detachment, preventing emotional involvement and keeping the reader at arm's length. As a result, the reader observes her appearance in an almost clinical manner, with a sense of ironic amusement or even contempt. Unlike in the next case study, the narrator does not guide the reader's gaze to foster empathy or intimacy with Maritornes as a person.

Cervantine Staring Back

The *descriptio puellae* trope, which Cervantes subverts in his portrayal of Maritornes, is ultimately a narrower variant of *effictio*, a classical rhetorical convention rooted in ancient Greek and Roman traditions that provides a detailed and vivid description of a person's physical appearance. Cervantes's narrative bias against deviant corporealities—evident in his *effictio* of Maritornes, as well as those of Cañizares and Clara Perlerina—was common for his time but contrasts with his own physical difference and diverges from the approach of other bodily deviant authors, such as Juan Ruiz de Alarcón, who had a pronounced spinal curvature and a keel-shaped ribcage yet did not reflect this bias in his works. While Cervantes unreservedly subjects deviant fictional bodies to the intrusive gaze, he takes a markedly different approach when portraying himself, actively shaping how his own physical difference is perceived in an effort to curb or reframe that gaze.

As is well established, Cervantes sustained a significant physical injury at the battle of Lepanto against the Ottoman fleet on October 7, 1571. He received three harquebus wounds—two to the chest and one to his left hand—which severed a nerve, leaving the hand immobile and ultimately leading to its ankylosis and withering over time. Living with a withered arm, Cervantes became acutely aware of the scrutiny his physical difference attracted. In his petitions, he often felt compelled to provide vivid descriptions of his disfigurement as proof of his military service. His left arm also became a target of mockery from literary rivals, including Lope de Vega and the anonymous author writing under the pseudonym Alonso Fernández de Avellaneda. Notably, a year before the latter published a biting satirical *effictio* of Cervantes in his spurious *Don Quijote* (1614), Cervantes composed his self-portrait in the prologue to the *Exemplary Novels* (1613).

In the "Prologue to the Reader," Cervantes recounts—somewhat begrudgingly—that he had no choice but to write the prologue.[15] The book was originally intended to feature an engraved frontispiece based on a portrait by the painter Juan de Jáuregui, but this was ultimately omitted. To compensate for its absence, Cervantes composes a verbal self-portrait. In a distinctly Cervantine fashion, this self-portrait functions less as a conventional *effictio* and more as an *ekphrasis*, either describing Jáuregui's portrait or constructing a notional *ekphrasis* of the missing engraving. Cervantes's self-portrait retains elements of *effictio*, following the conventional head-to-toe structure. He begins with his face, describing it as aquiline, with chestnut hair, a smooth forehead, and lively eyes. His nose is curved yet well proportioned, his beard silver, and his mustache prominent. His mouth is small, with only six misaligned teeth. He describes his body as average in size and acknowledges being somewhat stooped and lacking agility. He concludes by recounting the loss of his left hand without detailing the injury—which he considers unsightly—choosing instead to emphasize its symbolic value as a mark of honor and bravery.

Cervantes employs the same technique he uses for his fictional characters, linking physical traits to inner nature. The first set of features—his aquiline face, broad forehead, and lively eyes—conventionally signified cleverness and ingenuity.[16] The second set—his sparse, crooked teeth and hunched back—is presented with a humorous and self-deprecating tone.[17] Some Cervantine critics interpret these unflattering traits as part of his *captatio benevolentiae* strategy, arguing that by adopting a burlesque tone to satirize his self-portrait, Cervantes deflects any suspicion of self-aggrandizement and endears himself to the audience.[18] The initially lighthearted tone, however, shifts to a more solemn register when Cervantes introduces his withered arm. Although he acknowledges that it may appear unsightly, he takes pride in his injury—never described in detail—presenting it as a testament to his courage and sacrifice. Elizabeth Bearden interprets this section of Cervantes's *self-effictio* as a means of establishing his authorial ethos as a disabled writer.[19] She argues that Cervantes melds his authorial and martial identities, framing his battle wound as an integral part of both. By proudly displaying his left arm, she contends, he transforms his disability into a source of empowerment through the transgressive reappropriation of what is conventionally perceived as bodily deviance—a strategy Bearden terms "crip authority." While Cervantes indeed employs this strategy, I argue that he also shifts how he directs the reader's figurative gaze at divergent corporealities. Rather than allowing his physical difference to be subjected to the same detached scrutiny that invites amusement or contempt—as in the case of Maritornes—he deliberately dictates how his audience should interpret his own bodily deviance.

In *Staring*, Garland-Thomson argues that individuals with unusual appearances—whom she labels as "stareable"—develop relational strategies to assert control in situations where they are subjected to scrutiny.[20] These individuals often use charm, friendliness, humor, formidability, or wit to counteract being stared at, easing interpersonal tension and shaping how they are perceived. Garland-Thomson describes this practice as "staring back," a strategy that transforms the passive experience of being stared at into an active assertion of presence and identity. When starees engage actively with those who stare at them, she contends, they transform the interaction from a one-sided gaze into a reciprocal exchange.[21] By meeting the gaze of the starer, they assert their individuality and agency, encouraging the starer to move beyond initial reactions of shock or discomfort. In this mutual recognition, both parties acknowledge each other's humanity.

Documenting historical instances of "staring back" in its most direct sense is challenging, as first-person testimonies from individuals with physical differences in early modern Spain are rarely preserved. However, as Garland-Thomson argues, visual art—particularly portraiture—provides a structured and deliberate means of enacting this dynamic.[22] Portraits create a simulacrum of direct staring, allowing sitters to control their representation. Through eye contact, expression, and pose, they guide the viewer's gaze and reclaim agency in the act of looking. In his analysis of Velázquez's portraits of court dwarfs, particularly that of Sebastián de Morra, Maximilian Derksen argues that the subject's intense, almost defiant gaze directly engages the viewer. By positioning de Morra as the starer, Velázquez challenges the conventional dynamic in which individuals with atypical bodies are passive objects of the gaze.[23] This shift, Derksen contends, compels the viewer into an encounter on equal terms, disrupting the traditional hierarchy that renders sitters mere objects of observation.

Working within the limitations of written expression, Cervantes seeks to evoke in the reader the same engagement and empathy that visual portraiture achieves through simulated eye-to-eye interactions. Unlike paintings, which present a static moment for simultaneous perception and prolonged contemplation, *effictio* unfolds sequentially, guiding the reader's perception through a linear narrative that requires temporal progression. Since the immediacy of visual art is difficult to replicate, Cervantes employs alternative strategies to elicit the empathy generated by the intense eye contact characteristic of painted portraits. In the opening of his *self-effictio*, he introduces himself as "the man you see here" ("éste que veis aquí").[24] To create the illusion that the reader is directly observing Jáuregui's portrait, Cervantes shifts from the first-person perspective used in the prologue to the third person, thereby distancing himself from his self-portrait. As the reader figuratively examines the portrait, they encounter a dual Cervantes: both the subject depicted in the painting and the guide directing the observation. He constructs the illusion of his presence beside the reader, as though he were pointing out and interpreting specific physical traits, guiding their attention while remaining aware of their gaze. To alleviate any unease his presence might provoke, he cultivates a sense of familiarity, an approach that Porqueras Mayo describes as "tuteo amistoso."[25] Indeed, he addresses readers with great warmth, calling them "lector amantísimo" (most beloved reader) and "lector amable" (kind reader). This effort to ease interpersonal tension—allowing the reader/starer to feel comfortable while observing his divergent physicality—mirrors the relational strategies that, according to Garland-Thomson, stareable individuals employ to present themselves positively.

Conclusion

The playful mockery of Cervantes's physical imperfections serves as a lighthearted prelude to the core of the *effictio*: his withered arm. Having gained the reader's sympathy through his self-deprecating humor, Cervantes presents his withered arm as a testament to his military courage—transforming his disability, as Bearden explains, into a source of empowerment. Scars could be interpreted in various ways—from signs of a life marked by violence among the marginalized to evidence of corporal punishment. This may explain why Cervantes felt compelled to present his withered arm in a particular way, ensuring that the reader did not simply stare at it without guidance. In his portrayal of Maritornes, Cervantes treats congenital physical imperfections—seen as reflections of an individual's inner nature—as acceptable subjects of jest. His battle wound, however, falls into a different category of bodily divergence, one that demands respect. Indeed, as Fadrique Furió Ceriol observes in *El concejo y consejeros del príncipe* (1559) regarding individuals with congenital physical differences, "those who are born this way (I'm not referring to those who later became so due to calamity) always exhibit countless flaws in their understanding, behavior, and way of life."[26] This quote underscores the distinction, prevalent in Cervantes's time, between congenital deformities and those resulting from external causes. As reflected in the *effictiones* of Maritornes and Cervantes himself, this distinction shaped societal attitudes toward bodily difference, often fostering contrasting sentiments toward those born with physical anomalies and those who acquired them later in life. Faced with persistent scrutiny of his withered arm, Cervantes likely recognized that, rather than being seen as a testament to his bravery, it had instead become a source of unwelcome attention. To counter this, he deliberately shaped its meaning, emphasizing what he saw as the true essence of his identity.

NOTES

1. de Armas, ed., *Writing for the Eyes*; de Armas, ed., *Ekphrasis in the Age of Cervantes*; de Armas, *Quixotic Frescoes*; Laguna, *Cervantes and the Pictorial Imagination*; Alcalá Galán, "Retórica visual"; Botello López-Canti, *Literatura y pintura*; Michalski, "El retrato retórico"; and Stoopen Galán, "Cervantes retratador."
2. Garland-Thomson, *Staring*, 3.
3. Garland-Thomson, *Staring*, 10.
4. Cervantes, *Don Quijote*, 138.
5. Mata Induráin, "El revés burlesco"; Mayoral, "La imagen física de las mujeres"; Mendeloff, "The Maritornes Episode."
6. Veres d'Ocón, "Los retratos."
7. Johnson, *Affective Geographies*, 104.
8. Juárez-Almendros, "Entre con-fusiones corporales."
9. Rodríguez and Ruzicka, "Ecos de la Magdalena."
10. Juárez-Almendros, "Entre con-fusiones corporales," 51.
11. Michalski, "El retrato retórico," 42–43.
12. Michalski, "El retrato retórico," 42–43.
13. Colombí-Monguió, "Los 'ojos de perlas' de Dulcinea," 396.
14. Mata Induráin, "Revés burlesco," 261–62.
15. Cervantes, *Novelas ejemplares*, I: 50–51.
16. Arellano Torres, "Fisionomía múltiple," 63–65.
17. Arellano Torres, "Fisionomía múltiple," 66.
18. Canavaggio, *Cervantes, entre vida y creación*, 68; Salgado, "De lo jocoso a lo joco-serio," 214; Arellano Torres, "Fisionomía múltiple," 64.
19. Bearden, "Monstrous Births and Crip Authority," 78.
20. Garland-Thomson, *Staring*, 84.
21. Garland-Thomson, *Staring*, 84–94.
22. Garland-Thomson, *Staring*, 84–85.
23. Derksen, "Induction and Reception of Dignity," 191–92.
24. Cervantes, *Novelas ejemplares*, I: 51.
25. Porqueras Mayo, *Estudios sobre Cervantes*, 121.
26. Furió Ceriol, *Obra completa*, 122.

BIBLIOGRAPHY

Alcalá Galán, Mercedes. "Retórica visual: Ékfrasis y teoría de la ilustración gráfica en el *Quijote*." In *Autour de "Don Quichotte" de Miguel de Cervantes*, edited by Philippe Rabaté and Hélène Tropé. Presses Sorbonne Nouvelle, 2015.

Arellano Torres, Ignacio. "Fisionomía múltiple de un autorretrato cervantino." *RILCE* 34, no. 1 (2018): 58–68. https://doi.org/10.15581/008.34.1.58-68.

Bearden, Elizabeth. "Monstrous Births and Crip Authority: Cervantes, the *Persiles*, and the Representation of Disability." *eHumanista/Cervantes* 5 (2016): 69–84.

Botello López-Canti, Jesús. *Literatura y pintura en Cervantes y Lope de Vega*. Edition Reichenberger, 2021.

Canavaggio, Jean. *Cervantes, entre vida y creación*. Centro de Estudios Cervantinos, 2000.
Cervantes Saavedra, Miguel de. *Don Quijote de la Mancha*. Edited by Francisco Rico. Real Academia Española, 2004.
Cervantes Saavedra, Miguel de. *Novelas ejemplares*, vol. I, 24th ed. Edited by Harry Sieber. Ediciones Cátedra, 2005.
Colombí-Monguió, Alicia de. "Los 'ojos de perlas' de Dulcinea (*Quijote*, II, 10 y 11): El antipetrarquismo de Sancho (y de otros)." *Nueva Revista de Filología Hispánica* 32, no. 2 (1983): 389–402. https://doi.org/10.24201/nrfh.v32i2.558.
De Armas, Frederick A., ed. *Writing for the Eyes in the Spanish Golden Age*. Bucknell University Press, 2004.
De Armas, Frederick A., ed. *Ekphrasis in the Age of Cervantes*. Bucknell University Press, 2005.
De Armas, Frederick A. *Quixotic Frescoes: Cervantes and Italian Renaissance Art*. University of Toronto Press, 2006.
Derksen, Maximilian. "Induction and Reception of Dignity in Diego Velázquez's Portraits of Court Dwarfs." *Journal of Literary & Cultural Disability Studies* 14, no. 2 (May 2020): 187–202. https://doi.org/10.3828/jlcds.2020.10.
Furió Ceriol, Fadrique. *Obra completa*, edited by Henry Mechoulan and Jordi Pérez Durà. Edicions Alfons el Magnànim, 1996.
Garland-Thomson, Rosemarie. *Staring: How We Look*. Oxford University Press, 2009.
Johnson, Paul Michael. *Affective Geographies: Cervantes, Emotion, and the Literary Mediterranean*. University of Toronto Press, 2020.
Juárez-Almendros, Encarnación. "Entre con-fusiones corporales: A vueltas con Maritornes y Don Quijote." *Cervantes: Bulletin of the Cervantes Society of America* 39, no. 1 (Spring 2019): 47–60. https://doi.org/10.1353/cer.2019.0005.
Laguna, Ana María G. *Cervantes and the Pictorial Imagination: A Study on the Power of Images and Images of Power in Works by Cervantes*. Bucknell University Press, 2009.
Mata Induráin, Carlos. "El revés burlesco de la mujer y el amor en el *Quijote*: Algunos retratos femeninos grotescos." In *De mi patria y de mí mismo: Actas del X Congreso Internacional de la Asociación de Cervantistas (Madrid, 3–7 de septiembre de 2018)*, edited by Daniel Migueláñez and Aurelio Vargas Díaz-Toledo. Editorial Universidad de Alcalá, 2022.
Mayoral, Marina. "La imagen física de las mujeres en el *Quijote*." In *El "Quijote" en clave de mujer/es*, edited by Fanny Rubio. Editorial Complutense, 2005.
Mendeloff, Henry. "The Maritornes Episode (DQ: I, 16): A Cervantine Bedroom Farce." *Romance Notes* 16, no. 3 (Spring 1975): 753–759. https://www.jstor.org/stable/43801387.
Michalski, André. "El retrato retórico en la obra cervantina." In *Cervantes, su obra y su mundo. Actas del I congreso internacional sobre Cervantes*, edited by Manuel Criado de Val. EDI-6 S.A, 1981.
Porqueras Mayo, Alberto. *Estudios sobre Cervantes y la Edad de Oro*. Centro de Estudios Cervantinos, 2003.
Rodríguez, Alfred, and James Ruzicka. "¿Ecos de la Magdalena en Maritornes?" *Romance Notes* 30, no. 1 (Fall 1989): 77–82. https://www.jstor.org/stable/43802053.
Salgado, María A. "De lo jocoso a lo joco-serio: El autorretrato literario en los Siglos de Oro y la Ilustración." In *Actas del XII Congreso de la Asociación Internacional de Hispanistas: 21–26 de agosto de 1995, Birmingham*, vol. 3, edited by Jules Whicker. Department of Hispanic Studies, University of Birmingham, 1998.

Stoopen Galán, María. "Cervantes retratador." In *Cervantes creador y Cervantes recreado*, edited by Emmanuel Marigno, Carlos Mata Induráin, and Hugo Hernán Ramírez Sierra. Servicio de Publicaciones de la Universidad de Navarra, 2015.

Veres d'Ocón, Ernesto. "Los retratos de Dulcinea y Maritornes." *Anales Cervantinos* 1 (1951): 249–71.

CHAPTER 8

Cervantes's Cure

Reimagining Empathy, Medicine, and the Art of Healing

ANA LAGUNA

Cervantes's life, library, and literary imagination were profoundly shaped by the medical realities of his time.[1] As the son and grandson of surgeons who witnessed some of the era's most devastating epidemics, Cervantes grew keenly aware of the precarious balance between sickness and health, life and death.[2] In his fiction, medical tropes pervade the narrative not merely as passing references but as powerful forces shaping characters' fates. Don Quijote's delusions and malnourishment, the poisoning of Isabella in "La española inglesa," and Campuzano's venereal affliction in "El coloquio de los perros" all exemplify Cervantes's sustained engagement with disease, not just as a thematic device but as a lens through which the novelist explores individual journeys, collective discoveries, and emerging (often ambiguous) fields of knowledge.

Yet Cervantes's relationship with medical thought extended beyond the fictional realm. In 1588, he directly contributed to the publication of *Tratado nuevamente impresso de todas las enfermedades de los riñones, vexiga y carnosidades de la verga y vrina*, a pioneering treatise on renal diseases by Dr. Francisco Díaz (1527–1590). Widely viewed as the father of modern urology for his groundbreaking treatments and surgical instruments, Díaz would have exerted a profound impact on Cervantes that went well beyond friendship. In the "Canto de Calíope" of *La Galatea*, Cervantes extolled Díaz's medical genius, and in the sonnet prefacing the *Tratado*, the novelist underscored his friend's legacy with a moving sonnet:[3]

Tú, que con nuevo y sin igual decoro
tantos remedios para un mal ordenas,
bien puedes esperar de estas arenas,
del sacro Tajo, las que son de oro,

y el lauro que se debe al que un tesoro
halla de ciencia, con tan ricas venas
de raro advertimiento y salud llenas,
contento y risa del enfermo lloro;

que por tu industria una deshecha piedra
mil mármoles, mil bronces a tu fama
dará sin envidiosas competencias;

daráte el cielo palma, el suelo hiedra,
pues que el uno y el otro ya te llama
espíritu de Apolo en ambas ciencias.

You, who with new and unmatched grace,
So many cures for ailments arrange,
May well expect from this sacred range,
Golden sands from the Tagus to embrace,

And the laurel crown that's rightly placed
Upon one who discovers wisdom's stage,
Where rare insight and health engage,

Turning the sick's sorrow to smiling face.
For by your skill, a shattered stone
Will to your fame a thousand marbles raise,
And bronzes too, without envious tone;

Heaven shall grant you palms, earth its praise,
As both now call you their own,
Spirit of Apollo in twin fields of praise.[4]

Few writers would compose a poem to celebrate a friend's ability to transform stone into sand as precious as the golden sand of the holy Tajo River. With characteristic wit, Cervantes likens medical science to a treasure, exalting Díaz through the figure of Apollo ("espíritu de Apolo"), the deity of both poetry and healing. By doing so, he casts Díaz as a visionary yet humble physician, mastering two interdependent "sciences" ("en ambas ciencias"): the near-sacred art of healing ("por tu industria") and the rigorous pursuit of knowledge ("raro advertimiento"). His mastery of both should guarantee enduring and undisputed fame, commemorated in "mil mármoles" and "mil bronces."

Equally central to this praise is the emotional and moral dimension of Díaz's medical practice, suggested by Cervantes's poignant description of his impact: "salud llenas, / contento y risa del enfermo lloro." Here, healing is not merely a physical process, but one that restores joy and alleviates suffering, transforming the patient's tears into laughter. This framing suggests that true medical expertise extends beyond technical proficiency, encompassing a holistic understanding of the patient's well-being—one that attends to both body and spirit. This view on healing as both a physical and emotional process could illuminate Cervantes's broader engagement with medicine. His exploration of the subject in and beyond this poetic portrayal may signal not just a general familiarity with medical practice, but a deep awareness of the shifting medical paradigms of early modern Spain. Living at a pivotal moment of clinical evolution, Cervantes witnessed a gradual shift that took medicine from an informal, experience-based practice to a more structured and regulated profession. Central to this transformation was not only the institutionalization of medical authority—through bodies like the Royal *Protomedicato,* which sought to license and oversee practitioners—but also an increasing recognition of the physician's role in understanding and responding to the patient's suffering. During this shift, traditional Galenic and humoral theories increasingly clashed with emerging experimental approaches.[5]

Cervantes, in fact, does not merely acknowledge this transition but actively interrogates its implications.[6] In *Don Quijote,* Dr. Pedro Recio de Agüero—the so-called physician who zealously restricts Sancho Panza's meals—becomes a satirical embodiment of rigid medical dogma, exposing the risks of an authoritative yet detached application of expertise. Similarly, "El licenciado Vidriera" dramatizes the precarious boundary between sanctioned medical authority and the more intuitive, empathetic dimensions of care. Both figures illustrate stereotypical positions of the evolving medical field, revealing the tensions between institutional validation and individual suffering. By depicting physicians, healers, and patients caught between competing notions of expertise, Cervantes suggests that true mastery—whether in medicine or literature—requires not only intellectual rigor but also an understanding of the lived experience of illness. In doing so, his work anticipates contemporary debates on the ethics of care, urging the medical profession to balance clinical protocols with a deeper, more empathetic understanding of the patient's emotional needs.

This call for a more humane approach to medicine resonates with the twenty-first-century principles of health humanities, a field that prioritizes the role of empathy and patient experience in medical education. By integrating literature, history, and philosophy into clinical training, health humanities fosters a patient-centered ethos, recognizing the emotional and psychological dimensions of illness as essential to effective care. From this perspective, Cervantes's works compel us to question the boundaries of clinical frameworks, demonstrating how literature and the humanities enrich medical discourse by illuminating the ethical, narrative, and experiential dimensions of illness and care. Early modern texts illustrate how the figure of the professional physician—and the public's expectations of medical authority—is reshaped by shifting cultural attitudes and evolving paradigms of care. By embracing the interdisciplinary spirit of this volume, this essay argues that a close reading of Cervantes's exploration of the pressing anxieties of his own era can help us critically reevaluate the ever-changing intersections of medicine, performance, and empathy in our own.

A Medical Cervantes?

Cervantes's insights into health and disease have long been recognized by both doctors and clinical educators. As early as the seventeenth century, Thomas Sydenham (1624–1689), often referred to as the "English Hippocrates," recommended *Don Quijote* to medical students seeking a deeper understanding of the profession. In our time, medical educators like Johanna Shapiro and Lloyd Rucker have acknowledged the novel's impact, coining the term "Quixote Effect" to describe its influence. This effect essentially refers to a "temporary infusion of idealism" that recharges the empathy and social awareness of health students and professionals—qualities often depleted by the demands of daily practice.

In literary and cultural studies, Cervantes's engagement with medicine has traditionally been examined through explicit references to treatments and disease. Emerging scholarship, however, is expanding this scope. In this volume alone, Alani Hicks-Bartlett explores "El licenciado Vidriera" through the lenses of disability studies and early modern medical thought, and Margaret E. Boyle situates Cervantes's representations of diagnosis and care within broader discourses of disability, fragility, and cure in early modernity. Building on these perspectives, my own chapter considers Cervantes's treatment of medical knowledge not merely as thematic content but as part of a larger epistemological and ethical inquiry into the profession itself.

This ethical dimension is particularly evident in Cervantes's attention to how illness is experienced, perceived, and narrated. Early modern texts provide crucial insights into shifting conceptions of disease over time, demonstrating that medical knowledge is never static but deeply embedded in social and cultural contexts. José Pablo Barragán Nieto, for example, reminds us that while "syphilis" today refers to a specific disease caused by *Treponema pallidum*, in Cervantes's time, it encompassed a range of afflictions—including gonorrhea and leprosy—commonly referred to as "el mal francés" (the French disease). Cervantes's empathetic lens is especially evident when these ailments become central to his characters' identities and narrative trajectories, offering a perspective that blends historical specificity with a more empathetic concern for the human condition.

We all remember how in "El casamiento engañoso" the harshness of the illness's effects contrasts with the sensibility of its narrative voice. Campuzano is, for example, introduced as a debilitated patient of compromised masculinity (his sword only serves now as a cane) who leaves a hospital with wobbly legs and pale color ("su espada de báculo y por la flaqueza de sus piernas y amarillez de su rostro") after enduring a draconian, twenty-day-long mercury treatment for an ailment contracted in only one hour of passion ("haber sudado en veinte días todo el humor que quizá granjeó en una hora").[7] In this regard, as Barragán Nieto notes, "there is nowhere in Cervantes the cruel satire of the effects of this condition on the body that we can find in the poetry of Quevedo or the misogynistic picaresque novels like *La lozana andaluza* and *Pícara Justina*."[8] "Notably absent as well," Barragán Nieto continues, "are the moralizing extrapolations that view disease as the somatic manifestation of the corruption of the kingdom," a claim normally associated with the "corrupting effect" of certain social groups as the cause of contagion.[9] From the stark realities of early modern misogyny, antisemitism, and Islamophobia to contemporary authoritarian narratives that construct "the other," Cervantes's work often presents a more nuanced and empathetic perspective—one that, mediated through irony and ambiguity, leaves the final interpretations of his work open-ended.[10]

This dynamic interplay between irony and ambiguity extends to Cervantes's portrayal of doctors. By juxtaposing genuinely skilled practitioners with ignorant or even dangerous professionals, he highlights the rarity and inherent value of true medical expertise. Evoking the same reverence found in the sonnet to Díaz, Sancho Panza expresses deep respect for medical authority during his brief tenure as governor, declaring that "a los médicos sabios, prudentes y discretos, los pondré sobre mi cabeza y los honraré como a personas divinas" (wise, prudent, and intelligent doctors I'll respect and honor as if they were divine).[11] Yet Cervantes, ever attuned to the tension between idealized professions and their flawed realities, tempers this admiration with sharp critique. The scarcity of trained medical professionals in rural areas—and even within the royal court—made competence a privilege rather than an expectation.

Even with the clearly flawed Doctor Recio, Cervantes leaves room for ambiguity; while he appears fanatically strict to Sancho, his actions are driven more by obedience to the Duke's orders than by his own medical judgment. Yet his exaggerated performance aligns with a long literary tradition of satirical portrayals of physicians, reinforcing the very criticisms that Andrés Laguna leveled against incompetent practitioners. In *Dioscorides*—a pivotal medical text that Cervantes repeatedly references—Laguna emphasizes the necessity of professionalizing medicine through rigorous study and extensive practice.[12] Cervantes appears to share this perspective, as seen in "El rufián dichoso," where Doña Ana acknowledges the paradox of medicine: while the science itself is praiseworthy, its practice is often fraught with danger due to the rarity of truly knowledgeable doctors ("la medicina yo alabo, pero los médicos no, porque ninguno llegó, con lo que es ciencia al cabo").[13]

Like Laguna—and unlike Quevedo and other satirists—Cervantes critiques individual failings rather than discrediting the medical profession as a whole. However, his work does highlight one broader ethical concern: the lack of civil and legal accountability in the profession. By exposing this absence of oversight, Cervantes reveals how it could compromise both the integrity of medical practice and the well-being of patients. This critique is particularly evident in "El licenciado Vidriera," where Tomás Rodaja bitterly denounces the unchecked power of doctors, remarking that they alone have the privilege of killing "sin desenvainar otra espada que la de un récipe. Y no hay descubrirse sus delitos, porque al momento los meten debajo de la tierra" (without baring any sword more lethal than a prescription).[14]

This specific concern lies at the heart of Sancho and Recio's increasingly heated exchanges, culminating in Governor Sancho Panza's furious threat to murder Recio by smashing his head with the very chair he sits on—a potent symbol of his authority. Sancho even argues that killing Recio, whom he pointedly calls a "verdugo de la República" (executioner of the Republic), would be an act of public service, asserting that "yo me descargaré con decir que hice servicio a Dios en matar un mal médico" (I'll clear myself by saying that I did a service for God when I killed a bad doctor, who's the same as an executioner).[15] The idea is driven home once more when Sancho, determined to cleanse the island of medical incompetence, declares before his court: "voto al sol que tome un garrote, y que a garrotazos, comenzando por el doctor Pedro Recio de Malagüero, no me ha de quedar médico en toda la ínsula, a lo menos aquellos que yo entienda que son *ignorantes*" (I swear by the sun that I'll take a cudgel, and starting with you, I'll beat all the doctors so hard there won't be a single one left anywhere on the *ínsula*, at least the ones I know to be *ignorant*).[16]

The critique of the medical profession goes beyond mere incompetence a few chapters later, however, as Sancho is turned into an unlikely healer. In the episode of Altisidora's supposed death and resurrection, the Duchess's maid pretends to have died of a broken heart due to unrequited love for Don Quijote. Through an elaborate ruse orchestrated by the Duke and Duchess, the aristocrats aim to cruelly mock both Don Quijote and Sancho Panza one more time. In this complex setup, Sancho is informed that in order to "resurrect" Altisidora, he must endure a bizarre and painful ritual, which includes being pinched and whipped by the maidservants. The news is doubly unsettling for Sancho, since he was already expected to whip himself to liberate another lady, Dulcinea, from her supposed enchantment. Through Sancho's abuse, the episode not only satirizes the absurdity of certain medical practices but also involves a critical exploration of the workings (or absence) of empathy: while the aristocrats view Sancho's suffering as a source of amusement, the reader is compelled to empathize with his plight, recognizing the cruelty masked by the pretense of healing.

A profound irony also emerges from this development: Sancho, who had so vehemently criticized the bad representatives of the medical establishment a few chapters earlier, like Doctor Recio, is now forced into the very role he despised. Despite his strong aversion to Recio, the pressures of Altisidora's adventure convince Sancho of his newfound "healing" powers, embodying the very absurdity and superficiality he once criticized. The squire, now ironically transformed into a "martyr doctor," goes on to invert the usual association of disease with pain, since as a healer, he is the one expected to restore life and health through *his own* suffering. Lamenting the paradox of his predicament, Sancho voices the plight of impoverished and unrecognized doctors who must endure great hardship without fair compensation:

> En verdad, señor, que *soy el más desgraciado médico* que se debe de hallar en el mundo, en el cual hay físicos que, con matar al enfermo que curan, quieren

> ser pagados de su trabajo, que no es otro sino firmar una cedulilla de algunas medicinas, que no las hace él, sino el boticario, y cátalo cantusado; y a mí, que la salud ajena me cuesta gotas de sangre, mamonas, pellizcos, alfilerazos y azotes, no me dan un ardite. Pues yo les voto a tal que *si me traen a las manos otro algún enfermo*, que, *antes que le cure*, me han de untar las mías; que el abad de donde canta yanta, y no quiero creer que me haya dado el cielo la virtud que tengo para que yo la comunique con otros de bóbilis, bóbilis.
>
> The truth is, Señor, *that I'm the most unfortunate doctor* one could find anywhere in the world, where a physician can kill the sick person he's treating and wants to be paid for his work, which is nothing but signing a piece of paper for some medicines that are not by him but the apothecary, and that's the whole swindle; but then other peoples' well-being cost me drops of blood, slaps, pinches, pinpricks, and lashes, they don't give me an *ardite*. Well, I swear that *if they bring me another patient, before I cure anybody* they'll have to grease my palm, because if the abbot sings, he eats his supper, and I don't want to believe that heaven gave me this virtue to use for others at no charge.[17]

This critique of the performative aspect of medicine within the court raises questions about the recognition and compensation of good doctors outside such theatrical displays. Were competent physicians, those who truly understood the art and science of healing, like Cervantes's friend, Francisco Díaz, ignored and poorly paid in favor of those who excelled merely in the spectacle of courtly medicine? Through Sancho's complaint, Cervantes may subtly expose the empty rhetoric and performance of court doctors, suggesting that true healing demands genuine knowledge, skill, *and* empathy. In orchestrating this cruel charade, the Duke and Duchess exploit Sancho's empathy, turning his concern for a fellow being in distress into a mandated flagellation. In doing so, the aristocrats embody the closest thing to the absolute negation of empathy. The callous manipulation of the situation highlights their complete disregard not only for Don Quijote and Sancho, but also for the humanity and well-being of anyone in their court, reduced to a mere pawn in their twisted game of amusement.

In stark contrast to this cruel indifference, Cervantes offers a quiet vindication for the link between healing and empathy in one of the most striking medical cases in his corpus: that of "licenciado Vidriera." The poisoned protagonist, Tomás Rodaja, who had been exceedingly critical of doctors, ends up regaining his health and judgment not at the hands of a good doctor but through the compassion of a religious man who possesses both "gracia" and "ciencia." This religious figure, moved by charity, restores Rodaja's health after two years of madness:

> Dos años o poco más duró en esta enfermedad, porque un religioso de la Orden de San Jerónimo, que tenía gracia y ciencia particular en hacer que los mudos entendiesen y en cierta manera hablasen, y en curar locos, tomó a su cargo de curar a Vidriera, *movido de caridad*; y *le curó y sanó*, y volvió a su primer juicio, entendimiento y discurso.

> The illness lasted about two years, until a monk of the Hieronymite order, who had a particular gift and skill of making the deaf hear and the mute speak, as well as curing madness, took it upon himself *out of charity to* cure the Glass Graduate. He *cured him and restored* him to health and to his previous good sense, intelligence, and reason.[18]

Thus, in a tale that so explicitly voices a recurrent critique of the medical profession, true healing does not stem from the title of "doctor" alone but from a blend of grace, knowledge, and, crucially, compassion—qualities often missing in the satirical depictions of court doctors. Through "Licenciado Vidriera," Cervantes narrates a case in which the most effective healer may not be the one who bears the professional title but rather the one who approaches his duty with genuine charity and understanding. The message reinforces a deeper claim in Cervantes's work, the consideration that true healing—like all true wisdom—is not the result of ostentatious shows of expertise, or rigid clinical mandates, but rather lies in the humble and compassionate application of knowledge.

Cervantes's view of empathetic healing—along with his questioning of medical authority and clinical competence—is strikingly modern, aligning his opus with key contemporary concerns in health-related disciplines. By reading Cervantes through the interdisciplinary lens of health humanities, we see that his work does more than depict medical practice; it compels us to reconsider the intersection of disciplines, occupations, and the ethical imperatives of care, ultimately revealing a deeper humanistic (or humanizing) need at the heart of all clinical practice. Ultimately, authors like Cervantes remind us that restoring both health and humanity requires addressing something beyond vital signs alone. In the works explored in these pages, Cervantes underscores how clinical competence and essential empathy—our ability to interpret and emotionally engage with human experience—are not only central to literature but also intrinsic to the very nature of healing. In a world increasingly shaped by the dehumanizing forces of technological advancement and shifting societal values, this holistic vision of healing—the Cervantine cure—serves as a timely reminder that, despite all obstacles and complexities, the essence of human experience remains recognizable, valuable, and perhaps, even fully healable.

NOTES

1. According to Eisenberg, Cervantes inherited some of his father's medical manuals, such as the *Tratado de las cuatro enfermedades cortesanas* by Lobera de Ávila (1544), *La Práctica y Theórica de la Cirugía* (1582) by Daza Chacón, *Práctica en Arte Chirurgica Copiosa* by Giovanni Vigo (trans. by Miguel Juan Pascual, 1537), and the celebrated *Dioscórides*, illustrated and edited by Andrés Laguna (1555). See Eisenberg, "Notas," 189–204 and Montes Santiago, "Saberes médicos," 294.
2. Astrana Marín, *Vida ejemplar y heroica*, 257.
3. Cervantes, *Galatea*, VI:563–89, 568.
4. Miguel de Cervantes, "Al doctor Francisco Díaz," in *Viaje al Parnaso*, 244–45. My translation.
5. The Royal *Protomedicato* was a central regulatory body established by the Spanish Crown to oversee medical practice, licensing, and the distribution of medicines. Originally founded in the late fifteenth century, it underwent considerable institutional development throughout the sixteenth and seventeenth centuries, setting and enforcing standards for physicians, surgeons, apothecaries, and other medical practitioners across Spain and its territories. See López Piñero, *Ciencia y técnica*, 65–85; and Lanning, *The Royal Protomedicato*.
6. See, for example, Cascardi, *The Cambridge Companion to Cervantes*; Chavaroche, "Midwives and Spin Doctors," 305–328; Matteo, "Professional Identity," 113–29; Pender and Struever, *Rhetoric and Medicine*, 31–55; Slater, "Don Quixote in the Pharmacy," 96–107; and Smith, "Staging Authority," 141–59.
7. Cervantes, "El casamiento engañoso," *Novelas ejemplares*, 221; "The Deceitful Marriage," *Exemplary Stories*, 237.
8. Barragán Nieto, "Sudar," 661.
9. Barragán Nieto, "Sudar," 661.
10. At times, Cervantine irony has been interpreted as cruel humor, as Vladimir Nabokov famously argued in his lectures on *Don Quijote*, seeing it as evidence of the author's "crude sensibility" and lack of compassion toward his protagonist; Nabokov, *Lectures on Don Quixote*, 7–8. However, the same passages that Nabokov criticizes can, conversely, be read as implicit calls for empathy, challenging the reader to respond with a more humane perspective. This interpretive duality reflects the complexity of Cervantes's narrative style, where irony serves both as mockery and moral inquiry. Scholars such as Martín de Riquer (*Aproximación al Quijote*, 67) and Carroll B. Johnson (*Madness and Lust*, 12) have emphasized Cervantes's ability to weave satire, compassion, and metafiction into a single, layered text. Ultimately, no single work of Cervantes can be confined to one definitive stance or dismissed outright, as his opus at large invites multiple, often contradictory, readings.
11. Cervantes, *El ingenioso hidalgo*, II, 47: 389; *Don Quixote*, II, 47: 760.
12. Andrés Laguna gets to the point of advocating a government rule requiring freshly minted doctors to "practice" for six or seven years in foreign lands or highly reputed hospitals before working independently; *Dioscorides*, 9.

13. Cervantes, *Obra completa*, 424.
14. Cervantes, "El licenciado Vidriera," *Novelas ejemplares*, 129; "The Glass Graduate," *Exemplary Stories*, 121.
15. Cervantes, *El ingenioso hidalgo*, II, 47: 389; *Don Quixote*, II, 47: 760.
16. Cervantes, *El ingenioso hidalgo*, II, 47: 389, emphasis added; *Don Quixote*, II, 47: 759–60.
17. Cervantes, *El ingenioso hidalgo*, II, 71: 570; emphasis added; *Don Quixote*, II, 71: 919.
18. Cervantes, "El licenciado Vidriera," 142; "The Glass Graduate," 128–29; my emphasis.

BIBLIOGRAPHY

Astrana Marín, Luis. *Vida ejemplar y heroica de Miguel de Cervantes Saavedra*. 7 vols. Reus, 1948.

Barragán Nieto, José Pablo. "Sudar catorce cargas de bubas: Mal francés, verosimilitud y empatía en *El casamiento engañoso* y *el Coloquio de los perros*." *Janus: Estudios sobre el Siglo de Oro* 9 (2020): 643–66.

Cascardi, Anthony J., ed. *The Cambridge Companion to Cervantes*. Cambridge University Press, 2002.

Cervantes Saavedra, Miguel de. *Don Quixote*. Translated by Edith Grossman. HarperCollins, 2005.

Cervantes Saavedra, Miguel de. *Exemplary Stories*. Translated by Lesley Lipson. Oxford University Press, 2018.

Cervantes Saavedra, Miguel de. *La Galatea*. Cátedra, 2006.

Cervantes Saavedra, Miguel de. *El Ingenioso hidalgo Don Quijote de la Mancha*. 2 vols. Edited by Luis Murillo. Castalia, 1978.

Cervantes Saavedra, Miguel de. *Novelas ejemplares*. 3 vols. Edited by Juan Bautista Avalle-Arce. Castalia, 1982.

Cervantes Saavedra, Miguel de. *Obra completa*, vol. 1. Edited by Florencio Sevilla Arroyo and Antonio Rey Hazas. Centro de estudios cervantinos, 1995.

Cervantes Saavedra, Miguel de. *Viaje del Parnaso: Poesías Sueltas*. Edited by Vicente Gaos. Castalia, 2001.

Chavaroche, Olivier. "Midwives and Spin Doctors: The Rhetoric of Authority in Early Modern French Medicine." In *New Directions in Literature and Medicine Studies*, edited by Stephanie Shirilan and M. R. Crane. Palgrave Macmillan, 2017

Eisenberg, Daniel. "Notas para la biblioteca de Cervantes: Husillos y Laguna." In *Actas del IV Congreso Internacional de la Asociación de Cervantistas: Alcalá de Henares, 1–5 de octubre de 2001*, 189–204. Centro de Estudios Cervantinos, 2002.

Johnson, Carroll B. *Madness and Lust: A Psychoanalytical Approach to Don Quixote*. Vanderbilt University Press, 1983.

Laguna, Andrés. *Pedacio Dioscórides Anazarbeo, Acerca de la materia medicinal y de los venenos mortíferos*. 1555.

Lanning, John Tate. *The Royal Protomedicato: The Regulation of the Medical Professions in the Spanish Empire*. Duke University Press, 1985.

López Piñero, J. M. *Ciencia y técnica en la sociedad española de los siglos XVI y XVII*. Labor, 1979.

Matteo, Marie N. "Professional Identity and Public Image: Medical Practice in the Court of Philip III." In *Medical Cultures of the Early Modern Spanish Empire*, edited by John Slater, Marie N. Matteo, and José Pardo Tomás. Ashgate, 2014.

Montes Santiago, Julio. "Miguel de Cervantes: Saberes médicos, enfermedades y muerte." *Anuario de Medicina Interna* 22, no. 6 (2005): 293–97.

Nabokov, Vladimir. *Lectures on Don Quixote*. Edited by Fredson Bowers. Princeton University Press, 1983.

Orobitg, Eusebio. "Las metamorfosis de Baco en la emblemática hispana. Sobre un epigrama de Juan de Mal Lara y los emblemas IX y LXX de Alciato." *RILCE: Revista de Filología Hispánica* 24, no. 4 (2008): 943–62.

Pender, Stephen, and Nancy S. Struever. *Rhetoric and Medicine in Early Modern Europe*. Routledge, 2012.

Riquer, Martín de. *Aproximación al Quijote*. Editorial Juventud, 1967.

Shapiro, Johanna, and Lloyd Rucker. "The Don Quixote Effect: Why Going to the Movies Can Help Develop Empathy and Altruism in Medical Students and Residents." *Families, Systems, & Health* 22, no. 4 (2004): 445–52. https://doi.org/10.1037/1091-7527.22.4.445.

Slater, John. "Don Quixote in the Pharmacy: Novel Reading and Early Modern Medical Culture." *Journal for Early Modern Cultural Studies* 11, no. 3 (2011): 96–107.

Smith, Dorothee E. "Staging Authority: Medical Praxis and the Performance of Knowledge in Early Modern Spanish Theatre." *Early Theatre* 18, no. 2 (2015): 141–59.

PART III

NEW MATERIALISMS

CHAPTER 9

Naturecultures *quijotescos*

Toward a New Materialist Reading of Don Quijote de la Mancha

LUIS RODRÍGUEZ-RINCÓN

> This is indeed why we feel so close to the sixteenth century, as if we were back before the "epistemological break," before the odd invention of matter.
>
> BRUNO LATOUR, "Compositionist Manifesto"

The early modern period has long been considered a touchstone for theorists like Bruno Latour who question the nature-culture divide, and the works of Miguel de Cervantes are a telling example why. Given the diversity of disciplines that have responded to new materialist theory over the last decades, it is difficult to give a single definition for this rather heterogeneous critical trend.[1] Nevertheless, a great deal of theory that follows in the wake of the material turn focuses on defining concepts that bridge the nature-culture divide and permit an assessment of what critics like Latour and Donna Haraway have called nature-cultures.[2] Naturecultures are hybrid entities both conceptual and concrete that demonstrate the interconnectedness of nonhuman nature with human culture. In my mind, a natureculture is best understood as a garden; as a green space that has been partially cut off from nonhuman nature and which evidences clear signs of human aesthetic and utilitarian intervention. When thinking about spaces, naturecultures remind us that seemingly natural spaces and constructs often have a human history that has been naturalized and thus forgotten with time. Likewise, this critical approach makes plain the human aesthetic categories that are brought into play whenever Cervantine characters like Don Quijote pine after beauty in human and nonhuman nature. It will be proposed here that the new materialist paradigm of a natureculture offers a productive framework for assessing the Cervantine notion of a Third Nature as an answer of sorts to the question posed repeatedly in both parts of Cervantes's famous novel *Don Quijote de la Mancha*: What impact do literary texts have on the material world around them?

Though a modern coinage, the term natureculture overlaps productively with the Cervantine understanding of *tercia naturaleza*. A term adapted from the language used in Italy to describe Mannerist gardens, Cervantes repeatedly references Third Natures in his fiction, starting with his pastoral romance, *La Galatea* (1585).[3] The beauty of the River Tagus, according to Elicio in the sixth book of *La Galatea*, is enhanced by "la industria de sus moradores," which, "ha hecho tanto, que la naturaleza, encorporada con el arte, es hecha artífice y connatural del arte, y de entrambas a dos se ha hecho una tercia naturaleza, a la cual no sabré dar nombre" (the skill of its inhabitants [which] has wrought so much that nature, incorporated with art, is become an artist and art's equal, and from both together has been formed a third nature to which I cannot give a name).[4] With its blending of nature with art, the category of *tercia naturaleza* can be productively considered an early modern natureculture, but one which stresses the constructed nature of such hybrid entities. Certainly, Cervantes's definition of Third Nature develops from classical understandings of the relation of nature to art, concepts which were consistently defined in relation to each other from antiquity to the early modern period.[5] Given that Elicio is describing the idyllic countryside along the banks of the Tagus that leads to the gardens of the *valle de los cipreses*, it becomes clear that Third Nature is one name Cervantes gives to a variety of human-constructed hybrid landscapes that merge nature with art to varying degrees and for divergent ends. Elicio's final gesture toward Galatea and the assertion of a bond between the wrought beauty of the Tagus and the shepherdesses' physical beauty highlights furthermore the parallels between human attempts at literary self-fashioning and a terraforming imagination that did not just find beauty in nature but sought to distill and recreate it in both people and places.

Cervantes's understanding of naturecultures develops over the course of his literary career with the beguiling sincerity of *La Galatea* giving way to more critical appraisals in his later fictions. According to Alban Forcione, Cervantes describes nature and art as harmoniously intertwined in *La Galatea*, but by the time of *Don Quijote* and *Persiles y Sigismunda* (1616), it is art which dominates nature.[6] In these later novels, Forcione identifies a nascent understanding of art for art's sake as Cervantes strove to free himself from rigid Aristotelian precepts of artistic theory.[7] Implicit in Forcione's analysis is an evolutionary model for Cervantine mimesis that has modernity and its artistic values as its vanishing point. A useful contrast to Forcione's evolutionary model for Cervantine mimesis are the insights of Elizabeth Rhodes, who understands Third Nature as a key paradigm for understanding the relation between Cervantes's notions of fiction and the question of human nature.[8] For Rhodes, *La Galatea* is marked by a pendular movement between moments of contemplation where the ideals of pastoral life are showcased and moments of action where such ideals must confront the shortcomings of the real, of history.[9] In the back-and-forth between these two poles, what emerges is the possibility for characters to change their individual natures and escape the static, idealized world of poetry and enter the dynamic world of history. A dynamic relation between the poles of poetry and history, art and nature, is thus at the heart of what makes Cervantes's characters so compelling for readers even in his earliest works. Such a model posits human and nonhuman nature alike not as fixed entities but as malleable constructs open to artful development as later characters like Don Quijote exemplify.

Don Quijote has been rightfully called a new Adam by critics who note the radical ruptures that mark this character's debut.[10] His penchant for renaming people, animals, objects, and places according to his preferred textual models is a telling example of his Adamic role. The Adamic power of names, of words over matter, is evoked every time a new name is given and an old one removed. Rocinante's renaming is instructive in this regard. First, the hidalgo visits the horse and observes his condition: "Fue luego a ver a su rocín, y aunque tenía más cuartos que un real y más tachas que el caballo de Gonela, que 'tantum pellis et ossa fuit,' le pareció que ni el Bucéfalo de Alejandro ni Babieca el del Cid con él se igualaban." (Then he went to look at his nag, and though its hooves had more cracks than his master's pate and it showed more flaws than Gonnella's horse, that *tantum pellis et ossa fuit*, it seemed to him that Alexander's Bucephalus and El Cid's Babieca were not its equal).[11] Readers here witness the knight's peculiar mode of apprehending the world as he negotiates the evidence presented by his senses alongside his textual ideal of what the horse can and should be. The ontological-semantic negotiation that then occurs as the knight squares the perceived nature of his horse with his textual models indicates the malleability of the world to semiotic transformations: "después de muchos nombres que formó, borró y quitó, añadió, deshizo y tornó a hacer en su memoria e imaginación, al fin le vino a llamar 'Rocinante'" (after many names that he shaped and discarded, subtracted from and added to, unmade and remade in his memory and imagination, he finally decided to call the horse *Rocinante*).[12] The process of fashioning a new name for Rocinante suggests that the transformations undergone by words implicate the ontological status of the living being described. A change in name denotes not just a change in identity but a change in nature, and, furthermore, literary texts seemingly play a guiding role in catalyzing such transformations.

Readers of *Don Quijote* are repeatedly reminded that for Cervantes, reality is constructed largely upon the basis of the names and stories humans create for themselves and the world around them. Some of those stories are true, but many are false. Certainly, the adventures of Don Quijote are defined by a striking disconnect between the knight's perception of the world and its material-historical reality. The novel's many narrators rarely miss an opportunity to underscore this disconnect. Nevertheless, the novel also foregrounds the ways in which characters change their external reality to better suit their internal perception of it. Over the course of both parts of *Don Quijote*, readers glimpse a cohort of characters like Sancho and various literary shepherds who learn to see the world like the knight through the lens of literary fictions. Like Don Quijote, these characters strive to reify their desires and prior readings in a world that is described by Cervantes as remarkably open to their mimetic interventions. As Foucault described the situation in semiotic terms, Don Quijote the character searches for signs in the material-historical world that prove the fictions animating his textual understanding of himself.[13] The knight himself functions like a sign in the novel in search of a material signified to ground his fictional signifiers, but a sign whose realization, I argue, aims to bring nature and art into ever greater convergence. It is this recurring desire to combine nature with art that leads us to identify in Don Quijote's chivalric mission a latent terraforming imagination, one which seeks to produce natureculture landscapes in the world that reflects the knight's desired literary identity.

From the perspective of naturecultures, Don Quijote's chivalric persona appears oriented toward bringing nature and art, world and word, into harmony both in his own person and in the world around him. Throughout his adventures, the knight exudes joy at being outdoors and away from established settlements. Readers witness this affinity for wilderness when he and Sancho enter the Sierra Morena: "así como don Quijote entró por aquellas montañas, se le alegró el corazón, pareciéndole aquellos lugares acomodados para las aventuras que buscaba." (As soon as Don Quixote entered those mountains his heart filled with joy, for it was a landscape that seemed suited to the adventures he was seeking).[14] For Don Quijote, wilderness is an ideal setting for knight errantry, for he understands that enterprise as representing an order that transcends the borders of any single kingdom and encompasses instead the entire world. Their laws are universal and knights errant traverse the natural world as lawgivers in seemingly lawless domains. The laws defended by the knight focus largely on policing damsels but extend as well to a natural world reimagined in the image of the beautiful and the good. One repeatedly stated goal for Don Quijote is to return nature and human society to what they were in the lost Golden Age. In this model, the art of knight errantry perfects the inchoate beauty of fallen nature and attempts to fabricate Third Natures as approximations of a lost Eden.

The knight's desire to inhabit natureculture landscapes that correspond to his chivalric textual identity is evidenced whenever Don Quijote is alone in nature. In settings such as the Sierra Morena and the Cave of Montesinos, readers witness a negotiation between two landscapes: one inside the knight's mind and sourced from his textual models and another existing outside his mind and described in relative detail by the novel's narrators. Rather than describing such scenes as moments of opposition between idealism and realism in narrative fiction—literary categories which are easily misconstrued as part of a modernist teleology—I turn instead to Barry Lopez's understanding of an outer and an inner landscape.[15] The knight's inner landscape is sourced from his textual models while the outer landscape is described by the narrator. What interests me is the curious way in which Cervantes illustrates the relation of the knight's inner landscapes to the outer ones and, in particular, the ability of the inner landscape to shape the knight's perception of the material-historical world outside himself. This echoes Harry Berger Jr.'s understanding of the function of green worlds in Renaissance fictions. For Berger, English writers from More to Shakespeare demonstrated that the value of green worlds stemmed from their ability to transform the material-historical world: "fiction can fulfill itself only by going beyond itself and invading life."[16] But what happens when fictions invade life? Does that mean a return to an enchanted view of the world, one where reality is crowded out of view by illusion and fiction? Not necessarily. As Jodi Cranston has demonstrated in the context of Renaissance Venice: "The concept of green world allows us to think less about landscape as peripheral components and more about the process through which spaces, places, and their representations become meaningful."[17] To think of green worlds as naturecultures brings to the fore the myriad ways in which humans imbue landscapes and nature more generally with meaning by elucidating the literary models and aesthetic ideals guiding such ventures. This was certainly true in Iberia during Cervantes's lifetime. Aguilar Pardomo highlights the tight mimetic dialogue that existed in the early modern period between the fictional gardens described in sixteenth-century chivalric romances and the historical gardens nobles in Iberia and Italy built for themselves in the period.[18] In this back-and-forth between historical gardens and early modern literary fictions, what comes to the fore are the parallels between historical gardening practices and Don Quijote's manner of apprehending nature and reimagining natureculturеs that reify his privileged literary models.

The knight's desire to inhabit a natureculture landscape that reflects his chivalric Third Nature is exemplified by key episodes in the Sierra Morena. Critics are in agreement that these episodes, in particular chapter 25, are a focal point in the novel that gathers together various narrative threads of Part One of *Don Quijote.*[19] In chapter 25, having decided to feign madness like his chivalric heroes, Don Quijote comes face-to-face with a pleasing mountainscape: "Llegaron en estas pláticas al pie de una alta montaña, que casi como peñón tajado estaba sola entre otras muchas que la rodeaban. Corría por su falda un manso arroyo, y hacíase por toda su redondez un prado tan verde y vicioso, que daba contento a los ojos que le miraban." (As they were conversing, they came to the foot of a high mountain, which, almost like a peak carved out of the rock, stood alone among the many others that surrounded it. At its base there flowed a gentle stream, and all around it lay a meadow so green and luxuriant it brought joy to the eyes that gazed upon it).[20] Here readers glimpse a landscape seemingly untouched by humans where nature's beauty inspires, in turn, the knight's literary-pastoral ruminations and the desire to insert himself definitively into a transformed landscape:

> Éste es el lugar, ¡oh cielos! que diputo y escojo para llorar la desventura en que vosotros mesmos me habéis puesto. Éste es el sitio donde el humor de mis ojos acrecentará las aguas de este pequeño arroyo, y mis continos y profundos suspiros moverán a la contina las hojas de estos montaraces árboles, en testimonio y señal de la pena que mi asendereado corazón padece.
>
> This is the place I designate and choose, O heavens, to weep for the misfortune to which you have condemned me. This is the place where the humor of my eyes will increase the waters of this small stream, and my continual deep sighs will constantly move the leaves of these untamed trees in testimony to and as proof of the grief that afflicts my troubled heart.[21]

The knight declares his intention to merge with the landscape: to join his tears with the mountain streams and to have his laments traverse the forests like a gentle breeze forevermore. In other words, the knight desires a landscape transformed in his emotional image. The knight's evocation of rustic pagan gods points to the imagined interlocutors of his dialogue with nature:

> ¡Oh vosotros, quienquiera que seáis, rústicos dioses que en este inhabitable lugar tenéis vuestra morada: oíd las quejas de este desdichado amante, a quien una luenga ausencia y unos imaginados celos han traído a lamentarse entre estas asperezas, y a quejarse de la dura condición de aquella ingrata y bella, términos y fin de toda humana hermosura!
>
> And O you rustic gods, whoever you may be, who dwell in this desolate place, hear the laments of this unfortunate lover, brought by long absence and imagined jealousy to this harsh terrain to complain and weep over the unyielding nature of that ungrateful beauty, the culmination and perfection of all human comeliness.[22]

The rustic gods that Don Quijote interpolates are the same beings that appear in the lyric poetry that inspired the knight, particularly the verses of Garcilaso de la Vega. These divine interlocutors exist at the blurred frontier between nature and art as poetic conceits that are reified and made into the natural counterpoint to the knight's narcissistic lament. To engrave a forlorn lover's lament in tapestries woven by nymphs of algae and gold, as the knight imagines and perhaps desires for himself here, is to offer a curious form of material immortality to human emotional concerns in a transformed nature. Such is the artistically transformed natureculture that Don Quijote seeks to inhabit. No longer the idealized landscapes produced by divine intelligences for human habitation, Cervantine naturecultures are human constructs that reflect personal values, needs, and the limitations there implied. Such spaces might recall the harmony of Eden, but their human-all-too-human underpinnings are ever evident.

For Cervantes, naturecultures are the product of human ingenuity taking over the role of the godly creator. This foregrounding of human concerns undergirding the fabrication of humanized landscapes is evident as well in the famous scene from the Second Part in the Cave of Montesinos. There, Don Quijote unearths the human origins of the lagunas of Ruidera and the river Guadiana. The trapped Montesinos conveys the etiologies of these bodies of water: "Solamente faltan Ruidera y sus seis hijas y sobrinas, las cuales llorando, por compasión que debió de tener Merlín de ellas, las convirtió en otras tantas lagunas." (The only ones missing are Ruidera and her daughters and nieces, who wept so much that Merlin must have taken pity on them, for he transformed them into lakes).[23] Here mournful tears metamorphose into bodies of water that serve as enduring monuments across time for human memories of love and loss. The etiology of the river Guadiana is explained in a similar vein:

> Guadiana, vuestro escudero, plañendo asimismo vuestra desgracia, fue convertido en un río llamado de su mismo nombre, el cual cuando llegó a la superficie de la tierra y vio el sol del otro cielo, fue tanto el pesar que sintió de ver que os dejaba, que se sumergió en las entrañas de la tierra; pero, como no es posible dejar de acudir a su natural corriente, de cuando en cuando sale y se muestra donde el sol y las gentes le vean.

> Guadiana, your squire, also lamented your misfortune and was transformed into a river that bears his name; when he reached the surface of the earth and saw the sun in another sky, the grief he felt at leaving you was so great that he descended again to the bowels of the earth; but since it is not possible to resist the natural course of his current, from time to time, he emerges and shows himself where the sun and all people may see him.[24]

The fate of Guadiana, the squire of the knight Durandarte, mixes together emotional, imperial, and natural histories. Because of his tears, the page became a river that seeks to be near his enchanted master underground but is forced back to the surface by the natural course of his river body. The squire's fluvial fate recalls Don Quijote's penance in the Sierra Morena and indicates the hybrid products that emerge from attempts to merge human stories and memories with natural phenomena. One has only to recall the lake of blood that concludes Cervantes's play *Numancia* to get a concrete sense of how the author understood human stories intermixing with liquid matter in Iberian history.[25] But the later Cervantes is more critical of this dream of reconciling nature and art under the guise of a Third Nature. Given the tongue-in-cheek nature of the Montesinos episode, readers are advised to interpret the knight's account of the river Guadiana and the lagunas of Ruidera with a healthy dose of skepticism. Modern readers can suppose that Cervantes here attempts to raise a reader's critical awareness about etiologies and poetic fables that posit a human origin to natural phenomena. But that does not mean that Cervantes is urging readers to abandon these natureculture constructs, but rather to be more aware of the stakes involved with them as well as the ability of individuals like Don Quijote to fabricate natureculture for themselves.[26] Like the river Guadiana making its way to the surface, the inner and outer experience of a landscape can be bent toward each other and their opposing poles reconciled in both symbolic and material-historical terms.

It has been argued here that the Cervantine understanding of Third Nature represents a prescient historical iteration of the new materialist notion of a natureculture. To approach early modern naturecultures from the perspective of Cervantes highlights their artificiality as constructs that reflect human emotional, political, and aesthetic imperatives. While new materialist theory largely aims to question anthropocentrism today, we note that naturecultures in the early modern period served primarily to center the human form and values in the natural world. In the historical gardens of the period, nature was actively transformed into novel and aesthetically pleasing forms guided by literary-artistic models and human desires. Further afield, the expansion of mercantile capitalism across the globe likewise resulted in the production of historical natures like sugar plantations that transformed tropical landscapes in the image of capital.[27] Cervantes was certainly attuned to these parallel terraforming processes occurring in his lifetime as his works remind readers today that the poles of nature and art, like the difference between fiction and reality, are only as static and universal as humans make them.

NOTES

1. Connolly, "New Materialism," 399: "the 'new materialism' is the most common name given to a series of movements in several fields that criticize anthropocentrism, rethink subjectivity by playing up the role of inhuman forces within the human, emphasize the self-organizing powers of several nonhuman processes, [and] explore dissonant relations between those processes and cultural practice" in order to, among other aims, "rethink the sources of ethics" from an ecologically informed perspective.
2. Latour, *We Have Never Been Modern*, 7; Haraway, *Companion Species Manifesto*, 12. At the macro level, naturecultures have been called hyperobjects by critics like Timothy Morton, who seeks categories capacious enough to encompass global phenomena like climate change. But naturecultures also exist at the micro level, as Stacy Alaimo (2010) and Astrida Neimanis demonstrate when discussing the permeable chemical-organic frontiers of the human body as trans-corporeality.
3. Montero ed., *La Galatea*, 345n17; Beck, "Gardens as a 'Third Nature,'" 327–34. Commentators identify a letter written in 1541 by the Italian Jacopo Bonfadio as an important source from which Cervantes derives the term *tercia naturaleza*. In this letter, which was printed several times by Aldus Manutius starting in 1545, Bonfadio describes the beauty of an Italian landscape that merges nonhuman nature with agricultural industry.
4. Cervantes, *La Galatea*, 240, 345.
5. Tayler, *Nature and Art*, 23–36. In this classic study, Tayler explains how the variable meaning of both nature and art resulted from a shifting valuation of human reason. From antiquity to the early modern period, any "controversy over the relative values of Nature and Art is thus in effect a controversy over man's role in the order of nature." If human reason was deemed corrupt, then art was considered a corruption of a divinely ordained natural order.

By contrast, if nature was understood to be inchoate, then human reason was called upon to perfect and refine the raw stuff of the world.

6. Forcione, *Cervantes, Aristotle, and the Persiles,* 224.
7. Forcione, *Cervantes, Aristotle, and the Persiles,* 245.
8. Rhodes, "'Tercia Realidad,'" 20.
9. Rhodes, "'Tercia Realidad,'" 22.
10. Avalle-Arce, *Don Quijote como forma de vida,* 48–50.
11. Cervantes, *Don Quixote,* 22; Cervantes, *Don Quijote,* 35.
12. Cervantes, *Don Quixote,* 22; Cervantes, *Don Quijote,* 45.
13. Foucault, *The Order of Things,* 47: "If he is to resemble the texts of which he is the witness, the representation, the real analogue, Don Quixote must also furnish proof and provide the indubitable sign that they are telling the truth, that they really are the language of the world."
14. Cervantes, *Don Quixote,* 174; Cervantes, *Don Quijote,* 273–74.
15. Lopez, "Landscape and Narrative," 5–6: "I think of two landscapes—one outside the self, the other within. The external landscape is the one we see– not only the line and color of the land and its shading at different times of the day, but also its plants and animals in season, its weather, its geology, the record of its climate and evolution. . . . The second landscape I think of as an interior one, a kind of projection within a person of a part of the exterior landscape."
16. Lopez, "Landscape and Narrative," 37.
17. Cranston, *Green Worlds of Renaissance Venice,* 14.
18. Aguilar Perdomo, *Jardines en tiempos de los Austrias,* 30.
19. Dudley, "Don Quijote as Magus," 356–57; Jiménez Fajardo, "The Sierra Morena as Labyrinth," 214; Avalle-Arce, *Don Quijote como forma de vida,* 151.
20. Cervantes, *Don Quixote,* 195; Cervantes, *Don Quijote,* 237–38.
21. Cervantes, *Don Quixote,* 195–96; Cervantes, *Don Quijote,* 238.
22. Cervantes, *Don Quixote,* 196; Cervantes, *Don Quijote,* 238.
23. Cervantes, *Don Quixote,* 608; Cervantes, *Don Quijote,* 726.
24. Cervantes, *Don Quixote,* 608; Cervantes, *Don Quijote,* 727.
25. Rodríguez-Rincón, "Cervantes after the Material Turn," 411–227.
26. Egido, *Cervantes y las puertas del sueño,* 150; 155.
27. Moore, *Capitalism in the Web of Life,* 19, 59: "the history of capitalism is one of successive *historical natures,* which are both producers *and* products of capitalist development." In turn, capitalist historical natures have a distinctly early modern history: "From the sixteenth century, the law of value began to take shape out of the global extensions of commodity production and exchange, stretching from the silver mines of Saxony and Potosí to the sugar plantations of Brazil and Barbados, and the timber frontiers of Scandinavia and the Baltic."

BIBLIOGRAPHY

Aguilar Perdomo, María del Rosario. *Jardines en tiempos de los Austrias: De la ficción caballeresca a la realidad nobiliaria.* Centro de Estudios Europa Hispánica, 2022.

Alaimo, Stacy. *Bodily Natures: Science, Environment, and the Material Self.* Indiana University Press, 2010.

Avalle-Arce, Juan Bautista. *Don Quijote como forma de vida.* Fundación Juan March and Editorial Castalia, 1976.

Beck, Thomas E. "Gardens as a 'Third Nature': The Ancient Roots of a Renaissance Idea." *Studies in the History of Gardens and Designed Landscapes* 22, no. 4 (2002): 327–34.

Berger, Harry Jr. "The Renaissance Imagination: Second World and Green World." In *Second World and Green World: Studies in Renaissance Fiction-Making*. University of California Press, 1988.

Connolly, William E. "The 'New Materialism' and the Fragility of Things." *Millennium: Journal of International Studies* 41, no. 3 (2013): 399–412. https://doi.org/10.1177/0305829813486849.

Cervantes, Miguel de. *Don Quijote de la Mancha*. Edited by Francisco Rico. Real Academia Española, 2004.

Cervantes, Miguel de. *Don Quixote*. Translated by Edith Grossman. HarperCollins-Ecco, 2005.

Cervantes, Miguel de. *La Galatea*. Edited by Juan Montero. Real Academia Española, 2014.

Cervantes, Miguel de. *La Galatea*. Translated by H. Oelsner and A. B. Welford. Gowans and Grey, 1903.

Cranston, Jodi. *Green Worlds of Renaissance Venice*. Pennsylvania State University Press, 2019.

Dudley, Edward. "Don Quijote as Magus: The Rhetoric of Interpolation." *Bulletin of Hispanic Studies* 49, no. 4 (1972): 355–68.

Egido Martínez, Aurora. *Cervantes y las puertas del sueño: Estudios sobre La Galatea, El Quijote, y El Persiles*. Promociones y Publicaciones Universitarias, 1994.

Fajardo, Salvador Jiménez. "The Sierra Morena as Labyrinth in Don Quixote I." *Modern Language Notes* 99, no. 2 (1984): 214–34.

Foucault, Michel. *The Order of Things: An Archeology of the Human Sciences*. Pantheon Books, 1970.

Forcione, Alban K. *Cervantes, Aristotle, and the Persiles*. Princeton University Press, 1970.

Garrote Pérez, Francisco. *La naturaleza en el pensamiento de Cervantes*. Ediciones Universidad de Salamanca, 1979.

Haraway, Donna. *A Companion Species Manifesto*. Prickly Paradigm Press, 2003.

Latour, Bruno. "An Attempt at a 'Compositionist Manifesto.'" *New Literary Criticism* 41 (2010): 471–90.

Latour, Bruno. *We Have Never Been Modern*. Translated by Catherine Porter. Harvard University Press, 1993.

Lopez, Barry. "Landscape and Narrative." In *Vintage Lopez*. Vintage Books, 2004.

Morton, Timothy. *Hyperobjects: Philosophy and Ecology After the End of the World*. Minnesota University Press, 2013.

Moore, Jason W. *Capitalism in the Web of Life: Ecology and the Accumulation of Capital*. Verso, 2015.

Neimanis, Astrida. *Bodies of Water: Posthuman Feminist Phenomenology*. Bloomsbury Academic, 2016.

Tayler, Edward William. *Nature and Art in Renaissance Literature*. Columbia University Press, 1964.

Rhodes, Elizabeth. "*La Galatea* and Cervantes's 'Tercia Realidad.'" *Cervantes: Bulletin of the Cervantes Society of America* 8 (1998): 17–28.

Rodríguez-Rincón, Luis. "Cervantes after the Material Turn: River Gods, Lakes of Blood, and Other Personified Bodies of Water in *Numancia*." *Journal of Spanish Cultural Studies* 23, no. 4 (2022): 411–28.

CHAPTER 10

Necropastoral and Conflicting Modes of Testimony

Don Quijote's Tale of Grisóstomo and Marcela

ELIZABETH SPRAGINS

A sheep bleats. A shepherd strums his lute. A beautiful woman, barefoot, trips gracefully behind her flock over the green landscape dotted with oaks and cork trees, whose shed bark affords easy shelter where needed. Plentiful, clear water flows in abundance throughout these lands. Agriculture—that hard, daily toil against the plow—is unknown in these parts, for the land is so fertile that food springs readily and bountifully all over. At lunchtime, poetry abounds. And there, right there at the center of it all, lies a man's dead body. For all its apparent simplicity and transparency, the pastoral proves remarkably slippery to define. Simultaneously a literary genre, setting, aesthetic, mode, and way of life, the pastoral is as much defined by what it is not as what it is: Paul Alpers claims that it is not the Golden Age or idyllic landscapes, but its herdsmen and their lives; David M. Halperin argues that "critics are justifiably unsure" where and how to locate the pastoral; and Annabel Patterson eschews definition entirely, claiming that critics of the pastoral have been failing to define it since the sixteenth century.[1] This essay does not endeavor to clarify this issue of genre definition, but rather considers one of the darker sides of the pastoral mode: the necropastoral.

The necropastoral reframes the site of supposed Arcadian bliss as a space just as focused on death and destruction as the world it is meant to escape. Poet Joyelle McSweeney introduces what she terms the "necropastoral" mode by proposing that the pastoral's rural idyll is centered on death itself: "For all the pastoral's shoring up of separations, and despite the *cordon sanitaire* it purports to erect between unhealthy urban lifestyle and wholesome rural peace, we must remember that the premier celebrity resident of Arcadia is Death."[2] This is certainly true of the episode of Grisóstomo and Marcela in Part I of *Don Quijote*, the spurned, dead lover and the decidedly unimpressed object of his love, whose pastoral sojourn in Arcadia takes a necropastoral turn with Grisóstomo's suicide.[3] I use the necropastoral to understand the dead as epistemological support for the stories told about them. Grisóstomo's corpse posthumously anchors his autobiographical account of his love and Marcela's scorn, which competes with Marcela's version of the events. Grisóstomo's account is triply supported by his corpse, the text of his diary, and the spectacle of the funeral itself, while Marcela is forced to make her case orally, with the compurgatory support of other shepherdesses around her.[4] The public that attends the funeral is asked to assess these conflicting models of testimony (textual, supplemented by the presence of Grisóstomo's corpse; oral, undermined by Marcela's relative lack of juridical standing as female), and delivers a resounding verdict on the relative value of these systems. While the mad knight vows to defend Marcela's side of the case, the remainder of the male audience prefers Grisóstomo's modern epistemological system and reinscribes Marcela within the confines of conventional love tropes. As eulogy morphs into testimony in the necropastoral with its narrower focus on the truthfulness of words spoken at the graveside, Grisóstomo's corpse is one medium by which the credibility of that testimony is judged, revealing Arcadia's logically dubious worldview that, by centering the corpse of its victim, only succeeds in drawing attention to the absurdity of his death and adjudicating whether his death was justifiable or blameworthy. Though never explicitly stated, at stake in this mock trial is whether Grisóstomo's death is truly a suicide and he has only himself to blame, or whether the love conventions that drove him to take his own life can lay that blame at Marcela's feet instead.

The Necropastoral

The tale of Grisóstomo and Marcela has long been recognized as a parody of the pastoral that brings the mad knight and other supporting characters into an Arcadia in which unrequited lovers don't just say they're dying of their pain but really do so, rich women dressed as shepherdesses actually herd their own sheep, and shepherd poets set their legal affairs in order.[5] Normally, the pastoral space establishes an idealized, external society apart from the corrupting, constraining influences of the urban, a "place of spiritual and artistic 'recreation' where the lovelorn poet seeks respite from his grief as he tests his skills against the past achievements of pastoral authors."[6] Grisóstomo's Arcadia, however, is not a place of respite for the poet, but rather concentrates and exacerbates his grief. He repeatedly exposes himself to the source of that grief—Marcela—by following her into the pastoral space and eventually driving himself to pay the ultimate price for that choice. Because of this, the episode "exposes the central and destructive 'paradox' of pastoral: that Arcadia looks back to the bliss of the Golden Age, and yet takes as theme 'the unbearable suffering of unrequited love.'"[7] This Cervantine pastoral represents the failure of Arcadia: "The two central characters pursue incompatible variants of the pastoral ideal, and neither of them realizes the Arcadian promise of poetic accomplishment."[8] Indeed, while Grisóstomo's poetic accomplishments are mediocre at best, Marcela steps entirely out of literary aspirations and seeks to undermine the foundation of the poetic artifice as a whole.

Viewed through the lens suggested by McSweeney, this core episode of Part I of *Don Quijote* should be understood as a necropastoral. McSweeney primarily discusses her concept in terms of twentieth- and twenty-first-century poetics and the aesthetics of the Anthropocene, arguing that the pastoral "spasms" time on itself:

> The necropastoral stages strange meetings. The dead meet the living or the dead meet the more or-less-than-dead . . . the speaker and Death mean together, the worms/words move through bodies and continually produce new masticating/speaking heads; thus temporal qualities, "before," "after," "during," and even "event" itself are also spasmed and distended.[9]

For McSweeney, the pastoral is thus never truly a place of bucolic ease, but instead an unsettling world that facilitates living characters' significant and signifying encounters with the dead, encounters that prove necessary for the poetic and literary production of the pastoral space. Identifying the necropastoral as a site of encounter between the living, the almost-dead, and the dead points to the paradox of this setting as an ultimately futile flight from the painful realities of the real world. McSweeney's insight that death is at the heart of the pastoral also perfectly encompasses the Cervantine or, more broadly, as Hernan Iventosch would have it, the Renaissance pastoral: "Bucolic funeral scenes, in fact, are of the very essence of the Renaissance pastoral [and] the pastoral elegy . . . a permanent monument of the Renaissance."[10] Don Quijote's lengthiest sojourn in the pastoral centers on not just a funeral, but on its dead, present, and according to its spectators, celebrity resident: Grisóstomo's yet-to-be-interred corpse. As I will show, that corpse is the key object that acts as the gravitational center of these four chapters of part I of the novel.

To continue to draw on McSweeney's necropastoral language, the spasming of time at the bucolic funeral scene enables the juridical encounter the reader witnesses at Grisóstomo's funeral. The necropastoral space becomes the site of discursive exchange among the living and the dead, and that funereal space transmutes into a spontaneous, makeshift courtroom in which the voice of the dead is revivified and considered alongside those of the living. In this liminal zone, Grisóstomo appears "as a decomposing author, shedding words and commas" in his "Canción desesperada" (Desperate Song).[11] This eulogy, declaimed on Grisóstomo's behalf by a friend, puts forth his version of his unrequited love for Marcela as sufficient justification for his suicide. Grisóstomo's corpse anchors this autobiographical account, standing as seemingly incontrovertible proof of the truth that he literally died for. Put in other terms, this eulogy morphs into testimony in the juridical necropastoral of his funeral scene, where Grisóstomo's corpse intervenes as a legible piece of evidence through which the credibility of the dead Grisóstomo's testimony can be judged. Grisóstomo's will blocks the scene so that his corpse sits visibly front and center for the presentation of his written testimony, yet another piece of evidence he presents against Marcela. Ultimately, however, the need for the presence of that corpse also points to a crisis in the worldview presented by the body and its accompanying mountain of text.

Grisóstomo's concerns for the strength of his case are borne out when Marcela comes on the scene. Unwilling to let the dead man have the last word, she questions the validity of his case, his standing as a witness, and his worldview. While Grisóstomo's martyrdom is erected on the edifice of conventional love tropes that portray the object of his love as necessarily distant, cruel, and disdainful, Marcela delivers an indictment of the logic of conventional love: a woman beloved for her beauty by all cannot reciprocate all that love; such indiscriminate reciprocation of love would violate the principle that love should be undivided and voluntary; if love feeds on hope, she can be found guilty of having provided no such thing. She prosecutes not only the sanity of one of its adherents, something that has already been called into question by his friends, but demonstrates the speciousness of the whole worldview. Most tellingly, she delivers this invective by stepping out of the textual conventions of literary love and proffering her testimony in viva voce, supported by her co-shepherdesses, whose compurgatory presence attests to her competence to give evidence in this matter.

Understanding the legal underpinnings by which those assembled at this bucolic funeral scene assess Grisóstomo's and Marcela's testimony reveals that the question under debate in this scene is that which has caused the most controversy among modern scholars: whether Grisóstomo should be considered guilty of his own death. Sanity, physical presence, mode of delivery, and gender all impact the credence their audience lends the protagonists. The legal basis of their testimony at times cooperates with and ignores the epistemically rich substance that Grisóstomo's corpse brings to the proceeding. The appearance of this celebrity resident of Arcadia proves to be the undoing of its entire system, not only by bringing the bureaucracy and jurisdiction of the outside world to bear on its bucolic peace, but by allowing Marcela to testify to the unsustainable paradox of this necropastoral space. While Marcela gives it an emphatic push over the edge, Grisóstomo's death-centered Arcadia was already on the verge of collapsing under the weight of its own contradictions.

Text as Masculine Space of Expression

While not all elements of the funereal gathering around Grisóstomo's graveside meet the requirements for a judicial hearing of a crime, the legal grounds for evaluating the ethical and epistemic standing of witnesses provides a useful framework for deciding the dispute at the heart of the episode and its outcome. The *Siete Partidas* defines witnesses as "Testigos son homes ó mugeres que son atales que non se pueden desechar de prueba, que aducen las partes en juicio para probar las cosas negadas ó dubdosas" (men and women who are of such character that their evidence, introduced by parties in court to prove matters which are denied or doubtful, cannot be dispensed with).[12] As seen in this framing, the pre- and early modern witness was assessed in terms of their character, social standing, and relationship to the party against whom they were to testify. Although gender factored into the mode of testimony—oral or written—that was accepted, women were not excluded from serving as witnesses, so long as they satisfied certain ethical, social requirements. There were also certain basic expectations for the witness's epistemic standing: that they could testify to the events or dispute in question. Finally, how the testimony was delivered and how it was documented mattered: the *Siete Partidas* and its derivative legal systems preferred oral testimony—that was then captured in writing by the judge for posterity—to submitted written testimony.[13] All of these factors are critical elements of the case presented to the attendees of Grisóstomo's funeral, who are assessing Marcela's guilt in provoking his suicide.

Throughout the Marcela/Grisóstomo episode, the question of the protagonists' social and ethical standing is paramount to the proceedings. This reflects the early modern period as a transitional moment in the role of witnesses within juridical, historiographical, and bureaucratic contexts. The modern understanding of the role of a witness in a legal context is an epistemological one—the witness is there to testify to the facts of the matter.[14] In contrast, medieval and early modern eyewitnesses were more often called upon to testify in ethical terms to the character of the accused.[15] But Andrea Frisch argues that medieval assumptions about the ethical and social role of the eyewitness carried well into the early modern period:

> Medieval forms of juridical "proof" were designed to establish . . . an "ethical truth" based on social consensus and not some approximation of the "facts." . . . rather than presupposing rational actors, it required parties who had established ethical relations with one another. . . . *This legitimacy was not based on a witness's epistemic capacities, but rather on his socio-ethical status.*[16]

Pre- and early modern testimony was deployed as a performative act that created truth rather than merely attesting to it. Although early modern eyewitness testimony gained prestige as a source of truth alternate to accepted textual authorities, that shift was gradual, and the *ad hominem* evaluation of witnesses' standing remained important well into the early modern period.[17]

Although pre- and early modern witnesses were not primarily called to contribute knowledge to the facts of the case, basic epistemic standards still had to be met for the court or magistrate to consider them competent. A witness's competence was narrowly defined—they could not merely contribute hearsay evidence but rather needed to weigh in directly on the contract or dispute in question.[18] It was expected that they give concrete details about where and when the events in question took place and to name other witnesses that were present there.[19] If those witnesses disagreed, all of their testimony would be thrown out. Crucially, where the witness's character was in question, the judge is encouraged to subject them to further epistemic scrutiny.[20] In this model of testimony, the witness's epistemic capacity is consubstantial with their ethical stature rather than being the primary characteristic under scrutiny.

The concern for and constraints around a witness's character were even more pronounced when the witness was female. Despite the severe restrictions a patriarchal society could impose upon women's legal standing, Iberian women, especially women of property, enjoyed legal privileges nearly unmatched for women in almost any other part of Western Europe at the time.[21] Those women were still almost exclusively defined according to their familial and sexual relationships with men, but they were nonetheless acknowledged as valuable contributors to the judicial process. For example, the *Siete Partidas* stipulates that a woman's testimony could be accepted from "Muger de buena fama puede ser testigo en todo pleyto, fueras ende en testament . . ., mas si contra la muger fuese dado juicio de adulterio, ó fuse vil et de mala fama, non debe seer cabido su testimonio en ningunt pleyto así como desuso deximos" (a woman of good reputation . . . in any suit except one relating to a will, . . . but if she has been convicted of adultery, or is degraded, or of bad reputation, her testimony will not be competent in any case, as we stated above).[22] This ethical and social assessment of women's standing was broadly applied even beyond the secular arm of the law.[23] While "legally, a woman in early modern Portugal was not an appendage of her father, husband, or other male in the family," "socially, . . . she was generally viewed as such, and this social construct was perpetuated by many public officials, including notaries."[24] Unsurprisingly for a society that so closely intertwined male social standing and advancement and the chastity of the women of their family, a woman's reputation for legal purposes was primarily defined by her relationships, sexual and otherwise, with men.

In addition to the ethical limitations on what kinds of women could testify, the situations in which they could offer their testimony and the modes in which that testimony was accepted were also circumscribed. Specifically, women's interventions were largely kept out of the textual sphere: "women were acceptable witnesses only in oral testaments, and in cases of testaments from soldiers engaged in battle—that is, in dire circumstances. Thus, the legal transactions under discussion were open to women as property owners, not as citizens."[25] Furthermore, female testimony was marginalized within the legal process: "the male protagonists did all the negotiating, made all the necessary arrangements, provided all the essential details, drew up all the important documents, and then the women were brought into the picture, minor characters on the edges of the momentous occasion, almost as an afterthought."[26] Their capacity to intervene in legal proceedings were more geographically and socially circumscribed, a fact that reflects both the legal system's preference for in-person testimony and women's more strictly trammeled movement in the world.[27] Thus, even if women retained relatively equitable status with men according to the letter of the law, the cultural and social limitations placed on their interactions with the world meant that their testimony was framed in terms of their sexual purity and the social status of their male relatives, while the evidence they were permitted to give was kept to the margins, both literally and figuratively, of the legal process.

To be sure, the Iberian legal tradition generally expressed a preference for in-person, oral testimony, by men as well as women, that would be entered into the formal record by notaries present for their statement, but makes an exception for written testimony if a witness cannot be present.[28] While the end result is that the testimony is "facer escrebir ó escrebirlo él mismo bien et lealmente" (faithfully reduced to writing), the overwhelming preference for oral testimony reflects a belief that the interaction between judge and witness may impact upon the witness's testimony, as shown in the recommendation that the judge "debe . . . oirle mansamente, et callar fasta que haya acabado catandol todavia en la cara" (should listen to [the witness] kindly, and be silent until he has finished, looking him all the time in the face).[29] In-person testimony thus allows the judge and the notary to apply social pressure to the witness, as well as to ensure epistemic reliability: they could repeat the witness's account back to them to fact-check, ask for the witness to add more detail they may have previously omitted, ascertain how the witness came by this information, and, through close visual scrutiny of their embodied reactions, judge the witness's sincerity. The preference for this mode of testimony applied regardless of the witness's exalted or debased social standing.[30]

Despite the fact that oral testimony best allowed for the judge and other officials of the court to establish the facts of the case in a dialogic manner, the *Siete Partidas* and its derivative legal codes recognized that it would not always be possible for witnesses to appear in person on the appointed day. In such a situation, that witness is permitted to "débelos facer jurar ante homes buenos, et facer escrebir lo que dixieren, et seellar lo con su seello porque sean guardados los dichos dellos fasta el tiempo en que sean meester" (be sworn in the presence of good men, have their testimony reduced to writing, and seal it with his seal, that their statements may be kept until the time when they are required).[31] As this stipulation makes clear, however, the strong preference was still for oral testimony given in the presence of purgatory witnesses that could attest to the competence of that witness, which would only subsequently be submitted in writing. Indeed, it is noted later that evidence put in writing is significantly less valuable than that given in person: "Testimonio que sea dado ó enviado por carta decimos que bien lo pueden desechar aquellos contra quien lo dieren; ca *no tenenos por derecho que ninguno envie su testimonio por escripto al judgador*" (We decree that evidence put in writing, or sent in a letter, can be rejected by those against whom it is given; for *we do not consider it just that any one should send his testimony in writing to a judge*).[32] The deciding factor in assessing the relative value of the testimony presented by Marcela and Grisóstomo is the presence of Grisóstomo's corpse. At play here, in addition to the balance of ethical and epistemological testimony in dispute at the grave site, is also the power of that dead body as a necroepistemological resource.[33] The presence of Grisóstomo's corpse in this episode can be understood as an effort to shift the epistemological balance of power. By orchestrating the public display of his own body at this funeral, Grisóstomo demonstrates his understanding of the power of the corpse to influence epistemologically and ethically on an audience's assessment of a piece of testimony. And, by directing his own funeral, Grisóstomo endeavors to literally throw his own dead weight around. He does this with an eye toward influencing the juridical outcome of the judgment of Marcela's guilt in his death.

When reading the Marcela/Grisóstomo episode as a kind of informal legal proceeding that sets out to determine Marcela's complicity in Grisóstomo's untimely death, crucial elements to attend to in determining the trial's final outcome include: the protagonists' social standing and thus competence as witnesses as assessed by those in attendance at the funeral; their capacity to offer epistemically reliable testimony; the impact of gender on their right to testify; and the mode—written or spoken—in which that testimony is offered. Grisóstomo's corpse becomes a key element in the delicate balance being struck among all of these different factors. The stakes of the determination the audience arrives at are high—as a suicide, Grisóstomo risks eternal damnation unless he can offload blame for his actions onto Marcela as his effective murderess. Revivifying Grisóstomo's corpse as the central celebrity of the necropastoral space not only establishes a monument to his life and work, but also makes a more targeted testimonial intervention into a legal dispute.

NOTES

1. Alpers, *What Is Pastoral?*, 11; Halperin, *Before Pastoral*, 76; and Patterson, *Pastoral and Ideology*, 7. Irigoyen García argues that the early modern Spanish pastoral is a site for constructing a pure cultural, racial, and religious Spanish identity apart from the realities of its Jewish and Muslim legacies. He also gives a substantial review of the extensive consideration by a range of literary and art historical critics of the rising prestige of the genre of the pastoral and the figure of the shepherd in the Iberian world over the course of the sixteenth century. Irigoyen García, *The Spanish Arcadia*, 75–111.
2. McSweeney, *The Necropastoral*, 3. While McSweeney does not make mention of the trope, her conceptualization of the pastoral gestures to the axiom of *et in arcadia ego*, that death still reigns over the pastoral and is, perhaps, the very source of its art. See Panofsky's classic essay about the Nicolas Poussin painting named after the axiom, "Et in Arcadia Ego," 295–320. Damiani and Mujica have studied this as a Renaissance phenomenon in *Et in Arcadia Ego*.
3. This essay does not engage with Cervantes's exploration of the pastoral in *Galatea*, nor other examples of the significant dead in Cervantes's oeuvre or even in *Don Quijote* (e.g.,

Don Quijote's dream in the Cave of Montesinos dealing with Durandarte's heart, the hanging corpses in part II, encounters with corpses in both parts I and II, etc.) due to length considerations.

4. Unlike witnesses to matters of fact (what can be understood as the epistemological matter of a case), compurgatory witnesses attest to the character and credibility of a defendant (the ethical matter of a case). While her companions do not speak during the scene, I argue that their presence stands as a kind of communal affirmation of Marcela's socio-ethical status. See Frisch's discussion of compurgation and its accompanying epistemological considerations in "The Ethics of Testimony," 43–47.
5. To name only a few: Forcione, "Cervantes en busca," 1,028–36; Iventosch, "Cervantes and Courtly Love," 64–76; and McGaha, "Cervantes and Virgil," 96–109.
6. Rupp, "True and False Pastoral," 6.
7. Rupp, "True and False Pastoral," 5.
8. Rupp, "True and False Pastoral," 8.
9. McSweeney, *The Necropastoral*, 7.
10. Iventosch, "Cervantes and Courtly Love," 67.
11. McSweeney, *The Necropastoral*, 10.
12. *Siete Partidas*, Partida III, Title XVI, Law I.
13. This can also be seen in the *Ordenações Filipinas*, which were promulgated under the Philippine regime in Portugal in the days of the Iberian Union.
14. Frisch, "The Ethics of Testimony," 36.
15. Frisch, "The Ethics of Testimony," 39–43.
16. Frisch, "The Ethics of Testimony," 43, my emphasis.
17. Pagden's work on *autoptic* testimony argues that the stakes of trustworthy information forced participants in colonial processes to develop strategies that supported their claims to credibility by emphasizing corporeal access or presence at events they narrated. Pagden, *European Encounters*, 51. See also Adorno, "Discourses of Colonialism," 239–58, especially 245–46; Campbell, *The Witness and the Other World*; and Folger, *Writing as Poaching*.
18. *Siete Partidas*, Partida III, Title XVI, Law XXVIII.
19. *Siete Partidas*, Partida III, Title XVI, Law XXVIII.
20. *Siete Partidas*, Partida III, Title XVI, Law XXVIII.
21. Abreu-Ferreira, "Women, Law," 293–94.
22. *Siete Partidas*, Partida III, Tit. XVI, Law XVII. This and subsequent translations are from *Las Siete Partidas*, vol. 3.
23. Perry, *Gender and Disorder*, 120. See, too, Abreu-Ferreira, "Women, Law," 306, 308.
24. Abreu-Ferreira, "Women, Law," 305.
25. Abreu-Ferreira, "Women, Law," 308.
26. Abreu-Ferreira, "Women, Law," 305.
27. Abreu-Ferreira, "Women, Law," 308.
28. *Siete Partidas*, Partida III, Title XVI, Law II.
29. *Siete Partidas*, Partida III, Title XVI, Law XXVI.
30. *Recopilacion de las Leyes destos Reynos*, 102. As Johnson points out, the embodied nature of testimony could also make the judge susceptible to manipulation, whether through "the rhetorical prowess of those under oath," or other "more improvisational aspects of self-presentation." "Feeling Certainty, Performing Sincerity," 51.
31. *Siete Partidas*, Partida III, Title XVI, law II.

32. *Siete Partidas,* Partida III, Title XVI, Law XXXII, my emphasis.
33. *Necroepistemology* is a system of knowledge grounded in or transmitted through firsthand experiences of the material dead. See my discussion of this phenomenon in Spragins, *A Grammar of the Corpse,* 1–23.

BIBLIOGRAPHY

Abreu-Ferreira, Darlene. "Women, Law and Legal Intervention in Early Modern Portugal." *Continuity and Change* 33 (2018): 293–313.

Adorno, Rolena. "Discourses of Colonialism: Bernal Díaz, Las Casas, and the Twentieth-Century Reader." *MLN* 103, no. 2 (1988): 239–58.

Alpers, Paul. *What Is Pastoral?* University of Chicago Press, 1996.

Campbell, Mary B. *The Witness and the Other World.* Cornell University Press, 1988.

Damiani, Bruno, and Barbara Mujica. *Et in Arcadia Ego: Essays on Death in the Pastoral Novel.* University Press of America, 1990.

Folger, Robert A. *Writing as Poaching: Interpellation and Self-Fashioning in Colonial relaciones de méritos y servicios.* Brill, 2011.

Forcione, Alban. "Cervantes en busca de una pastoral auténtica." *Nueva revista de filolofía hispánica* 36, no. 2 (1988): 1,028–36.

Frisch, Andrea. "The Ethics of Testimony: A Genealogical Perspective." *Discourse* 25, no. 1/2 (2003): 36–54.

Halperin, David M. *Before Pastoral: Theocritus and the Ancient Traditions of Bucolic Poetry.* Yale University Press, 1983.

Irigoyen García, Javier. *The Spanish Arcadia: Sheep Herding, Pastoral Discourse, and Ethnicity in Early Modern Spain.* University of Toronto Press, 2013.

Iventosch, Herman. "Cervantes and Courtly Love: The Grisóstomo-Marcela Episode of Don Quixote." *PMLA* 89, no. 1 (1974): 64–76.

Johnson, Paul Michael. "Feeling Certainty, Performing Sincerity: The Emotional Hermeneutics of Truth in Inquisitorial and Theatrical Practice." In *The Quest for Certainty in Early Modern Europe: From Inquisition to Inquiry, 1550–1700,* edited by Barbara Fuchs and Mercedes García-Arenal. University of Toronto Press, 2020.

McGaha, Michael D. "Cervantes and Virgil: A New Look at an Old Problem." *Comparative Literature Studies* 16, no. 2 (1979): 96–109.

McSweeney, Joyelle. *The Necropastoral: Poetry, Media, Occults.* University of Michigan Press, 2014.

Pagden, Anthony. *European Encounters with the New World: From Renaissance to Romanticism.* Yale University Press, 1992.

Panofsky, Erwin. "Et in Arcadia Ego: Poussin and the Elegiac Tradition." In *Meaning in the Visual Arts.* University of Chicago Press, 1983.

Patterson, Annabel. *Pastoral and Ideology: Virgil to Valery.* University of California Press, 1987.

Perry, Mary Elizabeth. *Gender and Disorder in Early Modern Seville.* Princeton University Press, 1990.

Recopilacion de las Leyes destos Reynos, hecha por mandado de la Magestad Catholica del Rey don Philippe Segundo nuestro Señor. Alcalá de Henares, 1581.

Rupp, Stephen. "True and False Pastoral in 'Don Quijote.'" *Renaissance and Reformation* 16, no. 3 (1992): 5–16.

Las siete partida: Edición de 1807 de la Imprenta Real, Tomo II, Partida segunda y tercera. Real Academia de la Historia, 2021.

Las Siete Partidas. Vol. 3, *Lawyers and Their Work* (Partida III). Translated by Samuel Parsons Scott, edited by Robert I. Burns, SJ. University of Pennsylvania Press, 2000.

Spragins, Elizabeth. *A Grammar of the Corpse: Necroepistemology in the Early Modern Mediterranean*. Fordham University Press, 2023.

CHAPTER 11

Cervantes's Animal Menagerie

STEVEN WAGSCHAL

Animal studies is a capacious interdisciplinary field, allied to environmental studies, that brings together research in the humanities, social sciences, and natural sciences to understand human-animal relationships and, as Linda Kalof puts it, "to rethink and reconfigure [these] relationships with other animals." The field thus reveals the commodification of animals throughout history in various contexts; demonstrates how human-caused loss of habitat has led to the decline of autochthonous animal populations, including the extinction of numerous species; and envisions better ways "to coexist with other animals in urban, rural, and natural contexts."[1] As some practitioners articulate their work, animal studies puts nonhuman animals in focus, "centering" them as crucial elements of human history, culture, and science, while seeking to understand animals as beings with their own meaningful existences, apart from human interest.[2]

While critics had noted the presence of certain animals in *Don Quijote*, it was historian Abel Alves, in his groundbreaking *The Animals of Spain*, who drew attention to the plethora of animal species in Cervantes's novel and the activities in which they engage. Alves rightfully concludes that "*Don Quixote*'s animals are the animals of Spain in literary microcosm."[3] While his focus was not *Don Quijote*, he importantly brought to the fore the human-animal relationships that demonstrate interspecies emotional bonds. Adrienne Martín was the first Cervantes scholar to center nonhuman animals in Cervantes's oeuvre explicitly from the perspective of animal studies. Martín draws out the way in which Cervantes's novel recaptures for us how animals were an integral part of the fabric of human existence and early modern daily life.[4] In this essay, I will show how Cervantes demonstrates a surprisingly nuanced depth of understanding of several nonhuman animals' minds and behavior. Given his appreciation of nonhuman animals and of their concerns *qua* animals, it is thus fruitful to approach *Don Quijote* from the theoretical perspective of animal studies.

There are, indeed, many and varied animals in the novel. Most of them are valued primarily as commodities. For instance, the herd of sheep that Don Quijote attacks in part I, chapter 18 are being raised for their value as wool, milk, and meat. And in part I, chapter 11, the protagonists will share a goat-meat stew with the goatherds to whom Don Quijote directs his first grandiloquent speech. There are also passages in which animals are interpreted in a symbolic manner, much like they would have been in a Homeric epic. In this vein, Don Quijote reads the hare's motion (part II, chapter 70) as meaningful to his current circumstances. It is not my claim that Cervantes, in describing and narrating these commodified or symbolic animals, is doing anything original with animals. Yet throughout *Don Quijote*, Cervantes introduces a slew of particularly interesting individual animal characters, inviting the reader to reflect on what could be broadly referred to as their cognition. I will focus on four of these animals—the cat, the lion, the horse Rocinante, and the donkey—to highlight what is special about how the author portrays each one and how these constitute an innovative representation of animals. In subtle ways, Cervantes presents animal emotion, thought, and intentional agency, developing what I term "animal embodiment." He opens up, in fiction, a world of possibilities for representing animals' minds, creating nonhuman characters that merit the reader's consideration, reflection, and empathy.

One important way that Cervantes approaches animal embodiment is by treating them as individuals, rather than as a mass or herd. Thus, from the sack stuffed with cats that are used to torture Don Quijote (part II, chapter 46), there is one cat who literally gets out of the bag, "viéndose" (seeing himself) being attacked by the knight. Such a focus on the individual cat character emphasizes the animal's perspective toward the knight: "uno, viéndose tan acosado de las cuchilladas de don Quijote, le saltó al rostro y la asió de las narices con las uñas y los dientes" (one of them, finding himself [literally: "seeing himself"]) so hounded by Don Quijote's sword thrusts, leaped at his face and sank his claws and teeth into his nose).[5] The cat reacts in a way that other combatants are portrayed in the novel, for instance, the Vizcayan, in part I, chapter 9, where the gerund of "ver" (literally "seeing") is also employed. However, while there is something human-like about the cat's activity, this treatment is far from the "gratuitous anthropomorphism" typical of talking-animal fables, to employ the term coined by primatologist Frans de Waal; rather it is a reasonable, common-sense, folk psychological way of portraying a cat.[6] The cat has eyes and can obviously see that Don Quijote is a threat, so why would he not "see himself"? As Charles Darwin argued in *The Descent of Man* in 1871, rather than privileging a view of human exceptionalism, we should observe the "continuity" of many cognitive abilities across species; that is, given the fact of evolution, humans must share a great deal in common with other animals: "there is no fundamental difference between man and the higher animals in their mental faculties."[7]

The episode with a much larger feline invites additional questions of animal sentience too. In this particular instance (part II, chapter 17), the reader has little direct access to what the lion is thinking. In a certain way, the lion's mind seems impenetrable. Yet what is perhaps more interesting is that some characters first implicitly deny that the lion is thinking and then begin to think about his motivations (thinking about what the lion is thinking), affording the reader the same opportunity. At the beginning of the episode, important but skeletal pieces of background information are revealed by the royal cart driver: "Son hembra y macho; el macho va en esta jaula primera, y la hembra en la de atrás; y ahora van hambrientos porque no han comido hoy" (They're male and female; the male's in the first cage and the female's in the one behind, and they're hungry now because they haven't eaten today).[8] From Don Quijote's perspective, the lions are not particularly sentient. As he challenges them in his act of insane bravery, he calls the felines "bestias" (beasts), a term used in period treatises to mean that an animal specifically lacks reason. Don Quijote expects that, with the cage open, the lion will rush out and attack him. As in the episode of the cat who escaped from the bag, only one of the lions is centered through his challenge. Despite Don Quijote's own apparent beliefs in the animal's "bestial" instinctual behavior, this nonhuman animal is individuated and becomes a character with a mind.

Other characters hold a similar belief to Don Quijote's—that the lion will definitely rush out and attack. Thus, the carriage driver only unlocks the lion's cage under duress, fearing that the lion will kill his mules, those who allow him to do his job. Don Diego thinks Don Quijote is out of his mind; Sancho fears that the lions will kill Don Quijote and then him. All four of these characters are certain that the lion will rush out of the cage and attack. Such certainty implies that they believe, at least implicitly, that the lion cannot choose to do otherwise. That is, they do not believe that this "beast" has any thought process at all but, rather, that *it* will mechanistically charge and kill. But the reader learns that these assumptions are wrong when that is not what happens:

> Lo primero que hizo fue revolverse en la jaula, donde venía echado, y tender la garra, y desperezarse todo; abrió luego la boca y bostezó muy despacio, y con casi dos palmos de lengua que sacó fuera se despolvoreó los ojos y se lavó el rostro; hecho esto, sacó la cabeza fuera de la jaula y miró a todas partes con los ojos hechos brasas . . . Pero el generoso león, más comedido que arrogante, no haciendo caso de niñerías ni de bravatas, después de haber mirado a una y otra parte, como se ha dicho, volvió las espaldas y enseñó sus traseras partes a don Quijote, y con gran flema y remanso se volvió a echar en la jaula.

> The first thing the lion did was to turn around in the cage where he had been lying and unsheathe his claws and stretch his entire body; then he opened his mouth, and yawned very slowly, and extended a tongue almost two spans long, and cleaned the dust from his eyes and washed his face; when this was finished, he put his head out of the cage and looked all around with eyes like coals . . . But the magnanimous lion, more courteous than arrogant, took no notice of either the childishness or bravado, and after looking in both directions, as has been said, he turned his back, and showed his hindquarters to Don Quixote, and with great placidity and calm went back inside the cage.[9]

What went wrong with the humans' predictions? It appears they underestimated the lion's ability to choose. The sentences contain a series of actions, mostly avoiding explicit inferences about the lion's thoughts. In an analogous scene at the end of part I, Don Quijote is let out of the cage to speak with the Canon of Toledo, at which point, like the lion now, the first thing he does is stretch; indeed, the lion's actions are a foil for those of the novel's protagonist.[10] Since Don Quijote clearly possesses intentional agency, this implicit comparison develops the lion's agency. Like the smaller cat, the lion has a moment that we could only call reflection, as "he put his head out of the cage and looked all around." A few sentences later, the narrator emphasizes the reflective moment stating that the lion was "looking in both directions." Again, the narrator implies that the lion had a choice to make, expressing intentional agency, a capacity oft believed to be only human. The lion then turns around, demonstrating his hinder parts. While Cervantes may have selected this action as a comical insult, he may also have been familiar with lion behavior or debates about animal agency.

The narrator suggests that the lion has multiple emotions, calling him, as quoted earlier, "generoso león, más comedido que arrogante" (magnanimous lion, more courteous than arrogant). The term "generoso" implies that the lion chooses not to kill the knight out of something like clemency, calling to mind a *topos* popularized in Pliny's *History* and in the hagiographic tradition. In such stories, lions engage in improbable friendships with humans. That the lions have not eaten on this day is a significant detail, and with it, we have the outlines of the early modern debate about animal sentience, which specifically asked whether animals deliberate and make choices, first taken up by Gómez Pereira (1554) contra Pliny, and later by René Descartes and his disciple Nicolas Malebranche.[11] When a lion doesn't kill a human, it is never because of "clemency" as Pliny suggests, but merely because the lion has been "stuffed" (ahíto).[12] While Pereira may be right that in most cases a hungry lion will try to kill a person for nourishment, his claim that a lion who does not do this must be "stuffed" is based on an unfounded assumption that animals lack decision-making. Pereira's schema is logically deficient if it is applied to the Cervantine episode, since the narrator has carefully countered it: the reader knows that the "stuffed" explanation is false since the lions, in fact, "van hambrientos" (they are famished).[13] Cervantes's reader is left face-to-face with the difficulty of scrutinizing the animal mind. In the absence of a common language between humans and the lion, we cannot know for certain why he chooses one thing over another. Yet we see him make a choice, looking one way and then the other, before acting. The fact that the lion does not automatically rush out and kill Don Quijote, in opposition to what characters predict and what Pereira would have predicted, suggests that the lion possesses richer mental processes: reflection, intention, and emotion. Thus, focusing clearly on one specific lion, offering some of the lion's perspective, and having him act in an unexpected way, Cervantes demonstrates subtly the complexity of the lion's mind. An individuated character is created, and while he does not speak, the lion is a most memorable one.

While the cat and the lion only come into the story for a short while, Rocinante and the donkey appear repeatedly and are the most thoroughly treated animal characters in *Don Quijote*. Reflecting on the friendship between these two animal characters and, specifically, on the chapter in which the two equines rub each other's necks (part II, chapter 12), both Martín and Alves purposively employ anthropomorphizing terms to describe the bonds. Martín calls this passage "one of the warmest and friendliest descriptions of the novel's equine protagonists."[14] Alves goes further, alleging that the passage shows that Cervantes's equids experience love: "Cervantes' beasts understand, feel and love."[15] Much of the creation of character of these two equids, I would argue, stems from Cervantes's careful treatment of their sensation and cognition, through what I call "constructive anthropomorphism."[16] A key experience here is their suffering—that is, the experience of pain is fundamental. Indeed, both *el rucio* and Rocinante are cognitively embodied beings, showing species-typical functioning and individual personality. Their cognition is a complex, multifaceted representation in which consciousness, intentional agency, memory, and multiple emotions come together, and which is very much in line with what today is considered species-typical equine cognitive functioning.

The equids have a varied emotional experience.[17] In the interest of brevity, I will focus on just two emotions: joy and suffering. The equids enjoy each other's company, often being spared the separation that would likely occur in most stabling settings. Comparative psychologist Michel-Antoine Leblanc discusses the horse as a "supremely social animal," which in the wild "never lives alone."[18] Leblanc views stabling as a hindrance to the emotional flourishing of horses and critiques the "constraints imposed on domesticated horses (such as confinement, social isolation, and relative inactivity)" that can "ultimately overwhelm their natural capacity to adapt."[19] In Cervantes's passage, the freedom that the pair has to enjoy each other's company is thus salutary, and helps explain why these animals are flourishing emotionally. Their well-being is not only caused by being together in each other's company, but also by the grooming behaviors in which they engage, which are mentioned by the narrator. The scholarly appraisals of the animals' emotions, by Alves and Martín, rely on constructive anthropomorphic inferences, based on explicit actions—"rascarse el uno al otro . . . cruzaba Rocinante el pescuezo sobre el cuello del rucio . . . mirando los dos atentamente" (scratch each other . . . Rocinante would lay his neck across the donkey's . . . staring intently . . . the two of them)—rather than on an explicit representation of the animals' thought processes.[20] The behaviors of Rocinante and *el rucio* are not ambiguous. Reasonable people can understand their feelings toward one another. While not identical to human caresses, the animals' scratching of each other and the crossing of their necks, as well as their maintaining of these postures for a lengthy period of time, have broad correlatives in human actions based on emotion, which humans know intuitively and believe others to hold as well. Beyond such constructive anthropomorphism and folk animal psychology, ethological research shows that grooming behaviors performed on specific "preferred grooming sites" have a calming effect on horses, resulting in significant physiological benefits.[21] Grooming fulfills multiple functions, including cleaning and removal of parasites, establishing and deepening bonds, and avoiding potential aggressions. Contrasting social grooming in equids and in many primates, Leblanc notes that in the latter group, grooming involves the entire body and "thus appears especially to be related to hygiene,"[22] whereas region-specific equine grooming is even more social and entails "a hedonic reward element designed to maintain the behavior."[23] This "hedonic reward" involves something similar to the neuronal release of endorphins in humans, documented in experiences of love and of eating chocolate.[24] Cervantes's lengthy paragraph, then—allegedly abridged for "la decencia y decoro" (decency and decorum)—is an apt folk psychological appraisal of the joy of equine friendship or love that has been validated by contemporary cognitive science.[25]

Turning to the second experience I will discuss, pain is one of the most potent indicators of phenomenal consciousness, that is, of the qualitative nature of experience. As philosopher Kristin Andrews explains, paraphrasing Thomas Nagle, a creature has an experience of phenomenal consciousness "if and only if there is something that it is like to be that creature." Measures of phenomenal consciousness therefore have to do with qualia or awareness, and a paradigmatic measure of this, in scientific animal studies, is that of pain. Unlike the times of Gómez Pereira and Descartes, the overwhelming evidence concerning whether vertebrates (including equids) have phenomenal consciousness is no longer an issue of scientific debate.[26] As Andrews points out, in 2012 a large group of international experts signed "The Cambridge Declaration of Consciousness in Non-human Animals," stipulating that "humans are not unique in possessing the neurological substrates that generate consciousness."[27] For these reasons, it is significant that Cervantes's equids suffer in various ways the slings and arrows of their human masters' misfortunes. Both animals suffer in numerous scenes from physical and emotional pain, sometimes indicating as much with "intentional behaviors." For just one such example, the equid duo suffer the deliberate malice of others. Alves points out the importance of the scene with the furze, highlighting the narrator's tender remarks about the "poor animals" who are helped by the knight and squire after they are thrown from their mounts:

> Al entrar [en la ciudad] . . . [dos muchachos] traviesos y atrevidos, se entraron por toda la gente, y, alzando el uno de la cola del rucio, y el otro la de Rocinante, les pusieron y encajaron sendos manojos de aliagas. Sintieron los pobres animales las nuevas espuelas, y, apretando las colas, aumentaron su disgusto de manera, que, dando mil corcovos, dieron con sus dueños en tierra.

> [A]s they entered [the city] . . . [two boys] who were particularly mischievous and impudent made their way through all the people, and one lifted the gray's tail and the other lifted Rocinante's, and there they placed and inserted branches of furze in each one. The poor animals felt these new spurs, and when they

> passed down their tails, they increased their discomfort to such an extent that they reared and bucked a thousand times and threw their riders to the ground.[28]

In terms of conscious awareness, anthropomorphizing the animals' reactions to the furze is scientifically sound, as they react with intentional behaviors including rearing and bucking. Here and in other scenes, as Ordóñez and others have pointed out, the animals' suffering is directly linked to that of their human riders who get knocked off their mounts. In another case of such emotional pairing, after the final battle with the Knight of the White Moon, the narrator first describes Don Quijote's defeat and then Rocinante's: "Levantaron a don Quijote, descubriéronle el rostro y halláronle sin color y trasudando. Rocinante, de puro malparado, no se pudo mover por entonces" (They picked up Don Quixote, uncovered his face, and found him pale and perspiring. Rocinante had been so badly hurt that he could not move).[29] This narrative technique sets up Don Quijote and Rocinante as a pair of characters about whom the narrator feels obliged to comment, in parallel experiences of pain.[30]

In conclusion, animals are an important, albeit traditionally overlooked, feature of Cervantes's oeuvre. Their experiences are relevant, and appreciating them leads to a deeper understanding of *Don Quijote*. First, in order of importance, Rocinante accompanies Don Quijote in more episodes than does his squire; the horse sometimes decides where Don Quijote will travel, while at other times he involves him and Sancho inadvertently in adventures (like that of the Yanguesans). Second, the donkey, for whom Sancho professes love and other emotions, explicitly feels fear and pain himself. Both equids demonstrate love to each other and experience their own peripeteia that are interwoven into many episodes and adventures. Their feelings, desires and behaviors are brought to the fore multiple times; for example, in the adventure of the enchanted boat, when the narrator tells of their psychological suffering at being left behind by their human counterparts. In particular here Rocinante, reckless like his master, wants to jump into the river where he might drown; in turn, the donkey utters sounds in complaint but does little, echoing Sancho Panza's protests combined with the squire's lack of action in the episode. Not paying attention to how these animal characters are foils to Don Quijote and Sancho leads to a diminished reading of *Don Quijote*, similar to reading the novel without observing that Cardenio and Diego de Miranda bring to the fore the eponymous character's attributes or deficiencies.

Beyond these two important nonhuman supporting characters, there are many other equids in the novel who play important parts in the plot and more.

For instance, the Vizcayan's rental mule stumbles and occasions the man's failure against Don Quijote; the Knight of the Mirrors' horse is slow to charge and leads to the twenty-something Sansón Carrasco's loss in battle to the fifty-something Don Quijote (part II, chapter 14), an event that prompts an elaborate scheme that ultimately results in Don Quijote's end. In addition, sheep, bovines, and pigs all act in separate episodes in which Don Quijote and Sancho ultimately get pummeled or trampled. Without listing all of the animals exhaustively, a cat attacks Don Quijote's face and evinces self-consciousness, another character looks into the eyes of a goat who seems to understand him, Sancho climbs a tree to escape an enraged boar, a monkey obeys commands to jump on a trickster's shoulder as part of his hoax, and the episode of the lion engages a contemporaneous philosophical debate about animal sentience in a scene that thematizes perspectivism, in this case, about whether animals are purely instinctual or have intentional agency. These animals are characters, and they are portrayed with forms of phenomenal consciousness, in resonance with a contemporary cognitive ethological understanding of nonhuman animals. Cervantes's treatment of animals as characters involves a sophisticated appreciation of how animals perceive, think, and feel. Analyzing the myriad, complex, and often behaviorally-accurate representations of animals in *Don Quijote* brings to the fore not only Cervantes's deep interest in nonhuman animals—most likely based on his personal experiences seeing and engaging with animals in his travels around Spain and other parts of the Mediterranean—but also helps us to appreciate aspects of *Don Quijote* that we might otherwise ignore.

NOTES

1. Kalof, ed., *The Oxford Handbook of Animal Studies*, 1.
2. Few and Tortorici, eds., *Centering*, 1.
3. Alves, *The Animals of Spain*, 58.
4. Martín, "Zoopoética," 448–64. Other significant contributions to animal studies and Cervantes include Beusterien, *Canines*, Rodríguez Mansilla's guest-edited volume of *Romance Notes* and the contributions therein by several authors, including Julia D'Onofrio; and my own *Minding Animals*, especially chapter 4.
5. Cervantes, *El ingenioso hidalgo*, 2, 46: 385; Grossman, trans., *Don Quixote*, 756.
6. De Waal, "What I Learned," n.p.
7. Darwin, *Descent*, 448.
8. Cervantes, *El ingenioso hidalgo*, 2, 17: 160; Grossman, trans., *Don Quixote*, 560.
9. Cervantes, *El ingenioso hidalgo*, 2, 17: 164; Grossman, trans., *Don Quixote*, 563–64.
10. Cervantes, *El ingenioso hidalgo*, 1, 49: 577.
11. See Wagschal, *Minding Animals*, 10, for Pereira, Descartes, and Malebranche.

12. Pereira, *Antoniana Margarita*, 49; see also Alves, *Animals of Spain*, 42.
13. Cervantes, *El ingenioso hidalgo*, 2, 17: 160 (my translation).
14. Martín, "Zoopoética," 459.
15. Alves, *Animals of Spain*, 58. Ordóñez Vila was the first to argue that Rocinante and the donkey should be considered "characters" ("Rocinante y el asno," 57). She provides an excellent case for the animals being almost omnipresent in the two parts and, while not making an argument from the point of view of animal studies, she does mention their suffering.
16. Wagschal, *Minding Animals*, 6.
17. Rocinante is portrayed as having a range of emotions including sadness, fear, joy, lust, love, and fury.
18. Leblanc, *Mind of the Horse*, 11.
19. Leblanc, *Mind of the Horse*, 10.
20. Cervantes, *El ingenioso hidalgo*, 2, 12: 122; Grossman, trans., *Don Quixote*, 528.
21. The most important of which is the lowering of the heart rate, indicating a calming effect. This occurs especially through the sense of touch, at the equids' "preferred grooming sites" (LeBlanc, *Mind of the Horse*, 380).
22. Leblanc, *Mind of the Horse*, 383.
23. Leblanc, *Mind of the Horse*, 383.
24. "A large part of this activation is opioid mediated, accompanied by activation of the serotonergic neurons in the raphe nuclei section of the reticular formation." Leblanc, *Mind of the Horse*, 384.
25. Cervantes, *El ingenioso hidalgo*, 2, 12: 122; Grossman, trans., *Don Quixote*, 528.
26. Andrews rehearses the arguments of biologist Victoria Braithwaite and philosopher Gary Varner, which are based on (a) the presence of nociceptors in the skin of vertebrates that send signals to the spinal cord, and (b) a corresponding area of the animal's brain, usually involving a dopamine system, that is activated along with the nociceptors. Andrews, *Animal Mind*, 63–65.
27. Andrews, *Animal Mind*, 51.
28. Cervantes, *El ingenioso hidalgo*, 2, 61: 508; Grossman, trans., *Don Quixote*, 863.
29. Cervantes, *El ingenioso hidalgo*, 2, 64: 535; Grossman, trans., *Don Quixote*, 887.
30. The equids also seem to suffer from psychological pain (e.g., in the enchanted boat episode). On psychological pain in animals, see Pierce, "Emotional Pain."

BIBLIOGRAPHY

Alves, Abel A. *The Animals of Spain: An Introduction to Imperial Perceptions and Human Interaction with Other Animals, 1492–1826*. Brill, 2011.

Andrews, Kristin. *The Animal Mind: An Introduction to the Philosophy of Animal Cognition*. Routledge, 2015.

Beusterien, John. *Canines in Cervantes and Velázquez*. University of Illinois Press, 2013.

Cervantes Saavedra, Miguel de. *Don Quixote*. Translated by Edith Grossman. Harper Collins Publishers Inc., 2003.

Cervantes Saavedra, Miguel de. *El ingenioso hidalgo don Quijote de La Mancha*. Edited by Luis Murillo. 2 vols. Castalia, 1978.

Darwin, Charles. *The Descent of Man, and Selection in Relation to Sex*. 2 vols. John Murray, 1871.

De Waal, Frans. "What I Learned from Tickling Apes." *New York Times*, April 10, 2011.
Few, Martha, and Zeb Tortorici, eds. *Centering Animals in Latin American History*. Duke University Press, 2013.
Kalof, Linda, ed. *The Oxford Handbook of Animal Studies*. Oxford University Press, 2017.
Leblanc, Michel-Antoine. *The Mind of the Horse: An Introduction to Equine Cognition*. Harvard University Press, 2013.
Martin, Adrienne L. "Zoopoética quijotesca: Cervantes y los estudios de animales." *eHumanista/Cervantes* 1 (2012): 448–64.
Ordóñez Villa, Montserrat. "Rocinante y el asno, personajes cervantinos." *Razón y Fábula* 8 (1968): 57–75.
Pereira, Gómez. *Antoniana Margarita: Reproducción facsimilar de la edición de 1749*. Edited and translated by José Luis Barreiro Barreiro et al. Universidad de Santiago de Compostela, 2000.
Pierce, Jessica. "Emotional Pain in Animals: An Invisible World of Hurt." *Psychology Today* 24 April 2012.
Rodríguez Mansilla, Fernando, ed. "Los estudios de animales y el Siglo de Oro." Special issue of *Romance Notes* 60, no. 3 (2020).
Wagschal, Steven. *Minding Animals in the Old and New Worlds: A Cognitive Historical Analysis*. University of Toronto Press, 2018.

CHAPTER 12

Materializing Cervantes

Object Lessons from His Mediterranean World

CATHERINE INFANTE

> We have to follow the things themselves, for their meanings are inscribed in their forms, their uses, their trajectories. It is only through the analysis of these trajectories that we can interpret the human transactions and calculations that enliven things.
>
> ARJUN APPADURAI, *The Social Life of Things*

What can objects divulge about the communities and lived experiences of the many individuals who crisscrossed the diverse places and spaces of the Mediterranean world? Human and material lives were undeniably interwoven into the fabric of the Sea that Cervantes characterizes so poignantly in many of his works. The accounts of captives, slaves and corsairs, renegades, merchants, and exiles were intimately entangled with objects that made similar trajectories between the shores of the Mediterranean Sea, giving meaning to human experiences and illuminating their encounters and exchanges. In fact, many of the most enigmatic characters that populate the pages of Cervantes's fiction and who live within these borderlands would be largely unrecognizable without the objects that give shape to the characters' narratives. To name just a few, we can think of the Morisco Ricote who returns to Spain to retrieve his buried treasure made up of gold coins and other riches, unsettling the nation's official discourse related to the expulsion of the Moriscos.[1] Other Cervantine characters inhabiting the in-between spaces of Christianity and Islam, such as Rafala, Zoraida, and the Murcian renegade, display a reed or metal cross at crucial points of their narratives to complicate or externalize a certain aspect of their identity.[2] The performance of the false captives in the *Persiles* revolves around their painted canvas, engaging the spectators to make meaning of their theatrical act.[3] In *La gran sultana*, Catalina's dress and accessories illuminate how questions surrounding lineage and blood purity are articulated visually.[4] Finally, one cannot forget Cide Hamete Benengeli's pen that the fictional Muslim historian used to write *Don Quijote*.[5] In sum, Cervantes materializes the frontier spaces that his characters inhabit, and we must follow these objects to untangle "the human transactions and calculations that enliven things," to borrow Arjun Appadurai's phrasing from the epigraph to this essay.[6]

This article responds to a growing interest in early modern "global" objects and considers how these things and their trajectories offer a nuanced understanding of interfaith relationships in Cervantes's Mediterranean world through a new materialist reading of "El amante liberal" (1613).[7] This novella offers a fascinating case study to uncover how references to material culture mark how identities are negotiated within the work and influence cultural encounters among the characters. Amid these objects, Leonisa's North African dress ("hábito berberisco") is described in detail and is of particular importance as it gains protagonism throughout the novella.[8] After Leonisa is taken captive by a crew of Turkish pirates off the coast of Trapani, she eventually becomes the property of a Jewish merchant who lavishly dresses her in gold-embroidered silk attire and a crimson taffeta veil. Like her owner's richly colored garments and fine linens traveling on board the vessel, Leonisa is subjected to the same fate of being avidly desired and exchanged. In fact, as a female captive, her potential buyers objectify her ornately clothed body, blurring the porous boundary between subject and object. In my reading of "El amante liberal," I pause at three points along the dress's trajectory from Cyprus to Sicily to show how it is much more than just a way to add colorful details to her account; Leonisa's dress and its movements play an active role in shaping the social relations among the cast of Muslim, Christian, and Jewish characters.

Dress as Participant

The novella is filled with many references to costume and accessories that initially appear to mark individual membership in collective groups defined by ethnicity, origin, or religion. Right as the story opens, the Sicilian renegade Mahamut explains to his childhood friend Ricardo that he has renounced his Christian beliefs, which is why he now finds himself in a new set of clothes that he detests.[9] Mahamut continues to cite his attire as a visible manifestation of his religious identity as a Muslim, even if he plans to convert back to Christianity and change his clothing once he returns home.[10] "In a culture obsessed with identifying difference through outward signs," as Barbara Fuchs has convincingly argued, "dress became a loaded marker of identity for all involved."[11] In fact, as Inquisition trials reveal, garments were oftentimes interpreted as one of the first signs of "proof" of one's adherence to Islam.[12] Dress was also used to visually catalog alterity in costume books, satiating early modern Europeans' desire to render the world legible and classify diverse sartorial costumes and customs, whether or not it always reflected the reality of how different communities actually clothed themselves in the early modern world.[13]

In Cervantes's novella, however, the ways in which alterity is articulated visually through costume become less important as the problems attached to categorizing differences are made more apparent. As the story develops, Muslims dress as Christians, and Christians clothe themselves in Muslim attire, complicating any notion that dress could superficially define ethnicity, origin, or religion.[14] Within this context of dressing and undressing, Leonisa's North African garb gains increased relevance as a participant. Even though her costume is described as more exquisite than that of the "más rica mora de Fez ni de Marruecos" (richest Moorish woman in Fez or Morocco) and the narrator emphasizes the "foreignness" of her accessories by translating the Arabic *carcajes* as golden bracelets for the audience, there is still no ambiguity surrounding her status as a captive Christian.[15] Furthermore, once we shift our focus from the origin of her dress to the trajectory, the meaning of her costume cannot just be understood as a passive object that either reinforces cultural divides or signals belonging. Instead, the trajectory and movements of her dress tell a much more complicated story of connectivity in the Mare Nostrum, one in which her costume acts as a key participant in the storyline alongside the human characters. Thus, while past scholarship has examined dress in this novella as a means to question identities, this essay instead focuses on the trajectory and materiality of Leonisa's dress as a way to act out human relations.

The role of Leonisa's dress as an active member in the plot becomes evident during the ceremony of the transfer of power to the new viceroy of Cyprus, where Ricardo and Mahamut are among the engaged spectators in the audience. The tent where the ritual takes place amplifies the theatricality of the episode as different characters pass through this makeshift stage, putting on a spectacle for the public. Accompanied by the five hundred janissaries marching in two lines with their muskets and scimitars drawn, the two pashas appear on scene to greet one another with bows and shouts of praise. In the midst of this ceremony, Leonisa and her gown also form part of the action as she is brought on stage by the Jewish merchant. Her North African attire emphasizes the performative aspect of the occasion, acting as a prop to frame Leonisa with the veiling and unveiling of her face. As an active participant in the chain of events, her dress incites intense emotions to possess her, exchange her for money, and ultimately objectify Leonisa. In fact, the language that many of the characters use strengthens this idea as each of them refers to the female captive as a "prenda" (darling, prize) at different points of the novella, using verbal cues to erode the boundaries of subject and object even further.[16] In this sense, her dress functions as an "actant," to use Bruno Latour's language; that is, her clothing participates by provoking others to act in certain ways.[17] The important presence of the dress does not just illuminate some of the connections among the characters, but, rather, it forms part of a network of relations that actively molds and transforms the relationships among individuals in this episode.

The active participation of the costume reveals that there is a shared visual language among the characters. Despite their different backgrounds and circumstances, a variety of Muslim, Christian, and Jewish individuals in the text equally recognize the titillating value of Leonisa's exotically attired body to incite desire. The two pashas and the qadi are quick to admire her, and, according to Leonisa's account, the Jewish merchant clothes her in this way wholly knowing that the costume will intensify her appeal.[18] For Ricardo, encountering Leonisa dressed in this manner revives his passion for her, which he believed to be lost forever.[19] This idea is extended further when the Jewish merchant insists that Leonisa is worth more with the North African dress on her body, and the qadi agrees to pay the additional price specifically because he wants to present her "de aquella manera" (in that way) to the Grand Turk Selim.[20] As such, the qadi hints at the capacity of the dress to act upon others, to provoke certain reactions and emotions, and that the Grand Turk would also admire the detail of the costume adorning the captive's body. Thus, the shared visual language underscores the function of the dress as a participant in negotiating the network of social relations among the characters that buy, sell, and desire to possess the human/object. Returning to the Latourian concept of the dress as actant, her clothing mediates the relationships among the diverse cultures of the Mediterranean, underscoring its capacity not just to connect, but also to transform this network of relations.[21]

Dress as Memory

This initial scene of Leonisa's clothed body presented before the audience is later brought up by the narrator and other characters who, as we will see, call to memory this first moment in which Leonisa appears in the pashas' tent, thus highlighting the close connection between dress and memory. This occurs for the first time when Leonisa and Ricardo have a moment to convene and the presence of the North African apparel bookends their conversation at Halima and the qadi's house. The narrator focuses the reader's attention on Leonisa's body, attired "del mismo modo y traje que cuando entró en la tienda del bajá" (just as she had been when she entered the pasha's tent).[22] Since the scene is marked by a deafening silence, the visual cues are intensified as they guide the characters' interactions with each other. When Ricardo enters the room, Leonisa is looking in the opposite direction and initially perceives nothing except "un mudo y sosegado silencio" (a quiet and calm silence), underscoring the ekphrastic nature of the episode.[23] Finally, as his eyes catch a glimpse of Leonisa donning the dress, the silence breaks in an instant, and all of the memories of the past return to him. As a consequence of the silence that marks the initial meeting of the two captives, the audience is forced to listen to the dress as a messenger of meaning.[24] Clothing and textiles such as Leonisa's attire, as Ann Rosalind Jones and Peter Stallybrass have demonstrated, functioned as "material memory" in the early modern world, storing potent memory systems that connected the past to the present through the garments.[25] In the case of Ricardo, Leonisa's costume goes beyond inciting desire as it did in its first iteration in the novella; this time, it serves as a mnemonic device that conjures his memory of what he had believed to be lost, seeing his soul up for "auction."[26] Ricardo is overcome with a mix of fear and happiness that reminds him of this recent past encoded in Leonisa's dress.

The North African costume also acts as a repository of memory for Leonisa as she carries traces of her experience as a captive on her body. After Ricardo finally has a chance to ask Leonisa to tell him the story about how she escaped from the corsairs and ended up with the Jewish merchant, she relies on her clothing as a material reminder of this incident. When Leonisa reaches the end of her account and begins to describe how and why the merchant sold her, she recalls the uncomfortable sexual advances and the fear she experienced during these exchanges. As she remembers, the merchant finally decided to get rid of her with the hope of selling her to one of the two pashas. At this moment in the narrative, Leonisa makes reference to her dress as proof of her account, assuring Ricardo that she is standing before him, attired in North African costume, because the merchant believed that this would increase her purchase price, as was the case.[27] For Leonisa, then, the dress participates in the production of memory of her experience as a captive, acting as a prop to validate her account. The gown that has accompanied her throughout her journey abroad continues to take on new meanings with each movement but always carries with it the memory of captivity.

Dress as Nexus

The last stop on the gown's trajectory takes place upon the characters' return to their native Trapani. Ricardo recreates a parallel spectacle to that of the transfer of power in the pashas' tent back in Cyprus, with Leonisa's dress serving as the centerpiece and material connection between the shores of the Mediterranean. When the crew sees their homeland, Ricardo richly decorates the vessel with colorful streamers and silk flags, gaining a large audience's attention at the harbor. As if taking advantage of the multitude of spectators, Ricardo then orders Leonisa to put on her North African dress, arousing admiration and wonder in the onlookers. When they finally disembark in a procession, Leonisa is the main attraction, accompanied by Mahamut and Ricardo attired in Turkish fashion. This spectacle mirrors the one that took place in Cyprus, not just because Leonisa is dressed "de la misma manera que cuando entró en la tienda de los bajáes" (in the same way as when she entered the pashas' tent), but also because of the heightened theatricality of both episodes.[28] Like the audience gathered to witness the celebration of the new viceroy, now a large crowd assembles to observe the arrival of the vessel and to listen "con gusto y con silencio" (with pleasure and silence) to Ricardo's presentation alongside the elegantly dressed cast of characters.[29] This time, however, Ricardo lifts Leonisa's taffeta veil from her face at just the right moment to highlight the dramatic tension of his performance. Finally, instead of the pashas and the qadi disputing over who will present Leonisa as a gift, Ricardo offers the Christian captive before admitting that she is not his to give away.

Despite his claims to have Leonisa dress up to enact a "graciosa burla" (amusing trick), Ricardo's actions suggest that he is actually more interested in watching how the townspeople will react and take in his performance.[30] In fact, the effect of his perplexing "trick" appears to be more for the audience in early modern Spain; inciting them to question engrained assumptions about fashioning collective identities, it lays bare the performative nature of recounting

Mediterranean experiences. With the North African dress as an active participant in the performance, it unveils some of the similarities among the diverse troupe of characters that are only superficially masked with their colorful costumes. As Barbara Fuchs and Carroll Johnson, among others, have suggested, the captives' parallel experience in Cyprus and Trapani underscores the dissipating frontiers between Christianity and Islam, effectively weaving together the interconnected shores of the Mediterranean.[31] Expanding on this idea, I want to pause for a moment to focus on the materiality of Leonisa's dress and its particular role in mediating Mediterranean cultures and subjectivities. Given its movements and trajectory between places and peoples, Leonisa's North African costume intertwines the lives of characters while also connecting the narrative threads of the novella.

Looking back at the genesis of her dress, it begins with the Jewish merchant who first clothes her in it. Including this character as a relevant part of the plot does not seem to be a coincidence, as various contemporary records attest to Jewish merchants' connections to the interwoven world of the textile trade.[32] In addition to Leonisa's dress, the merchant in "El amante liberal" travels on board his ship with finely spun woolen fabric in a variety of colors, linen cloth made for different uses, and other items to trade on his routes between North Africa and the eastern Mediterranean.[33] We could, of course, look at many sources illuminating the historical connections brought to light through Cervantes's fiction, as various scholars have done.[34] However, what interests me here is not necessarily the historical reality of the Jewish merchant connected to the textile market in Cervantes's novella, but rather how we might read the materiality of Leonisa's dress within this context.

The mobility of different clothes and garments, including the captive's North African costume, alongside the circulation of slaves and merchants, subtly hints at the regular exchanges and reuses of the materials that make up Leonisa's dress. Even though the attire first appears in the possession of the Jewish merchant, the very nature of this character's trade activities makes delineating a certain point of the dress's origin more convoluted and much less relevant to define. Cervantes alludes to a similar case in *La gran sultana* (1615) when another female captive, doña Catalina de Oviedo, dons a dress in "Spanish" fashion.[35] The captive's apparel is also brought to her by a Jewish merchant in Algiers, who, in turn, bought it from loot stolen off a corsair boat. Thus, despite qualifiers like "berberisco" that initially appear to mark the origin of Leonisa's dress (or "español" in the case of Catalina's gown), the very materiality of the garments reveals the porousness of any superficial boundaries of belonging attributed to the clothing. In fact, as fashion designer and cultural anthropologist Leyla Belkaïd-Neri has shown, attire in Mediterranean port cities such as Algiers was constantly transforming into what she calls "entangled styles," reflecting the ethnic mixes of the peoples and cultures of each region.[36] The migratory movements of Jews and Muslims from Spain to North Africa initiated by the Catholic kings' conquest of the Iberian Peninsula, followed later by the Morisco expulsion at the start of the seventeenth century, significantly influenced the evolution of North African dress. From exiled Moriscos' contributions to silk production to Sephardic Jews' manufacture of gold thread, Leonisa's green silk dress covered in gold-embroidered braids participates in this economy transformed by the migrations of peoples, techniques, and materials.[37] Considering the materiality of the captive's costume and its movements around the Mediterranean thus actively points to the interwoven human relations of the characters that form part of this world.

The Futures of Objects in Cervantes's Mediterranean

This brief incursion into "El amante liberal" shows us how these object lessons revolving around Leonisa's dress provide a framework for how material culture defines the human dimensions of Mediterranean experiences in unique and meaningful ways. As we have seen, the North African costume acts as an active participant in the plot, producing memory and weaving together the threads of diverse communities, thus reworking deep-rooted notions about fashioning collective identities in the early modern world. As Bruno Latour suggests, literature, in particular, constitutes "a vast playground to rehearse accounts of what makes us act."[38] Cervantes's fiction, then, is an especially productive laboratory to explore the ontological dimension of objects and how individuals and objects interact because human and material lives were so closely interwoven in his Mediterranean and were often subjected to the same fate within this space. Thus, if we continue to follow these objects and consider their active roles beyond mere literary adornment, we will necessarily be in a much better place to unravel the networks of entangled human relations that crisscrossed the same routes of the Sea.

NOTES

1. On the materiality of Ricote's coins, see Leahy, "Dineros en cruzados."
2. Infante, *The Arts of Encounter*, 39–42, 152–56.
3. Infante, "Captive Audiences," 228–30.
4. Infante, "Relatos de cautiverio."

5. López-Baralt, "The Supreme Pen," 505–18.
6. Appadurai, "Introduction," 5.
7. The rapidly expanding bibliography on early modern "global" objects is extensive. For a general introduction, see Findlen, "Early Modern Things;" Gerritsen and Riello, "The Global Lives of Things;" Martin and Bleichmar, "Objects in Motion."
8. Cervantes, "El amante liberal," 129.
9. Cervantes, "El amante liberal," 111.
10. Cervantes, "El amante liberal," 126, 134.
11. Fuchs, *Passing for Spain*, 7.
12. Bennassar and Bennassar, *Los cristianos de Alá*, 368–76.
13. Wilson, *The World in Venice*, 70–132.
14. Cervantes, "El amante liberal," 151, 155.
15. Cervantes, "El amante liberal," 129. All translations into English are my own unless otherwise noted.
16. Cervantes, "El amante liberal," 132, 138, 140, 157.
17. Latour, *Reassembling the Social*, 54–55.
18. Cervantes, "El amante liberal," 129, 144.
19. Cervantes, "El amante liberal," 141.
20. Cervantes, "El amante liberal," 132.
21. Latour, *Reassembling the Social*, 39. Unlike mere intermediaries, as Latour explains, mediators have the capacity to "transform, translate, distort, and modify the meaning or the elements they are supposed to carry."
22. Cervantes, "El amante liberal," 141.
23. Cervantes, "El amante liberal," 141.
24. I draw on Lorraine Daston's urging that we listen to "things that talk." Daston, "Introduction: Speechless," 9–24.
25. Jones and Stallybrass, *Renaissance Clothing*, 200.
26. Cervantes, "El amante liberal," 132.
27. Cervantes, "El amante liberal," 144.
28. Cervantes, "El amante liberal," 155.
29. Cervantes, "El amante liberal," 156.
30. Cervantes, "El amante liberal," 155.
31. Fuchs, *Passing for Spain*, 73–80; Johnson, *Cervantes and the Material World*, 119–42. As I alluded to in the previous two paragraphs, Leonisa is not the only one dressed in colorful attire; the former captives also don the garments of the Turks they have killed. However, as I argue, the meaning of Leonisa's dress arises from its trajectory and materiality—elements that Cervantes emphasizes specifically with Leonisa, in contrast to the other costumes in the plot.
32. Hegyi, *Cervantes and the Turks*, 238–44.
33. Cervantes, "El amante liberal," 143.
34. See especially Ottmar Hegyi's comprehensive analysis in *Cervantes and the Turks*, 215–76.
35. Cervantes, *La gran sultana*, 427.
36. Belkaïd-Neri, "Entangled Styles," 116.
37. Belkaïd-Neri, "Entangled Styles," 119–24; Jansen, "Keswa Kebira," 102–4; Mann, "Textiles Travel," 49–53.
38. Latour, *Reassembling the Social*, 55.

BIBLIOGRAPHY

Appadurai, Arjun. "Introduction: Commodities and the Politics of Value." In *The Social Life of Things: Commodities in Cultural Perspective*, edited by Arjun Appadurai. Cambridge University Press, 1986.

Belkaïd-Neri, Leyla. "Entangled Styles: Mediterranean Migration and Dress in Premodern Algiers." In *The Mobility of People and Things in the Early Modern Mediterranean: The Art of Travel*, edited by Elisabeth A. Fraser. Routledge, 2019.

Bennassar, Bartolomé, and Lucile Bennassar. *Los cristianos de Alá: La fascinante aventura de los renegados*. Translated by José Luis Aristu. Nerea, 1989.

Cervantes Saavedra, Miguel de. "El amante liberal." In *Novelas ejemplares*, edited by Jorge García López. Galaxia Gutenberg / Círculo de lectores, 2005.

Cervantes Saavedra, Miguel de. *La gran sultana*. In *Teatro completo*, edited by Florencio Sevilla Arroyo and Antonio Rey Hazas. Planeta, 1987.

Daston, Lorraine. "Introduction: Speechless." In *Things That Talk: Object Lessons from Art and Science*, edited by Lorraine Daston. Zone Books, 2004.

Findlen, Paula. "Early Modern Things: Objects in Motion, 1500–1800." In *Early Modern Things: Objects and Their Histories, 1500–1800*, 2nd ed., edited by Paula Findlen. Routledge, 2021.

Fuchs, Barbara. *Passing for Spain: Cervantes and the Fictions of Identity*. University of Illinois Press, 2003.

Gerritsen, Anne, and Giorgio Riello. "The Global Lives of Things: Material Culture in the First Global Age." In *The Global Lives of Things: The Material Connections in the Early Modern World*, edited by Anne Gerritsen and Giorgio Riello. Routledge, 2016.

Hegyi, Ottmar. *Cervantes and the Turks: Historical Reality Versus Literary Fiction in* La Gran Sultana *and* El amante liberal. Juan de la Cuesta, 1992.

Infante, Catherine. *The Arts of Encounter: Christians, Muslims, and the Power of Images in Early Modern Spain*. University of Toronto Press, 2022.

Infante, Catherine. "Captive Audiences: Performing Captivity in Cervantes's Prose Narrative." In *Drawing the Curtain: Cervantes's Theatrical Revelations*, edited by Adrienne L. Martín and Esther Fernández. University of Toronto Press, 2022.

Infante, Catherine. "Relatos de cautiverio y la circulación de objetos de lujo." In *Un mar de objetos, un mar de personas: musulmanes y cristianos en el Mediterráneo en las edades media y moderna*, edited by Borja Franco Llopis and Francisco J. Díaz del Campo. Universidad de Granada, 2024.

Jansen, M. Angela. "Keswa Kebira: The Jewish Moroccan Grand Costume." *Khil'a* 1 (2005): 79–105.

Johnson, Carroll B. *Cervantes and the Material World*. University of Illinois Press, 2000.

Jones, Ann Rosalind, and Peter Stallybrass. *Renaissance Clothing and the Materials of Memory*. Cambridge University Press, 2000.

Latour, Bruno. *Reassembling the Social: An Introduction to Actor-Network Theory*. Oxford University Press, 2005.

Leahy, Chad. "'Dineros en cruzados': The Morisco Expulsion, Numismatic Propaganda, and the Materiality of Ricote's Coins." *Hispanic Review* 84, no. 3 (Summer 2016): 273–98.

López-Baralt, Luce. "The Supreme Pen (Al-Qalam Al-A'lā) of Cide Hamete Benengeli in *Don Quixote*." *Journal of Medieval and Early Modern Studies* 30, no. 3 (2000): 505–18.

Mann, Vivian B. "Textiles Travel: The Role of Sephardim in the Transmission of Textile Forms and Designs." In *From Catalonia to the Caribbean: The Sephardic Orbit from Medieval to Modern Times*, edited by Federica Francesconi, Stanley Mirvis, and Brian M. Smollett. Brill, 2018.

Martin, Meredith, and Daniela Bleichmar. "Objects in Motion in the Early Modern World." *Art History* 38, no. 4 (2015): 604–19.

Wilson, Bronwen. *The World in Venice: Print, the City, and Early Modern Identity*. University of Toronto Press, 2005.

PART IV

BURIED HISTORIES

CHAPTER 13

Cervantine Allusions

SUSAN BYRNE

Late twentieth-century scholars described the "aesthetic distance" between readers and texts from earlier centuries, and called for reconstructive readings to allow for perception of a literary work "within its discursive space."[1] These critical voices implicitly affirmed a much earlier paradigm for textual understanding, that of sixteenth-century Italian jurist Andrea Alciato, who insisted that for full comprehension, the legal volumes of sixth-century Emperor Justinian should be read alongside contemporaneous writings in philosophy, history and creative letters.[2] That is, the optimum method for deep textual understanding is a historically informed philological interdisciplinarity. Closing the aesthetic distance between ourselves and the writings of Miguel de Cervantes is best achieved with that same hybrid approach, as the Spanish author manipulates not only language, but also genre norms and theoretical principles of his day to structure sociohistorical commentaries into his fictional texts. Exploiting Aristotelian rhetorical maxims on *inventio*, *elocutio* and *dispositio*, Cervantes highlights specific words (*elocutio*) to signal ideas (*inventio*) inserted into literary passages. Close philological study of these lexical ciphers reveals the complexity of his textual structures (*dispositio*). The *elocutio* are allusions, tropes around which the author builds his texts. It is notoriously difficult for later readers to grasp the deliberately enigmatic references contained in such allusive messaging, but Cervantes's *elocutio* function as covert clues to his deeper meanings. Classically considered a substitution or misdirection to indicate a secondary expressive meaning, Cervantine allusions literally do signal *sub-rosa* cultural connotations.

Don Quijote, for example, contains multiple references to contemporaneous legal matters.[3] Some are explicit statements by the protagonist, who asserts that the very goal of literature (*letras humanas*) is to assure for society "la justicia distributiva y . . . hacer que las buenas leyes se guarden" (distributive justice . . . and give surety that good laws are followed).[4] That is, this new prose genre is a place of not only poetic but true justice. Further to such open statements, Cervantes inserts carefully couched hints on specific legal processes, such as a one-word change to Don Quijote's motto, from "desfacer tuertos" (undo wrongs) to "desfacer fuerzas" (undo forcings).[5] This understated yet substantial allusion signals a commentary on a contentious legal process regarding the refusal of ecclesiastical courts to grant appeals. For centuries, critical editions glossed this changed phrasing in the episode of the galley slaves as merely synonymic. However, that one-word change in motto (*elocutio*) reveals an inner message (*inventio*), critical of the king and of the controversial appellate court procedure called "way of force" (*vía de fuerza*). The author's creative *dispositio* in the episode includes a dramatized appeals court replete with religious and civil forensic language leading to a chaotic, anarchic resolution. One restrained yet very precise juridical allusion hints at the deeper, multi-layered commentary that governs the passage's structure.

A second example from the same novel glosses an artistic disciplinary and philosophical topic. In the *Quijote*'s episode with Knight of the Green Cloak Don Diego de Miranda, Cervantes's protagonist signals a complex theoretical observation on creative letters with one intellectually informed allusion. The pointed *elocutio* in this case is the use of the term "essences" for "sciences." While recommending the proper education for guardians in books VI and VII of the *Republic*, Plato privileges dialectic as the apex of all sciences, the primary route to the ultimate good, and the science to which all others are in service. In his fifteenth-century commentary on that text, Italian philosopher Marsilio Ficino agrees, further placing dialectic in the exalted company of theology and metaphysics. For both the Greek philosopher and his Italian translator, dialectic is served by the other sciences and it serves them.[6] Esteemed as the optimum higher-order intellectual activity, it is unique in its principles and functioning. Ficino adapts the reasoning of Saint Thomas of Aquinas regarding "essence" as the object of intellectual thought, as he further develops the concept.[7] More than an ideal for the Italian philosopher, essence is principle and cause, existence and agent: "in terms of the intellect, 'science' means the essence acquired by the dialectician, and true knowledge follows this essence."[8]

The echo and adaptation of the above in Cervantes's novel is remarkable. Don Quijote directly follows Ficino with his own use of "essences" for "sciences," but he replaces dialectic with poetry: "La poesía . . . es como una doncella tierna . . . a quien tienen cuidado de enriquecer, pulir y adornar otras muchas doncellas, que son todas las otras ciencias, y ella se ha de servir de todas, y todas se han de autorizar con ella . . . quien la sabe tratar la volverá en oro purísimo" (Poetry . . . is like a sweet damsel . . . who should be enriched, polished and adorned by many other damsels, who are all the other sciences; she must serve herself of them, and they must all find their authority in her . . . he who knows how to treat her will turn her into the purest gold).[9] As with dialectic for Plato and Ficino, Cervantes's one most important essence-science, poetry, serves and is served by all others.[10] It also leads to the ultimate good, or as Cervantes calls it here, the "purest gold." The key difference in Cervantes's novel is that poetry has replaced dialectic. Having studied Latin and Greek, Don Diego's son has made it through "el primer escalón de las esencias" (the first rung of the essences) that will lead him to the mountain peak of human letters, his chosen career in poetry.[11]

As the art of dispute that aims to discern truth and differentiate it from falsehood, dialectic implies two or more interlocutors. In contrast, Cervantes opts for the pinnacle of human endeavor as poetry, the art of a single voice. Eclipsing the invention versus mimesis debates of his day, the Spanish author privileges the voice of one human artist refracting the world through an individual perspective, and thus advocates for constitutive rather than mimetic art, truth as seen through and in that one human lens. Further, this truth comes from rather than being revealed to the human artist; art is made and judged by terrestrial rather than celestial criteria. Following the acquisition of the essences, a literary theurgy can be realized. Such a secular celebration of the power of one creative voice will not be commonplace until the Romantic period, two centuries later. The very precise use of essences for sciences is a richly nuanced allusion directing readers to the philosophical poetics embedded in the creative text.

At times, the sheer amount of cultural referents buried in one Cervantine text can be breathtaking. A prime example of such abundance is the detailed socioreligious praxis coded into a plethora of clues in Cervantes's short story "El coloquio de los perros."[12] In this case, multiple details announce the encrypted allusion: the title word *coloquio*; the use of two dogs as interlocutors; the seemingly off-hand mention of a Jesuit school attended by the son of one character; and the critiques of gossip and ambition. Those choices (*elocutio*) highlight the narrative structure and theme (*dispositio*) that confirm Cervantes's *inventio*, which in this case is recovered by reading the story in parallel with Jesuit documentation on the *conspectus*, or examination of conscience.

The Company, as the Society of Jesus was known, was formally founded with just ten members in 1540 but by 1599 it had grown to over eight thousand.[13] When Miguel de Cervantes was six years old, his hometown of Alcalá de Henares became the site for the first Jesuit building dedicated specifically to the practice of Ignatius's Spiritual Exercises, and documentation shows rotating waiting lists of twenty men at a time for the building at Alcalá.[14] To announce public lectures, members would parade through the streets with children ringing bells and singing the catechism. Some sectors of Spanish society opposed the Company as a polemical, theatrical newcomer.[15] During the same years that Cervantes studied in Madrid, his own teacher tried to impede the founding of a Jesuit *colegio* in that city as it would have been in direct competition with his own school.[16] In Italy shortly thereafter, Cervantes served as steward in the house of Julio Acquaviva, brother of Jesuit Rodolfo and nephew of another, Claudio, who by 1581 would be elected Superior General of the Society of Jesus.[17]

Given those personal connections and the public-facing theatricality, it cannot surprise us that in "El coloquio de los perros," Cervantes displays a highly engaged knowledge of Jesuit practices. In the preceding story of the collection, a soldier undergoing treatment for syphilis at the Hospital of the Resurrection in Madrid catches up on news with a friend. He relates a conversation overheard through the hospital window and, astonishingly, tells his friend that the speakers were two dogs named Cipión and Berganza. That novel then commences with those two canine characters remarking on the miracle of speech suddenly afforded them. As Berganza speaks, Cipión offers both critical and supportive commentary.

Cervantes's "El coloquio de los perros" has most frequently been read in formal relation to sixteenth-century dialogue models, but those readings have always come with caveats regarding the limited quality and quantity of Cipión's interventions. That same contra-dialogic distinction, however, offers a neat parallel to a different formal model: the spiritual conversation and catechesis practiced by Ignatius and the Jesuits. The Company called its proselytizing tactics "fishing" for souls to confess, and their efforts were quite successful: "En cinco días uvo una vez cerca de 400 destas confessiones" (In five days there were once close to 400 of these confessions).[18] The practice was mandated in the Jesuit *Constitutions* as the first step for one who wished to enter the Company. In a conversation with an existing member, the postulant would confess his life trajectory up to that point of entry. This model plainly fits both the formal and thematic aspects of Cervantes's story: Berganza makes his examination of conscience because he wishes to emulate Cipión's life of good works, and Cipión is Berganza's temporal coadjutor. The two dogs comply in all respects with the mandated roles for each party in such a confession.

A postulant to the Company was asked for his name, age, place of birth, and its nature: legitimate or not.[19] He would provide the names and professions of parents and siblings, clarify his ancestry and reveal any possible heretical findings against predecessors.[20] Questions were posed to the postulant about trade skills, literacy and ethical proclivities, including general mode of conduct from a young age onward, the health of his conscience, and his intellectual sociability along with his suitability for good conversation. Specific academic disciplines, authors and doctrines were addressed, along with prowess in Latin, length of study, natural or willful inclination toward it, agility of memory, and capacity for understanding.

Cervantes's Berganza begins with these last qualities: his memory, understanding, and inclination for study. He highlights canine instincts, understanding and proclivity for discourse, quoting commonplaces about the strong memories of dogs. Berganza makes it personal: "desde que tuve fuerzas para roer un hueso tuve deseo de hablar, para decir cosas que depositaba en la memoria . . . a decir todo aquello que se me acordare" (from the moment I was old enough to gnaw on a bone I wanted to speak, to reveal the things retained in my memory . . . to tell everything I might remember).[21] Throughout the story the canine character emphasizes these factors: "me dejes ahora filosofar un poco; porque si dejase de decir las cosas que en este instante me han venido a la memoria . . . no sería mi historia cabal" (let me philosophize a bit here; for if not allowed to say those things that right now have come into my memory . . . my history will not be complete).[22] Linking these qualities to prowess in Latin, he explicitly notes that reviewing Latin lessons in his memory improved his understanding.

Throughout "El coloquio de los perros," Berganza includes all details required by the Jesuits for the *conspectus*: he was born in Seville to parents of known heritage who worked in the city's slaughterhouse; he had a series of jobs in which, from the start, he demonstrated enough natural inclination so as to be "un águila" (an eagle) in results.[23] He studied at the Jesuit school where he learned Latin, and he also provides details and commentary on other readings, specifically the pastoral novels read aloud by the girlfriend of one of his owners. Berganza reveals the workings of his conscience from an early age by stressing his own judgments on the misdeeds of others, such as butchers who "con la misma facilidad matan a un hombre que a una vaca" (will just as easily kill a man as a cow).[24] He expresses horror at a realization that "los pastores eran los lobos" (the shepherds were the wolves), rather than guardians.[25] He confesses his failures in accepting bribes and in working for miscreants, including a witch whose behavior shocked him into a plea to the heavens for relief. With striking specificity, the final experience related by the canine character offers a direct parallel to the life of Ignatius of Loyola, who was wounded in battle then converted: as a performing dog in a theater, Berganza suffered a nearly mortal wound that brought about his conversion. Repenting and recovering, he observed Cipión's service to hospital patients and decided to follow in his footsteps. This final factor provides yet another parallel, as from the start such hospital service was one of the Company's predilective activities.

For his part, Berganza's interlocutor Cipión perfectly conforms to the prescribed Jesuit coadjutor role for a confessor, who is directed to speak infrequently and only when necessary, with the goal of helping the postulant recognize and amend his greatest defect.[26] In Berganza's case this is "murmuring" or "gossip," a quite pointed allusion by Cervantes as the Jesuits prided themselves on avoiding it at all costs. In the *Constitutions*, in their letters and in their shared advice to each other, they consistently tout their avoidance of gossip (*murmuración*), and references to this vice are found throughout the novella.[27] Cipión counsels: "Vete a la lengua" (watch your tongue) and Berganza insists: "que no me tengas por largo y por murmurador" (I don't wish to be taken for a mouthy gossip), only for Cipión to relent: "consentiré que murmures un poco de luz y no de sangre" (I will let you gossip just a little, but only if your manner and presentation is lighthearted).[28] Berganza begins to catch himself as he falls into the act, and Cipión interjects to praise this self-restraint: "Aprovechándote vas, Berganza, de mi aviso" (You are doing well, Berganza, in following my advice).[29] Both dogs stress the need to judge the intention of a gossiper and, tellingly, Cervantes's fullest exploration of the topic takes place during the section of the story dedicated to the merchant of Seville who, due to ambition, yet another topical concern of the Company's members, sends his children to a Jesuit school.[30] Berganza complains of the difficulty in avoiding gossip: "con ser un animal, como soy, a cuatro razones que digo me acuden palabras a la lengua como mosquitos al vino, y todas maliciosas y murmurantes . . . el hacer y el decir mal lo heredamos de nuestros primeros padres y lo mamamos en la leche" (being an animal, as I am, even for four points I might make, words stick to my tongue like mosquitoes to wine, all of them malicious and gossipy . . . this doing and speaking of evil we inherit from our parents, and we drink it in at our mother's breast).[31] Cipión responds "no murmuremos de aquí adelante" (let's not gossip from here on), but only to quickly add, "sigue tu cuento, que le dejaste en la autoridad con que los hijos del mercader tu amo iban al estudio de la Compañía de Jesús" (continue with your story, which you left off at the attitude with which the sons of the merchant your master went to the Jesuit school).[32] The dogs speak of biting their tongues to avoid gossip, as they correlate the vice to two key activities that further emphasize the Jesuit connection: preaching and philosophizing. At one point Cipión accuses Berganza of being a hypocrite for his broken promise on gossiping and once more, the lexical specificity is noteworthy: the word hypocrite was used early on to insult Ignatius and his followers, with even the word "Jesuit" taking on a pejorative meaning of "religious hypocrite."[33]

In short, in "El coloquio de los perros" Cervantes dramatizes a Jesuit confession of conscience, with explicit praise for the Company's educational practices accompanied by a canine study of the traits most shunned by the members of the same group: ambition, gossip, and hypocrisy. Use of the word colloquy in the title confirms the author's intent, as the daily Jesuit spiritual exercises were stipulated to begin with a prayer followed by precepts, key points to consider, then a colloquy to close. Company members stressed the importance of these colloquies, and praised those who excelled at them: supposedly, those of Jesuit co-founder Peter Faber were powerful enough to draw water from a stone.[34]

One final point on Cervantes's use of canines as interlocutors: although Spain already had a long history of groups insulting each other as "dogs," during the second half of the sixteenth century the epithet became commonly used throughout Europe for the Jesuits, apparently beginning with Peter Canisius, whose last name held the Latin root word "can," or dog. The Jesuits themselves began to appropriate the moniker, and one early Jesuit writer, referencing the biblical Isaías, described his companion Jesuits as "canes muti" or "mute dogs."[35] Cervantes gave those dogs the gift of speech. The allusions to contemporaneous Jesuit practices would have been very hard for his early public to miss, yet the chronological distance between his day and our own has buried this social message, leaving later readers with an entertaining but inscrutable tale. Full cultural contextualization clarifies this story's thematic underpinnings and also allows us to grasp the extraordinary sophistication of its artistic and generic structure. Whether to see admiring allegory or parody of the confessional practice is left, as such choices always are with Cervantes, to the individual reader.

For critical literary praxis, everything old should be new again. An interdisciplinary philological approach that incorporates the author's sociohistorical context as well as theoretical and rhetorical principles of his day is optimum for Cervantes's complex creative texts with their manifold enigmatic allusions. With this hybrid critical approach, we close the aesthetic distance between his day and our own. The reward is a deeper understanding of the author's artistic prowess in both formal and thematic terms.

NOTES

1. For "aesthetic distance" see Jauss, "Literary History," 14. For "discursive space" see Olivares, "Soy un fue," 389.
2. Drysdall, "Alciato and the Grammarians," 695.
3. See Susan Byrne, *Law and History in Cervantes'* Don Quixote.
4. Cervantes, *El ingenioso hidalgo*, 339. All translations of this and other Spanish texts are my own, unless otherwise noted.
5. Cervantes, *El ingenioso hidalgo*, 183.
6. Ficino, *Divini Platonis*, 419.
7. Sepich, "Estudio preliminar," 22. For Aquinas, the essence as object of study is an exploration of the category of being.
8. "Rursus in intelligentia scientiam quidem dicit essentiam consequi ad dialecticum pertinentem, cognitionem vero sequi essentiam." Ficino, *Divini Platonis*, 419.
9. Cervantes, *El ingenioso hidalgo*, 565–66. The use of "essences" with this meaning is unique for Cervantes's day: see Byrne, "'Essentiae,'" 14–19.
10. Ficino, *Divini Platonis*, 419.
11. Cervantes, *El ingenioso hidalgo*, 566.
12. See also Byrne, "Coloquio, murmurar, *canes muti*: Cervantes y los jesuitas."
13. Padberg, "Development of the *Ratio Studiorum*," 80.
14. O'Malley, *The First Jesuits*, 55 and 129; Iparraguirre, *Historia de los ejercicios de san Ignacio*, II:235.
15. Astrain, *Historia de la Compañía de Jesús*, 1905, 73–127; and 1909, 307–46.
16. Alvar Ezquerra, *Un maestro en tiempos de Felipe II*, 297.
17. Aldea Vaquero, *El cardenal infante Don Fernando*, 62n86.
18. Polanco, *Polanci complementa*, I:209.
19. The specific *conspectus* steps are found in the Jesuit *Monumenta* series of the Constitutions: *Monumenta Ignatiana*. I use the pronouns "he" and "his" for ease of reference, although we know that the ranks of Jesuit postulants did include women.
20. These two factors were obviously related to the blood purity statutes, although there is no specific indication of rejection on either basis: "si uiene de christianos antiguos o modernos" and "algunos herrores contra la nuestra religión christiana"; Jesuits, *Monumenta*, II:31.
21. Cervantes, *Novelas*, II:301.
22. Cervantes, *Novelas*, II:318.
23. Cervantes, *Novelas*, II:302.
24. Cervantes, *Novelas*, II:303.
25. Cervantes, *Novelas*, II:311.
26. Cipión's minimalist interventions have problematized readings of "El coloquio de los perros" as dialogue. Iparraguirre recommends infrequency of interjections in *Historia*, II:251. On goals, see O'Malley, *The First*, 142.
27. Byrne, "Coloquio," 88. Other scholars have addressed the attention paid to *murmuración* in the text, but none in relation to the Jesuits.
28. Cervantes, *Novelas*, II:304, 306, and 306, respectively.
29. Cervantes, *Novelas*, II:308.
30. Saint Ignatius of Loyola, *Constitutiones Societatis Jesu*, *Monumenta*, CXXV-CXXVII.
31. Cervantes, *Novelas*, II:315.

32. Cervantes, *Novelas*, II:315.
33. *Diccionario histórico*, I:179.
34. Rosephii, "P. Gregorii Rosephii promptuarium," 3:516.
35. Ramírez de Oviedo, in a letter to Laínez. Laínez, *Lainii monumenta*, 314.

BIBLIOGRAPHY

Aldea Vaquero, Quintin. *El cardenal infante Don Fernando o la formación de un príncipe de España: Discurso leído el día 16 de febrero de 1997 en su recepción pública*. RAE, 1997.

Alvar Ezquerra, Alfredo. *Un maestro en tiempos de Felipe II: Juan López de Hoyos y la enseñanza humanista en el siglo XVI*. La Esfera de los Libros, 2014.

Astrain, Antonio. *Historia de la Compañía de Jesús en la Asistencia de España*. Administración de Razón y Fe, 1905.

Byrne, Susan. *Law and History in Cervantes' Don Quixote*. University of Toronto Press, 2012.

Byrne, Susan. "Coloquio, murmurar, canes muti: Cervantes y los jesuitas." In "Un paseo entre los centenarios cervantinos," edited by Robert Lauer and Caterina Ruta, special issue of *Cuadernos* AISPI 5 (2015): 81–95.

Byrne, Susan. "'Essentiae' in Ficino y en el Quijote (II, 6)," in *La obra de Cervantes ayer y hoy*, edited by Nuria Murgado and Lía Schwartz. Hispanic Seminary of Medieval Studies, 2016.

Cervantes Saavedra, Miguel de. *El ingenioso hidalgo Don Quijote de la Mancha*. 2 vols. Edited by Celina Sabor de Cortazar and Isaías Lerner. Eudeba, 2005.

Cervantes Saavedra, Miguel de. *Novelas ejemplares*. 2 vols. Edited by Harry Sieber. Cátedra, 1997.

Diccionario histórico de la Compañía de Jesús. Edited by Charles E. O'Neill and Joaquín María Domínguez. Institutum Historicum, 2001.

Drysdall, Denis L. "Alciato and the Grammarians: The Law and the Humanities in the *Parergon iuris libri duodecim*." *Renaissance Quarterly* 56 (Autumn 2003): 695–722.

Ficino, Marsilio. *Divini Platonis Opera Omnia: Marsilii Ficini interprete*. Antonium Vicentium, 1557.

Iparraguirre, Ignacio. *Historia de los ejercicios de san Ignacio*. El mensajero del corazón de Jesús, 1955.

Jauss, Hans Robert. "Literary History as a Challenge to Literary Theory." Translated by Elizabeth Benzinger. *New Literary History* 2, no. 1 (1970): 7–37.

Jesuits. *Monumenta Ignatiana, ex autographis vel ex antiquioribus exemplis collecta. Series tertia: Sancti Ignatii de Loyola Constitutiones Societatis Jesu*, vol. II. Typis Pontificiae Universitatis Gregorianae, 1936.

Laínez, Diego. *Lainii monumenta*. G. López del Horno, 1912.

Loyola, Saint Ignatius of. Constitutiones Societatis Jesu. Monumenta Constitutionum Praevia. Borgo S. Spirito, 1934.

Olivares, Julián. "Soy un fue, y un será, y un es cansado: Text and Context." *Hispanic Review* 63, no. 3 (1995): 387–410.

O'Malley, John W. *The First Jesuits*. Harvard University Press, 1993.

Padberg, John W., SJ. "Development of the Ratio Studiorum." In *The Jesuit Ratio Studiorum: 400th Anniversary Perspectives*, edited by Vicent J. Duminuco, SJ. Fordham University Press, 2000.

Polanco, Juan Alfonso de. *Polanci complementa, Epistolae et commentaria.* G. López del Horno, 1916.

Rosephii, Gregorii. "P. Gregorii Rosephii promptuarium." In *Fontes narrativi de S. Ignatio de Loyola et de Societatis Iesu Initiis.* Edited by Candidus de Dalmases, SJ. Monumenta Historica Societatis Iesu, 1906.

Sepich, Juan R. *Estudio preliminar (Preliminary Study) to Santo Tomás de Aquino: El ente y la esencia.* Universidad de Buenos Aires, 1940.

CHAPTER 14

Epic Bodies and Tombs

Material Readings of Don Quijote, XIX through Juan Latino's Funeral Poetry

MAXIM RIGAUX

Cervantes's allusion to the Black poet and schoolmaster Juan Latino in the preliminaries of the first part of *Don Quijote* (via the fictitious poem by Urganda the Unknown) has often been cited as a curiosity, without attributing much real importance to it. At no point has the possibility that Cervantes would have known, let alone read, the Latin poetry of the former enslaved man of Granada been seriously considered.[1] On the contrary, the image of a Cervantes uncomfortable with Latin dominates our perception and is partly enhanced by the author himself in a series of ironic remarks throughout his oeuvre about the use of Latin in his day. Indeed, Urganda's mock poem, in the passage in question, discourages the author from engaging with Latin in any possible form, since he is no Juan Latino at all:

> Pues al cielo no le plu-
> que salieses tan ladi-
> como el negro Juan Lati-
> hablar latines rehú-.
>
> Since Heaven it hath not pleased on thee
> Deep erudition to bestow,
> Or black Latino's gift of tongues,
> No Latin let thy pages show.[2]

Nevertheless, Cervantes may have had the work of Juan Latino closely in mind when writing the chapter of the "dead corpse" (chapter 19). In particular, the Black poet's second volume of Latin poetry, published in 1576 in Granada by Hugo de Mena, shows affinities with the chapter of the "dead corpse" and helps us to read and interpret Don Quijote's reactions in the episode.

In the winter of 1573–1574, four corpses were transferred from Granada's Royal Chapel to Philip II's El Escorial.[3] This was part of a meticulous plan the king had prepared for several of his deceased relatives to arrive simultaneously from different places at the palace-monastery under construction.[4] On December 28 and 29, the bodies of Isabella of Portugal (1503–1539), Maria Manuela of Portugal (1527–1545), John of Austria (1528–1530) and Ferdinand of Austria (1535–1538), were solemnly bid farewell in Granada. On January 15, the same fate befell the body of Eleanor of Austria (1498–1558) in Mérida. In what must have been a well-organized event, the two processions arrived together in Yuste, between January 25 and 27, from where they would continue their journey to the Escorial in the company of yet another corpse: that of Charles V (1500–1558). Simultaneously, on January 26, the body of Maria of Austria (1505–1558) was removed from her burial place in Valladolid to be sent first to Tordesillas, where the body of Joanna I of Castile (1479–1555) would be added to the procession. Finally, the two bodies were to arrive in the Escorial at exactly the same time as the other six corpses that had been gathered in a single procession.

Juan Latino narrated this event in Latin hexameters. The epic grandeur he bestows on the ceremony becomes clear from the opening lines:

> Catholicum cineres canimus sibi corpora regum,
> Ossaque iungentem mira pietate Philippum,
> Hispanae gentis columen regemque potentem.
> Qui patrem, matrem, fratres cum coniuge sacra,
> Reginasque duas Caroli patrisque sorores,
> Ex variis populis templum transcripsit in unum.
> Quique et avos quondam disiunctos lege maritos
> Coniunxit pompa regali et funere grandi
> Regibus Isabel, Fernando et funere iunctis.

> We sing of Catholic Philip, the cornerstone and mighty king of the Spanish people,
> who unified around him with wondrous piety the ashes, bodies and bones of the royals.

> He transferred his father, his mother, his brothers together with his sacred spouse,
> and the two queen sisters of his father Charles, out of various cities into one temple.
> He also reunited in royal procession and splendid funeral his grandparents,
> once separated though joined in lawful marriage,
> together with the monarchs Isabella and Ferdinand, who were already united in funeral.[5]

The second part of the proem refers to the transfer of the corpse of Philip II's grandmother to Granada. There, as Latino indicates, she would be reunited not only with her husband, Philip I of Castile, but also with her parents, the Catholic Kings. The subject of Latino's heroic poetry is, of course, very different from classical epics like Virgil's *Aeneid*. And yet it came much closer to the historical reality of Philip II, who, unlike his father Charles V, did not intervene personally on the battlefield after his presence at Saint-Quintin (1557). The (re)united corpses of the royal family, both in Granada and the Escorial, are the weapons (*arma*) by which Philip II sought to terrify the heretics of his time.[6]

Cervantes, as a man of his time, was undoubtedly familiar with the many processions and transfers of corpses that took place during his lifetime, especially during the reign of Philip II, who was obsessed with relics and the religious symbolism of the corpses of his deceased family members.[7] In 1587, to give just one example, Cervantes must have witnessed the arrival of the remains of Saint Leocadia in Toledo. As Alban Forcione has observed, Cervantes "was living at the time in the neighboring town of Esquivias, where three days earlier the party escorting the remains of St. Leocadia arrived."[8] From his home, he might have experienced a reaction of surprise and anxiety similar to that of Don Quijote and Sancho Panza with respect to the "dead corpse" of chapter 19. However, perhaps more importantly, Cervantes must have seen as well the many ephemeral decorations such as triumphal arches adorned with (mostly) Latin poetry. His familiarity with the material world of festivities, ephemeral architecture, and writing was certainly enhanced by the numerous accounts that the festive events generated. Cervantes could thus have read the historical account of the festivities in Toledo in Miguel Hernández's *Vida, martyrio, y translación de la gloriosa Virgen, y Mártyr Santa Leocadia* (1591).

In addition to the Latin poems inserted in the final chapters, dedicated to the procession of the corpse of Saint Leocadia through the streets of Toledo, the Jesuit Miguel Hernández added poems in both Latin and the vernacular that were composed for a poetry contest organized by Toledo's Church, as well as the author's epitomized version of the history in Latin hexameters. In writing Chapter 19 of *Don Quijote*, I argue that Cervantes was parodying this "new" mode of epic discourse. Juan Latino calls himself a "*poeta novus*," who will sing of things previously unseen in his age (*res nova*). The *translatio* of eight corpses of royal family members by Philip II was indeed an epic endeavor that had no historical parallel.[9] It is hard to think that Cervantes would not have been informed of this enterprise. Rumors of the event probably reached him as a soldier in Italy. But it is not unlikely that, at a later stage in his life, perhaps in the 1580s after his captive years in Algiers, he came across a copy of Juan Latino's 1576 printed book.

It is generally accepted in modern scholarship that Cervantes was not a good Latinist. Thus, if we read a reference to the classics, it is assumed that Cervantes acquired that knowledge via translation. For example, in the second part of *Don Quijote* (chapter 41), the knight errant refers to an episode of Virgil's *Aeneid* as follows: "*Yo he leído en Virgilio aquello del Paladión de Troya*" (I have read in Virgil of the Palladium of Troy).[10] While much of classical literature had been translated into Spanish by Cervantes's time, such as Virgil's *Aeneid* by Gregorio Hernández de Velasco (1555), the vast body of so-called Neo-Latin literature would have been, if not inaccessible, at least of little interest to a Cervantes ignorant of Latin. However, Cervantes had enjoyed a humanist education at pre-university level under Juan López de Hoyos, so he must certainly have acquired a basic knowledge to read and even write some Latin. In addition, Don Quijote's humanistic discourse in the episode with the Caballero del Verde Gabán underscores the importance of mastering other languages such as Latin. Referring to Don Lorenzo, the knight suggests that Don Diego's son is likely not opposed to vernacular poetry in itself but rather to poets whose expertise is limited to their own vernacular language.[11] It is difficult to imagine, therefore, that an autodidact like Cervantes would automatically have neglected (Neo-)Latin writing, if there was no translation available.

Furthermore, it was almost impossible for Cervantes not to have been confronted with the Latin production of his time. In addition to the Latin texts used for ephemeral architecture, many of the festive accounts included Latin poetry next to vernacular compositions. Indeed, Cervantes's first poems, published in his former teacher's *Historia y relación verdadera de la enfermedad, felicísimo tránsito y suntuosas exequias de la Serenísima Reina de España Isabel de Valois* (1569), a prose account in which the royal corpse of Philip's third wife plays a central role, are printed alongside Latin poems. Cervantes must have shown at least to a certain extent interest in the Latin poetry of his time and the experimental writing of "new" epics, such as the one Juan Latino's 1576 book reveals.

It is ironic, then, that in this particular chapter Don Quijote argues that he does not know any Latin at all, when the *bachiller* Alonso López starts pronouncing a Latin decree that was approved during the Council of Trent:

> —Olvidábaseme de decir que advierta vuestra merced que queda descomulgado por haber puesto las manos violentamente en cosa sagrada, *iuxta illud, «Si quis suadente diabolo»*, etcétera.
>
> —No entiendo ese latín—respondió don Quijote—, mas yo sé bien que no puse las manos, sino este lanzón; cuanto más que yo no pensé que ofendía a sacerdotes ni a cosas de la Iglesia, a quien respeto y adoro como católico y fiel cristiano que soy, sino a fantasmas y a vestiglos del otro mundo.

> I forgot to mention that before he did so he said to Don Quixote, "Remember that you stand excommunicated for having laid violent hands on a holy thing, *juxta illud, si quis, suadente diabolo.*"
>
> "I do not understand that Latin," answered Don Quixote, "but I know well I did not lay hands, only this pike; besides, I did not think I was committing an assault upon priests or things of the Church, which, like a Catholic and faithful Christian as I am, I respect and revere, but upon phantoms and specters of the other world."[12]

Although Don Quijote claims not to understand the Latin of his adversary, in his reply he seems to be aware of the charges that are held against him. The knight's supposed ignorance of Latin resonates with Urganda's advice in the preliminaries to stay as far as possible from Latin. This is impossible, however, given the context in which a basic knowledge of the classical language was paramount in order to correctly interpret the situation.

Frederick A. de Armas has convincingly demonstrated that the episode of the "dead corpse" fits within a larger dialogue that Cervantes holds with the epic tradition in the third part of the novel (chapters 15 through 22). For the specific passage, as de Armas rightly points out, one possible source of influence is the Italian humanist Maffeo Veggio's sequel book XIII to the *Aeneid*, which had been translated into Spanish together with the rest of Virgil's epic by Hernández de Velasco. In book XIII, the Italian humanist narrated the funeral procession by which Turnus's body was returned to his father Daunus. De Armas further notes that "many of the ingredients used by Cervantes come directly from the translation: the dark and silence of the night, the empty fields, the strange sight, the mourning of the participants, and the lighted torches."[13]

More recently, Luce López-Baralt has interpreted chapter 19 in light of the historical transfer of San Juan de la Cruz's corpse from Úbeda to Segovia in 1593. According to López-Baralt, the historical parallels of the episode are intentional and Cervantes's decision to refer to the dead body as "caballero" is an implicit call to the reader to conjure up the mystical texts of San Juan de la Cruz, in particular his poem "Noche oscura."[14] However, the textual allusions that clearly stand out—the darkness of the night, the threatening light of the torches, etc.—are all very similar to those that Maffeo Veggio (and Hernández de Velasco in his translation) put forward in his epic description of the funeral procession of Turnus's body. Instead of looking for concrete parallels with the historical transfer of San Juan de la Cruz, which, I acknowledge, has been very helpful in reading the "dead corpse" passage, we may go one step further and examine how Cervantes anticipates and parodies the expected contemporary reaction to dead bodies in chapter 19. It is evident that Cervantes questions the adequate response one should have when confronted, as are Don Quijote and Sancho Panza, with a dead body in the middle of the night. Without (con)text, the corpse is only a meaningless object to which one must react through an interpretative act.

Juan Latino's 1576 volume of Latin poetry on the transfer of royal bodies from Granada to El Escorial not only describes the historical circumstances of the event in epic discourse, but also offers us a key for how to interpret Don Quijote's (comical) response in the "dead corpse" episode in light of contemporary expectations. Latino's opening Latin hexameters recall many of the ingredients encountered in Veggio's epic description of the funeral procession of Turnus's body and in the historical testimonies relating the transfer of San Juan de la Cruz in the middle of a night in 1593.[15] In the first elegy to his former enslaver, Gonzalo Fernández de Córdoba, the third Duke of Sessa, Latino describes the event with clear references to the burning torches of the servants and the darkness of the night:

> Expectata dies aderat, funusque paratum,
> Regali in templo regia, et ossa suo.
>
> . . .
>
> Tunc et lecticis componunt corpora patres,
> Et proceres humeris, ut retulere suis.
> A dextra laevaque faces portare ministros
> Cernas ardentes, qui vehebantur equis.
>
> . . .

Illic nocte duces servantes pia corpora sanctè,
Pervigilique vices in statione tenent.

The long-awaited day had come, and the funeral was prepared;
the royal bones rested in their proper place in the Royal Chapel.
. . .
Then the priests laid the bodies on litters,
and the nobles bore them back upon their own shoulders.
On the right and left you would see attendants,
who were riding on horseback, carrying burning torches.
. . .
There, at night, the nobles stand guard over the pious bodies
with reverence,
and in sleepless vigil they take turns at their post.[16]

The moment the procession is to leave the Royal Chapel, a personified Granada intervenes and interrupts the narrative. Granada's speech is full of rhetorical pathos and, like Don Quijote, she tries to stop the funeral procession from moving forward. She believes that she is done injustice and urgently demands that the king's delegates correct the unfair situation. A note in the margin affirms this idea: "*Garnata iniuriam cum ducibus Philippi expostulare visa est*" (Granada was seen to be disputing the wrong with Philip's officials).[17]

In addition to the similar "ingredients" we discover between Latino's description of the royal transfers in the winter of 1573–1574 and Don Quijote's fictional encounter with the "dead corpse" in chapter 19, I believe that Latino's 1576 book is also of supreme interest for giving a wealth of material on how Cervantes's contemporaries were prescribed to respond emotionally to the tombs and what they represented. Indeed, Latino's *De Augusta* contains many epigrams that served as epitaphs for the tombs or were placed on ephemeral arches. The poems provided the necessary context for (at least a part of) the public on how to react to the "vision" or visual spectacle of the tombs and dead bodies. The curious Don Quijote wanting to look at the bones of the dead corpse—"Quisiera don Quijote mirar si el cuerpo en la litera era huesos o no" (Don Quijote would have looked to see whether the body in the litter were bones or not)—is similar to the fictional character Viator asking several questions in the epigrams of Latino.[18] In one poem, for example, Viator asks impatiently for more information on whose bodies the tombs contain:

Dic, age, qui reges? Quae nomina? Regna virorum?
Reginasque refer, quae pia vita fuit?

Come on, say it, who are the Kings? Which names do they have?
The kingdoms of which men?
And
tell me of the Queens: whose life was virtuous?[19]

Finally, the idea of life as a spiritual battle is repeatedly mentioned in Latino's poetry. This comes very close also to the image of San Juan de la Cruz as a "caballero espiritual" and the genre of spiritual chivalry books in general. In an epigram for the tomb of Empress Isabella of Portugal, wife of Charles V, the metaphorical concept of "life is a battlefield" (*militia est vita*) is elaborated in more detail:

Militia est hominum, durat dum vita, per orbem,
Non visos hostes, quique videntur habet.
Invisae apparent facies, vultusque duorum,
Non est visibilis tertius in tenebris.

Man's life is a battlefield across the world, enduring as
long as life itself.
It has enemies both unseen and seen.
Loathsome faces appear—the visages of two.
The third is not visible in the darkness.[20]

The heroic image here evoked is taken from the book of Job. The two visible faces are to be understood as the world and the flesh. The third invisible element Latino refers to is the Devil.[21] Like Job, the Catholic Kings of the Habsburg family fight against visible and invisible enemies. As Ann Astell has convincingly demonstrated, the biblical model of Job, together with Boethius's *Consolation of Philosophy*, has had an important influence on the epic tradition in the Middle Ages and the Renaissance, one all too often overlooked in recent literary history.[22] The fact that Cervantes is given the name "Caballero de la Triste Figura" by Sancho in this episode may also be an allusion to this "new" epic model, one that prioritizes the virtues of suffering and consolation.

In conclusion, taking Cervantes's allusion to Juan Latino in the preliminaries of the first part of *Don Quijote* as a serious intertextual hint can be the first step toward considering not only the influence of Neo-Latin literature on the novelist, but also an additional epic-chivalric model for the knight errant: the biblical figure of Job. The quest for "epic truth" is also Don Quijote's quest, and his suffering from both visible and invisible enemies takes on a whole other meaning if we recall Job's sufferings and the role of consolation in Boethius. Moreover, this insight may also inspire new interpretations of Juan Latino's poetry. The "dead corpse" chapter, then, may reveal close affinities of the poet-schoolmaster from Granada with the poetry of San Juan de la Cruz and a more intimate and inner experience of the religious. Despite the obvious ceremonial context of a funeral procession and the spectacle of ephemeral architecture, Latino's epigrams often seem to encourage a personal moment of inwardness.[23] Taking into account Cervantes's engagement with not only the poetic voice of an Afro-Hispanic author but also the larger Neo-Latin tradition may pave the way for a broader discussion, in future Cervantine studies, of two aspects that pervaded the author's life and work: Black people and Latin writings.

NOTES

1. This can be partly explained by the complete neglect, until recently, of critical scholarship on Juan Latino and, more broadly, on Black Africans in Europe. For recent scholarship on Juan Latino and his epic poem, see Wright, *The Epic of Juan Latino*; Lemons, "Juan Latino's Worldly Poetics"; and Rigaux, "Casting the Reader as Eyewitness." On (the recovery of) Black voices in early modern Europe, see, e.g., Lowe and Earle, *Black Africans*, and, more recently, Smith et al., *Early Modern Black Diaspora Studies*.
2. Cervantes, *Don Quijote*, 105. I quote the original Spanish from the *Quijote* edition by John Jay Allen; for the English translation, I refer to John Ormsby's, which is available online at Biblioteca Virtual Miguel de Cervantes.
3. For a synopsis of the historical circumstances, refer to Rigaux, "*Prosopopoeia*," 249–50, and the bibliography quoted there.
4. Construction ended in 1584. For a brief history of the building, see Kubler, *Building the Escorial*.
5. Latinus, *De Augusta*, fol. 1r. All translations into English are mine.
6. The proem is a clear allusion to Virgil's famous opening passage of the *Aeneid*, in which he announces that he will sing of the arms and the man (*arma virumque cano*). For a more detailed discussion of the epic resonances, see Rigaux, "*Prosopopeia*," 251–59.
7. See Eire, *From Madrid to Purgatory*, 260–62, for a brief discussion of this event within the broader framework of the king's ideas about death and the afterlife.
8. Forcione, *Cervantes and the Humanist Vision*, 326–27.
9. If Philip II had a historical model in mind for his enterprise, namely the one Charles the Bold had undertaken a century before, he clearly surpassed his ancestor. In 1473–74, the Duke of Burgundy had removed his parents, Philip the Good and Isabella of Portugal, from their respective burial places in Bruges and Gosnay to Dijon.

10. Cervantes, *Don Quijote,* II:365. Barnés Vázquez uses part of this sentence for the title of his book on Cervantes's engagement with the classical tradition and its literature in translation.
11. Cervantes, *Don Quijote,* II:160: "Pero vuestro hijo, a lo que yo, señor, imagino, no debe de estar mal con la poesía de romance, sino con los poetas que son meros romancistas, sin saber otras lenguas ni otras ciencias que adornen y despierten y ayuden a su natural impulso." (But your son, senor, I suspect, is not prejudiced against Spanish poetry, but against those poets who are mere Spanish verse writers, without any knowledge of other languages or sciences to adorn and give life and vigour to their natural inspiration.)
12. Cervantes, *Don Quijote,* I:275–76.
13. De Armas, *Don Quixote Among the Saracens,* 90.
14. López-Baralt, "Don Quijote ante la caballería espiritual," 23–27.
15. Cervantes, *Don Quijote,* I:272, makes an explicit comparison with the material world of festivities: "Comenzaron a correr por aquel campo, con las hachas encendidas, que no parecían sino a los de las máscaras que en noche de regocijo y fiesta corren" (they set off at a run across the plain with their lighted torches, looking exactly like maskers running on some gala or festival night.)
16. Latino, *De Augusta,* fol. 26v-27r.
17. Latino, *De Augusta,* fol. 27v.
18. Cervantes, *Don Quijote,* I:276.
19. Latino, *De Augusta,* fol. 21v.
20. Latino, *De Augusta,* fol. 24r.
21. Cervantes, *Don Quijote,* I:272 makes the ironic remark by which it is Don Quijote who is seen as the Devil: "porque todos pensaron que aquel no era hombre, sino diablo del infierno, que les salía a quitar el cuerpo muerto que en la litera llevaban" (for they all thought it was no man but a devil from hell come to carry away the dead body they had in the litter).
22. See Astell, *Job, Boethius, and Epic Truth,* 2. However, her book is solely focused on Italy and England. To my knowledge, the reception and influence of Job and Boethius in the early modern Iberian world have not been systematically examined.
23. Interestingly, a nineteenth-century short story, published in the journal *La Alhambra* and entitled "El Campo de los Mártires," narrates the (fictional) encounter between Juan Latino, San Juan de la Cruz, and Diego Hurtado de Mendoza.

BIBLIOGRAPHY

Astell, Ann W. *Job, Boethius, and Epic Truth.* Cornell University Press, 1994.

Barnés Vázquez, Antonio. "Yo he leído en Virgilio." *La tradición clásica en el Quijote.* Editorial Academia del Hispanismo, 2009.

Cervantes, Miguel de. *Don Quijote de la Mancha,* vol. I, 29th ed., edited by John Jay Allen. Cátedra, 2010.

Cervantes, Miguel de. *Don Quijote de la Mancha,* vol. II, 28th ed., edited by John Jay Allen. Cátedra, 2009.

De Armas, Frederick A. *Don Quixote among the Saracens: A Clash of Civilizations and Literary Genres.* University of Toronto Press, 2011.

Eire, Carlos M. N. *From Madrid to Purgatory: The Art and Craft of Dying in Sixteenth-Century Spain.* Cambridge University Press, 1995.

Forcione, Alban K. *Cervantes and the Humanist Vision: A Study of Four Exemplary Novels.* Princeton University Press, 1982.

Kubler, George. *Building the Escorial.* Princeton University Press, 1982.

Latinus, Joannes. *Ad catholicum et invictissimum Philippum Dei gratia Hispaniarum Regem, de Augusta, memorabilia, simul et catholica regalium corporum ex variis tumulis in unum regale templum translatione.* Hugo de Mena, 1576.

Lemons, Andrew. "Juan Latino's Worldly Poetics: Lepanto, Lucretius and Literary Tradition." *Calíope* 21, no. 1 (2018): 57–88.

López-Baralt, Luce. "Don Quijote ante la caballería espiritual de San Juan De La Cruz." *Teoliterária* 12, no. 27 (2022): 20–42.

Lowe, Kate J. P., and Thomas Foster Earle, eds. *Black Africans in Renaissance Europe.* Cambridge University Press, 2005.

Rigaux, Maxim. "Casting the Reader as Eyewitness: Apostrophe and Visualization in Juan Latino's *Austrias Carmen* (1573)." *Hispanic Review* 84, no. 4 (2016): 405–25.

Rigaux, Maxim. "*Prosopopoeia* in the Funeral Poetry of Juan Latino." *eHumanista* 39 (2018): 248–60.

Smith, Cassander L., Nicholas R. Jones, and Miles P. Grier, eds. *Early Modern Black Diaspora Studies: A Critical Anthology.* Palgrave Macmillan, 2018.

Wright, Elizabeth. *The Epic of Juan Latino: Dilemmas of Race and Religion in Renaissance Spain.* University of Toronto Press, 2016.

CHAPTER 15

Visual and Material Culture in Cervantes's Works

The Painted Sargas in Don Quijote

MERCEDES ALCALÁ GALÁN

Studies examining visual culture, material culture, and ekphrasis in Cervantes's works delineate an extensive terrain that remains largely uncharted, notwithstanding the commendable contributions of extant scholarly endeavors concerning artistic representations in his texts.[1] Artworks are frequently portrayed in the literature of the Golden Age in general, and notably within Cervantes's oeuvre. Cervantes intricately problematizes the relationship between the visual and the verbal, delving into the representation of textual images or ekphrasis pertaining to paintings to an unprecedented degree. Within visual studies, there has been a profoundly fruitful exploration of the intricate interplay between image and word. For instance, W. J. T. Mitchell asserts, "all media are mixed media, and all representations are heterogeneous; there are no 'purely' visual or verbal arts, though the impulse to purify media is one of the central utopian gestures of modernism."[2] He further adds in another work, "There are deep and fundamental differences between the verbal and visual arts. But there are also inescapable zones of transaction between them."[3]

In Cervantine criticism concerning artistic images, the social context, history of the images, their mode of perception, and, above all, their materiality and status as objects with their own history, are often overlooked. Moreover, studies focusing on pictorial ekphrases in Cervantes frequently address pictorial images through the aesthetic frameworks governing the discipline of art history, without distinguishing between textual images and textual artworks. The notion of art has its own historiography dating from the late eighteenth century, owing to the development of aesthetics as a discipline. The idea of art, and implicitly of artwork, seeks to universalize the value of certain cultural artifacts privileged within the category of "Art." Visual studies are necessarily and productively interconnected with the discipline of art history. Yet Keith Moxey argues that visual culture is not concerned with any foundationalist theory of knowledge, nor with the universalist theme of aesthetics. Instead, it recognizes different subject positions, emphasizing that subjectivity is always embedded in history. As he states, "once this is understood, visual studies becomes a situated knowledge rather than a knowledge that claims universality."[4]

To comprehend many Cervantine passages featuring pictorial images, it is imperative to consider material culture and everyday practices, and to understand how ordinary people related to pictorial images. Toward the conclusion of this study, I will briefly discuss the *sargas pintadas* at the inn in *Don Quijote* part II. Critics have questioned the plausibility of mythological motifs in such a modest setting. However, early modern Spain's visual culture was highly philoscopic, exposing people to artworks of varying quality. This aspect remains understudied, significantly affecting how literary criticism interprets artistic images in Cervantes. The cultural significance of painting in the Golden Age thus warrants closer examination.

Visual and Material Culture in Early Modern Spain

In the early seventeenth century, Madrid and other Spanish cities were filled with painters' workshops mass-producing low-cost paintings of mythological, historical, and religious themes, mirroring elite tastes. From Santiago Street in Madrid, carts of such paintings were shipped daily across Spain and to the Americas. As Miguel Morán Turina has stated, "no matter how poor, there was no home in those times that was not adorned with paintings."[5] Individuals in Cervantes's era were deeply entrenched in an art-centric milieu. Morán Turina explains that in seventeenth-century Madrid, paintings were so prevalent that they were sold on sidewalks near Plaza Mayor, Puerta del Sol, and Plaza del Palacio, just as they adorned churches and major buildings.[6] Numerous accounts confirm that the popular classes integrated painting into daily life. The Counter-Reformation devoted immense energy to filling churches with religious art, making artistic representations a near-daily presence in people's lives, especially in churches and religious festivals. But people were also in continuous contact with visual codes of *non*religious art—secular art with mythological or historical themes, as well as other genres such as the landscape and still life.

It is essential to recognize that, despite the lack of formal education among the popular classes, visual cultural expressions remained deeply embedded in daily life. The inhabitants of early modern Spain engaged with a highly codified culture in which iconography, mythological and sacred references, and classical motifs were omnipresent in public festivals and civil and religious ceremonies. This structured visual culture permeated diverse spaces, from palace and church façades adorned with valuable paintings and tapestries on special occasions to triumphal arches erected for royal entrances and processions rich in symbolic imagery. Javier Portús and Miguel Morán Turina, in their exploration of popular involvement in visual cultural forms during the Spanish Golden Age, introduce the concept of "semantic discrimination."[7] This concept suggests that all social classes shared the dominant culture's manifestations—the same theatrical productions, public festivities, rituals, and even artworks—but with varying levels of comprehension based on their social and cultural standing. Importantly, there was no cultural estrangement to a degree that hindered the participation, within certain limitations, of the lower classes in a collective culture where the portrayal of motifs from the classical tradition and the Bible constituted a shared heritage.

During Cervantes's time, art was not confined solely to church exhibitions or the grand collections of the monarchy and nobility. Even in towns of moderate size, numerous art shops offered inexpensive paintings. These paintings varied in quality, imitating prevalent artistic trends and schools of the time. They encompassed diverse genres such as devotional pieces, portraits, still lifes, landscapes, as well as depictions of historical and mythological themes. For instance, Alonso de Alcalá Yáñez's *El donado hablador* narrates an encounter with a shop painter in Toro who sold mediocre paintings depicting secular themes for a humble clientele.

> Tenía costumbre de pintar la casa otomana, los emperadores romanos, los dioses de los antiguos. Y yo entonces . . . reprehendía su trabajo y la vana curiosidad de algunos, diciéndole: "En verdad, señor, que no tanto me admiro de que vuesa merced pinte al Soldán, a Rosa su mujer, a Bayaceto, a Nero, a Julio César, a Júpiter y a Venus, sino de que haya tantos que los compren."

> He would paint the Ottoman royal family, the Roman emperors, the gods of the ancients. And I then . . . would reprimand his work and the vain curiosity

> of some paintings, saying: "In truth, sir, I am not so much amazed that you painted the sultan, his wife Rosa, Bayezid, Nero, Julius Caesar, Jupiter and Venus, as that there are so many who buy them."[8]

The subjects depicted by master painters had become commonplace, almost mundane, and easily recognizable. Prints (*estampas*) were another widespread form of iconographic dissemination, not restricted solely to devotional purposes. Literary and historical examples, including those listed in wills, also attest to the familiarity with paintings across all social strata during the period.

Paintings recurrently appeared in Golden Age theater, often being integral to the plot.[9] Sometimes a painting mentioned in the narrative, though unseen by the audience, required no elaborate description and propelled the dramatic action forward. The subject matter depicted in such a painting automatically intertwined with the story. In instances where a painting did appear on stage, stage directions often simply stated the subject of the painting and added "as it's painted." Morán Turina writes that "'as it's painted' is entirely normal in stage directions. The iconographic tradition of painting—the sort of painting that . . . was seen in the streets and was the object of much discussion in daily life—constituted a fundamental point of reference when conceiving the dramatic action of the theatre itself."[10] Both Emilio Orozco and Miguel Morán Turina delve into the integration of art within theater. They highlight that the pictorial image in theater ceased to be singular, instead becoming generic based on the represented subject, a notion well understood by theater companies and explicitly detailed in inventories of early modern wills in which artworks are categorized thematically. This reflects what José Antonio Maravall characterizes as a Baroque mass culture, typified by standardized repetition of genres. In sum, historical, mythological, or religious paintings of the era did not merely inform but interpreted, evoked, and re-presented cultural motifs or themes, ingrained within a shared hermeneutical culture. This shared memory of conventional representations formed a codification assimilated by the popular classes, evident in both artistic and theatrical spheres.

Critical oversight of the tremendous vitality inherent in the visual culture of the early modern era leads Cervantine scholarship into serious methodological quandaries. Foremost among these is the reliance on erudite textual sources to trace influences within Cervantes's texts. This tendency means that literary criticism relies almost exclusively on written sources, largely ignoring the immense influence of visual culture on the literary works of Cervantes and his contemporaries. At times, it appears implausible to assume that Cervantes consciously engaged with a plethora of influences, each substantiated by a litany of textual antecedents. There seems to be an irrational assumption that Cervantes necessarily had to have perused every text published before he died, regardless of its obscurity or rarity. Consequently, this neglects his unquestionable, albeit untraceable, life experiences. Moreover, it is crucial to consider the existence during this period of a formidable and omnipresent visual culture in which society at large participated, which served as a conduit for shared knowledge between Cervantes and his readers. As previously stated, the art of this era also constituted a source of historical, mythological, and biblical references among a wide variety of topics. The inability to explicitly trace these references in many instances does not invalidate their existence.

A second critical issue arises from the artificial separation of the textual and the visual when studying Cervantes's oeuvre. Literary criticism has often sidelined the visual aspect of Baroque culture, thus missing half of the narrative when contemplating sources, influences, and meanings. Furthermore, in the analysis of artistic images, there is a prevalent tendency to seek concrete references from high culture, a procedure that, barring a few exceptional cases, presents complications. All Cervantine references to artists, paintings, prints, and other media are intricately intertwined with visual culture, art consumption practices, and their contexts. The painter Orbaneja and the itinerant—and inept—painter referenced by Teresa Panza are testimonies to the presence of images in the lives of all Spaniards during Cervantes's time.[11] Likewise, the "Licenciado Vidriera" refers to a poor street painter displaying his canvases on a sidewalk. In the interlude of *El viejo celoso*, the *guadamecíes* or leather paintings play a pivotal role in the plot. The *Persiles* features painting in various guises: canvases painted by captives to recount a story, the canvas depicting the protagonists' adventures; innumerable portraits of Auristela; aristocratic portraits and *retratos de faltriquera* (pocket portraits), showcasing the rise of portraiture as a genre adopted across nearly all strata of society. Additionally, there is a portrait of Auristela *a lo divino* in Rome which poses significant challenges from the standpoint of Catholic orthodoxy and its Counter-Reformation context, leading us to devotional painting.[12]

These instances, among myriad others, reflect a series of artistic practices and consumption needs related to art's role as a vehicle for religious propaganda. However, in the *Persiles* two fantastic museums emerge, transporting us to the past and future of painting: the museum of nonexistent portraits belonging to Monseñor de la Cámara and Imperia's museum, which brings together famous lost paintings from classical antiquity as well as those by Renaissance masters Michelangelo and Raphael. This singular instance encapsulates eminent figures from art history within a space—the museum—that simultaneously mirrors the collecting fervor of its time and the aspiration to render its artistic images accessible.

> Abrieron la sala y, a lo que después Periandro dijo, estaba la más bien aderezada que pudiese tener algún príncipe rico y curioso en el mundo. Parrasio, Polignoto, Apeles, Ceuxis y Timantes tenían allí lo perfecto de sus pinceles, comprado con los tesoros de Hipólita, acompañados de los del devoto Rafael de Urbino y de los del divino Micael Angelo: riquezas donde las de un gran príncipe deben y pueden mostrarse.
>
> The room was opened, and according to what Periandro said later, it was the most finely decorated room that any wealthy and curious prince in the world could possess. Parrhasius, Polygnotus, Apelles, Zeuxis, and Timanthes had their finest masterpieces there, acquired with the treasures of Hippolyta, alongside those of the devout Rafael of Urbino and the divine Michelangelo: treasures where the riches of a great prince should and can be shown.)[13]

The sargas pintadas

I have selected one example among many to demonstrate how visual and cultural studies offer new and meaningful interpretations of Cervantes's work. In *Don Quijote*, part II, as the protagonists return to their village, they stay at an inn where two *sargas*—outmoded cloth paintings—adorn the walls.

> Apeáronse en un mesón, . . . Alojáronle en una sala baja, a quien servían de guadameciles unas sargas viejas pintadas, como se usan en las aldeas. En una dellas estaba pintada de malísima mano el robo de Elena, cuando el atrevido huésped se la llevó a Menalao, y en otra estaba la historia de Dido y de Eneas, ella sobre una alta torre, como que hacía de señas con una media sábana al fugitivo huésped, que por el mar sobre una fragata o bergantín se iba huyendo. Notó en las dos historias que Elena no iba de muy mala gana, porque se reía a socapa y a lo socarrón, pero la hermosa Dido mostraba verter lágrimas del tamaño de nueces por los ojos.
>
> They dismounted at an inn . . . He was lodged in a ground-floor room where, in place of painted leather hangings [guadameciles] there were some old cloth paintings [sargas] such as are used in villages. On one of them was painted,

> very badly, the abduction of Helen, when the audacious guest was taking her away from Menelaus, and on another was the story of Dido and Aeneas, she on a high tower signaling with a half-sheet to the fugitive guest who was escaping by sea on a frigate or brigantine. In the two stories Don Quijote noted that Helen was not reluctant to leave as she laughed mockingly on the sly, but the lovely Dido was shown to shed tears the size of walnuts from her eyes.[14]

In the following chapter, Don Álvaro Tarfe arrives at the inn on horseback, and the text mentions that he is given a room opposite Don Quijote's, equally adorned with *sargas*, although it does not specify the motifs represented: "El caballero se apeó, y frontero del aposento de don Quijote la huéspeda le dio una sala baja, enjaezada con otras pintadas sargas como las que tenía la estancia de don Quijote" (The gentleman dismounted, and the landlady gave him a room on the ground floor, across from Don Quijote's lodging, which was adorned with painted sargas like those in Don Quijote's chamber).[15] Although this passage has received little critical attention, it has been studied from a scholarly standpoint for its references to the *Iliad* and especially the *Aeneid* within the context of classical culture in *Don Quijote*, with particular emphasis on Virgil.[16] The mythological motifs in the inn's *sargas* are interpreted as a parodic counterpoint to the protagonist's adventures. Adrián Sáez has linked one of them to a tapestry owned by Philip II depicting Dido and Aeneas and suggests other models in lost tapestries of Helen's abduction.[17] Studies on these *sargas* highlight the contrast between their erudite themes, poor artistic quality, and the modest setting, emphasizing the improbability of classical motifs in a rural inn. While the passage is clearly parodic, using the bad painter trope as a critique of Avellaneda, alternative readings, without contradicting previous ones, shed light on how the popular classes engaged with painting in the early modern period. In this sense, the presence of poorly painted *sargas* with classical themes in a humble setting is not only plausible but entirely credible.

This specific example serves, among numerous others, to underscore the necessity of a critical perspective that considers the visual culture of Cervantes's Spain. The inherent interdisciplinary nature of visual studies in relation to art history and cultural studies offers a theoretical path that can illuminate not only this but also many other Cervantine instances presenting pictorial ekphrases. The inn's *sargas* constitute verbal images, ekphrases, which, besides influencing the interplay between the textual and the visual, occupy their own social, cultural, and historical context. As W. J. T. Mitchell states: "Visual culture is the visual construction of the social, not just the social construction of vision."[18] The *sargas* not only narrate the story of Helen's abduction and Dido and Aeneas's farewell but also tell their own story. What are these paintings of little artistic value doing there? What do they tell us about a rural society that adorns its walls with paintings whose themes belong to a cultural sphere presumably unrelated to its own? The *sargas* recount their own history as objects stemming from a historical process entwined with the material culture of their time. Painted *sargas* are often mistaken for humble substitutes for woven tapestries but are distinct unprimed canvas paintings, typically unstretched and executed in glue-based tempera. Unlike oil paintings, their lower elasticity led to paint detachment, so they were hung unframed, like *guadameciles*—leather paintings also left unstretched.

By Cervantes's time, *sargas* had become obsolete, replaced by low-cost oil paintings. Wills and inventories from the early sixteenth century confirm their presence in modest households, featuring cultured motifs like Lucretia.[19] This evidence validates the plausibility of the inn's *sargas*, with their classical themes and poor execution, as part of daily life in Cervantes's Spain. Their antiquity reflects both geographical isolation and neglect in the inn's decor, suggesting it was last updated decades earlier when such adornments were more fashionable. In Don Quijote and Sancho's time, low-quality oil paintings, as poorly executed as *sargas*—like those possibly painted by Orbaneja—were mass-produced and served as the cheapest, most common form of decoration. The significance of *sarga* painting declined with the emergence of the "canvas" as a historical object, which fueled the rise of early modern painting. This innovation combined flexible, durable, fast-drying oil paint with waterproofed linen mounted on a stretcher. The combination of these two factors, oil and canvas, made possible the art's evolution by enabling the mobility of paintings, which, due to their lightness, could assume considerable dimensions.[20] Thus it materially facilitated the development of painting collections beyond the church's patronage. Themes broadened, and the collections of kings and nobles, relatively accessible in Spain, played a pivotal role in fostering an entire industry of low-quality paintings that imitated themes and motifs drawn from these collections.

Sancho and Don Quijote observe and comment on the *sargas*. It is interesting that after the narrator describes the *sargas* and remarks upon their "malísima mano" (very poor execution), the text shifts the focus to Don Quijote's perspective as quoted earlier: "In the two stories Don Quijote noted that Helen was not reluctant to leave as she laughed mockingly on the sly, but the lovely Dido was shown to shed tears the size of walnuts from her eyes."[21] Indeed, there is an initial assessment by the narrator regarding the *sargas*' antiquity, their rustic nature, and their poor execution, alongside the thematic description, followed by Don Quijote's observation capturing the grotesqueness of the scenes. Additionally, while observing the images, Sancho visualizes a future in which he and Don Quijote are portrayed in inns, hostelries, and barber shops. He concludes by appraising the images' quality, stating, "but I would like it if they were painted by a better hand than the one that painted these," prompting Don Quijote to refer for the second time to Orbaneja, the painter from Úbeda who painted "whatever comes out" and had to put a sign below saying "this is a rooster."[22] The attentive gaze of the two protagonists modulates into the condemnation of the false *Don Quijote* by Avellaneda. However, the *sargas* narrate multiple stories simultaneously: that of Dido and Aeneas and the abduction of Helen, as well as the story of the humble painter who, like Orbaneja, filled many modest spaces with ludicrous images. They also recount their own tale as material objects of a bygone era, supplanted by new oil painting techniques. Likewise, the *sargas* indicate that the inn is distant from fashion trends and, despite being clean, is unpretentious and has long lacked care in refurbishment. They also suggest that in the Golden Age, there was scarcely a space, no matter how impoverished, untouched by the need to hang images on walls, aspiring to make painting an integral part of daily life.

James Elkins writes that visual studies suffers from presentism, often neglecting the past, adhering to a predictable canon, and utilizing images "too cursorily, as illustrations or information; its images continue to merely illustrate or exemplify theories articulated in the texts, and they do not, so far, live up to the hopes that a number of writers have about them, namely that they contain, provoke, direct, or engender thoughts, theories, and arguments."[23] There is no singular solution for these shortcomings in visual studies, which nonetheless remain the most suitable critical instrument for the study of visual culture. But I want to conclude with a note expressing my belief that the textual images present in Cervantes's work have much to contribute to this critical trend, since his writing has confronted intentionally, and from multiple perspectives and genres, the problems of literary representation of the visual in such a profound, original, and innovative manner.

NOTES

1. Frederick De Armas's work is probably that which has made the most valuable and abundant contributions to the study of the relationship between the art of Italian Renaissance master painters and Cervantes's work. Through a series of seminal studies, he has significantly enriched research on ekphrasis in Golden Age literature. De Armas, *Cervantes, Raphael and the Classics*; *Ekphrasis*; and *Quixotic Frescoes*.
2. Mitchell, *Picture Theory*, 5
3. Mitchell, *What Do Pictures Want?*, 55.

4. Moxey, "What Does Visual Studies Do?," n.p.
5. My translation. Morán Turina and Portús, *El arte de mirar*, 49.
6. Morán Turina and Portús, *El arte de mirar*, 47.
7. Morán Turina and Portús, *El arte de mirar*, 83.
8. Alcalá Yáñez, *El donado hablador*, 290.
9. Regarding the significant and intricate presence of artworks, particularly portraits, in Spanish Golden Age theater see Laura Bass's important study, *The Drama of the Portrait*.
10. My translation. Morán Turina, "Velázquez," 58–59.
11. Orbaneja appears twice in the second part of *Don Quijote*, first in chapter 3 and later in chapter 71. He is such a bad painter that when asked what he is painting he says, "whatever comes out," and then needs to clarify with a written sign saying, "This is a rooster."
12. Regarding the portrait of Auristela "a lo divino" and Counter-Reformation Spain, see Alcalá Galán, "From Literary Painting," 2–21; and "La vida secreta," 27–53.
13. Cervantes, *Persiles* IV, 7: 670–71.
14. Cervantes, *Don Quijote*, II, 71: 1087.
15. Cervantes, *Don Quijote*, II, 72: 1089.
16. Those who have studied the classical echoes of this passage include Luis Gómez Canseco, Juan Diego Vila, Antonio Barnés Vázquez, and María Rosa Lida de Malkiel.
17. See Sáez, "Las 'sargas pintadas.'"
18. Mitchell, "Showing Seeing," 237.
19. Anonymous, *Inventario de bienes*, 313.
20. See Bruquetas, *Técnicas y materiales*, and Stoichita, *La invención*.
21. Cervantes, *Don Quijote*, II, 71: 1087.
22. "pero querría yo que la pintasen manos de otro mejor pintor que el que ha pintado a estas"; "lo que saliere"; "Este es gallo" (II, 71: 1087).
23. Elkins, *Visual Studies*, 9.

BIBLIOGRAPHY

Alcalá Galán, Mercedes. "La vida secreta de las imágenes: de los retratos de Auristela en el *Persiles* a los límites del neoplatonismo." *Boletín de la Biblioteca de Menéndez Pelayo* 99, no. 2, (2023): 27–53.

Alcalá Galán, Mercedes. "From Literary Painting to Marian Iconography: The Cult of Auristela in Cervantes' *Persiles*." In *Millennial Cervantes*, edited by Bruce Burningham. University of Nebraska Press, 2020.

Alcalá Galán, Mercedes. "The Deceived Gaze: Visual Fantasy, Art and Feminine Adultery in Cervantes' Reading of Ariosto (*El curioso impertinente* and *El viejo celoso*)." In *Goodbye Eros: Reassessing the Ethos of Love in Early Modern Spanish Literature*, edited by Ana Laguna. University of Toronto Press, 2020.

Alcalá Galán, Mercedes. "Painting Turned into Theatre: *Tableaux vivants* in Cervantes's Narrative." In *Cervantes's Theatrical Revelations*, edited by Esther Fernández and Adrienne Martín. University of Toronto Press, 2022.

Alcalá Yáñez, Jerónimo de. *El donado hablador: Alonso, mozo de muchos amos*, edited by Enrique Suárez Figaredo. Scribd, 2007.

Anonymous. *Inventario de bienes* [Documentación municipal de la cuadrilla de Salvatierra]. Eusko Ikaskuntza (Donostia), 2001.

Armstrong-Roche, Michael. *Cervantes' Epic Novel: Empire, Religion, and the Dream Life of Heroes in "Persiles."* University of Toronto Press, 2009.

Barnés Vázquez, Antonio. "'Yo he leído en Virgilio': La tradición clásica en el *Quijote*." Academia del Hispanismo, 2009.

Bass, Laura R. *The Drama of the Portrait: Theater and Visual Culture in Early Modern Spain.* Pennsylvania State University Press, 2009.

Bruquetas Galán, Rocío. *Técnicas y materiales de la pintura española en los Siglos de Oro.* Fundación de Apoyo a la Historia del Arte Hispánico, 2002.

Cervantes Saavedra, Miguel de. *Don Quijote de la Mancha.* 2nd ed. Edited by Francisco Rico. Crítica, 1998.

Cervantes Saavedra, Miguel de. *Los trabajos de Persiles y Sigismunda.* 2nd ed. Edited by Carlos Romero Muñoz. Cátedra, 2002.

De Armas, Frederick A. *Cervantes, Raphael and the Classics.* Bucknell University Press, 1998.

De Armas, Frederick A., ed. *Ekphrasis in the Age of Cervantes.* Bucknell University Press, 2005.

De Armas, Frederick A. *Quixotic Frescoes: Cervantes and Italian Renaissance Art.* University of Toronto Press, 2006.

Elkins, James. *Visual Studies: A Skeptical Introduction.* Routledge, 2003.

Gómez Canseco, Luis. "*Don Quijote* II, 72: Ficciones, inverosimilitudes y moralidades." *Philologia Hispalensis* 18, no. 2 (2004): 197–206.

Lida de Malkiel, María Rosa. *Dido en la literatura española: Su retrato y defensa.* Tamesis, 1974.

Mitchell, W. J. T. *Picture Theory: Essays on Verbal and Visual Representation.* University of Chicago Press, 1994.

Mitchell, W. J. T. *What Do Pictures Want? The Lives and Loves of Images.* University of Chicago Press, 2006.

Mitchell, W. J. T. "Showing Seeing: A Critique of Visual Culture." In *Art History, Aesthetics, Visual Studies,* edited by Michael Ann Holly and Keith Moxey. Sterling and Francine Clark Art Institute, 2002.

Morán Turina, Miguel. "Velázquez, la pintura, y el teatro del Siglo de Oro." *Boletín del Museo del Prado* 19 (2001): 47–71.

Morán Turina, Miguel, and Javier Portús. *El arte de mirar: La pintura y su público en la España de Velázquez.* Istmo, 1997.

Moxey, Keith. "What Does Visual Studies Do? Interview with Keith Moxey." Center for Visual Studies. Reprinted from *Handwerker Gallery Newsletter* 1, no. 3 (Fall 1999). https://www.visual-studies.com/interviews/moxey.html.

Orozco Díaz, Emilio. *El teatro y la teatralidad del Barroco.* Editorial Planeta, 1969.

Sáez, Adrián. "Las «sargas pintadas» de la venta: Écfrasis y tapicería en el *Quijote* (II, 71)." *Rivista di Filologia e Letterature Ispaniche* 20 (2017): 85–98.

Stoichita, Victor I. *La invención del cuadro: Arte, artífices y artificios en los orígenes de la pintura europea.* Translated by Anna Maria Coderch. Cátedra, 2011.

Vila, Juan Diego. "Didon et Énée dans le *Quichotte* de1615." *Classica: Sociedade Brasileira de Estudos Clássicos* 4 (1991), 185–202.

CHAPTER 16

The Quixotic Sensorium

VÍCTOR SIERRA MATUTE

Don Quijote begins with a deliberate omission whose resonance extends across time. By withholding the exact name of the village in La Mancha, the novel embraces uncertainty and incompleteness, unsettling the reader's sense of stability and highlighting the fragility of human perception.[1] Cervantes's book is not about greatness but rather the mundane aspects of life. In fact, right after its famous opening, *Don Quijote* continues with a description of the main character based exclusively on what he eats: "Una olla de algo más vaca que carnero, salpicón las más noches, duelos y quebrantos los sábados, lentejas los viernes, algún palomino de añadidura los domingos, consumían las tres partes de su hacienda" (An occasional stew, beef more often than lamb, hash most nights, eggs and abstinence on Saturdays, lentils on Fridays, sometimes squab as a treat on Sundays—these consumed three-fourths of his income).[2] With the second sentence of *Don Quijote*, Cervantes not only "opens the door to understanding better Spain's culinary and, in a larger sense, cultural and social history," but also brings us closer to the universe of this Cervantine character through an exploration of human sensation.[3] Taste and smell initiate a sensory experience where the five external senses participate in a highly descriptive and engaging way, making the reader complicit in the character's trajectory.[4] All of them are already present in the first chapter of the novel: after *smelling* and *tasting* his meal, we are invited to *touch* the quill of the "ingenioso hidalgo," to *visualize* his skinny nag, and even to *listen* to how the name he invents for the animal sounds: "al fin le vino a llamar Rocinante, nombre, a su parecer, alto, *sonoro*" (he finally decided to call the horse

Rocinante, a name, in his opinion, that was noble, *sonorous*).[5] In this first chapter, as in the rest of the novel, the senses are everywhere. Cervantes thus plays upon the Renaissance topos of the "banquet of the senses."[6] It is unsurprising that Cervantine critics have not hesitated to underscore *Don Quijote*'s "sensorial richness,"[7] and more generally, "Cervantes's highly sensorial, corporal literary creations."[8]

Critical studies have addressed the relationship between Cervantes's work and the history of the senses in many and varied ways.[9] And while the presence of the senses in *Don Quijote* is certainly overwhelming, we would be making a mistake if we reduced them to a mechanism for describing the real world, falling in yet another Cervantine trap. I argue that Cervantes's goal was not mimetic. Rather, I believe he was trying to radically question our way of relating to the world, as well as our tendency to trust our senses often unquestioningly. As I will demonstrate in this chapter, through Don Quijote's eyes—and ears, and hands, and nose, and tongue—Cervantes invites us to participate in a process of sensory inquiry. The form of sensory organization he puts forth to guide us in this process is what I have termed "the quixotic sensorium": an intense, deliberately paradoxical sensory order that challenges the prevailing philosophies of the senses of the time, namely the Aristotelian and Neoplatonic sensory hierarchies, in order to play with audience expectations.[10]

Sensory Shifts and Quixotic Realities

In an essay dedicated to the exemplary novel *La española inglesa*, Charles Victor Ganelin claims that, throughout all his oeuvre, "Cervantes draws attention to sensory perception and reception."[11] Creating a play on words with the name of the literary genre Cervantes coined, the "exemplary novel," Ganelin refers to the Cervantine sensorium as an "exemplary sensorium," one whose goal is to portray "realistic worlds."[12] While I subscribe in part to Ganelin's analysis, I propose an alternative approach to the Cervantine sensorium.[13] Specifically, I suggest that, rather than portraying realistic worlds, Cervantes utilizes sensory perception to subvert our understanding of the real world and create alternative realities. This subversion of sensory perception in Cervantes's work allows us to understand *Don Quijote* as a cautionary tale about the dangers of imitation, where the protagonist's misguided emulation of chivalric romances ultimately results in a distorted understanding of reality, suggesting that what I have termed "the quixotic sensorium" is not a tool for creating realistic worlds but rather for the destabilization of our own senses.

Building on foundational work on the history of the senses, particularly Walter J. Ong's concept of sensorium as "the entire sensory apparatus as an operational complex," we see how a culture's sensory organization can shift over time.[14] Ong's notion of "The Shifting Sensorium" is helpful for understanding *Don Quijote*, where the characters' perceptions—and our own as readers—continuously evolve. The quixotic sensorium is not only determined by the Cervantine narrative universe but is precisely what produces its entire fictional ecosystem and, at the same time, a powerful and sensual reading experience.[15] The sensorium also varies throughout the course of the novel, reflecting its ever-changing nature. For example, the knight errant undergoes a shifting sensorium as his perception of reality becomes increasingly distorted—from a "normative" point of view—in the first part of the novel but clearer and less distorted toward the end of the second part, as he becomes more grounded and his perceptions align more with the other characters' shared reality.[16] All these moments and processes of sensory confusion highlight the fact that our understanding of the world is not fixed or objective, but rather subjective and dependent on our individual experiences and perceptions.

One of the recurring topics in *Don Quijote* is the quest for authenticity, as the novel ultimately raises questions about the nature of reality.[17] In fact, Américo Castro noted that the primary theme of *Don Quijote* is what he termed the "oscillating reality," a concept that is closely aligned with the shifting nature of the quixotic sensorium.[18] Avalle-Arce specifies that this reality only oscillates when viewed from Don Quijote's perspective, an opinion that further reinforces my main point about the shifting nature of the quixotic sensorium.[19] However, as I noted earlier, we must never equate our world with the world depicted in the novel. As Steven Wagschal has shown, the many temporal and spatial inconsistencies found in the novel lead us to think that "Time and Space are radically different" in *Don Quijote*.[20] Wagschal asserts that Cervantes employed methodological skepticism, paralleling Descartes's approach in his *Meditations* (1641) and applying "epistemic doubt" almost half a century before Cartesianism.[21] It may sound paradoxical, but skepticism is precisely what provides the novel's thematic unity and coherent structure.[22] The narrator consistently demands that the reader challenge the authenticity of the events portrayed through the use of the human senses, creating an atmosphere of ambiguity that allows for multiple interpretations of the text.

Building on the idea of authenticity and reality in *Don Quijote*, the shifting sensorium experienced by characters and readers—contemporary and otherwise—raises the question of whether the Cervantine novel can be considered a reliable source for exploring the history of the senses. In other words, if the sensory experience is affected by epistemic doubt, how does the quixotic sensorium relate to the Aristotelian and Neoplatonic hierarchies of the senses? While the quixotic sensorium was built as an alternative to the early modern sensorium, it was also heavily influenced by early modern models precisely to challenge them. The following discussion will use various examples from the novel to explore how Cervantes employs and challenges early modern hierarchies of the senses.

Entering the Quixotic Sensorium

Cervantes presented his own sensory model by building on the existing theory of the senses, but he did not replicate that framework in his own. Instead, he subverted the dominant theories of the senses to create a quixotic sensorium that effectively challenged normative views, especially the "canonical and hierarchical Western five-sense model, inherited from Aristotle."[23] Aristotle ranked the senses in order of their perceived importance and reliability: 1. sight; 2. hearing; 3. smell; 4. taste; 5. touch. While there were competing theories of the senses in the period, this hierarchy was widely accepted in early modern Europe and has had vast cultural implications, as the Aristotelian model of the senses became deeply ingrained in the region and was also exported through colonialism to other parts of the world.[24] As a result, culture not only influenced the way the senses were perceived, but it also modified the hierarchy itself: the cultural context in which the hierarchy existed affected how the different senses were ranked and valued, and how they related to each other. Cultural historian Constance Classen provides an example of this interaction between the hierarchy of senses and their cultural context in her brilliant explanation of the distribution of perception in early modern Europe, which was based on a symbolic division between "masculine" and "feminine" senses:

> In the European hierarchy of the senses, the sensibilities of women traditionally ranked low. While men had mastery of the "higher" senses of sight and hearing, women were linked with the "lower" senses of touch, taste and smell. Both men and women were understood to make practical use of all of their senses: men could touch, women could see. Nonetheless, touch, along with taste and smell, was imagined to be essentially feminine in nature: nurturing, seductive, dissolute in its merging of self and other. Sight, and to a lesser

extent hearing, was essentially masculine: dominating, rational, orderly in its discrete categorization of the world.[25]

Let us take a moment to recall that Cervantes introduced Alonso Quijano by describing his eating habits. Cervantes challenged the traditional symbolic hierarchy of the senses from the outset by characterizing his male protagonist based on his sense of taste, which was associated with women and considered to be one of the lowest senses, second to last. It is ironic that from this point forward in the narrative Alonso Quijano elects to prioritize his higher senses over his lower senses, at the cost of making the misguided decision of becoming a knight errant: when he becomes Don Quijote, he starts to *see* fantastical enchanters and towering giants, to *hear* sounds coming from fierce battles and vast armies.[26] Cervantes "elevates" his hidalgo to the status of a pitiful antihero through the senses of sight and hearing, which were traditionally ranked much higher than taste. In a subtle manner, Cervantes appears to suggest that overindulging in our higher senses can lead to tragic consequences, despite this idea being contrary to more conservative traditions that brought attention to the perils of the lower, bodily, "seductive" senses. As readers, we accompany Don Quijote on his journey. We go up to go down. Don Quijote insists on relying on his higher senses, so his suffering intensifies. This emotional journey is one that the reader shares with Don Quijote, feeling his pain and hardship along the way.

At times, the quixotic sensorium shifts its focus to the lower senses, and the difference with the higher ones becomes blurred. This often happens in episodes that involve Sancho. For instance, in chapter 22 of the first part, when Don Quijote and Sancho are sleeping after their encounter with the fulling mills, the sense of smell comes to the fore. The narrator tells us that they were sewn together when Don Quijote notices that Sancho is trying to defecate, first sensing a sound and then an odor:

> —¿Qué rumor es ése, Sancho?
>
> —No sé, señor—respondió él—: alguna cosa nueva debe de ser, que las aventuras y desventuras nunca comienzan por poco.
>
> Tornó otra vez a probar ventura, y sucediole tan bien, que sin más ruido ni alboroto que el pasado se halló libre de la carga que tanta pesadumbre le había dado. Mas como don Quijote tenía el sentido del olfato tan vivo como el de los oídos, y Sancho estaba tan junto y cosido con él que casi por línea recta subían los vapores hacia arriba, no se pudo escusar de que algunos no llegasen

a sus narices, y apenas hubieron llegado cuando él fue al socorro apretándolas entre los dos dedos, y con tono algo gangoso dijo:

—Paréceme, Sancho, que tienes mucho miedo.

"What sound is that, Sancho?"

"I don't know, Señor," he responded. "It must be something new; adventures and misadventures never begin for no reason."

He tried his luck again, and things went so smoothly that with no more noise or disturbance than the last time, he found himself rid of the burden that had caused him so much grief. But since Don Quixote had a sense of smell as acute as his hearing, and Sancho was joined so closely to him, and the vapors rose up almost in a straight line, some unavoidably reached his nostrils, and as soon as they did he came to the assistance of his nostrils and squeezed them closed between, and in a somewhat nasal voice, he said:

"It seems to me, Sancho, that you are very frightened."[27]

As we see here, Sancho tries to hide his defecation and flatulence by directing Don Quijote's attention to an upcoming adventure and, at the same time, indicating his discomfort with attention being paid to his bodily activities, which are perceived through the lower senses. This comparison of Sancho's routine bodily functions and Don Quijote's elevated aspirations emphasizes the striking difference between their perspectives while underscoring their coexistence in the quixotic sensorium. In the end, their bodies are metaphorically sewn together, and their sensory experiences are confused.

Don Quijote's observation about Sancho's fear not only acknowledges emotion in relation to the alteration of the human senses, but also serves to highlight the significance of fear in the sensory experiences of the characters throughout the novel. In fact, fear is one of the emotions that fuel the quixotic sensorium, as it can temporarily alter the established hierarchy of the senses.[28] This is not the first time that Don Quijote notices Sancho's fear as related to sensory perception. Just a couple of chapters before, Don Quijote had explicitly warned Sancho that "el miedo que tienes . . . te hace, Sancho, que ni *veas* ni *oyas* a derechas, porque uno de los efectos del miedo es *turbar los sentidos* y hacer que las cosas no parezcan lo que son" (it is your fear, Sancho . . . that keeps you from *seeing* or *hearing* properly, because one of the effects of fear is to *cloud the senses* and make things appear other than they are).[29] It goes without saying that, once again, the two senses that Don Quijote considers to be in danger—the senses he associates with rightness and that he, as a knight errant, has to protect—are sight and hearing. Sancho, on the other hand, does not hesitate to rely on all five senses—especially the lower ones—to avoid any conflict, as he explicitly states even while still in pain from being struck: "Cuanto más que no pienso ponerme en ocasión de haberle menester, porque pienso guardarme con *todos mis cinco sentidos* de ser ferido ni de ferir a nadie" (I don't intend to put myself in the position of needing it, because I plan to use *all my five senses* to keep from being wounded or wounding anybody else).[30] Sancho values self-preservation above all else, while Don Quijote prioritizes his chivalric duties. This further underscores the quixotic nature of their relationship, as they both navigate the sensory experiences of the world around them in their own unique ways.

As readers, we are often left with a question: Whose sensory perception should we trust, Sancho's or Don Quijote's? The narrator's deliberate presentation of the conflict between their sensory perceptions raises that question for readers, leaving them with an impossible choice. This intentionally creates confusion and mirrors Sancho's internal struggle as he, according to Don Quijote, experiences uncertainty that affects his sensory perception. By presenting this unanswerable question, the narrator invites the reader to interrogate their own perception and understanding of reality, much like the characters in the novel. This creates a sense of instability, reflecting the unpredictable nature of the sensory experiences within the novel. In this way, the narrator effectively immerses readers in the quixotic sensorium, allowing them to examine their own sensory perceptions.

The quixotic sensorium encompasses all the potential sensory experiences available to both characters and readers, as well as the specific hierarchy of the senses they rely on to experience the world they occupy. Since the quixotic sensorium represents the conditions that make every sensation possible, we cannot fully describe them all. However, we can identify a few key elements that constitute the core of the quixotic sensorium up to this point, that is, in the first half of the novel. In other words, the quixotic sensorium is an ever-changing complex. As such, it persistently mirrors canonical models in order to challenge them. This happens in different ways. First, by showing that an excess of trust in our higher senses leads to an unavoidable fall. Second, by portraying characters who possess a different hierarchy of the senses, as seen both in their acts and in their words, since they explicitly speak about their perceptions. And third, by introducing intense emotions that temporarily suspend any hierarchy of the senses. Finally, it is in all these moments of empathy and dissent that readers realize they should not trust their own senses.

And Yet Another Twist: The Cave of Montesinos

While readers constantly question their own sensory perceptions, Don Quijote does not—until the Cave of Montesinos. This episode, marking a turning point in his character, parallels a major shift in the quixotic sensorium. As he descends physically into the cave, he experiences a symbolic ascent, confronting the limitations of his senses. Previously, he had relied entirely on perception to construct his chivalric world. After emerging from the cave, however, he recognizes the fallibility of his senses, foreshadowing his eventual abandonment of knight errantry and return to Alonso Quijano. Cervantes highlights this shift through metaphors of inversion and paradox. The episode's title, "la grande aventura de la Cueva de Montesinos, que está en el corazón de La Mancha, a quien dio felice cima el valeroso Don Quijote" (the great adventure of the Cave of Montesinos that lies in the heart of La Mancha, which was successfully concluded by the valiant Don Quixote), suggests both penetration into the depths of La Mancha and an elevation of self-knowledge.[31] Sancho's remark about Lucifer's fall serves as another hint: just as Lucifer descended into the abyss, Don Quijote undergoes a reversal that unsettles his previous worldview. The cave functions as an epistemological test, particularly in regard to sight. Don Quijote, for the first time, doubts his own perceptions. When recounting his visions inside the cave, his words leave Sancho, the student, and the reader unsure of what to believe. This moment of uncertainty—both for the protagonist and for those who hear his story—reinforces Cervantes's larger meditation on the instability of sensory experience. From this point forward, Don Quijote is irreversibly altered. This transformation is once again related to a shift in the quixotic sensorium, which we become aware of when Don Quijote wakes up inside the cave after an undetermined period of deep sleep:

> Despabilé los ojos, límpiemelos y vi que no dormía, sino que realmente estaba despierto; con todo esto, me tenté la cabeza y los pechos, por certificarme si era yo mismo el que allí estaba o alguna fantasma vana y contrahecha; pero el tacto, el sentimiento, los discursos concertados que entre mí hacía me certificaron que yo era allí entonces el que soy aquí ahora.

> I opened my eyes wide, rubbed them, and saw that I was not sleeping but really was awake; even so, I felt my head and chest to verify whether it was I myself or some false and counterfeit phantom sitting there, but my sense of touch, my feelings, the reasoned discourse I held with myself, verified for me that, there and then, I was the same person I am here and now.[32]

In contrast to the first part of the novel, where sight was the dominant sense for confirming reality, the latter part of *Don Quijote* elevates touch to a higher position in the quixotic sensorium.[33] Don Quijote touches his head and chest to make sure that he is himself and not a ghost. This act of touch, considered the lowest sense in the canonical early modern hierarchy of senses, now elevates this sense to be one of the highest—alongside sight—in the quixotic sensorium. This new hierarchy is reinforced when Sancho questions the veracity of Don Quijote's narrative, and the protagonist responds that "lo que he contado lo vi por mis propios ojos y lo toqué con mis mismas manos" (what I have recounted I saw with my own eyes and touched with my own hands).[34] Equating touch and sight in the sensory hierarchy challenges the sensory orders of the time and highlights the fallibility of sensory perception by making us realize that hierarchies can shift.

After this new shift in the quixotic sensorium, there is no turning back for Don Quijote. He cannot revert to his previous ways of perceiving the world, even if he wished to. The realization of the unreliability of his perceptions has permanently transformed him, which is evident in his subsequent conduct throughout the novel. He becomes more self-aware and grounded in a reality shared by the other characters. This new version of Don Quijote is vastly different from the delusional knight errant who embarked on his first sally, making Cervantes's *Don Quijote* a tool for sensory exploration. The transformation of the quixotic sensorium throughout the novel highlights the idea that our sensory experiences are not fixed and can be shaped by both internal and external factors, such as our thoughts and emotions, as well as cultural and historical influences.

NOTES

1. Several Cervantes scholars have defined the novel in similar terms. For instance, Hessel describes the novel as the "praxis of aporia without the limits of theory because it does not afford any reading a stable footing" (Hessel, "Paradigms," 230). For a cognitive approach to the works of Cervantes, see the special issue of *Cervantes: Bulletin of the Cervantes Society of America* devoted to this topic: "Cognitive Cervantes" (vol. 32, no. 1), especially Jaén, "Cervantes and the Cognitive."
2. Cervantes, *Don Quijote,* I, 1: 27; Cervantes, *Don Quixote,* I, 1: 19. All quotations will be taken from *Don Quijote,* ed. Francisco Rico. English translations in parentheses come from *Don Quixote,* trans. Edith Grossman.
3. Nadeau, *Food Matters,* 190.
4. In this essay, I will ground my discussion on the five external senses (sight, hearing, taste, smell, and touch) and the four internal senses (common sense, imagination, memory, and estimation) that Cervantes inherited from the Aristotelian and Neoplatonic traditions, which

are the ones challenged in his quixotic sensorium. Nevertheless, I want to acknowledge upfront that humans have more senses than these, including proprioception or vestibular sense, among others.

5. Cervantes, *Don Quijote*, I, 1: 32; Cervantes, *Don Quixote*, I, 1: 22, my emphasis.
6. Wagschal, "The Smellscape," 125.
7. Johnson, *Affective Geographies*, 39.
8. Ganelin, "Cervantes's Exemplary Sensorium," 167.
9. An excellent introduction to the history of the senses in relation to Cervantes's work and his time can be found in Giles and Wagschal, ed., *Beyond Sight: Engaging the Senses in Iberian Literatures and Cultures, 1200–1750*.
10. As Susan Byrne has demonstrated, Cervantes's literary works—particularly his early writings—bore the distinctive imprint of Neoplatonic philosopher Marsilio Ficino's influence, whose ideas about the human senses held considerable sway during that period. Byrne, "Sight," 105. Ficino's sensory hierarchy, coexisting with the Aristotelian framework, epitomized the prevailing philosophical perspectives on the senses in early modern Spain, sharing several foundational principles. Despite nuances, both the Aristotelian and Ficinian Neoplatonic hierarchies highlighted the primacy of sight and hearing as fundamental external senses. However, Ficino's Neoplatonist perspective aligned the hierarchy with degrees of materiality, situating the most abstract senses—understanding, hearing, and sight—at the pinnacle of human perception; Byrne, "Sight," 105. In contrast, early modern Aristotelian thinkers tended to prioritize sight over hearing.
11. Ganelin, "Cervantes's Exemplary Sensorium," 174.
12. Ganelin, "Cervantes's Exemplary Sensorium," 181.
13. To be totally fair, Ganelin's assertion concerning touch as a "site of mixed reception" ("Cervantes's Exemplary Sensorium," 172) is in fact very consistent with my main thesis. However, Ganelin appears to have omitted elaborating on this concept in his essay, or at least not to the extent that I intend to do so in this chapter.
14. Ong, "The Shifting Sensorium," 28.
15. Two articles that showcase how *Don Quijote* could create impactful and engaging experiences for readers are Gasta, "Writing to Be Heard," and Wagschal, "The Smellscape."
16. This "decline from illusion to reality" has been generally formulated as "the Sanchification of Don Quixote," while Sancho experienced a parallel but opposite process called "the Quixotization of Sancho"; Pope, "Metamorphoses," 94. Both processes could easily be related to my idea of a quixotic sensorium.
17. Levin, "The Example," 141.
18. Castro in Avalle-Arce, *Don Quijote*, 110.
19. Avalle-Arce, *Don Quijote*, 112.
20. Wagschal, "*Don Quixote*," 153.
21. Wagschal, "*Don Quixote*," 142.
22. Lorca, *Neo-Stoicism and Skepticism*, 20.
23. Skeates and Day, "Sensory Archaeology," 2.
24. Skeates and Day. "Sensory Archaeology," 8.
25. Classen, "The Witch's Senses," 70.
26. It is important to clarify that, according to the medical treaties of the time that Cervantes was familiar with, Alonso Quijano's external senses are not damaged, but rather his internal senses process the information obtained by sight and hearing incorrectly. See Domínguez, "The Internal Senses."

27. Cervantes, *Don Quijote*, I, 20: 182; Cervantes, *Don Quixote*, I, 20: 148.
28. For a pivotal study on Cervantes and the history of emotions, see Johnson, *Affective Geographies*.
29. Cervantes, *Don Quijote*, I, 18: 161; Cervantes, *Don Quixote*, I, 18: 129; my emphasis.
30. Cervantes, *Don Quijote*, I, 21: 191; Cervantes, *Don Quixote*, I, 21: 155; my emphasis.
31. Cervantes, *Don Quijote*, II, 22: 714; Cervantes, *Don Quixote*, II, 22: 597.
32. Cervantes, *Don Quijote*, II, 23: 723–24; Cervantes, *Don Quixote*, II, 23: 605.
33. As Anthony Cascardi has noted in his close reading of this episode, when Don Quijote states "vi que no dormía, sino que realmente estaba despierto," we fall, as readers, into another Cervantine aporia: "not only do we know that Don Quixote is utterly mistaken, we know that his dream is as unverifiable from 'inside' as from 'outside.' Dreams are like suppositions, essentially unverifiable" (Cascardi, "Cervantes and Descartes," 121).
34. Cervantes, *Don Quijote*, II, 23: 730; Cervantes, *Don Quixote*, II, 23: 611.

BIBLIOGRAPHY

Avalle-Arce, Juan Bautista. *Don Quijote como forma de vida*. Fundación Juan March, 1976.

Byrne, Susan. "Sight, Hearing and Higher Truths in Cervantine Narrative Structures." In *La vida como obra de arte: Essays in Memory of John Jay Allen*, edited by Moisés Castillo. Juan de la Cuesta, 2021.

Cascardi, Anthony J. "Cervantes and Descartes on the Dream Argument." *Cervantes: Bulletin of the Cervantes Society of America* 4, no. 2 (1984): 109–22.

Cervantes, Miguel de. *Don Quijote de la Mancha*. Edición Conmemorativa IV Centenario Cervantes. Edited by Francisco Rico. Real Academia Española, 2015.

Cervantes, Miguel de. *Don Quixote*. Translated by Edith Grossman. HarperCollins, 2003.

Classen, Constance. "The Witch's Senses: Sensory Ideologies and Transgressive Femininities from the Renaissance to Modernity." In *Empire of the Senses: The Sensual Culture Reader*, edited by David Howes. Routledge, 2004.

Domínguez, Julia. *Quixotic Memories: Cervantes and Memory in Early Modern Spain*. University of Toronto Press, 2022.

Domínguez, Julia. "The Internal Senses in *Don Quixote* and the Anatomy of Memory." In *Beyond Sight: Engaging the Senses in Iberian Literatures and Cultures, 1200–1750*, edited by Ryan D. Giles and Steven Wagschal. University of Toronto Press, 2018.

Ganelin, Charles Victor. "Cervantes's Exemplary Sensorium, or the Skinny in *La Española Inglesa*." In *Beyond Sight: Engaging the Senses in Iberian Literatures and Cultures, 1200–1750*, edited by Steven Wagschal and Ryan D. Giles. University of Toronto Press, 2018.

Gasta, Chad M. "Writing to Be Heard: Performing Music in *Don Quixote*." In *Cervantes in Perspective*, edited by Julia Domínguez. Iberoamericana-Vervuert, 2013.

Hessel, Stephen. "Paradigms, Aporia, and the Limiting of Cervantes." In *Metacritical Cervantes*. Juan de la Cuesta, 2018.

Jaén, Isabel. "Cervantes and the Cognitive Ideas of His Time: Mind and Development in *Don Quixote*." *Cervantes: Bulletin of the Cervantes Society of America* 32, no. 1 (2012): 71–98.

Johnson, Paul Michael. *Affective Geographies: Cervantes, Emotion, and the Literary Mediterranean*. University of Toronto Press, 2021.

Levin, Harry. "The Example of Cervantes." In *Cervantes's Don Quixote*, edited by Harold Bloom. Chelsea House, 2001.

Lorca, Daniel. *Neo-Stoicism and Skepticism in Part One of* Don Quijote: *Removing the Authority of a Genre*. Lexington Books, 2016.

Nadeau, Carolyn A. *Food Matters: Alonso Quijano's Diet and the Discourse of Food in Early Modern Spain*. University of Toronto Press, 2016.

Ong, Walter J. "The Shifting Sensorium." In *The Varieties of Sensory Experience: A Sourcebook in the Anthropology of the Senses,* edited by David Howes. Toronto: University of Toronto Press, 1991.

Pope, Randolph D. "Metamorphosis and *Don Quixote*." *Cervantes: Bulletin of the Cervantes Society of America* 8 (1988): 93–101.

Simerka, Barbara, Julien Simon, and Howard Mancing, eds. "Cognitive Cervantes." Special issue of *Cervantes: Bulletin of the Cervantes Society of America* 32, no. 1 (2012): 11–275.

Simon, Julien. "The Intersection of Mind and *Don Quixote*: Overview and Prospects." In *Don Quixote: Interdisciplinary Connections,* 19–34. Juan de la Cuesta, 2013.

Skeates, Robin, and Jo Day. "Sensory Archaeology: Key Concepts and Debates." In *The Routledge Handbook of Sensory Archaeology,* edited by Robin Skeates and Jo Day. Routledge, 2020.

Wagschal, Steven. "*Don Quixote,* the Skeptical Reader and the Nature of Reality." In *Cervantes in Perspective,* edited by Julia Domínguez. Iberoamericana-Vervuert, 2013.

Wagschal, Steven. "The Smellscape of *Don Quixote*: A Cognitive Approach." *Cervantes: Bulletin of the Cervantes Society of America* 32, no. 1 (2012): 125–62.

PART V

MEDIA FUTURES

CHAPTER 17

Cervantes and Inflationary Media

DAVID CASTILLO AND WILLIAM EGGINTON

In 2016 we published a book called *Medialogies: Reading Reality in an Age of Inflationary Media*. When we argued in that book that we are living in a time of inflationary media, what we meant is that our current media saturation is eroding the commons at a breathtaking pace, and with it any collective sense of truth. While today's digital media technologies came with the promise of increased connectivity, the practical effect of their pervasiveness has been the opposite. Today, our media-saturated world is plagued by divisive, polarizing, fringe discourses and increased feelings of disunity, isolation, depression, and anxiety—a sort of doom mentality that popular media monetize in a never-ending series of apocalyptic products, from miracle cures for our aching bodies and souls to fundamentalisms of all kinds, ethnic, racial, religious, and nationalistic.

Perhaps the most pervasive and dangerous of our medialogy's products, in some ways its dominant presupposition, is something we call reality entitlement, or reality-on-demand: a way of receiving information that allows us to curate our world in accordance with our own beliefs and biases. Our media feeds can be a sort of combination of diminished and augmented realities: a diminished reality that protects us from what we don't want to see, say climate change, poverty, homelessness, social injustice, etc., and an augmented reality that reinforces our beliefs by providing us with all the scapegoats we need so that we don't have to adjust those beliefs. Here we're thinking of scapegoating notions about immigrants and refugees stealing "our" jobs and ruining the economy; secularists destroying "our" true values and debasing our nation; or racial minorities taking "our" hard-earned tax dollars while living off welfare.

In many ways it's not too far to claim that reality itself has become a consumer good in our society. Let's take the example of misinformation or disinformation. While it is obvious that there are nefarious agents out there actively generating disinformation as a political weapon or even as a weapon of war, the reason that false information of all kinds spreads four to five times faster than factual information in certain social media circles is that this kind of disinformation tends to make the media giants more money.[1] The truth is boring and cannot compete with the titillation of scandals, conspiracy theories, and hate speech. In other words, disinformation is a for-profit business. The algorithms that run social media sites have been designed to attract more eyeballs and maximize profits using what industry insiders call "personalized amplification." This is why in the United States we need to disentangle First Amendment rights, such as freedom of speech, from efforts to regulate social media. The latter has nothing to do with freedom of speech, since the algorithms they use are effectively putting their thumb on the scale, artificially amplifying sensationalist, fringe, and outrageous discourse at the expense of truthful, evidence-based information that may not be deemed as "interesting" from a market perspective.

The currency of reality entitlement further leads to a widely distributed sense of isolation on the part of citizens. The absence of a commons where our ideas and beliefs can be tested through exposure to the ideas and beliefs of others makes it possible for us to ignore anything that doesn't fit our worldviews and to ascribe to those who do not agree with us some sort of nefarious intent. When others are not members of my group, my tribe, they are essentially my enemy, intent on destroying me and others like me. I must stand up to them with everything I've got. The result is a circularity that reinforces my own beliefs with ever higher walls. Then I can project those beliefs into some agency that anchors them. To put it plainly, in a Christian context for example, the question of "What would Jesus do?" comes with the default answer, "whatever I believe," since I know the "real" Jesus!

This cocoon-like structure and infallibility of the self underpins modern fundamentalisms, which increase isolation, making it difficult to work together on common goals. The result is a general weakening of our communities and an endemic inability to respond to emerging crises. The pandemic we have just experienced or are still experiencing is a perfect example, with all kinds of anti-vaccine conspiracy theories filling the airwaves and jeopardizing efforts to develop and follow common-sense strategies to protect ourselves and our communities. Our inability to change course to address the climate change emergency would be another example, with the caveat that climate change denialism is amplified by interest groups tied to corporations for whom climate change is, at best, an inconvenient truth.

We argue that a critical humanist thought can help us survive and even reverse our current situation. The set of distinct disciplines and fields of knowledge we call "the humanities" can help by illuminating our predicament more fully. The long view of history can prove to be very valuable to the extent that many of our current problems are the result of a sort of collective amnesia about our own past. Art and literature can help put things in perspective. A particularly apt illustration would be the body of modern dystopias of warning like *1984*, *The Handmaid's Tale*, or *A Brave New World*. We can say that these works of twentieth-century literature are still sounding the alarm. Their warnings feel just as timely today as at the time of their production. We can certainly relate to the dangers of authoritarian powers presented with such poignant clarity in *1984* and *The Handmaid's Tale*. At the same time, as Neil Postman wrote in 1985 in his prescient *Amusing Ourselves to Death*, the dystopian horizon of Aldous Huxley's early 1930s masterpiece *A Brave New World* appears to be gaining fresh ground in our time. As Postman wrote (again this is back in 1985): "Orwell feared those who would deprive us of information. Huxley feared those who would give us so much that we would be reduced to passivity and egoism. Orwell feared that the truth would be concealed from us. Huxley feared that the truth would be drowned in a sea of irrelevance."[2]

As we argue in both *Medialogies* and in *What Would Cervantes Do?*, the fictional works published at the dawn of modernity, in another age of inflationary media, can also help us put things in perspective in our own time. Our primary example here is, as the title of our second book indicates, the work of Miguel de Cervantes. The inventor of modern fiction was particularly concerned about the effects of the emerging mass media, with its awesome power to influence our thinking and behavior through their framing of the world. Of course, in the early modern period we are talking about print and the emerging mass spectacles we associate with the modern theater, with their appeal to raw emotions, rather than to our minds. We argue that Cervantes's works slow things down so that we can see the sleight of hand at work. We professors often talk about the importance of teaching our students to think outside the box. A Cervantine point to make would be that to think outside the box we have to be able to see the box first. The fictional awareness strategies that we attribute to the works of Cervantes can help us hone our interpretive skills today to understand how our own inflationary media frame, edit, and ultimately construct our reality. We've been calling this "reality literacy."

In one of our books, we quote Lorca's poem "Despedida":

> Si muero dejad el balcón abierto.
> El niño come naranjas.
> (Desde mi balcón lo veo).
> El segador siega el trigo.
> (Desde mi balcón lo siento).
> ¡Si muero,
> dejad el balcón abierto!
>
> If I die
> Leave the balcony open.
> The child is eating oranges.
> (From my balcony I hear him.)
> The reaper scythes the wheat.
> (From my balcony I listen.)
> If I die,
> Leave the balcony open![3]

Critics have often remarked on the "prescient" significance of the poem, which is obviously (and necessarily) there, but we have instead emphasized its "activist" stance. The poet refuses to be laid down to rest, asking instead to remain vigilant at his open balcony, watching, listening . . . The Cervantes of *Medialogies* and *What Would Cervantes Do?* is also, in this same sense, an activist presence, an ally we can turn to as we watch and listen for signs of reemerging authoritarianism, fascism, racism, and misogyny in our AI-assisted present/future. We are less interested in his work as a classic or timeless corpus of masterpieces than we are in its disruptive ability to reveal the frame, to make the strings visible, to remind us of how the game is played, be it the game of writing, as in the author's prologue to *Don Quijote*, part I, or the game of manipulation, Chanfalla's game in *El retablo de las maravillas*, and of course the sense-making game, as in *El coloquio de los perros*. Is there anything more urgent today than understanding how our AI-assisted media frame and make sense of the world? As Stuart A. Thompson, Tiffany Hsu, and Steven Lee Myers wrote in a *New York Times* article published on March 22, 2023: "Even as tech giants scramble to join the commercial boom prompted by the release of Chat GPT, they face an alarmed debate over the use—and potential abuse—of artificial intelligence. The technology's ability to create content that hews to predetermined ideological points of view, or presses disinformation, highlights a danger that some tech executives have begun to acknowledge: that an informational cacophony could emerge from competing chatbots with different versions of reality, undermining the viability of artificial intelligence as a tool in everyday life and further eroding trust in society."[4]

Indeed, isn't it the point of *Don Quijote*, especially the second volume, to show the framing power of the new media of the time, the guts of the printing press and their awesome reach? Isn't it the point of *El retablo de las maravillas* to make the strings of the spectacle visible, as Chanfalla uses the audience's own confirmation-bias as the hook? And isn't it the point of *El coloquio de los perros*, as one of us argued in *Un-Deceptions*, to remind us about our own libidinal investment in what we see, what we make of the world, and the beautifully fallible necessity (and responsibility) of interpreting? Readers can hardly be blamed if they see in *Don Quijote* a sort of literary analogue of (and a commentary on) the self-sustaining illusions that animate conspiracy theories inside familiar rabbit holes today. No amount of crashing reality is seemingly enough to dissuade our own Don Quijote-style vigilantes from tilting at windmills. Their clinging to alternative realities is indeed reminiscent of Don Quijote's trademark response to the inconvenient presence of windmills and other hard obstacles in what amounts to some version of *I believe and therefore it is true*:

> —¡Válame Dios!—dijo Sancho—. ¿No le dije yo a vuestra merced que mirase bien lo que hacía, que no eran sino molinos de viento, y no lo podía ignorar sino quien llevase otros tales en la cabeza?—Calla, amigo Sancho—respondió don Quijote—, que las cosas de la guerra más que otras están sujetas a continua mudanza; cuanto más, que yo pienso, y es así verdad, que aquel sabio Frestón que me robó el aposento y los libros ha vuelto estos gigantes en molinos, por quitarme la gloria de su vencimiento.

> "For God's sake!" said Sancho. "Didn't I tell you to be careful what you were doing, didn't I tell you they were only windmills? And only someone with windmills on the brain could have failed to see that!" "Not at all, friend Sancho," replied Don Quijote. "Affairs of war, even more than others, are subject to continual change. All the more so as I believe, and thus it is the truth, that the same sage Frestón who stole my library and my books has just turned these giants into windmills to deprive me of the glory of my victory."[5]

Later in the narrative, in chapter 21, Don Quijote cannot help but acknowledge that the shiny object he has decided is Mambrino's legendary helmet does indeed look like a barber's basin, just as Sancho says. Yet, since he knows the truth, the appearance of the object makes no difference: "parece bacía de barbero, como tú dices. Pero sea lo que fuere, que para mí que la conozco no hace al caso su trasmutación" (which seems as you say, like a barber's basin. But let it be what it will; for me, who knows it well, its transformation is of no consequence).[6]

Yet it is in the adventure of the enchanted boat, where Don Quijote's rationalizations may remind us most closely of the rationalizing verbiage of contemporary QAnon-style conspiracies. As Don Quijote and Sancho come upon the Ebro River, the knight errant spots a small boat tied to the trunk of a tree. The presence of the boat triggers a hilarious dialogue as Don Quijote expresses his conviction that the "enchanted boat" is an unmistakable signal that he is being beckoned to undertake a perilous journey to rescue some noble personage who must be in grave danger. Paying no heed to Sancho's objections, Don Quijote cuts the line and jumps into the boat followed by his faithful squire. As they start to drift from shore, Don Quijote laments their lack of navigation instruments with which to establish their location, to which Sancho retorts that all they really need is their own eyes to see that they haven't moved far from the place where they left their mounts. Such evidence is nonetheless discarded by Don Quijote in favor of his knowledge of astronomical signs: "tú no sabes qué cosa sean coluros, líneas, paralelos, zodiacos, eclíticas, polos, solsticios, equinocios, planetas, signos, puntos, medidas, de que se compone la esfera celeste y terrestre; que si todas estas cosas supieras, o parte dellas, vieras claramente qué de paralelos hemos cortado, qué de signos visto y qué de imágines hemos dejado atrás y vamos dejando ahora" (you don't understand about colures, lines, parallels, zodiacs, ecliptics, solstices, equinoxes, planets, signs, points and measurements of which the terrestrial and celestial globe is comprised, for if you did understand all these matters, or some of them, you would realize how many parallels we've crossed, how many signs we've seen and how many constellations we've left behind and are leaving behind even now).[7]

Needless to say, the conclusion of the adventure of the enchanted boat turns out rather differently from the outcome Don Quijote had anticipated, as the boat crashes against the physical reality of some watermills. Nevertheless, the self-made knight errant has one more rationalization up his sleeve: "en esta aventura se deben de haber encontrado dos valientes encantadores, y el uno estorba lo que el otro intenta: el uno me deparó el barco y el otro dio conmigo al través" (in this adventure two mighty enchanters must have clashed headlong, and one of them impedes whatever the other attempts: one provided me with the boat, the other knocked me out of it).[8] It bears repeating, for he who "knows" what things truly are regardless of their appearance, no amount of "debunking" by the Sanchos of the world or even physical evidence will mean a thing. As for the QAnon knights of our day intent on revealing the truth about the nefarious activities taking place in mattress stores all over the country or the child-trafficking operation run by the Clintons inside the basement of a Washington, DC, pizza parlor, appearances (such as the lack of an actual basement at the restaurant in question) will not distract them from what they know to be real. This is why debunking approaches fall short when we are dealing with the impact of disinformation.

Former editor of *Time* magazine and government official in the Obama administration Richard Stengel offered a sobering view of the problem from a national security perspective in his *Information Wars*, published in 2019. He reminds us that the reason disinformation sticks with predictable reliability in the internet age is that it appeals to our confirmation-bias; it can fit our worldview in the same way that when we make a purchase on our smart phone, we are automatically subjected to "information" about similar products. Inside our media echo chambers, truth is likely to be discarded when it goes against the beliefs that anchor our perception of the world, which is why, as he writes, "it's not enough to fight falsehood with truth; the truth does not always win."[9] For readers familiar with Cervantes's *El retablo de las maravillas*, Stengel's reflection that "the truth does not always win" will likely resonate as a Cervantine corrective to the "naïve" logic behind Hans Christian Andersen's *The Emperor's New Clothes* and its much older precedent "Lo que sucedió a un rey con los burladores que hicieron el paño" (What Happened to a King with the Conmen Who Made the Cloth), of *El Conde Lucanor* (1335). Once publicly expressed, the truth (that the king or emperor is naked) is accepted in these tales. But this is not at all what happens inside the paranoid world of Cervantes's *Retablo*, a comedic interlude that makes fun of the fantasy of Christian (i.e., racial) superiority in Counter-Reformation Spain. Here the con men sell a nothing spectacle (the stage of the magic tableau is empty) with a simple lie that plays into the expectations and beliefs of their audience: *those with tainted genealogies or lacking in pure Christian blood will by no means be able to see the magical figures of the tableau.* While the proud commoners who think of themselves as the true Christian-Spanish race will of course not see the tableau's "never seen wonders," they act as if they do on account of their racial biases. This is how, we would argue, Cervantes invites his "lectores avisados" (discerning readers) to make the connection between the theatrical reality of the (non)performance and the fantasies operative in the social reality they themselves inhabit. *These fantasies work not because they are in any way true but rather because we act as though they were true.*

Today, we may continue to read Cervantes's fictional strategy as an illustration of the truth of common racist beliefs, but also of the disinformation campaigns that use our own biases as hooks to manipulate us. Who are the blind people of the *Wondrous Tableau* if not those spectators who have been manipulated into willfully pretending to see? At some level, it does not even matter whether they or we truly believe the lies; those lies maintain their power if we simply fail to confront them. This is just the point that columnist Thomas Edsall seemed to make in a January 19, 2022 *New York Times* piece dealing with the Big Lies of our time: "The unwillingness of Republican leaders to challenge Trump's relentless lies, for whatever reason—for political survival, for mobilization of whites opposed to minorities, to curry favor, to feign populist sympathies—is as consequential as or more so than actually believing the lie."[10] Unlike in *The Emperor's New Clothes*, then, the deception of Chanfalla's tableau is as safe as Trump's lies because in both cases, once the conmen have succeeded in capturing the attention of their audiences and in stirring their sense of grievance, those audiences are ready to turn their backs on any truth that doesn't confirm their beliefs. This is what we argue is a key lesson of the Cervantine table of tricks, a lesson that we must encourage our students and the public to revisit today if we hope to survive our own age of inflationary media.

NOTES

1. Dizikes, "Study: On Twitter."
2. Postman, *Amusing Ourselves to Death*, xix.
3. García Lorca, "Despedida."
4. Thompson, Hsu, and Myers, "Conservatives."
5. Cervantes, *Don Quijote*, I:8 (our emphasis).
6. Cervantes, *Don Quijote*, I:xxi.
7. Cervantes, *Don Quijote*, II:xxix.
8. Cervantes, *Don Quijote*, II:xxix.
9. Stengel, *Information Wars*, 12–13.
10. Edsall, "Why Millions."

BIBLIOGRAPHY

Castillo, David R. *Un-Deceptions: Cervantine Strategies for the Disinformation Age*. Juan de la Cuesta Monographs, 2021.

Castillo, David R., and William Egginton. *Medialogies: Reading Reality in the Age of Inflationary Media*. Bloomsbury, 2017.

Cervantes, Miguel de. *Don Quijote de la Mancha*. Ed. Instituto Cervantes, dir. Francisco Rico. *Centro Virtual Cervantes*. https://cvc.cervantes.es/literatura/clasicos/quijote/.

Dizikes, Peter. "Study: On Twitter, False News Travels Faster than True Stories." *MIT News*, March 8, 2018. https://news.mit.edu/2018/study-twitter-false-news-travels-faster-true-stories-0308.

Edsall, Thomas. "Why Millions Think It Is Trump Who Cannot Tell a Lie" *New York Times*, January 19, 2022.

García Lorca, Federico. "Despedida." Poets.org. https://poets.org/poem/farewell-4

Postman, Neil. *Amusing Ourselves to Death: Public Discourse in the Age of Show Business*. 2nd ed. Penguin, 2005.

Thompson, Stuart A., Tiffany Hsu, and Steven Lee Myers. "Conservatives Aim to Build a Chatbot of Their Own." *New York Times*, March 22, 2023.

Stengel, Richard. *Information Wars: How We Lost the Global Battle Against Disinformation and What We Can Do About It*. Atlantic Monthly Press, 2019.

CHAPTER 18

(Non-)Cervantine Hoaxes

Discursive Populism and Don Quijote in the Internet Era

ANA FERNÁNDEZ-BLÁZQUEZ

The apocryphal, as a phenomenon, has coexisted and been entangled with literature in every era and tradition, yet some texts seem to be more entrapped by it. Since its genesis, Miguel de Cervantes's *El ingenioso hidalgo Don Quijote de la Mancha* has been one of those particularly tortuous novels, defying traditional notions of authorship through the appearance of Fernández de Avellaneda's unauthorized sequel, Cide Hamete Benengeli as a metafictional historian, and apocryphal quotes, mainly from the Arthurian and Castilian chivalric traditions.[1] Yet Cervantes could not have foreseen the varied, often disparate cultural representations and spurious references that emerged after his time. The apocryphal, tied to *auctoritas* and the search for historical, political, and artistic sources, also intersects with the efforts of Spanish popular culture to generate numerous paroemias ostensibly linked to Cervantes's work.[2] Although different manifestations of popular creativity have coexisted with the original Cervantine text for centuries, the arrival of the internet, social networks, and mass culture have fostered the creation of a new type of quixotic apocryphal quote, highly politicized and problematic.

Here I locate and explore two such texts that were created and disseminated in Spain, and which were subsequently flagged and discredited by the platform Maldita.es, part of the International Fact-Checking Network. Their political content, along with their widespread diffusion and populist discourse, leads me to read these texts, contrary to other forms of apocryphal quotes, as pieces of willful disinformation, cataloged in Peninsular Spanish as *bulos*, or "hoaxes."[3] Unlike other forms of apocryphal writing, hoaxes do not pretend to rewrite the text for leisure or disinterested purposes. They operate under pretensions of veracity and mask political and ideological motives under Cervantes's reputation and name recognition. Such forms of disinformation are usually studied within the fields of natural or social sciences, yet do exist in the humanities and literature, working as an evil twist of *auctoritas* and "act[ing] as a fuel which is able to ignite ideological polarization."[4]

There are multiple studies devoted to fake-news detection and the consequences of their dissemination in social and mainstream media, and David Castillo and William Egginton, in this volume and elsewhere, have mused at length on these phenomena and their relationship to Baroque Spain.[5] But there is currently a lack of research delving into those hoaxes that specifically use fake literary quotes as their main content. What could be considered a "literary hoax" has been excluded from a field justifiably concerned by the spread of scientific disinformation—such as that related to climate change or anti-vaccine campaigns—or by political fake news that misrepresents democratic policies and issues of public concern. Nevertheless, my main goal throughout this chapter will be to demonstrate that literary hoaxes participate in the political sphere in a manner similar to that of scientific ones, distorting the functioning of *auctoritas* and manipulating the history and prestige of authors and their writings to discredit public figures. In this case, the subjects of mockery and political victimization were politicians of the Spanish left wing. Cervantes's early fixation with the interaction between fiction and reality, facts and fakes, proves nowadays to be of extreme relevance in a time when the literary is being exploited as a political tool. This suggests the need for a Cervantine future in which the coexistence of these two dimensions is acknowledged and studied in the fields of literature and cultural studies as well. I argue that these literary hoaxes, spread through the internet and social media, channel populist fervor while inheriting a long tradition of quixotic political representations. Therefore, I attempt to situate my analysis of the sociological and political phenomenon of disinformation in twenty-first-century Spain within historical and literary understandings of *Don Quijote*'s many afterlives. My methodology throughout this chapter combines a close reading of the two hoaxes with their reception, in order to provide a comprehensive and informed analysis of their political, social, and cultural content.

The first hoax in this study was diffused through the social network and messaging platform WhatsApp, formatted as the text that follows:

> YA VIÓ DON QUIJOTE VENIR A LOS DE PODEMOS . . . HACE MÁS DE CUATROCIENTOS AÑOS: Tengo por costumbre querido Sancho que, en viendo el burro venir, ya de lejos me apercibo sin confundirme, de las patadas que pudiera propinarme, por tanto mi fiel escudero fijate en los andares y si viéndolo retorcido y mal encarado vieres que arranca sin compostura, hazte a un lado, que de estos con mala idea, sucios y desaliñados mejor no tener contacto. Y hay que tener cuidado con tal calaña, que de ser menester utilizan a las más tiernas criaturas y hasta pretenden adoctrinarlas y que salgan de su mala hueste con títeres y cabalgatas. Y cuidado amigo Sancho que son los mismos que luego cobran de berberiscos y de otros que más allá someten a sus pueblos y ello, tanto mal vestidos cuando procede el buen hábito, como vestidos de la más cursi casta, cuando no es tan menester. ¡¡¡¡¡¡ Grande CERVANTES !!!!!!!????????????????

> DON QUIJOTE ALREADY FORESAW THOSE OF PODEMOS . . . MORE THAN FOUR HUNDRED YEARS AGO: Dear Sancho, I have a habit that, foreseeing the donkey, even from afar I realize without mistaking myself, of the kicks that it could give me, therefore my loyal squire pay attention to its gait and if seeing it twisted and badly faced you, see that it starts off without composure, move aside, because of these people with bad ideas, dirty and disheveled, it is better not to have contact. And you have to be careful with such ilk, who if necessary use the most tender creatures and even try to indoctrinate people and get them out of their evil host with puppets and cavalcades. And be careful, Sancho my friend, they are the same ones who later get paid from Berbers and others who further subjugate their people, both poorly dressed when good habit is appropriate, and dressed in the corniest caste, when it is not so necessary. Great CERVANTES !!!!!!!????????????????[6]

This text was refuted on the web page of the organization Maldita.es on June 25, 2020, after contrasting it with several online editions of *Don Quijote* and making use of philological arguments. For instance, as proof of its fakeness it was noted that terms like *cursi* (corny) or *calaña* (low-life) were not part of the Spanish lexicon in the era of Cervantes, and Maldita.es also consulted the Cervantes scholars Emilio Martínez Mata and José Manuel Lucía Megías as another type of expert evidence.

The second hoax I will consider was disseminated in two different ways: as a text in the messaging application WhatsApp and as an image, superimposed on a traditional Spanish ceramic tile, mainly through the social network formerly known as Twitter, rebranded as X as of 2023. The text consisted of the following:

Figure 18.1. Convivencia Civica Catalana (@CCivicaCatalana), "Cervantes ya escribió sobre Iglesias y Sánchez." Twitter (now X), June 11, 2021, https://x.com/ccivicacatalana/status/1403477868789776392.

Sabio Don Miguel de Cervantes:

"Querido Sancho: Compruebo con pesar, como los palacios son ocupados por gañanes y las chozas por sabios. Nunca fui defensor de los reyes, pero peores son los que engañan al pueblo con trucos y mentiras, prometiendo lo que saben que nunca les darán. País este, amado Sancho, que destrona reyes y corona piratas, pensando que el oro del rey será repartido entre el pueblo, sin saber que los piratas solo reparten entre piratas."

Wise Don Miguel de Cervantes:

Dear Sancho: I see with regret how the palaces are occupied by ruffians and the huts by wise men. I was never a defender of kings, but worse are those who deceive the people with tricks and lies, promising what they know they will never give them. This country, beloved Sancho, that dethrones kings and crowns pirates, thinking that the king's gold will be distributed among the people, without knowing that pirates only distribute among pirates.[7]

Maldita.es refuted this apocryphal quote on December 12, 2020, relying once again on digital editions of the original text and the expertise of Lucía Megías as a consultant.

The organization's analysis classifies these hoaxes as part of a populist discourse, strongly influenced by *Don Quijote*'s mythos and its associated nationalism. In both hoaxes, the Spanish colors and flag are included, either as an emoticon in the text or following the illustration featuring Don Quijote and Sancho. Symbolically, the goal is to represent them as national heroes, affiliating the characters with "pure Spanishness." In contemporary Spain, *Don Quijote* is embedded in the national imaginary, used both by the left and the right. Nevertheless, its link with the notion of "Spanishness" has been subject to multiple changes and transformations. There is an academic consensus that the War of '98 was when Don Quijote's figure was first explicitly used in the service of a particular political movement. It was at this point that the authors of the Generation of '98, such as Ganivet, Unamuno, Maeztu, and Ortega y Gasset, inaugurated quixotism as an ideological faction, from a perspective that elevates Don Quijote and his creator as Spanish heroes.[8] At the turn of the century, Spain was not a favorable context for the development of nationalism in the same way that was occurring in the rest of Europe, something demonstrable, according to Eric Storm, in the late construction of monuments commemorating national figures.[9] However, in 1905 authors like Galdós and Benavente insisted on behalf of mainly liberal intellectuals on celebrating the third centenary of the publication of Part One of *Don Quijote.*[10] The celebrations included popular festivities, expositions, and official commemorations, concluding with an inaugural manifestation of patriotic sentiment. Moreover, this made for an opportunity for Unamuno, Azorín, and others to promote in public speeches their quixotic interpretation of Spanish society at the time.[11] At this point, and with the inauguration of the monument at the Plaza de España in Madrid, Don Quijote's figure is unanimously identified with national patriotism and Spanish nationalism.[12]

The ideological principles of quixotism are also present in the twenty-first-century hoaxes, both in the text and the elements that surround them. In each of them, the apocryphal quotes are included within a paratext, differentiated by the introduction of two dots and quotation marks, or using capital letters. The paratexts praise Cervantes through adjectives such as "sabio" (wise) or "grande" (great), and, at the same time, they also introduce a prophetic overtone to the quotes, using the formulas of "Don Quijote already foresaw those of Podemos . . . more than four hundred years ago," or, in the inscription on the tile, "written by Miguel de Cervantes five centuries ago." Through them, the quotes emphasize the symbolic authority of Cervantes over an imagined, hypothetical political argumentation. Historically, the prophetic and messianic overtones ascribed to Cervantes can be traced back to essays by the aforementioned Ganivet, Unamuno, Ortega y Gasset, and Maeztu, whose goal was that Spaniards reclaimed their destiny, becoming quixotic on the occasion of failure.[13] Unamuno specifically assimilated Don Quijote to a Messiah, whose madness would be cured by the resurrection, while Ortega y Gasset contemplated Cervantes as a master whose lessons had been ignored by Spaniards for too long.[14] Prophetism, whose first apparition in the history of the reception of the novel is quixotism, is explicitly present in the paratexts of the hoaxes from 2020, but is also implicit in the application of Cervantes to a modern political situation.

The paratexts also shape the interpretation of the quotes. The first one emphasizes its pretense, linking it to the political party Podemos. The second one, however, does not identify directly who it is addressing, but the allusion to crowned pirates, in essence, transports the reader to the beginning of the mandate of the political parties PSOE and Podemos, both situated on the left wing, after the Spanish general elections in November 2019. One can observe in the image included earlier how some of the anonymous users that promote it relate it directly to their leaders in 2020, Pedro Sánchez and Pablo Iglesias. But are these hoaxes isolated? Although their literary content makes them unique, they are situated in a much larger context of disinformation on the internet, where half of the information verified as problematic is created by anonymous users, unrelated to political parties and without public relevance, and 31 percent of the problematic information features politicians of the left as main characters portrayed in a negative manner.[15] The manufacture of these quotes advances the equation of left-wing politicians with pirates, criticism of their physical appearance and mode of dress, and an animalization that assimilates them to donkeys, with the large list of insults including *gañanes*, *sucios*, *desaliñados*, *adoctrinadores*, and *mentirosos* (ruffians, dirty, disheveled, indoctrinating, and liars, respectively).

The hoaxes also engage with some of the polemics of Spain's political context in 2020. The first hoax leverages a lexicon with pointed political connotations for its contemporaries. It describes the enemy as *retorcido* (twisted), which could be understood as a reference to Pablo Iglesias' nickname among the right wing as "el chepas," a trending hashtag on Twitter on the morning of July 7, 2020.[16] The catchword *casta* (caste) was specifically used by Podemos to designate the politicians against them, while *títeres* (puppets) would resonate with a polemic of March 2025, when the right-wing political party Vox published a tweet against Javier Bardem, Pedro Almodóvar, and Paco León calling them *titiriteros* (puppeteers).[17] The phrase "que luego cobran de berberiscos" (who later get paid by Berbers) is not innocent either, as in the year 2020 the political coalition Unidas Podemos was subject to criticism from media aligned with right-wing parties because of their relationships with Sultan Mohamed IV of Morocco.[18] The second hoax is more subtle, avoiding lexical references, but its mention of palaces and huts could allude to Pablo Iglesias' polemical acquisition in 2018 of a large house on the outskirts of Madrid.[19]

These insults and cross-references let us situate these hoaxes within Laclau's perspective on discursive populism. Laclau considers populist discourses to be those that try to construct a meaning of 'the people' based on the polarization of political space through an internal border that differentiates those people from an "other."[20] The others are present in the hoaxes as the pirates or the donkeys, antagonists that Don Quijote warns Sancho about, while these two characters would correspond to 'the people,' a notion reinforced by the use of the Spanish flag and the praise of Cervantes and *Don Quijote* that have already been discussed. The hoaxes are part, therefore, of two of the main characteristics of populist discourse, moral antagonism and the construction of otherness.[21] By way of all these elements, these hoaxes work as a tool for polarization, drawing a line between us and others, using cultural authority and the literary canon as a political and discursive weapon of right-wing populism.

However, the weaponization of *Don Quijote* is also rooted in tradition. During the twentieth century, the so-called two Spains interpreted and appropriated the novel in disparate manners. As the historian García Martín notes: "Conservatives, Republicans, anarchists, Communists, Falangists, and Carlists, residing in Spain or exiled, came to the Quijote to express their common worries."[22] On the one hand, during the Civil War the nationalist side perceived the novel as a crusade against the adversary, an aspect also present in the populist discourse of the hoaxes.[23] On the other hand, the Republic continued with the tradition of the Generation of '98, as a generalized national decadence brought about the need to find heroic and inspiring figures.[24] Don Quijote survived as a national myth to whom both contemporary politicians and popular culture look in their writings, songs, discourses, and arguments. In the twenty-first century, to cite merely one example, the left-wing musical group *La Raíz* published the song "Nuestra Nación," in which they make references to "a fairer island," "being knights of that squire," and "a thousand Dulcineas."[25] Varela Olea examines Don Quijote's triumph as a national mythologem against figures like the Cid, arguing that the knight errant's interpretation adapts readily to various ideological perspectives.[26] The figure's development as a myth, reinterpreted politically through the ages, has culminated in the creation of these apocryphal quotes that collect some of the characteristics associated with Don Quijote in the last century, the notion of national myth, the crusade against the enemy, and the messianic and prophetic aspects of the novel.

Despite the fact that the hoaxes analyzed in this chapter are apocryphal quotes from *Don Quijote*, evidence in the archives of the International Fact-Checking Network agencies suggests that the manufacture of apocryphal quotes for populist motives is a phenomenon spreading through other parts of the Hispanic world. In Spain, the foundation Maldita.es has also dedicated articles to a hoax falsely attributed to José Espronceda and a text allegedly written by Mario Vargas Llosa.[27] In Argentina, the organization Chequeado identified as apocryphal a poem attributed to Federico García Lorca that references Cristina Fernández de Kirchner, as well as quotes supposedly by Dante Alighieri and Albert Camus that referred to the government's management of the COVID-19 crisis.[28] In Colombia, there are examples of texts speciously attributed to George Orwell and Gabriel García Márquez.[29]

From the formal analysis of both quixotic hoaxes, it is evident that the characters of Don Quijote and Sancho Panza have been rewritten to configure a polarizing, populist discourse, the latest disturbing chapter in the evolving reception of Cervantes. Through explicit and implicit allusions, these hoaxes create an "us" and "them," aligning the former with the canonical Spanish author and the latter, with left-wing politicians. Yet these are but two examples of a growing phenomenon across the globe, in which populist discourses are fabulated based on canonical literary works. For the future of our discipline, not to mention the global democratic order, we would do well to be attentive to the increasing threat of these developments and to pursue further studies on the relationship of disinformation to *auctoritas* in literature and cultural studies.

NOTES

1. See Marín Pina, "Citas caballerescas apócrifas," 55.
2. One prominent example is "ladran luego cabalgamos" (they bark, then we ride). See Ugarte García, "Lo que Don Quijote nunca dijo," 200. This is not a phenomenon associated solely with Cervantine texts. The most famous paroemia is possibly "Elementary, my dear Watson," a phrase that never appeared in any of the Conan Doyle novels.
3. For an overarching introduction to hoaxes and their development, see Arlix and La Roche, *Hoax*. For insights into the Spanish context, see Olivas Osuna, "Populismo en España," 371.
4. Pérez-Escolar et al., "A Systematic Literature Review," 84.
5. See, for example, Anstead, *Fake News*; Chun and Drucker, *Fake News*; and Tandoc, Lim, and Ling, "Defining 'Fake News.'" Castillo, *Un-Deceptions*; Castillo and Egginton, *Medialogies* and *What Would Cervantes Do?* See also Castillo and Nelson, *Anti-Disinformation Pedagogy*.

6. Fundación Maldita.es, translation mine, as are those that follow, unless otherwise noted. After the text, the message distributed through WhatsApp included three emoticons of the Spanish flag. For coherence, I have decided to transcribe the hoaxes in the exact way in which they were shared and later refuted. Because of that, I have kept the same orthographic and quotation methods, even if they are not standard and contain mistakes.
7. Fundación Maldita.es, "No, esta cita en la que Don Quijote."
8. See, for example, Britt Arredondo, *Quixotism*, 197; and Stavans, *Quixote*, 81.
9. Storm, "El Tercer Centenario," 630. On the significance of monument-building for the transformation of a figure into a myth, consult Pérez Magallón, *Cervantes*, 16–31.
10. Guereña, "El nacionalismo español," 90; Storm, "El tercer centenario," 634.
11. Storm, "El Tercer Centenario," 647.
12. Guereña, "El nacionalismo español," 105; Storm, "El tercer centenario," 648; and Stavans, *Quixote*, 84.
13. Stavans, *Quixote*, 81.
14. Britt Arredondo, *Quixotism*, 143, 167.
15. Lava-Santos et al., "Crude, Anonymous, Partisan," 8–11.
16. See, for example, Ollero, "'Busca Rata Chepuda.'"
17. See Tremlett, "The Podemos Revolution"; "El Mundo de la Cultura se revuelve contra el polémico tuit de VOX sobre los «titiriteros»." *ABC*, March 25, 2020, https://www.abc.es/cultura/abci-mundo-cultura-revuelve-contra-polemico-tuit-sobre-titiriteros-202003251730_noticia.html.
18. See, for example, García Domínguez, "Podemos y Marruecos."
19. See Somolinos, "Pablo Iglesias e Irene Montero."
20. Laclau, *On Populist Reason*. See Olivas Osuna, "Populismo en España," 379.
21. Olivas Osuna, "Populismo en España," 381.
22. García Martín, "El Quijote en el nuevo orden del franquismo," 771.
23. García Martín, "El Quijote en el nuevo orden del franquismo," 763.
24. See Varela Olea, *Don Quijote*, 120.
25. "una isla más justa" / "ser caballeros de ese escudero" / "mil Dulcineas." *La Raiz*, my trans.
26. Varela Olea, *Don Quijote*, 122.
27. Fundación Maldita.es, "No, el poema"; and Fundación Maldita.es, "No, este texto titulado." For a detailed analysis, see Fernández-Blázquez, "Bulos literarios hispánicos," 215–30.
28. Chequeado, "¿García Lorca escribió'"; and Chequeado, "No, la frase que circula."
29. See for example Colombiacheck, "'El pueblo que elige."

BIBLIOGRAPHY

Anstead, Nick. *Fake News: What Do We Know and What Should We Do About It . . .?* Sage, 2021.

Arlix, Eric, and Jean de La Roche. *Hoax*. Ère, 2008.

ABC. "El Mundo de La Cultura Se Revuelve Contra El Polémico Tuit de VOX Sobre Los «titiriteros»." March 25, 2020.

Britt Arredondo, Christopher. *Quixotism: The Imaginative Denial of Spain's Loss of Empire*. State University of New York Press, 2005.

Cascardi, Anthony J. *Cervantes, Literature, and the Discourse of Politics*. Toronto Iberic. University of Toronto Press, 2012.

Castillo, David R. *Un-deceptions: Cervantine Strategies for the Disinformation Age*. Juan de la Cuesta, 2021.

Castillo, David R., and William Egginton. *Medialogies: Reading Reality in the Age of Inflationary Media*. Bloomsbury, 2017.

Castillo, David R., and William Egginton. *What Would Cervantes Do? Navigating Post-Truth with Spanish Baroque Literature*. McGill-Queen's University Press, 2022.

Castillo, David R. and Bradley Nelson, eds. *Anti-Disinformation Pedagogy: Tackling the Power of Manipulative Media*. Special issue of *Hispanic Issues On Line* 32 (2024).

Chequeado. "¿García Lorca escribió sobre CFK? Es #FalsoEnLasRedes que es autor del poema 'La dama de negro.'" *Chequeado* (blog), February 3, 2015. https://chequeado.com/el-explicador/igarcia-lorca-escribio-sobre-cfk/.

Chequeado. "No, la frase que circula no es parte de la novela La peste de Albert Camus ni fue escrita por él." *Chequeado* (blog), April 24, 2015. https://chequeado.com/el-explicador/no-la-frase-que-circula-no-es-parte-de-la-novela-la-peste-de-albert-camus-ni-fue-escrita-por-el/.

Chun, Russell, and Susan J. Drucker, eds. *Fake News: Real Issues in Modern Communication*. Peter Lang, 2020.

Colombiacheck. "'El pueblo que elige corruptos es cómplice,' una frase falsamente atribuida a George Orwell." *Colombiacheck* (blog), 11 January 2023. https://colombiacheck.com/chequeos/el-pueblo-que-elige-corruptos-es-complice-una-frase-falsamente-atribuida-george-orwell.

Fernández-Blázquez, Ana. "Bulos literarios hispánicos: Los casos de José de Espronceda y Federico García Lorca." In *Palabra y Código: Las Humanidades y el Horizonte Digital*, edited by Alberto Custodio Romero Vallejo and Lara Gallardo Calvo. Editorial Trea, 2025.

Fundación Maldita.es. "No, el poema de 'Oigo, patria, tu aflicción' no es del poeta José Espronceda." *Maldito Bulo* (blog), September 29, 2020. https://maldita.es/malditobulo/20240115/poema-oigo-patria-afliccion-poeta-jose-espronceda/.

Fundación Maldita.es. "No, esta cita en la que Don Quijote de la Mancha advierte a Sancho Panza sobre gente con 'mala idea, sucios y desaliñados' y que se utiliza para afirmar que Cervantes 'vio venir a los de Podemos' no es real." *Maldito Bulo* (blog), June 25, 2020. https://maldita.es/malditobulo/20200625/cita-don-quijote-de-la-mancha-cervantes-vio-venir-a-los-de-podemos/.

Fundación Maldita.es. "No, este texto titulado 'Sí, lloro por ti Argentina' no es del escritor Mario Vargas Llosa." *Maldito Bulo* (blog), May 9, 2023. https://maldita.es/malditobulo/20230509/mario-vargas-llosa-argentina-texto-falso/.

Fundación Maldita.es. "Querido Sancho compruebo con pesar . . . la cita falsa sobre reyes y piratas atribuida a Cervantes que no aparece en 'El Quijote.'" *Maldito Bulo* (blog), December 2, 2020. https://maldita.es/malditobulo/20240129/querido-sancho-reyes-piratas-miguel-cervantes-cita/.

García Domínguez, José. "Podemos y Marruecos." *Libertad Digital*, December 13, 2020. https://www.libertaddigital.com/opinion/2020-12-13/jose-garcia-dominguez-podemos-y-marruecos-6690002/.

García Martín, Pedro. "El Quijote en el nuevo orden del franquismo." *eHumanista: Journal of Iberian Studies*, no. 28 (2014): 759–89.

Gratchev, Slav N., and Howard Mancing, eds. *Don Quixote: The Re-Accentuation of the World's Greatest Literary Hero*. Bucknell University Press, 2017.

Guereña, Jean Louis. "El nacionalismo español y el Quijote: La génesis y la difícil realización del monumento al Quijote en la Plaza de España de Madrid (1905–1960)." *eHumanista / Cervantes,* no. 3 (2014): 90–116.

"La Raíz – Nuestra Nación." Posted to YouTube by La Raíz Oficial, March 1, 2013. https://www.youtube.com/watch?v=MTUmZhUaIRI.

Laclau, Ernesto. *On Populist Reason.* Verso, 2005.

Lava-Santos, David, Gamir-Ríos José, and Germán Llorca-Abad. "Crude, Anonymous, Partisan, Sectoral and Anti-Elitist: Electoral Disinformation in Spain (2019–2022)." *El Profesional de La Información,* September 2, 2023, e320506. https://doi.org/10.3145/epi.2023.sep.06.

Marín Pina, María del Carmen. "Citas caballerescas apócrifas en el 'Quijote.'" *Parole rubate: Rivista internazionale di studi sulla citazione. Speciale Cervantes,* no. 8 (December 2012): 51–67.

Olivas Osuna, José Javier. "Populismo En España: Fundamentos Teóricos y Relatos Dominantes." *Araucaria,* no. 47 (2021): 371–401. https://doi.org/10.12795/araucaria.2021.i47.17.

Ollero, Daniel. "'Busca Rata Chepuda En Google': Así Se Cocinó La Última Campaña de Acoso Contra Pablo Iglesias." *El Mundo,* August 25, 2020. https://www.elmundo.es/tecnologia/2020/08/24/5f43f186fdddff3b728b461c.html.

Pérez-Escolar, Marta, Darren Lilleker, and Alejandro Tapia-Frade. "A Systematic Literature Review of the Phenomenon of Disinformation and Misinformation." *Media and Communication* 11, no. 2 (March 16, 2023). https://doi.org/10.17645/mac.v11i2.6453.

Pérez Magallón, Jesús. *Cervantes, monumento de la nación: Problemas de identidad y cultura.* Cátedra, 2015.

Somolinos, Daniel. "Pablo Iglesias e Irene Montero: El Chalet de La Discordia." *El Mundo,* December 29, 2018. https://www.elmundo.es/loc/famosos/2018/12/29/5c1caec0fc6c83a0628b4605.html.

Stavans, Ilan. *Quixote: The Novel and the World.* W.W. Norton, 2015.

Storm, Eric. "El tercer centenario del Don Quijote en 1905 y el nacionalismo español." *Hispania* 58, no. 199 (March 2019): 625–54. https://doi.org/10.3989/hispania.1998.v58.i199.651.

Tandoc, Edson C., Zheng Wei Lim, and Richard Ling. "Defining 'Fake News': A Typology of Scholarly Definitions." *Digital Journalism* 6, no. 2 (2018): 137–53. https://doi.org/10.1080/21670811.2017.1360143.

Tremlett, Giles. "The Podemos Revolution: How a Small Group of Radical Academics Changed European Politics." *The Guardian,* March 31, 2015. https://www.theguardian.com/world/2015/mar/31/podemos-revolution-radical-academics-changed-european-politics.

Ugarte García, María del Carmen. "Lo que Don Quijote nunca dijo: Falsas atribuciones fraseológicas a Cervantes." *Paremia,* no. 25 (2016): 197–206.

Varela Olea, María Ángeles. *Don Quijote, mitologema nacional: Literatura y política entre la Septembrina y la II República.* Centro de Estudios Cervantinos, 2003.

CHAPTER 19

Cervantes, Crusade Apologist

Responding to La conquista de Jerusalén por Godofre de Bullón Today

CHAD LEAHY

La conquista de Jerusalén por Godofre de Bullón (circa 1581–1586) is a play that endorses and celebrates crusading. In contrast with its "amorous" elements, drawn from Tasso's *Gerusalemme*, Antonucci characterizes the play's historical, "epic" material as "ideologically Manichaean and shamefacedly propagandistic."[1] Brioso Santos similarly reads *La conquista* as triumphalist and inimical to the kinds of critique of crusading that we might levy today on humanitarian grounds.[2] The play's pro-crusade posture aligns with one of Cervantes's core concerns in the period following his Algerian captivity. The *manco de Lepanto*'s early production notably critiques Felipe II's 1581 peace treaty with the Ottomans for abandoning Spain's long-standing Mediterranean ambitions, thereby allowing the thousands of Christians held in captivity across North Africa—whose experiences Cervantes well understood—to languish.[3]

That said, *La conquista* also narrativizes humanizing interfaith border-crossings, grounded in (not-unproblematic) desire and love between Christians and Muslims. If the play's embrace of crusading feels proper to the ideological leanings of the former captive and proud veteran of Lepanto, then its gestures recognizing a more contradictory, fluidly "Mediterranean," interfaith social and affective matrix might feel, if anything, even more comfortably Cervantine.[4] Such strands align with well-studied aspects of Cervantes's captivity plays (*El trato de Argel*, *Los baños de Argel*, *La gran sultana*), and familiar episodes in *Don*

Quijote, *Novelas ejemplares*, and *Persiles*. Not surprisingly, those elements of the play that linger in the interstices of religious difference have found more favor with scholars. Castillo, for example, highlights how *La conquista* is rooted in a cultural contact zone in which interfaith desire relativizes dogmatic binaries.[5] Such approaches nevertheless demand bracketing the play's emphasis on holy war, a central aspect of *La conquista* which appears in loud tension with dominant notions of Cervantine multiculturalism. Taken together, such contradictions pose a dilemma for interpreting what this play might have meant in the 1580s and, even more so, what it might mean today. What follows is a call to reckon with these internal disjunctions with the aim of more fully fleshing out the futures to which this play might belong.

The work's jarring narrative layers might be read as markers of the inept rookie playwright working in an experimental time in Spanish theater before the post-Lope fixing of conventions.[6] I prefer instead to consider this friction as generative of important questions. *La conquista*'s uncomfortable assemblage of messier grays stuffed between layers of pulpit-thumping crusade apology forces us to reflect on the kinds of values, meanings, and uses we ascribe to Cervantes. Through its internal contradictions, *La conquista* places on the surface the divergent cultural and political work that the author function "Cervantes" has always been made to perform.[7] In sitting with such ideological tensions, we are faced with a very Cervantine *baciyelmo* problem that obliges us—audiences, readers, critics—to again consider what kind of Cervantes we want.[8] As a play that flies its crusade flag proudly, part of that reckoning implies acknowledging that in our contemporary context *La conquista* legitimizes—precisely through the tremendous capital of Cervantes's name—a deeply problematic set of images, values, and ideas from which groups and individuals including violent far-right white Christian ethnonationalists have drawn strength in recent years.[9] There is thus a fundamental ethical quandary here, both for how *La conquista* forces us to respond to assumptions we make about Cervantes and for how it compels us to confront this particular work's crusading content.

What does it mean in the twenty-first century to stage a crusade fantasy attributed to Cervantes? If we take Castillo and Egginton's provocation as our guide—*What Would Cervantes Do?*—this play leaves us contemplating the possibility that he might encourage us to envision potentialities that disrupt or frustrate essentialisms, rejecting dreams of divinely licensed slaughter.[10] Such an approach would align with well-established trends placing Cervantes's work in productive dialogue with urgent problems of the present from an angle often sympathetic to progressive sensibilities.[11] But Castillo and Egginton's question could just as well yield for us a Cervantes leading in the opposite direction, encouraging us to follow in the steps of the hate-filled murderers behind the 2011 Norway attacks or the 2019 Christchurch massacre, for example, both of whom sympathized with—and made very clear that their abominable actions were inspired by—precisely the same kinds of Christian holy war that *La conquista* dramatizes and celebrates.[12] Starkly divergent forms of present-facing praxis emerge from opposing readings of what Cervantes represents as model.

As a palpable instantiation of this problem, the remainder of this chapter reads the sixteenth-century text of *La conquista* against the 2016 staging of the play by theater company Antiqua Escena (AE), under the direction of Juan Sanz. Premiered on March 22, 2016, in Cuenca's Teatro Auditorio, the production was the first and only to stage the work since the late sixteenth century, enjoying a national tour with performances in Madrid, Alcalá de Henares, Almería, and Almagro. The production would not have been possible without the late Stefano Arata's recovery of *La conquista* more than three decades ago from a cache of theatrical manuscripts belonging to the Conde de Gondomar, housed in the Biblioteca de Palacio. Arata published two foundational articles presenting a first edition and advancing a powerful case that the anonymous play might be the work of Cervantes.[13] While it remains customary to note the lack of a smoking-gun autograph, the evidence supporting Cervantine authorship at this point is overwhelming.[14] I consider the matter of authorship interesting here only in view of how AE strategically harnessed the symbolic cachet of Cervantes's name, particularly in the setting of the collective Cervantine delirium that was the fourth centenary.[15] Insistent Cervantine attributions in publicity and press coverage invested the obscure work—which even specialists of Cervantes rarely care about—with a capital that it would not have otherwise enjoyed.[16]

The work that "Cervantes" as signifier performs interests me particularly as a social, critical, and affective guardrail directing our response, informing the kinds of questions that we feel inclined to bring to the play. I would offer that it is through "Cervantes" that *La conquista*'s basic ideological and structural bifurcation acquires meaning. AE's production in particular jockeys to contain the disquieting specter of a crusade apologist Cervantes while activating ideas of Cervantes as embodiment of "modern" values through his handling of desire across borders. In this way, it reflects particular—and popular—modes of reading that are selective and problematic because of how they short-circuit the difficult and necessary labor of thinking through and sitting with the internal contradictions that characterize Cervantes's work.

While much discourse around the Cervantine attribution tied to this production suggests circumspection, Cervantes is nonetheless everywhere here. The hedging "*atribuida a* Cervantes," or its variant "de atribución cervantina," are ubiquitous.[17] At a press conference at the Festival in Almagro, Sanz acknowledges we will never verify Cervantine authorship "from a scientific point of view."[18] An article in *El Mundo* thus tantalizes in the subjunctive: "¿Un Cervantes inédito? Pudiera ser" (An Unpublished Cervantes? Could be).[19] Sanz concludes a reflection published in *Nueva Revista* with this final wink-nod flourish: "The rest? The eloquence of an unsuspected text that manifests itself under the signature of Miguel de Cervantes . . . Or not?"[20] Such rhetorical moves operate even on a graphic scale on the several posters designed to advertise the production, which all feature the name of Cervantes in significantly larger scale than the diminutive "attributed to" that it follows.[21] The nature of such discourse centers the name of Cervantes even in the act of questioning it.

In contrast with such vacillations, others just go for broke. In her own reflections on the production, for which she played a key role as adviser and adapter of the script, Noguera Guirao doesn't mince words. Cervantes is the agent of her verbs: "Cervantes takes the audience by the hand," and "Cervantes creates situations that would be familiar to readers of the *Quijote*."[22] Sanz, for his part, admits that "I believe that what can most attract the audience to see *La Conquista* . . . is, one, the possible authorship of Cervantes."[23] This opinion on "Cervantes" as driver of interest and as publicity strategy, is channeled by Ruiz-Gallardón, president of the Consejo Social of Universidad Internacional de La Rioja (UNIR), one of the production's principal sponsors: "this discovery of this Cervantine work is a cultural event of the first order and of course . . . this fantastic opportunity is something that has to motivate us a little."[24] UNIR's own publicity couldn't be clearer: "The theatrical piece by Miguel de Cervantes is a total recovered gem" and we are in the humbling presence of "The best Cervantes."[25] *El Mundo* puts it artfully: "Cervantes conquers the Holy City."[26] The collective body of evidence, from advertisements, posters, interviews, press, and social media yields the ineluctable conclusion that whether or not *La conquista* is by Cervantes, it is.

This matters because "Cervantes" doesn't just drive ticket sales. He also catalyzes forms of reading. In the particular case of AE's production, "Cervantes" works to divert our attention from the play's crusading content in order to highlight, instead, its messier Mediterranean inter-religious love subplots. As Noguera Guirao puts it, *La conquista* "recreates the complexity of the human being beyond the conquest itself. A classic contemporary theater in which there is room to reflect on current times . . ., the eternal confrontation of two cultures sustained, in the end, by human beings."[27] For Sanz at Almagro, "Cervantes is always new, always modern, and always interesting and appealing."[28] And what appears most interesting, enjoyable, and perhaps useful, as a point of engagement with the present through Cervantes, is definitively not holy war but rather interfaith desire:

> [*La conquista*] deals fundamentally with . . . the theme of war, right? Of the war of the First Crusade. Unfortunately a theme about which I don't have to say anything, right?, [that's] unfortunately current because of the topic of religion, so unfortunately current and eternal because of the theme of . . . the cultures of the three religions of the Book having the city within their territory. . . But aside from this theme, which is there, it deals with various themes, and one, a really interesting one, [is] love, the possibility of love between two people of different religions. . . .So this theme of the impossibility of love . . . is a range of themes that the work touches on. But within this appearance of war, of the conquest of Jerusalem, what is really delicious, no? as with all delicious sandwiches, is inside, no? The meat, it's a play that has meat, because it has a story where the characters are very human and beyond the difference of religion. And Cervantes deals with this in an absolutely modern way allowing them to develop their relationship.

The repetition of "unfortunately" three times to refer to the crusades as the play's reluctantly necessary—perhaps superficial ("within this appearance of war")—frame contrasts with the description of the love theme as "interesting." The paraleptic rhetorical move of acknowledging the crusades while expressing disinterest in acknowledging them too much ("about which I don't have to say anything, right?"), as well as the disposition of the entire paragraph—sequentially subordinating crusading to privilege the more important topic of love—similarly telegraphs a set of priorities. What is "absolutely modern" here is not sacred violence but rather the human complexities that exceed and frustrate the logics of crusading. The delicious analogy of the play as a sandwich drives home the basic point that in confronting Cervantes's crusade fantasy, many of us would, I imagine, be just as happy to pick out the meat and throw away the bread. While religious violence may be a "current" topic, Cervantes's true "modernity"—what is "absolutely modern"—lies in the meat.

There is a politics of time at play here that bears acknowledging. Cervantes's recurrent framing not just by AE but by many Cervantes scholars as embodiment of new, "modern" modes of subjectivity, perception, literary form, and perhaps even qualified tolerance appears as fundamentally incompatible with the categories of the pre- or non-modern to which ideas such as crusading appear to belong.[29] *Don Quijote* obviously plays in the gaps between activating an imagined "medieval" as against a world in which such structures and values are no longer operative.[30] It is worth recognizing that the 'medieval' of *Don Quijote* includes *los nueve de la fama*, the Nine Worthies, among whom the titular protagonist of *La conquista* himself is counted.[31] *La conquista*'s historical crusading elements thus inhabit the temporal site against which Cervantine modernity is routinely positioned, and against which *Don Quijote* itself in some sense rails. From this vantage, the scholarly compulsion to yoke Cervantes to modernity may be generatively interrogated by considering the operation of the non-modern that *La conquista* embodies. I especially have in mind the work of scholars like Davis who have argued for viewing the "medieval" as modernity's temporal Other through which to symbolically legitimize problematic regimes of order, including justifications for racialized capitalism, ethnonationalism, colonialism, imperialism, and myriad other structures that draw strength from association with values such as "modern" empiricism, popular sovereignty, rationality, and secularism, in contraposition to "medieval" forms of superstition, violence, and the class imbalances of feudalism.[32] *La conquista* helpfully troubles Cervantes's location within this fraught temporal-political imaginary.

With this in view, it becomes clear that forms of reading that downplay crusading in order to recover what is more comfortably "modern" and "Cervantine" about *La conquista* deeply inform the choices that AE made in its adaptation. Beyond supplementing lacunae in the notoriously deficient manuscript or gently modifying some verses in order to correct evident copy errors, AE took significant liberties, reducing the number of verses by 28.5 percent, from 2,635 in the original to only 1,884.[33] The text's original length is well within the customary range for early modern Spanish theater, and was not a factor.[34] Sanz explains that "the density of almost episodic characters and subplots has obliged us to do away with those branches that didn't let us see the forest. . . . We've done a very respectful pruning with the meter and with some tertiary characters that have a single appearance in order to preserve the main story."[35] Cervantes's *repartos* are indeed legendary for their uncommon length—there are no less than thirty-one separate characters in the original text—and on a dramatic level, Cervantes is known in his early theater for uneven dramatic continuity between scenes in spatial and narrative terms, and a tendency for long static speeches.[36] That said, the tree pruning metaphor is not dissimilar to the sandwich metaphor and a careful reading of the well-landscaped forest leads to similar conclusions about what AE consider most "principal."

In the press conference at Almagro, Noguera Guirao insists that "we've tried . . . to be as rigorous as possible. For us that is always very important because fidelity to the author makes what you're showing be of the author and not what you want, what you would have wanted it to be, no? I mean, we haven't corrected Cervantes."[37] My aim is not to question the intentions of the team responsible for the adaptation but rather to note that a careful read of what was pruned in 2016—more than a quarter of the original play—reveals a set of assumptions about what can and should be left untouched in order to preserve "fidelity to the author," versus what might be snipped off without causing scruples. What AE cut while preserving Cervantine essence is, not surprisingly, a considerable volume of what we might call the play's most crusade-y bits. Before surveying specific cuts, I offer that in its choices, this adaptation materializes critical reading practices that extend beyond the particularities of AE, reflecting broader critical approaches that cultivate the Cervantes we need and want (the multicultural meat) while downplaying that other Cervantes who we might not always know exactly what to do with (the champion-of-sacred-violence and ontologies-of-religious-priority bread).

AE's interventions in pruning the play's ideological armature of crusading are considerable. For example, two rank-and-file crusaders, Charles and Fabricio, and a knight named Enrique de Volterra, are wholesale eliminated.[38] These characters operate as synecdochic stand-ins for the crusading army, embodying diverse military activities, asserting the historical appeal of crusading as a movement across social classes and geographies, and illuminating experiences of privation and suffering that would certainly provoke the sympathies of audiences. Two Christian captives, Teodoro and Anselmo, are similarly cut.[39] Though their presence is brief, as figures metonymically emblematizing the suffering of the Christian community under Muslim rule in Jerusalem, Teodoro and Anselmo activate notions central to crusade apology. While these characters are fictional, the adaptation also trims historical exposition tied to the crusades, including heroic profiles of Godfrey of Bouillon, Raymond of Saint-Gilles, and Boemund; references to the siege of Antioch, the discovery of the holy lance, the Seljuk governor of Antioch, and the Byzantine Emperor Alexios I Comnenus; the preaching of Peter the Hermit; and passing description of the Christian siege encampment.[40] A pair of key passages that are eliminated extol the ethics and spiritual virtues of the crusaders in almost hagiographic terms.[41] Through such perhaps minor moments, the material and ideological matrix of crusading nevertheless permeates the play.

Even more significant modifications relate to the play's opening and closing, when the allegorical characters of Jerusalem, Travail, Hope, Contentment, and Liberty provide an affective frame allowing for the dramatization of crusade history.[42] A number of select passages from the play's opening are cut, along with almost the entirety of the extended closing allegorical scenes.[43] In her move from miserable Muslim captivity to joyous Christian liberty, the dramatic arc of Jerusalem personified which bookends the play is, in essence, the Latin Christian story of the First Crusade itself. This particular framing is rooted in the very justifications for crusade laid out in Pope Urban II's famous sermon at 1095 Clermont, which have shaped the stock narratives and cultural imaginary of crusading ever since.[44] While the adaptation retains the play's initial allusion to Clermont, what it excises relating to Urban's sermon is substantive.[45] For example, we lose an entire stanza enumerating the topical anti-Muslim catalogue of horrors reflected in near contemporary chronicles and subsequent crusade histories: Jerusalem here is victim of the conventional abuses of tyrannical Muslims who topple churches, profane relics, and slit the throats of innocent Christians.[46] The adaptation retains just four verses of the subsequent stanza, in which Muslims appear as a "pueblo infame" (vile people) stomping on the Sepulchre of Christ with "pies sacrílegos" (sacrilegious feet) but it then eliminates a description of one of the linchpins undergirding all of crusading theology, the indulgences promised to those who take the cross.[47] The adaptation skips over an implied allusion to the famous spontaneous cry of "Deus vult" that those present at Clermont uttered, the first of no less than nine instances in which versions of the famous battle cry appear throughout the play, four of which are eliminated in the adaptation, largely through the aggressive trimming of the concluding allegorical sequence.[48] The gutting of the final allegorical sequence means that the symbolic opening of Jerusalem dragging chains on her feet, bearing a literal yoke, is no longer rounded out with the removal of her yoke by Travail at the end.[49] Contentment and Liberty are also cut, along with extended verses highlighting Christian joy at the crusaders' victory. Since most of the final siege is not acted out directly on stage in the original but is imaginatively conjured through the emotional responses of the allegorical characters, the elimination of the bulk of the allegorical sequence deprives audiences of the affective climax of the entire crusading endeavor as originally conceived. Throughout this exchange between allegorical figures, the battle also rages offstage. Cuts to this sequence thus imply the elimination of several stage directions aimed at evoking the heat of the battle, thereby neutering the cathartic moment of crusading victory.[50] Taken together, such modifications hack at the affective, ideological, and spiritual appeals basic to the crusading imaginary.

The adaptation also eliminates the original play's concluding scene: the coronation of Godfrey as king of Jerusalem.[51] Following the successful siege, the allegorical figures abandon the stage, and the victorious crusaders emerge to give prayerful thanks. They agree to elect Godfrey as their king, which he accepts while rejecting the crown of gold that they offer him, instead removing his shoes and kissing the sacred ground of Jerusalem, a gesture which the whole army imitates. The elimination of this conclusion erases the profound historical, political, and spiritual valence of the establishment of the Latin crusader kingdom in the East. Spain's possession of the crown of Jerusalem following the 1510 papal investiture of Ferdinand the Catholic with the title obliges us to read Godfrey's coronation as the origin story of an important strand of political mythology in Spain.[52] By eliminating this scene, the adaptation severs pretended historical continuities and obscures the culminating moment toward which the entire crusading project is appointed: the establishment of permanent Christian dominion in Jerusalem (with Spain playing a providentially central role).[53]

This is not an exhaustive catalogue of changes made to the play, but as this survey makes clear, AE's production encourages us to see *La conquista*'s crusading content as incidental to Cervantine essence. The play's non-crusade elements remain almost untouched, whereas the adaptation seems to assert that we can jettison holy war without jettisoning Cervantes. In line with this approach, AE concludes their production with one final strategy I suggest aims to manage critical anxieties around the specter of a crusade apologist Cervantes:

> At the end of the show . . . the actors stop playing their roles . . . Now they're human beings removed from the game of war. They advance in silence towards the audience, looking at their bloodied hands. It is the only and humble contribution we make to the *mise-en-scène* regarding the rabid currentness of the religiously-tinted conflict that our world has suffered for centuries.[54]

This gesture acknowledging the human cost of sacred violence through the somber symbol of bloodied hands appears dramatically impactful. What it is not, of course, is part of *La conquista*. As a creative choice, this modified ending is noteworthy not just as a laudable artistic and ethical response to crusade, but also as a mechanism for reaffirming a particular reading of Cervantes. What Sanz calls AE's "only and humble contribution" in effect replaces the original play's coronation of Godfrey—celebrating the providentially-ordained triumph of good over evil, imagining the dawn of a utopian Christian future in Jerusalem—with a symbolic interrogation of those very same narratives. Cervantes here is pressed into creative service to condemn that which the original text of *La conquista* celebrates, and that for which it advocates throughout: crusading.

Having expurgated many of the play's most committed elements of crusade apology, AE's decision to conclude the work in this fashion reads as a symptom of the desire to mollify the specter of crusade apologist Cervantes. By working to guide our own interpretation of what "Cervantes" should mean in these ways, however, it is worth considering if the adaptation does not also accidentally undercut the critical potentiality of the disharmonious narrative layers and ideological dispositions of the original themselves. Here we might consider, for example, how in the adaptation, Tancredo's tragic murder of the Muslim woman he loves and desires to be with, Clorinda, may be ciphered in the collective guilt of the crusaders expressed in this added scene.[55] Yet the original already invites serious questions in this direction thanks, precisely, to the juxtapositions that have sometimes been read as a flaw of *La conquista*. Ironically, perhaps the closest that the original comes to the sort of critical interrogation that the bloodied hands embody is also an element that was undermined through AE's pruning. In a brief but deeply poignant moment following Clorinda's death, Tancredo emerges in mourning, literally wearing her black outergarment and shield, standing sadly to the side just as Godfrey is in the midst of his rousing harangue before the final assault. Stage directions are explicit on Tancredo's affect here, which dramatizes in a visible and material way the tremendous gulf of tension between the play's narrative layers.[56] The violent contrast between a triumphant speech about the "dulce fin" (sweet end) of a providential victory over "bárbara fiereza" (barbarous savagery) and Tancredo's own wrenching human experience of love and loss across religious boundaries are allowed to exist simultaneously on stage. Rather than see this as a clumsy flaw, the friction itself invites questions and produces very Mediterranean meanings that generatively muddy singular interpretations.

To my mind this scene represents the play's most emotionally interesting and frankly "Cervantine" moment. This is unfortunately another moment that suffered considerable modifications in the adaptation, which edits out most of Godfrey's speech and moves the gutted Tancredo's emergence to just moments before the final siege begins.[57] My point here is that the seeds of something like a critical interrogation of sacred violence are evident in *La conquista*, even if they are directly contradicted by other internal elements such as those already discussed.

AE's creative—often interventionist—adaptation ultimately dramatizes the very fact that Cervantes remains difficult to reconcile even with Cervantes. In opting for a particular version of "Cervantes," AE responds to a problem that is basic to not just this play but to much of the *manco de Lepanto*'s work. This adaptation seeks to reduce the cognitive dissonance by trimming out as much crusade as possible from a play about crusading, while appending an acerbic final meditation on the horrors of holy war. The adaptation thus tenders a stark confession about how uncomfortable the idea of a crusading Cervantes might be for us today, though in its particular responses to this problem, AE ironically also undermines what is most deeply Cervantine about this play to begin with: its aporistic contradictions that interpellate us as subjects called on to render our own critical judgments.

That said, in particular view of the fact that this is a play about crusading by Cervantes, it is worth considering that this selective approach may be not just appropriate but perhaps even necessary. As I highlighted at the start, far-right extremist ideologies draw strength from the malleable notion of a divinely licensed battle against an absolute Other. Crusade has been explicitly marshaled as inspiration in justifying slaughter in recent years. In Spain, the narratives of not just "Reconquista" but also the conceptually related field of crusade operate as vehicles for imagining a pure Spanish ethno-state free from the contaminations of forces cast as external to it, justifying modes of violence both symbolic and real.[58] These are notions that feature routinely in public discourse and online culture, and are dear to Spain's resurgent right, emblematized in the Vox party.[59] The Falange's much earlier National-Catholic "cruzada" performed similar ideological duties during and after the Spanish Civil War, freighting "crusade" with a set of resonances proper to recent national history.[60] For all of these reasons, concerns over how a Cervantes enamored of crusade might play out in the public sphere go beyond the abstractions of academic debate. This play obliges us to confront the fact that, despite its complex border-crossings—and regardless of AE's efforts to downplay crusade—*La conquista* undeniably activates ideologies and images that circulate widely among the extreme right, and that feed violence and hate. And it does so under the authority of the name of "Cervantes."

I preface what follows by saying that I have not been able to identify any direct evidence of extremist expressions of appreciation for, or appropriations of, *La conquista*. This may not be too shocking since not even *cervantistas* seem aware of this play. Regardless, as an example of how natural the slippage might be, posters advertising AE's production, prominently featuring the so-called Jerusalem cross—with the name of Cervantes inscribed on it—perhaps ironically look at home alongside popular right-wing crusader memes. In Spain, crusader memes and allusions to "Deus vult" or to crusading in general abound online in places like Twitter/X and Facebook in reference to phenomena as wide-ranging as applauding Vox party leader Santiago Abascal's interview with Tucker Carlson or complaining about issues from Muslim immigration to the leftist woke agenda to Pedro Sánchez's agreement to secure the votes to be invested with the presidency.[61] Specific expressions of crusade ideology also manifested themselves in abundance following the start of the 2023 war in Gaza, with numerous Spanish commentators online noting that Felipe VI is titular king of Jerusalem, and that the time for a Spanish crusade to conquer the Holy Land has arrived.[62]

If *La conquista*'s crusading subject matter by its very nature resonates with such ideas, then the fact that it is the national icon Cervantes, of all figures, who is licensing crusade in this play only complicates matters further. In view of this broader social and political context, we might want to go easy on AE for its choices to creatively quarantine the play's crusading narrative in order to emphasize those aspects of the work that serve precisely to undermine such violent ideologies. In the end, to return to Castillo and Egginton's question of *What Would Cervantes Do?*, this particular play ultimately drives home just how much the answer to that question depends on who is doing the asking.

NOTES

1. Sincere thanks to Liz Spragins for her generous comments on this chapter.
1. Antonucci, "Reelaboración," 392. See also Antonucci, "La conquista," 187; Kahn, "Even Further"; and Arata, "*La conquista*," 26.
2. Brioso Santos, "Notas," 162.
3. For a summary, Kahn, "Attributions," 470–71; and Arata, "*La conquista*," 26. For a recentering of Jerusalem within Spain's sixteenth-century Mediterranean, see Devereux, *The Other Side*, especially chapters 1 and 5. On captivity as driver of a complex network that helped produce the early modern Mediterranean, see Hershenzon, *The Captive Sea*.
4. Brioso Santos's edition of Cervantes, *La conquista*, 98. For an introduction to a Mediterranean studies approach to the work of Cervantes, see Johnson, *Affective Geographies*.
5. Castillo, "Espacios," 139–40.
6. Antonucci, "La conquista," 190–91.
7. For example, Laguna, *Cervantes*; and Layna Ranz and Cortijo Ocaña, eds., *Cervantes*.
8. I have in mind here the question Mariscal posed twenty-five years ago: "What kind of Cervantes do we want? Or, put another way, what kind of Cervantes de we need?" Mariscal, "The Crisis," 205.
9. For an introduction, see Horswell and Awan, eds., *The Crusades*.
10. For two examples: Castillo, "Notes," and García Jordán, "*El trato*."

11. Aside from Castillo and Egginton, *What Would Cervantes Do?*, some works that reflect this trend include Burningham, *Tilting*; Childers, *Transnational*, part three, "Cervantes Now"; Clamurro, *Cervantes'* Novelas; Castillo, *Un-Deceptions*.
12. On crusade in the Norway terrorist's manifesto, see Wollenberg, "The New Knighthood." On Christchurch, see Leahy, "Reflections."
13. Arata, "*La conquista*" and "Nota"; and Brioso Santos's introduction to his edition of *La conquista*, 11–25.
14. Scholarship on *La conquista* obsesses on authorship. While Eisenberg, "¿Qué escribió Cervantes?," raised some initial doubts, his arguments are not based on a close reading of the text, and are thoroughly insufficient. Aside from Eisenberg, those few scholars who have engaged with the work appear in overwhelming agreement that signs point to Cervantes. See Arata, "*La conquista*" and "Notas"; Brioso Santos, "Análisis métrico"; Brioso Sánchez and Brioso Santos, "De Heliodoro a Tasso"; Castillo, "Espacios"; Cerezo Soler, "*La Conquista*"; Cerezo Soler and Calvo Tello, "Autoría" and "*La conquista*"; Kahn, "Towards a Theory" and "Even Further"; and Rodríguez López-Vázquez, "La *Jerusalén*."
15. The production was included among official acts of the National Commission for the Commemoration of the Fourth Centenary of the Death of Cervantes: Comisión Nacional, "Programa de Actividades."
16. *La conquista* remains marginal within Cervantes scholarship. Brioso Sánchez and Brioso Santos, "De Heliodoro," 165–66, suggest that disinterest stems from a lack of scholarly enthusiasm for Cervantes's theater, alongside lingering suspicions about authorship. Castillo, "Espacios," 101, shares this last opinion. Kahn, "Towards a Theory," 123, suggests the work is just not familiar to *cervantistas*. I would add to these hypotheses that perhaps the idea of a play about crusading does not align comfortably with how we prefer to read Cervantes. How comfortable are we, really, with the possibility of a Cervantes crusade apologist?
17. "La conquista," Madrid Es Teatro; Comisión Nacional, "Programa de actividades," 48.
18. All video transcriptions are my own. Festival de Almagro, "La conquista de Jerusalén."
19. Villán, "Cervantes inédito y morisco."
20. Sanz Ballesteros, "Propuesta escénica," 159.
21. I have identified three different posters produced for the production. See "La conquista," Madrid Es Teatro; "El mejor Cervantes," UNIR; and the photo section of AE's Facebook page: https://www.facebook.com/photo?fbid=1624333281190700&set=t.100054667950493.
22. Noguera Guirao, "Pinceladas," 15–16.
23. España Fascinante, "Juan Sanz Ballester."
24. UNIR, "TEASER."
25. "El mejor Cervantes," UNIR.
26. Gálvez, "Cervantes conquista."
27. Noguera Guirao, "Pinceladas," 156.
28. Festival de Almagro, "La conquista."
29. For example, the association between Cervantes and nascent modernity shapes Egginton's tellingly titled *The Man Who Invented Fiction: How Cervantes Ushered in the Modern World*.
30. See Palmer, "Don Quixote."
31. Manion, "'Perpetuel memorye,'" 123, notes the utility in late medieval and early modern Europe of the Nine Worthies—and particularly Godfrey—as vectors "to promulgate crusade ideology and to urge contemporary rulers and nobles to emulate those deeds." Don Quijote compares himself to the Nine Worthies in his famous "yo sé quién soy" speech (I:5).

32. Davis, *Periodization* and "Theory in Time."
33. For all references to the original, I have relied on Antonucci's edition. I have also consulted Brioso Santos's edition. For AE's adapted script, which does not indicate divergences from the original, see Cervantes, attributed to, "*Comedia de la conquista de Jerusalén*." To avoid confusion, I will use Cervantes, *La conquista* to refer to Antonucci's edition and Cervantes, "*Comedia de la conquista*," *Nueva revista*, to refer to the adaptation.
34. For comparison, Cervantes's contemporaneous *La Numancia* has 2,448 verses; Lope's *Fuenteovejuna*, 2,456; Tirso's *El burlador de Sevilla*, 2,978; and Calderón's *La vida es sueño*, 3,319.
35. Seoane, "'La conquista.'"
36. These characteristics already formed part of Arata's original arguments on behalf of Cervantine authorship.
37. Festival de Almagro, "La conquista."
38. Cervantes, *La conquista*, 1161–62, vv.1659–65 are cut; 1151–55, vv. 1329–440 are reassigned to Boemundo and Tancredo, though vv. 1389–400, 1421–22, and 1433–40 are also cut; Charles and Fabricio are removed from a scene in the third jornada, and Fabricio's lines there are reassigned to Boemundo, 1180–81.
39. Cervantes, *La conquista*, 1115–18, vv. 312–95
40. Cervantes, *La conquista*, 1107–11, 1140–44, 1156–57, vv. 137–68, 209–16, 1055–174, 1489–508, 1513–20.
41. Cervantes, *La conquista*, 1152–53 and 1158, vv. 1389–400, and 1545–60.
42. On Cervantes's allegorical figures, see Cerezo Soler, "*La Conquista*" and Kahn, "Even Further."
43. Cervantes, *La conquista*, 1103–4, 1107–11, and 1186–93, vv.7–14, 41–48, 113–20, 125–33, 136–77, 184–92, 209–20, 2402–46, 2453–83, 2486–91, 2504–21, 2537–42, and 2546–78.
44. On the historical sources informing *La conquista*, see Brioso Santos, "Notas" and Arata, "*La conquista*," 25. Crusade narratives continued to circulate widely in various forms through the seventeenth century in Spain. See Leahy and Tully, eds., *Jerusalem Afflicted*.
45. Cervantes, *La conquista*, 1106, vv. 105–12.
46. Cervantes, *La conquista*, 1107, vv. 113–20.
47. Cervantes, *La conquista*, 1107, vv. 121–24; Cervantes, "*Comedia de la conquista*," *Nueva revista*, 164, vv. 97–100. Cervantes, *La conquista*, 1107, vv. 129–34.
48. Cervantes, *La conquista*, 1107, v. 128 offers a passing reference, which the adaptation cuts, though it retains the play's later fulsome accounting of "Deus vult" at Clermont as one of the First Crusade's four miracles: 1151–52, vv. 1353–73; Cervantes, "*Comedia de la conquista*," *Nueva revista*, 158–59, vv. 823–43. Versions of "Deus vult" also appear five times in stage directions, Cervantes, *La conquista*, 1111, 1161, 1185–86, 1188–89, 1191, three of which are eliminated in the adaptation.
49. Cervantes, *La conquista*, 1103. Verses from the opening sequence in the adaptation are captured in the trailer: UNIR, "TEASER." The allegorical figure of Jerusalem in the adaptation appears adorned with a garment that symbolically evokes the city's walls and towers, whereas in the original the yoke and chains are central to her representation.
50. Cervantes, *La conquista*, 1188–91.
51. Cervantes, *La conquista*, 1193–95, vv. 2579–636.
52. For a brief overview, Leahy and Tully, *Jerusalem Afflicted*, 12–13, and 164–68.
53. Cervantes, *La conquista*, 1193, v. 2586–87.
54. Sanz, "Propuesta escénica," 159.
55. Cervantes, *La conquista*, 1182–84, vv. 2283–350.
56. Cervantes, *La conquista*, 1185, vv. 2362–74.

57. Cervantes, "*Comedia de la conquista*," *Nueva Revista*, 218.
58. García Sanjuan, "Rejecting al-Andalus" and Queimada e Silva, "The *Reconquista* revisited."
59. For a whirlwind meditation on the mercurial properties of nationalisms in contemporary Spain, see Batalla Cueto, *Los nuevos odres*.
60. See Reig Tapia, *La cruzada*, chapter 3.
61. For these specific examples, see the posts of @manuelcaper2014, @Classicus, and @BertiRods, and the eloquently named Facebook group page of "Neocruzados 'Deus Vult'" (Neo-crusaders Deus Vult). Links can be found in the bibliography.
62. For just two examples, see @AryanSpaniard @Padri's posts.

BIBLIOGRAPHY

@AryanSpaniard, "Tras lo de la iglesia cristiana destruida y medio millar de cristianos fallecidos hay suficiente motivo para convocar una Cruzada que establezca la paz en Tierra Santa y le deja la tutela de Palestina al legítimo Rey de Jerusalén (Felipe de Borbón)," October 20, 2023, 10:21 a.m., https://twitter.com/AryanSpaniard/status/1715402836370977003.

@BertiRods, "Wow! Excellent interview[.] Viva España! Deus Vult," November 20, 2023, 6:39pm, https://twitter.com/BertieRodz/status/1726777389877760291.

@Classicus, "La única solución que queda en España es la Santa Cruzada. No pierdan tiempo en darse cuenta y aprovechen para prepararse antes de que sea tarde. Dios lo quiere. ¡VIVA CRISTO REY! ¡ARRIBA ESPAÑA! DEUS VULT!," April 24, 2023, 8:44am, https://twitter.com/Classicus/status/1650511136427474947

@manuelcaper2014, "Viene apretando fuerte el sector nacionalcatólico del Reino de España. ¡Deus Vult!," Twitter / X, November 13, 2023, 3:12pm, https://twitter.com/manuelcaper2014/status/1723826139662008479.

@Padri, "Está llegando. A recuperar el Reino de Jerusalén del que Felipe VI es rey, por cierto," October 13, 2023, 8:45am, https://twitter.com/Padri__/status/1712841949986594933.

Antonucci, Fausta. "Reelaboración y reescritura de la 'Gerusalemme Liberata en La conquista de Jerusalén por Godofre de Bullón,' atribuida a Cervantes." In *Serenísima palabra: actas del X Congreso de la Asociación Internacional Siglo de Oro (Venecia, 14–18 de julio de 2014)*, edited by Anna Bognolo, Florencio del Barrio de la Rosa, María del Valle Ojeda Calvo, Donatella Pini, and Andrea Zinato, 383–94. Edizioni Ca'Foscari, 2017.

Antonucci, Fausta. "La conquista de Jerusalén por Godofre de Bullón." In Miguel de Cervantes, *Comedias y tragedias: volumen complementario*, coordinated by Luis Gómez Canseco, 182–94. Real Academia Española, 2015.

Arata, Stefano. "*La conquista de Jerusalén*: Cervantes y la generación teatral de 1580." *Criticón* 54 (1992): 9–112.

Arata, Stefano. "Notas sobre *La conquista de Jerusalén* y la transmisión manuscrita del primer teatro cervantino." *Edad de Oro* 16 (1997): 53–66.

Batalla Cueto, Pablo. *Los nuevos odres del nacionalismo español*. Trea, 2021.

Brioso Santos, Héctor. "Análisis métrico de *La conquista de Jerusalén* por Godofre de Bullón de . . . ¿Miguel de Cervantes?" In *Cuatrocientos años del* Arte Nuevo de Hacer Comedias *de Lope de Vega*, vol. 2, edited by Germán Vega and Héctor Urzáiz, 287–94. Universidad de Valladolid, 2010.

Brioso Santos, Héctor. "A propósito de la historicidad de *La conquista de Jerusalén*: Los cuatros Milagros de la primera cruzada." *Anuario de Estudios Cervantinos* 5 (2009): 101–24.
Brioso Santos, Héctor. "Notas sobre la historicidad de *La conquista de Jerusalén*, comedia atribuida a Miguel de Cervantes." In *La voz de Clío: Imágenes del poder en la comedia histórica del Siglo de Oro*, edited by Oana Andreia Sâmbrian, Mariela Insúa Cereceda, and Antonie Mihail, 158–87. Editura Universitaria, 2012.
Brioso Sánchez, Máximo and Héctor Brioso Santos. "De Heliodoro a Tasso y a ¿Cervantes?" *Philología Hispalensis* 21 (2007): 165–66.
Burningham, Bruce R. *Tilting Cervantes: Baroque Reflections on Postmodern Culture*. Vanderbilt University Press, 2008.
Castillo, David. *Un-Deceptions: Cervantine Strategies for the Disinformation Age*. Juan de la Cuesta, 2021.
Castillo, David, and Willliam Egginton. *What Would Cervantes Do? Navigating Post-Truth with Spanish Baroque Literature*. McGill-Queen's University Press, 2022.
Castillo, Moisés. "Espacios de ambigüedad en el teatro cervantino: *La conquista de Jerusalén* y los dramas de cautiverio." *Cervantes* 32, no. 2 (2012): 123–42.
Castillo, Moisés. "Notes on an Ethics of Theatricality in Cervantes: *El gallardo español* and *La Numancia*," in *Social Justice in Spanish Golden Age Theatre*. Edited by Erin Alice Cowling, Tania de Miguel Magro, Mina García Jordán, and Glenda Y. Nieto-Cuebas, 82–97. University of Toronto Press, 2021.
Cerezo Solar, Juan. "*La Conquista de Jerusalén* en su contexto: sobre el personaje colectivo y una vuelta más a la atribución cervantina." *Dicenda* 32 (2014): 33–49.
Cerezo Soler, Juan, and José Calvo Tello. "Autoría y estilo. Una atribución cervantina desde las humanidades digitales. El caso de *La conquista de Jerusalén*." *Anales Cervantinos* 51 (2019): 231–50.
Cerezo Soler, Juan, and José Calvo Tello. "*La conquista de Jerusalén* ¿de Cervantes? Análisis estilométrico sobre autoría en el teatro del Siglo de Oro español." *Digital Humanities Quarterly* 12, no. 1 (2019): 213–50.
Cervantes Saavedra, Miguel de. *Comedia de la conquista de Jerusalén por Godofre de Bullón*. In *Comedias y tragedias: Volumen complementario*. Coordinated by Luis Gómez Canseco. Edited by Fausta Antonucci, 1101–95. Real Academia Española, 2015.
Cervantes Saavedra, Miguel de. Attributed to. "*Comedia de la conquista de Jerusalén por Godofre de Bullón*." Version by Ana Martín Puigpelat, Dolores Noguera, and Juan Sanz Ballesteros. *Nueva Revista de Política, Cultura y Arte* 158 (2016): 160–220.
Cervantes Saavedra, Miguel de. Attributed to. *La conquista de Jerusalén por Godofre de Bullon*. Edited by Héctor Brioso Santos. Cátedra, 2009.
Clamurro, William H. *Cervantes'* Novelas ejemplares: *Reading Their Lessons from His Time to Ours*. Lexington, 2015.
Childers, William. *Transnational Cervantes*. University of Toronto University Press, 2006.
Comisión Nacional para la Conmemoración del IV Centenaria de la muerte de Miguel de Cervantes. "Programa de Actividades: IV Centenario de la muerte de Cervantes." Comisión Nacional, Ministerio de Educación, Cultura y Deporte, last modified May 2017, https://400cervantes.es/IV-CENTENARIO-CERVANTES-PROGRAMA-OFICIAL.pdf.
Davis, Kathleen. *Periodization and Sovereignty: How Ideas of Feudalism and Secularization Govern the Politics of Time*. University of Pennsylvania Press, 2008.
Davis, Kathleen. "Theory in Time," *PMLA* 130, no. 3 (2015): 59–67.

Devereux, Andrew. *The Other Side of Empire: Just War in the Mediterranean and the Rise of Early Modern Spain.* Cornell University Press, 2020.

Eisenberg, Daniel. "¿Qué escribió Cervantes?" In *Sobre Cervantes.* Edited by Diego Martínez Torrón, 9–26. Centro de Estudios Cervantinos, 2003.

Egginton, William. *The Man Who Invented Fiction: How Cervantes Ushered in the Modern World.* Bloomsbury, 2016.

España Fascinante. "Juan Sanz Ballester – Director de escena de 'La conquista de Jerusalén.'" YouTube, March 22, 2016, video, 1:04, https://www.youtube.com/watch?v=yIWf1LEZCQg.

Festival de Almagro. "La conquista de Jerusalén." YouTube, July 31, 2016, video, 14:29, https://www.youtube.com/watch?v=_CU6RJ87OQM.

Gálvez, Cristian. "Cervantes conquista la ciudad santa." *El Mundo,* May 17, 2016, https://www.elmundo.es/cultura/2016/05/17/572b2f72e2704ed3098b45cb.html.

García Jordán, Mina. "*El trato de Argel* and the Immigrant Crisis." In *Social Justice in Spanish Golden Age Theatre.* Edited by Erin Alice Cowling, Tania de Miguel Magro, Mina García Jordán, and Glenda Y Nieto-Cuebas, 157–74. University of Toronto Press, 2021.

García Sanjuan, Alejandro. "Rejecting al-Andalus, Exalting the Reconquista: Historical Memory in Contemporary Spain." *Journal of Medieval Iberian Studies* 10, no. 1 (2018): 127–45.

Hershenzon, Daniel. *The Captive Sea: Slavery, Communication, and Commerce in Early Modern Spain and the Mediterranean.* University of Pennsylvania Press, 2018.

Horsell, Mike, and Akil N. Awan, eds. *The Crusades in the Modern World: Engaging the Crusades,* vol. 2. Routledge, 2020.

Johnson, Paul Michael. *Affective Geographies: Cervantes, Emotion, and the Literary Mediterranean.* University of Toronto Press, 2021.

Kahn, Aaron M. "Attributions and Lost and Promised Works." In *The Oxford Handbook of Cervantes,* edited by Aaron M. Kahn, 467–88. Oxford University Press, 2021.

Kahn, Aaron M. "Even Further Towards a Theory of Attribution: Advancing the Cervantine Attribution of *La conquista de Jerusalén po Godofre de Bullón.*" *Cervantes* 33, no. 1 (2013): 133–66.

Kahn, Aaron M. "Towards a Theory of Attribution: Is *La conquista de Jerusalén* by Miguel de Cervantes?" *Journal of European Studies* 40, no. 2 (2010): 99–128.

"La conquista de Jerusalén atribuida a Cervantes." Madrid es teatro, accessed November 15, 2023, https://madridesteatro.com/la-conquista-de-jerusalen/.

Laguna, Ana María G. *Cervantes, the Golden Age, and the Battle for Cultural Identity in 20th-Century Spain.* Bloomsbury, 2021.

Layna Ranz, Francisco, and Antonio Cortijo Ocaña, eds. *Cervantes, política nacional y estética nacionalista.* Special issue of *eHumanista/Cervantes* 3 (2014).

Leahy, Chad. "Reflections on Iberian Studies, Christchurch, and Hate." *Contesting Hate: A Critical Response to Christchurch.* Edited by Chad Leahy. *Center for Middle East Studies: Occasional Paper Series* 11 (November 2020): 8–10. https://drive.google.com/file/d/1asNhQOD5Mq1G4OiqSAzpMkDAS4H2VeqE/view.

Leahy, Chad, and Ken Tully, eds. *Jerusalem Afflicted: Quaresmius, Spain, and the Idea of a 17th-Century Crusade.* Routledge, 2020.

Manion, Lee. "'Perpetuel memorye': Remembering History in the Crusading Romance." In *Remembering the Crusades and Crusading.* Edited by Megan Cassidy Welch, 114–28. Routledge, 2017.

Mariscal, George. "The Crisis of Hispanism as Apocalyptic Myth." In *Cervantes and His Postmodern Constituencies*. Edited by Caroll Johnson and Anne Cruz. Routledge, 2000.

Neocruzados. "Deus Vult," "'España cristiana y no musulmana' en Alicante. ¿Apoyas estos cánticos en contra del terrorismo de la Yihad Islámica?," November 10, 2023, https://fb.watch/o_1KA3PjVH/.

"El mejor Cervantes y 'La Conquista de Jerusalén,' llegan a Madrid de la mano de UNIR." UNIR La Universidad en Internet, May 13, 2016, https://www.unir.net/actualidad/vida-academica/la-conquista-de-jerusalen-y-el-mejor-cervantes-llegan-a-madrid-de-la-mano-de-unir/.

Noguera Guirao, Dolores. "Pinceladas sobre *La conquista de Jerusalén por Godofre de Bullón (1581–1585)*." *Nueva Revista de Política, Cultura y Arte* 158 (2016): 154–56.

Queimada e Silva, Tiago João. "The *Reconquista* Revisited: Mobilizing Medieval Iberian History in Spain, Portugal, and Beyond." In *The Crusades in the Modern World: Engaging the Crusades*, vol. 2. Edited by Mike Horswell and Akil N. Awan. Routledge, 2020.

Palmer, Donald D. "Don Quixote and the Remembrance of Things Medieval" *postmedieval* 5 (2014): 10–20.

Reig Tapia, Alberto. *La cruzada de 1936: mito y memoria*. Alianza, 2006.

Rodríguez López-Vázquez, Alfredo. "La *Jerusalén* de Cervantes: Nuevas pruebas de su autoría." *Artifara* 11 (2011).

Sanz Ballesteros, Juan. "Propuesta escénica: ¿un oratorio para la primera cruzada?," *Nueva Revista de Política, Cultura y Arte* 158 (2016): 157–9.

Seoane, Andrés. "'La conquista de Jerusalén por Godofre de Bullón' (Miguel de Cervantes). Cervantes inédito y musical." *Granada Hispánicas* (blog), accessed November 28, 2023, http://granadahispanicas.blogspot.com/2016/07/cervantes-inedito-y-musical.html.

Villán, Javier. "Cervantes inédito y morisco." *El Mundo*, May 26, 2016, https://www.elmundo.es/cultura/2016/05/26/5745e6f0e5fdea75388b467b.html.

Wollenberg, Daniel. "The New Knighthood: Terrorism and the Medieval." *postmedieval* 5, no. 1 (2014): 21–33.

Contributors

MERCEDES ALCALÁ GALÁN is professor of Spanish literature and culture at the University of Wisconsin–Madison, where she is an H.I. Romnes Fellow and senior fellow at the Institute for Research in the Humanities. She has served as president of the Cervantes Society of America. Her research focuses on poetics, gender, and visual culture in early modern Spain. She is the author of *Con esta carga nacemos las mujeres: Discursos sobre el cuerpo femenino en la España de Cervantes* and *Escritura desatada: Poéticas de la representación en Cervantes*, among other books, and more than eighty articles. She is completing a book on visuality and ekphrasis.

LUIS F. AVILÉS is emeritus professor in the Department of Spanish and Portuguese at the University of California, Irvine. He has published the books *Lenguaje y crisis: Las alegorías del Criticón* (1998), and *Avatares de lo invisible: Espacio y subjetividad en los Siglos de Oro* (2017). He is co-editor of *Representaciones de la violencia en América Latina* (2015), and a special issue of the journal *La Torre*. Apart from his work on authors such as Baltasar Gracián, Garcilaso de la Vega, Antonio de Guevara, and Sor Juana Inés de la Cruz, and his essays on *Abencerraje* and *Lazarillo de Tormes*, he has published several articles and book chapters on Cervantes.

MARGARET E. BOYLE is professor of Romance languages and literatures and Latin American, Caribbean and Latinx studies at Bowdoin College. Her primary interests include Hispanic women's literary history, *comedia* history and performance, and health humanities, including medical, spiritual, and food cultures. Boyle is the director of *Multilingual Mainers* and co-editor with Barbara Fuchs of *Bulletin of the Comediantes*. Her books include *Unruly Women: Performance, Penitence and Punishment in Early Modern Spain* (2014),

Health and Healing in the Early Modern Iberian World: A Gendered Perspective (with Sarah Owens, 2021), and *Sabor Judío* (with Ilan Stavans, 2024).

ISRAEL BURSHATIN is professor emeritus of Spanish and comparative literature, Haverford College. His writings on medieval and early modern Spanish literature and history explore issues of race, nationhood, and the politics of gender and embodiment. Notable among these is his collaboration with the Spanish artists Cabello / Carceller in *Anexo: Caso Céspedes/ Addendum: The Céspedes Case* (2019). He is currently at work on a personal chronicle of migration and displacement as captured in the family album.

SUSAN BYRNE is professor of Hispanic studies at the University of Nevada, Las Vegas. In her latest book, *The Aesthetic Turn in Cervantes* (2025), Byrne highlights the central role played by Cervantes in the modernization of aesthetic concerns. In prior monographs she has studied the reception of Neoplatonic philosophy in early modern Spain (*Ficino in Spain*); revealed a subtle juridical-historical substructure in Cervantes' masterpiece (*Law and History in Cervantes'* Don Quixote); and offered close philological study of Hermetic imagery in Renaissance Spanish mysticism (*El Corpus Hermeticum y tres poetas españoles*).

DAVID CASTILLO is a Spanish professor and founding co-director of the Center for Information Integrity at SUNY Buffalo, where he served as department chair (2009–2015) and Humanities Institute director (2016–2022). Castillo's latest book is *Un-Deceptions: Cervantine Strategies for the Disinformation Age* (2021). He also co-authored, most recently, *What Would Cervantes Do? Navigating Post-Truth with Spanish Baroque Literature* (2022) and *Medialogies: Reading Reality in the Age of Inflationary Media* (2016). Among his multiple co-edited essay collections are *Truth-Seeking in Our Age of (Mis)Information Overload* (2024) and *Anti-Disinformation Pedagogies: Tacking the Power of Manipulative Media* (2024). His current projects include the forthcoming volume *Building an AI Conscience? Critical Conversations on AI and Society Across the Disciplines*.

WILLIAM EGGINTON is the Decker Professor in the Humanities, chair of the Department of Modern Languages and Literatures, and professor of comparative thought and literature at Johns Hopkins University. He is the author of multiple books, most recently *The Rigor of Angels* (2023) and *Alejandro Jodorowsky: Filmmaker and Philosopher* (2024). He is co-author with

David Castillo of *Medialogies* (2016) and *What Would Cervantes Do?* (2022). In 2023, *The Rigor of Angels* was named to several best-books-of-the-year lists, including those of *The New York Times* and *The New Yorker*, was named as a runner-up to the ten best of the year by *The New York Times Book Review* podcast, and in 2025 was listed as recommended reading in the *Times*'s "Best 100 Books of the 21st Century."

ANA FERNÁNDEZ-BLÁZQUEZ is a PhD student in Spanish literature and cultures at Yale University and a fellow of the La Caixa Foundation. Her research examines the intersections of law, literature, and historical memory in the Hispanic world, with particular attention to guilt, acquittal, confession, and juridical imagination in modern Spain. Her dissertation, "Poetics of Acquittal," explores how literary and cultural texts negotiate innocence, responsibility, and exoneration. She is the recipient of the Premio Ana María Matute and author of the trade book *Anatomía del true crime*.

PABLO GARCÍA PIÑAR is an assistant instructional professor of Spanish language and literature at the University of Chicago. His research brings premodern disability studies into dialogue with early modern Spanish literature, performance history, and legal culture. He is currently completing *Unfit for Office: Divergent Bodies and the Embodiment of Authority in Early Modern Spanish Literature and Culture*, a monograph examining how bodily disqualification shaped officeholding and state authority in the Habsburg world. He is also developing a second project, tentatively titled *Utopias of Inclusion*, on the colonial imposition of Christian charity and hospital-based care on Indigenous populations in the Viceroyalty of Peru.

ALANI HICKS-BARTLETT is an assistant professor of comparative literature, French and Francophone studies, and Hispanic studies at Brown University, and affiliated faculty in Italian studies. She is one of the chairs of the Renaissance Studies Seminar at Harvard's Mahindra Humanities Center, and an editor-in-chief of *postmedieval*. She was recently awarded a Dibner Research Fellowship in the History of Science and Technology at the Huntington Library, and is completing *Writing the Disabled Self*, a book on medieval and early modern autobiographical discussions of disability. She has recently published on Cervantes, Garcilaso, Calderón, and Vélez de Guevara, and on premodern French, Portuguese, and Italian authors.

CATHERINE INFANTE is an associate professor of Spanish at Amherst College. She earned her PhD in Spanish with a minor in Arabic at the University of Wisconsin-Madison. Her research and publications center on the encounters of Christian and Muslim cultures in the early modern Mediterranean and on visual and material culture studies. She is the author of *The Arts of Encounter: Christians, Muslims, and the Power of Images in Early Modern Spain* (2022).

PAUL MICHAEL JOHNSON is an associate research professor of Spanish at Johns Hopkins University. His writing has encompassed such topics as the history of emotion, sound studies, race, gender, translation, public monuments, and popular culture. In addition to his book *Affective Geographies: Cervantes, Emotion, and the Literary Mediterranean* (2021), his work has appeared in such journals as *Renaissance Quarterly*, *PMLA*, *Atlantic Studies*, *MLN*, and *Exemplaria*. He is the editor of *Cervantes: Journal of the Cervantes Society of America*. Johnson's current book project explores the somatics of race across the early modern world.

NICHOLAS R. JONES is a professor of Spanish at Yale University and the former King Juan Carlos I of Spain Center's scholar-in-residence at New York University (2021–22). He is the author of *Cervantine Blackness* (2024) and the multi-award-winning *Staging "Habla de negros": Radical Performances of the African Diaspora in Early Modern Spain* (2019). A conceptual and theoretical thinker, Jones is a literary critic and cultural historian whose areas of specialty traverse Black European studies, Iberian studies, and the early African diaspora.

ELIZABETH S. LAGRESA-GONZÁLEZ is an assistant professor of Spanish and Romance literatures at the University of British Columbia. She holds a PhD in Romance languages and literatures from Harvard University and was a fellow at the Harvard Center for Renaissance Studies (Villa I Tatti), Freie Universität Berlin (Global Humanities), and Penn State University (Women's, Gender, and Sexuality Studies). Her research focuses on early modern Spanish literature, which she addresses at the intersection of gender, cross-cultural, and material studies. She received an SSHRC Insight Development Grant for her project "Re-Imagining the Spanish Novella: Early Modern Fiction by Women (1635–1700)."

ANA LAGUNA is a professor of Spanish at Rutgers University, Camden. Her work moves between Cervantes's Spain and the most pressing questions of our own time, from imperial reckonings to ethical crusades and epistemic crisis. Trained as a classical humanist and an applied one by vocation, she is a 2025–2026 Fulbright Scholar and the author of *Cervantes and the Pictorial Imagination* (2009) and *Cervantes, the Golden Age, and the Battle for Cultural Identity in 20th-Century Spain* (2021). She is co-editor of *Goodbye Eros* (2020) and *Más no pudiste vencerme* (2026). Her articles have won, among others, the Luis Murillo and the Martin Stevens Awards for Best Article of the Year.

CHAD LEAHY is an associate professor and chair of the Department of Spanish Language, Literary & Cultural Studies at the University of Denver. He is co-author, editor, and translator (with Ken Tully) of *Jerusalem Afflicted: Spain, Quaresmius, and the Idea of a 17th-Century Crusade* (2019) and co-editor (with Nicholas Jones) of *Pornographic Sensibilities: Imagining Sex and the Visceral in Premodern and Early Modern Spanish Cultural Production* (2020). His research has appeared in journals including *Anuario Lope de Vega*, *Bulletin of Spanish Studies*, *Cervantes*, *Criticón*, *Hispanic Review*, *Mediterranean Studies*, *Romance Notes*, *Symposium*, and others.

MAXIM RIGAUX is a Ramón y Cajal researcher at the University of Sevilla. He obtained his PhD from Ghent University in 2018 and held postdoctoral positions at the University of Chicago and the Universitat Autònoma de Barcelona. His research focuses on the cultural and literary histories of the Iberian world in early modernity. Rigaux has been the recipient of prestigious fellowships from the Fulbright Commission and the RSA-Virginia Fox Stern Center. He is a co-founder of the research group RELICS and serves as an editorial board member of the international peer-reviewed journals *JOLCEL* and *Neophilologus*.

LUIS RODRÍGUEZ-RINCÓN is an assistant professor of Spanish and comparative literature at Haverford College. His research explores animal personifications in literary contexts, the evolving role of poets as arbiters of knowledge in the early modern transatlantic world, and the intricacies of the question of the relation of nature to art in the works of Miguel de Cervantes.

VÍCTOR SIERRA MATUTE is an assistant professor of Spanish and comparative literature at Baruch College, CUNY. His research examines early modern Iberian and colonial cultures through the frameworks of materiality, sensory history, and transoceanic exchange. His work has appeared in journals such as *Latin American Research Review*, *Diacritics*, *Romance Studies*, the *Bulletin of Hispanic Studies*, *Romanic Review*, and the *Bulletin of Spanish Visual Studies*. He is the editor of *Soundscapes of the Early Modern Hispanophone and Lusophone Worlds* (2025) and the special issue "The Past Awakened: Cultural Reimagination in the Global Hispanophone" of the *Arizona Journal of Hispanic Cultural Studies* (2025).

ELIZABETH SPRAGINS is an associate professor of Spanish at the College of the Holy Cross. Her research on authority and identity in early modern Mediterranean narrative has appeared in *La Corónica*, *ConSecuencias*, *Medieval Encounters*, and *postmedieval*. She is the author of *A Grammar of the Corpse: Necroepistemology in the Early Modern Mediterranean* (2023), winner of the ACLA's Helen Tartar First Book Prize and the Sixteenth Century Society's Bainton Literature Prize. Other research is forthcoming in *Cervantes in Transit* and *The Kingdom of Xpaña*. A volume on *Cervantine Perversity*, with Leyla Rouhi and Sonia Pérez-Villanueva, is forthcoming with Palgrave.

CORNESHA TWEEDE is an assistant professor of Spanish and Portuguese at Arizona State University. She holds a PhD in Romance languages with a specialization in African studies from the University of Oregon. Her research agenda explores race, gender, sexuality, and the place of Africa in early modern cultural studies. Her work invites us to embrace the legacy of Blackness on the Iberian Peninsula within the early modern period. She is co-editor of *Iberia Negra: Textos para otra historia de la diáspora africana (siglos XVI y XVII)*, published in 2024.

STEVEN WAGSCHAL is a professor of Spanish at Indiana University Bloomington and affiliated faculty of cognitive science and Latin American & Caribbean studies. His most recent book, *Jaguar* (2026), traces this iconic animal in history, literature, and culture from ancient times to the present. He is also the author of *Minding Animals in the Old and New Worlds* (2018) and *The Literature of Jealousy in the Age of Cervantes* (2006), editor of Lope de Vega's *Peribáñez* (2004) and co-editor of *Beyond Sight: Engaging the Senses in Iberian Literatures and Cultures, 1200–1750* (2018).

Index

www.ingramcontent.com/pod-product-compliance
Lightning Source LLC
LaVergne TN
LVHW050833031026
849429LV00027B/219